China's Capitalism

CHINA'S CAPITALISM

A Paradoxical Route to Economic Prosperity

Tobias ten Brink

Translated by
Carla Welch

PENN

UNIVERSITY OF PENNSYLVANIA PRESS

PHILADELPHIA

Originally published in German in 2013 as
Chinas Kapitalismus: Entstehung, Verlauf, Paradoxien.
Copyright © 2013 by Campus Verlag.
English translation copyright © 2019 University of Pennsylvania Press

Published by
University of Pennsylvania Press
Philadelphia, Pennsylvania 19104-4112
www.upenn.edu/pennpress

Printed in the United States of America on acid-free paper
1 3 5 7 9 10 8 6 4 2

Library of Congress Cataloging-in-Publication Data

Names: Ten Brink, Tobias, author. Welch, Carla, translator.
Title: China's capitalism : a paradoxical route to economic prosperity / Tobias
    ten Brink ; translated by Carla Welch. Chinas Kapitalismus. English.
Translation of: Ten Brink, Tobias. Chinas Kapitalismus : Entstehung, Verlauf,
    Paradoxien.
Description: 1st edition. | Philadelphia : University of Pennsylvania Press, [2019]
    | Includes bibliographical references and index.
Identifiers: LCCN 2018033468 | ISBN 978-0-8122-5109-8 (hardcover)
Subjects: LCSH: Capitalism—China. | China—Economic conditions—2000-.
Classification: LCC HC427.95 .T4513 2019
LC record available at https://lccn.loc.gov/2018033468

The translation of this work was funded by Geisteswissenschaften
International—Translation Funding for Humanities and Social Sciences from
Germany, a joint initiative of the Fritz Thyssen Foundation, the German Federal
Foreign Office, the collecting society VG WORT and the Börsenverein des
Deutschen Buchhandels (German Publisher & Booksellers Association).

CONTENTS

ABBREVIATIONS

ACFIC	All-China Federation of Industry and Commerce
ACFTU	All-China Federation of Trade Unions
CCP	Chinese Communist Party
COE	collectively owned enterprise
CPE	comparative political economy
FDI	foreign direct investment
FIE	foreign-invested enterprise
GZFTU	Guangzhou Federation of Trade Unions
IPE	international political economy
LGFVs	local government financing vehicles
LSG	leading small group
MNC	multinational corporation
MOFCOM	Ministry of Commerce
MOFERT	Ministry of Foreign Economic Relations and Trade
MOHRSS	Ministry of Human Resources and Social Security
NDRC	National Development and Reform Commission
NGO	nongovernmental organization
OECD	Organisation for Economic Co-operation and Development
PBOC	People's Bank of China
POE	privately owned enterprise
PRC	People's Republic of China
R&D	research and development
RMB	Renminbi
SEZ	special economic zone
SME	small- and medium-sized enterprise
SOE	state-owned enterprise
SWRCs	Staff and Workers' Representative Congresses
TVE	township and village enterprise

WFOE   wholly foreign-owned enterprise
WTO   World Trade Organization

Introduction

Economic growth in China since the end of the 1970s has now outperformed every other long economic upswing in modern history. While the largest member countries of the Organisation for Economic Co-operation and Development (OECD) continue to struggle with the effects of the deepest recession since World War II, the People's Republic of China (PRC) is still enjoying growth rates that are massive by comparison. With these trends, China is leaving behind its role as "workshop of the world" and preparing to become a global engine for innovation.

Of course, beyond these developments is a different China, one still battling with social problems similar to those faced by other developing or large emerging countries. Nevertheless, according to criteria for measuring growth in economic efficiency, China is still the most successful and dramatic case of catch-up development in the world. Even experienced researchers in economics or industrial sociology are surprised by the scale of industrial expansion in some areas of the country. This particularly applies to the Pearl River and Yangtze River deltas, which over the past thirty years have seen the construction of the largest industrial zones in global history. Often the most astonishing fact for Western observers is that the second largest economy in the world has emerged in a country dominated by an authoritarian party-state where the unrestricted rule of the Chinese Communist Party (CCP) prevails to this day.

The renaissance of the Middle Kingdom triggered strong interest in China and raised a number of questions: What social structure has developed during the course of China's reform process, the length of which has now exceeded that of the Mao era (1949–78)? What have been the driving forces behind the country's development? What paradoxical consequences have been brought about by this "economic miracle"? The new China debate is characterized by a broad spectrum of different positions ranging from suspicion of an emerging China to "Sinomania" (Anderson 2010a). Today's enthusiasm about China's dynamic economic growth, although intermittently qualified by reports on political repression in the PRC, is reminiscent of the writings of seventeenth- and eighteenth-century thinkers such as Leibniz, Voltaire, and Quesnay. These philosophers were exceedingly impressed by the prosperity of imperial China, attributing to it a more advanced level of civilization than Europe. Even their slightly more skeptical contemporaries (Montesquieu and Adam Smith, for instance) admired the country's political regime and its wealth. However, in the nineteenth century, after parts of the country were colonized, there were dramatic shifts in attitude toward China, with the military, economic, and social backwardness of the crumbling empire coming to the fore. In the twentieth century, these antipathies escalated, culminating with the Maoist seizure of power. Today, though, admiration permeated by apprehension appears to be gaining the upper hand.

Research Interests

The progress of present-day China is, in many respects, reminiscent of other capitalist processes of catch-up development. In the country's smog-choked cities, against a backdrop of rapidly growing "collections of commodities" (Marx 1986, 49), a chaotic climate of buying and selling prevails. Tireless expansionism and inventiveness joins forces with an attitude of national euphoria where anything seems possible. The establishment of new business ethics transformed the "acquisition principle" (Sombart 1921, 320) and competition into quasi unquestioned and irreversible economic guiding principles.

In actual fact, however, China's unparalleled economic growth ought to silence every advocate of the free market. The Chinese economy is characterized by significant government intervention. In contrast to the transition countries of the former Eastern Bloc, in the PRC it was possible to avoid radical "big bang" liberalization, and, for a long time, there were no clearly defined private ownership rights. The sustained legacy of a bureaucratic command economy and the ruling party doubtless also require explanation.

A rich but controversial body of literature examining China's process of transformation has emerged. We can, however, identify a series of key issues that have not yet been adequately analyzed or that remain contentious:

- first, there is no plausible answer to the question regarding the main features of the socioeconomic system of the People's Republic;
- second, the question as to the key driving forces and dynamics of the country's rapid development remains controversial;
- third, more recent responses to the question about the paradoxes that are inherent in the growth process are also inconsistent.

There is an array of sophisticated insights and concepts to help us address these issues. As discuss below, I will link these concepts to a research framework, which in contrast to market- and/or business-centric approaches might be described as an extended analysis of capitalism. The aim of this framework is to contribute to a more in-depth understanding of the key features and growth dynamics of China's political economy, the different courses it has taken, and its paradoxical lines of development.

In my approach, I distance myself from the following arguments, which I have presented in an exaggerated ideal typical way here. In a number of journalistic but also scientific articles, market-economy aspects of the Chinese economy are contrasted with its "communist" politics. On the one hand, a combination of new entrepreneurial spirit and economic development are shaping social change. On the other hand, the party-state—which, contrary to the findings of China research, is frequently treated as a monolithic unitary state where all threads converge in the Central Committee of the CCP—continues to exert influence on this process of change. According to this line of argument, China's political system is seen as incompatible with the real demands of a market system. How can this perplexing juxtaposition be understood from a theoretical point of view? Is China's process of modernization in any way even comparable to the Western paths of modernization?

Another line of argument refers back to China's diverse civilizational roots, which, in the eyes of Western observers, enabled the country to relatively effectively combine market and party-state in a unique pairing. Critical China researchers have established that this culture-centric "China is China" perspective, which is reduced to Chinese traditions, is strictly speaking incompatible with a comparative social science angle (Kennedy 2011a). Even a postmodern perspective advanced in the media discourse really prevents any attempt to draw historical comparisons or make theoretical generalizations. This approach retells Chinese contemporary history as a chaotic, contingent process and disputes any kind of historical regularity. Consequently, wanting to make coherent statements about an incoherent reality where the fundamental constant is change seems like intellectual insanity.

And yet in China research and the areas of the economic and social sciences with a focus on China, a wide range of innovative perspectives have emerged. These have resulted in a much more convincing analysis of the processes of transformation based on far more than simply anecdotal evidence. There will be frequent reference to these approaches throughout the present work.

Undeniably, opinions on the current social structure in the PRC differ, in the advanced economic and social sciences as well as in the traditional field of China research. One of today's most renowned economists, Douglass C. North, even argues: "Yet none of the standard models of economic and political theory can explain China" (North 2005). Prominent China researchers are critical of the lack of effort to propose theory-based generalizations about the development of China, its dynamics, and its paradoxes. Political scientist David Shambaugh, former publisher of the *China Quarterly*, a leading scholarly journal in its field, describes this problem as "pervasive myopia and failure to generalize about 'China.' The field is, in my view, far too micro-oriented in its foci. . . . China scholars today know 'more and more about less and less' and see research methodologies as an end in itself rather than as a means to generate broader observations. . . . The result has been an unfortunate losing of the forest for the trees. Having deconstructed China over the past two decades in such considerable detail, scholars should begin to put the pieces of China back together again and offer generalizations about 'China' writ large" (Shambaugh 2009a, 916).

In many respects, China research presents factors that have contributed to economic growth, for example, only to then qualify them with a series of other well-founded arguments. This phenomenon could be attributed to China's continental scale and heterogeneity. However, it might also be explained by the excessive weight given to individual empirical positions, as argued by economic sociologists Fligstein and Zhang: "Given there is some empirical support for all these positions, this implies that the empirical work is probably based on a non-random or narrow sample. . . . This reflects the limits of empirical study and the lack of systematic, overarching theoretical thinking about what is happening" (Fligstein and Zhang 2011, 41).

In the light of this, highly promising analytical perspectives from political economy were recently applied for the first time in China research. The present analysis sets itself the challenge of systematically examining China's growth dynamics through a political economy lens. Although the term *capitalism* crops up in more recent studies on China, it is not generally conceptualized in detail. Even where there are more in-depth descriptions of the concept, "capitalism" is repeatedly reduced to "market economy," or the term is reserved for describing the behavior of individual social groups—the networks of overseas Chinese, other foreign investors, or the new private entrepreneurs in mainland China. But how should the state-owned enterprises (SOEs) and the political institutions of the party-state be depicted? Are we seeing the development of a "hybrid" capitalist-socialist transitional system in China? Do we have to subdivide the economy into capitalist private sectors and quasisocialist state sectors because public property is inherently noncapitalist? How does China's social order differ from other forms of capitalism and catch-up processes? What advantages did this social order enjoy over other emerging nations?

To address these and the other related questions mentioned at the outset, in the following sections, I outline a practicable approach. I begin with a discussion of relevant research works and research needs.

State of the Art and Research Needs

My objective is to identify the key features of the new Chinese economy, its driving forces, and paradoxes. To do this, I combine a range of theoretical insights to create a flexible set of analytical tools.[1] In order to do justice to the problems being addressed, I draw on empirical knowledge and innovative theoretical instruments that have so far rarely been associated with one another or interlinked across disciplines.

(1) Of central importance here is China research in the social sciences. A vast spectrum of academic literature, particularly from the Anglophone world with contributions from Chinese scholars, provides sound analysis. Research studies in this field depict different dimensions of the Chinese system.[2] The interface between the social and economic sciences and sinology has also been the subject of some significant research work by a number of German academics over the last few decades.[3]

(2) A strand of theoretical analysis that has rarely been associated with the field of China research is comparative political economy (CPE). Comparative analysis of Western capitalisms in the field of political economy, conducted by political scientists and economic sociologists, has now achieved canonical status. However, the use of CPE approaches for countries outside the OECD is a relatively recent phenomenon. Up until the 2010s, analysis of this type with a focus on China was rare (see Ahrens and Jünemann 2006; Chu 2010; McNally 2007a; Wilson 2007a). An interesting component of this strand of analysis is that it results in observations that go beyond business-centered studies.[4] These theories draw on insights that promote an understanding of the historical processes of business and market expansion in their wider institutional context. They invariably capture economic processes in terms of their relationship with the state and other noneconomic institutions. A valid point of departure to help us distinguish between the different varieties or variegations of capitalism is the reality of spatiotemporal inequalities in the regional subsystems of the global economy. The hypothesis that there are diverse types of capitalism that all develop their own characteristic features is an important basis for the present analysis.

Political economy approaches also give us an insight into the uneven geographies of crisis dynamics in national economies and the sociostructural conflicts of modern societies. These are manifested in tensions between market expansion and social integration (see R. Brenner 2006; Deutschmann 2009b; Dörre, Lessenich, and Rosa 2009; Streeck 2010a, 2010b). The assumption that the dynamics of capitalist social orders are unstable is paramount to this work. As there have been barely any studies of this kind in research on China (a country that regularly shows very rapid dynamics of change), the present work fills a gap in the literature. Contrary to the rampant Sinomania where GDP growth rates are prematurely extrapolated (Jacques 2009), I would like to examine the specific destabilization dynamics characteristic of the Chinese process of development.

(3) At the same time, there are also various instructive institutionalist concepts available that could be used to analyze gradual institutional change—to be understood in this context as socioeconomic and political change below the threshold of system change (see Mahoney and Thelen 2010; Streeck and Thelen 2005). These tools have only been applied to China's process of transformation in a small number of isolated cases, however (see Tsai 2007; Young 2011). This applies to a similar extent to pertinent new research on the transformation of the state in an age of

globalization, the concept of multilevel governance, and analysis on local statehood and other noneconomic institutions (Benz 2009; Brand 2006; N. Brenner 2004; Block 1994; Jessop 2007; Leibfried and Zürn 2006; Mackert 2006; Thompson et al. 1991). There is also a body of transformation research in former Stalinist countries (Eyal, Szelényi, and Townsley 2000; King and Szelényi 2005; Lane and Myant 2007) and various studies examining the processes of industrialization in the East Asian developmental states that refer to both similarities and striking differences between the different types of "Asian" capitalism (see Deyo 1993; Evans 1995; Hamilton and Biggart 1997; Pohlmann 2002; Wade 1990).

(4) The discipline of international political economy (IPE) provides us with insights that focus on the rise of China against a background of global economic restructuring and cross-regional and/or transnational institutions as well as regulatory and hegemonic structures. China's ascent cannot be explained without referring to the country's integration in the most important overarching macro process that took place in the latter part of the twentieth century, that is, liberal globalization.[5] A global analytical perspective would therefore refer to the extraordinary importance of specific stakeholders and processes acting or occurring beyond or at least not exclusively within Chinese territory and significantly impacting the dynamics and character of China's political economy. Neither the liberal success story of the marketization of China's domestic economy (see Hung 2008) nor more state-centric approaches (see D. Yang 2004) give due credit to the unique circumstances of the East Asian growth region and the process of advanced transnationalization of the global economy.

(5) Further, theories from historical sociology furnish the debate on the concept of "multiple modernities" with important insights, to which CPE and IPE have not given adequate consideration. In order to understand the concept of China's continuity *in* change, that is, the combination of path-dependent and path-shaping processes, we must take into account the concept of elements of modernization adapted from the West being reshaped by sociocultural and normative traditions (see Arnason 2003a, 2003b, 2005, 2008; Eisenstadt 2006; Knöbl 2007; Pomeranz 2000; Schwinn 2009). China's "adaptive" institutions can be properly grasped only if we view them in the context of their longer-term historical development (see Gates 1996; Hamilton 2006a).

In summary, we can conclude that there is a rich body of literature on the subject. My primary goal for the present study, therefore, is to tackle the inadequate link between the different research traditions and disciplines by synthesizing some of their theoretical and empirical findings.[6] My main aim here is to combine the questions developed at the start of this book within a research framework that I hope will help to lend coherence to China's incoherent reality. I am also keen to enrich the critical CPE and IPE literature with more nuanced insights into the "special case" of China.

Drivers of Global Capitalism and Divergent National Outcomes: Theoretical and Methodological Approach

Because there is no readily available existing research framework that reflects my approach, I will outline a number of general considerations that I consider to be vital. In Chapter 1, I will expand on these considerations to create a research framework. This will be followed by a historical account of the reform process in Chapter 2 and an analysis of current lines of development in Chapter 3. Building on this, I will use my Conclusion to question the validity of the aforementioned considerations and to identify gaps and/or potential areas for future research.

The general point of departure for my analysis of capitalist developments comprises the three key actors that played a decisive role in shaping the historical development of modern societies: companies, governments, and the working classes. "The comparative capitalism literature causes us to focus on three main actors in society: the government, firms, and workers. It may not tell us what that relationship will be, but it does argue that all economic development projects have produced stable institutions built around those relationships" (Fligstein and Zhang 2011, 50).[7] Consequently, beyond market- or company-centric theories of economic development, it is important for us to examine the social relationships between these groups of actors (which are inherently inhomogeneous and characterized by changing normative orientations), their structure, and relationships with other social groups as well as their historical evolution. With this contribution, I attempt to identify the institutional design or the competitive and cooperative relationships resulting from the interconnection between the three groups of actors. The complex interplay between companies, government actors, and the "subordinated" classes result in different forms of market activity, political regulation, and other types of coordination by social actors—in the world of work, for instance. Linked to this are also conflicts over guiding social principles and norms.

At the same time, these interactions always occur in social arenas that are, to a certain extent, already shaped and established. In other words, they arise under social conditions that have become independent from actors' conscious actions and desires and that affect both their perceptions and their actions. This social structure, though created by historical actors, had become an independent entity fostering an institutionalized compulsion to act and, at the same time, unevenly distributed scope for action. My hypothesis is that, particularly since the 1980s, this structure/agency nexus has largely been shaped (not determined) by the drivers of global capitalist development. A link between the insights outlined in the previous section is the idea that the drivers and fundamental components of capitalism must be viewed as an overarching dimension of societal modernization. These components include a boundless and infinite imperative to maximize accumulation and profit, competition, a structural propensity for social tension and crisis, and a reliance on noneconomic institutions such as the state.

In contrast to far-reaching historical contingency assumptions, I propose first, that capitalism as an all-encompassing social order has sustainably structured the various paths to modernity in different continents over the last century, including China's, even under Maoism. There are fundamental components of capitalism, without which it would be impossible to differentiate between different types of capitalism in the first place. In the context of global capitalist development, these various types should be viewed as different manifestations of common basic patterns, and in terms of the historical interrelations between the three groups of actors mentioned. At the same time, the overarching drivers and patterns of capitalism take on a specific form in different historical phases of capitalist development. These include the period of strong government interventionism that prevailed around the world from the 1930s or the period of liberalization that began in the 1970s, for instance.

Second, because the global drivers of capitalist development simultaneously encounter various historical development trajectories, I felt it was important to take into account the role of noneconomic institutions and historical traditions in order to understand the development of different types of capitalism. In this context, China research, for instance, emphasizes Sino-Marxism as well as the older Confucian traditions, traditions of a strong state, and the reciprocal system of social networks and influential relationships (*guanxi*) that facilitate business and other dealings.[8] Although it is true that historical and sociocultural traditions are reshaped by capitalist-driven processes of modernization (which calls into question the "China is China" argument mentioned above), global economic processes still develop unevenly because different local, national, and transregional areas provide different conditions for establishing capitalist social orders. These properties give rise to different forms of coordination of economic, political, and social processes and lend a political economy the distinctive character that develops over the course of history.

In light of all this, I therefore initially present a position that resembles convergence theory. According to this position, national capitalist development processes cannot reasonably be explored using comparative static analysis. Instead they must be approached as facets of a process of global capitalist socialization, that is, with reference to diverse driving forces or fundamental components that are universally inherent in capitalist development.

In a second step, however, this position is relativized because the overarching drivers of capitalism do not result in identical outcomes. The conflict between the main groups of social actors leads to different forms of coordination, for instance. These forms of coordination are based on completely different socioeconomic premises, each occupying a specific position in the global system, and so on. To enable me to describe the similarities and differences as well as the overall drivers and divergent outcomes of capitalist development, I draw on the concept of an international variegated capitalist world system (Jessop 2009; Streeck 2010a). I then incorporate a historical concept of institutions in my research framework that takes into account targeted human action beyond structuralism and intentionalism. To address the issues that are the crux of this study, I refrain from focusing exclusively on China's national economy but also examine how it is integrated in other East Asian and global economic spaces.

In a third step, in light of deficits and desiderata of both comparative capitalism analysis and China research, there is scope for a more detailed analysis of capitalist social relations in China. This analysis includes the aforementioned inter- and/or transnational analytical focus and the idea that the research perspectives presented here are incompatible with culturalism. This school of thought sees historical continuity prevailing in China where "unity between past, present, and future has become second nature"

(Weggel 1997, 122, my translation). I also draw on other recent CPE tools and concepts for instance. This allows me to examine different production regimes and the complementary cross effects between institutions, that is, the functional effects that occur between individual institutional spheres.

Furthermore, it is important to take account of the relationships between economic and noneconomic institutions on two additional levels:

(1) One problem with China and comparative capitalism research is the lack of proper analysis of the interplay between the economy and the state or companies and state institutions on different geographical and administrative levels and in informal networks. On the one hand, as I will demonstrate, market-centric approaches result in biased analysis of China's reform. Thus, predictions of an abrupt transition from the "plan" to the "market" proved to be flawed in light of the adaptability of state developmental regulation. Despite the transfer of functions from government agencies to companies and the dismantling of binding plan targets in favor of more indicative planning and market-led allocation, China can hardly be described as a liberal market economy. On the other hand, state-centric approaches attribute China's leadership with a degree of foresight and capacity to control that can in no way be reconciled with the anarchic reality of the Chinese reform process. This, albeit perhaps inadvertently, also correlates with the political leadership's self-perception. It is possible that the legacy of elite-centric totalitarianism research has thereby contributed to a stark contrast between the state and the economy and, in a wider sense, also society where the government is understood as an external regime rather than a social actor (see Fewsmith 2008).

The present work maintains that in order to analyze economic dynamics, we need to refer back to the interdependencies and overlaps between the economy and the state, which, during the course of reform, created close alliances between private actors and (local) government elites. For this reason, capitalist development in China (and elsewhere) cannot be seen as synonymous with markets and private enterprises. In certain phases of capitalist development and with some forms of capitalism, strong political steering plays a particularly important role, which may largely be determined by the drivers of capitalism. Further, political actors can, in certain situations, resemble market actors—particularly when they only have to devote themselves to managing redistributive functions to a limited extent because, for instance, social rights and civil society space is restricted or the social balance of power permits this. In this context, China research refers to the "entrepreneurial" state, "local state corporatism," and similar structures. In addition, the legal and de facto power of control over the means of production in China are diverging to the extent that legal owners are ceding control, partially or fully, to other actors. In contrast to hypotheses harnessing actors' preferences to their institutional form (to the "public" state sphere or "private" market sphere, for instance), I present an alternative explanation. I propose that the embedding of political actors in a broader capitalist system, while not determining all the preferences of these actors—state institutions have different criteria for reproduction than companies, and they also have differing development mechanisms—does have a powerful impact on them.

Bearing this in mind, I will later pose the question whether and to what extent a public-private hybrid regime and novel state-capitalist forms constitute an overarching dimension of Chinese capitalism reflecting the drivers of global capitalism and specific national and regional characteristics.[9] In a subsequent step, I explore the different mechanisms and strategies of state intervention and regulation in the Chinese system of multilevel governance, that is, the existence of many centers of power below the central government level, and of heterogeneous production regimes in the economy. Here I concentrate on the changing relationship between indicative or market-creating and imperative or market-restricting forms of political regulation. The objective of this approach is to examine the extent to which the new Chinese capitalism differs from coordinated or dependent varieties and other state-permeated forms of capitalism (see May, Nölke, and ten Brink 2013).

(2) A virtual absence of civil society and democratic conditions has led to the development of extremely unequal power relations in China. The workers have virtually no opportunity to participate. This has resulted in imperfect and fragmented coordination in the labor and employment systems. Any comprehensive analysis of the Chinese development process should incorporate this frequently neglected level of action. The last few decades have seen the emergence of an important body of literature on this. Drawing on, inter alia, corporatism research in industrial sociology, this literature examines the socioeconomic consequences of the relative powerlessness of the subordinate groups, as well as their sporadic empowerment (see Y. Cai 2010; A. Chan 2001; K. Chang, Lüthje, and Luo 2008; Friedman 2011; C. Lee 2007; Lüthje, Luo, and Zhang 2013; Perry and Selden 2003).

Finally, it is important to establish in this context whether the party-state generates sufficient social cohesion not only to foster a close alliance between the political and economic power elites but also to integrate the subordinated classes and to channel expectations of upward social mobility, or whether there is an indication of the limitations of China's model of subordination and of social counter movements.

From a methodological perspective, my analysis is based largely on studies of secondary literature. In the empirical sections of the study, I also analyze specialized economic literature and statistics including from the National Bureau of Statistics of China. Additionally, I incorporate findings from the numerous research and conference trips I made to China during the period from 2008 to 2016, visits to private and state-owned (Chinese and foreign) companies, and discussions with Chinese academics. As a partner in a research project conducted by the Frankfurt Institute for Social Research (coordinated by Boy Lüthje and funded by the German Research Foundation, DFG), I was also able to participate in several interviews with company and labor union representatives and members of nongovernmental organizations (NGOs).

To provide a historical account of China's socioeconomic dynamics, I use qualitative content analysis (see Hall 2008). Here, I combine empirical-historical analysis and theoretical generalizations in a way that "does not [seek] to identify statistical correlations between variables but rather attempts to find an *explanation* for unclear macro-phenomena by identifying the processes and interdependencies contributing to their *occurrence*" (Mayntz 2002, 13, my translation). In short, I reconstruct and systematize historical developments using a theory-based approach.

Main Hypotheses

To address the three research questions outlined at the beginning, I formulate the following hypotheses. These focus on the principal features of China's socioeconomic system (1a and b), on the key dynamics shaping this system (2a, b, and c), and on the current, at times paradoxical, lines of development (3a and b).

(1a) China's political economy is a competition-driven form of state-permeated capitalism with a heterogeneous internal structure. From the end of the 1970s onward, it was selectively integrated into global economic processes and consequently impacted by the phase-specific process of liberalization. Contemporary developments in China are therefore fundamentally based on the drivers of capitalism observed in other processes of modernization yet, in many respects, have also taken on their own distinctive form. As the somewhat cumbersome expression *variegated state-permeated capitalism*[10] suggests, the party-state in China does not retreat from liberalization and marketization tendencies but has contributed and is continuing to contribute to the establishment of a new type of capitalism.

(1b) In this respect, the party-state itself is an integral part of Chinese capitalism and should be treated as such in our analysis. In order to acquire an understanding of China's political economy, the importance of the drivers of capitalism in China's public-private system of multilevel governance must therefore be borne in mind. Here, there is evidence of distinctive forms of capitalism, such as local state-permeated capitalism. This is defined by (local) state and private entrepreneurs and characterized by the coexistence of competition and planning as well as nonmarket institutions, which, at the same time, are themselves also subject to competition. Considerations stemming from state theory and CPE, of the actual cross effects of institutions that are built (at least at first glance) on less than solid foundations give us a clearer view of the aforementioned types of capitalism. Further assumptions, linked to the institutional basis and contextual conditions of market expansion, focus on other distinctive characteristics of the PRC. Examples of this are a less stringent interpretation of contracts in contrast to strictly enforceable rules in the West and the significance of informal networks and consultation between the political leadership, administration, companies, and party-run labor unions.

(2a) To respond in more detail to the question as to the causes, contexts, and repercussions of the country's economic dynamics, I propose an interpretation of the modernization of China that does not see the turning point at the end of the 1970s as a complete break with the past, but rather as a gradual, albeit ultimately profound, process of restructuring. Contrary to the notion of a sudden leap from a command to a market economy, I believe that a transition took place from one form of national modernization in classical Maoism to a unique form of capitalist modernization. The aforementioned modernization under Mao already imitated capitalist mechanisms although market forms were largely not included ("protocapitalism"). After the 1970s, China's key institutions were undergoing a process of change that led to a novel polycentric mixture of plan, market, and other forms of coordination. The subsequent market expansion was not exclusively funded by the new private sector. The figure of the risk-taking, rule-breaking entrepreneur, who, over time, increasingly became symbolic of expertise, moral authority, professionalism, and commercial success also maintained an important position in the state-owned enterprise sector and in government institutions.

(2b) Another factor that is of paramount importance when endeavoring to explain economic dynamics is the existence of favorable global economic circumstances. As well as a number of advantageous domestic institutional and sociostructural preconditions for growth in national income, a range of external factors come into play here. These include the dynamic East Asian economies, "patriotic" ethnic Chinese, and, in the second phase of reform beginning in the 1990s, the transfer of capital from the major OECD economies.

(2c) I also make the assumption that the relative continuity of the economic and political elites secured the reform process. According to economic criteria, this process was a success but the dynamics of the process were uneven and combined and driven by crisis rather than predictable planning. Yet the public-private power elite seen in various segments proved to be a contributing factor in maintaining the status quo. Here, capital valorization processes as key determinants of government policy initiated a series of bureaucratic restructuring measures. At the same time, China's political system was reorganized to facilitate *institutional learning*. This was implemented via processes of institutional layering through, for example, new entrepreneurs circumventing formal rules. Up until the 2000s, we frequently heard assumptions (founded on theories of democracy) of a probable regime change in China. Counter to these opinions, on the whole, there is evidence of a continuity of power elites and the political system that have ensured a relatively stable reform path and fostered economic growth. According to a different hypothesis, a key basis for this is the segmentation of the working class and the segregation of the labor market.

(3a) The restructuring of government institutions in the context of a reconfigured yet stable power elite and a rigid political environment contributed to a situation where the Chinese central government and its local counterparts were equipped with greater capacity than in other emerging countries to process the paradoxes of capitalist development. At the same time, however, the discrepancies in the country's regional development and the multiscale government apparatus have created a social structure that is not free of conflict. The Chinese central government has only temporarily and partially succeeded in gaining control of the internal competition to attract business and investment. Associated with this are the high-risk growth and fiscal policies of the country's subnational governments, and in the financial system and corporate sector. Hence, the steering capacity of the heterogeneous party-state cannot be hypostasized, and contradictory macroeconomic lines of development as well as limitations of political regulation can be discerned. I will therefore identify factors that have recently contributed to destabilization. In order to attenuate the effects of capitalist modernization, the Chinese central government has been pushing for a comprehensive restructuring of the economy and a reinforcement of domestic consumption. In normative terms, this is motivated by the objective of achieving a "harmonious society" (*hexie shehui*). As I will attempt to demonstrate, this endeavor is rather difficult to realize in practice, however, also under the Xi Jinping administration.

(3b) In addition to the paradoxical effects of market expansion and political macroregulation, the mechanisms of conflict resolution within the labor system are flawed. There are limitations to Chinese-style labor subordination, which puts the rule of the party-state under considerable strain.

The present work[11] pursues two further objectives: first, my intention is to target readers with an interest in the social sciences and, at least to some degree, help them to decipher China's path to a modernity, which is shaped by capitalism. My second aim is that the research framework developed here and some of the findings resulting from this study may also arouse interest in political economy considerations. For me, the optimal outcome would be for my account and explanations of the fundamental dynamics of China's capitalist development to act as a preliminary work and an aid for further, more specialized empirical analyses of individual sectors of the economy or policy areas that could then substantiate more specific causalities.

At this juncture, I think it is important to comment on the limitations of this study. The present work does not examine all dimensions of China's process of capitalist modernization. For example, it does not cover in any detail the emergence of a consumer society, the development of the welfare state, the evolution of new middle classes, or the agriculture issue. I also only sporadically refer to the valorization of the environment and the long-term costs of the exploitation of natural resources. The same applies to the colonization of the lifeworld and the development of gender relations. The study also tackles the global implications of the rise of China only to a limited degree and, with regard to the political system, only selectively discusses the role of the Chinese People's Liberation Army (PLA) and the security apparatus. Finally, the role played by ideational orientation, motives for social upward mobility, and the question of normative integration and leadership legitimacy are also not adequately acknowledged.

Outline

In Chapter 1, I develop a research framework based on insights, gaps, and desiderata in China research and using theoretical tools from, inter alia, the fields of CPE and IPE. In order to avoid a state/market dualism, I combine insights from various disciplines and approaches that I feel benefit the analysis of China's new capitalism. I refer here to the notion of a capitalist-driven modernity and an international variegated capitalist world system. To help me describe the unstable dynamics of China's process of development, I draw on a global perspective, the notion of uneven, combined and interconnected development, and a concept of institutions that takes account of targeted human action. To operationalize the research framework, I introduce five dimensions of capitalist economies:

1. unstable dynamics of markets and enterprises;
2. types of industrial relations;
3. the financial system;
4. interaction between economic and political actors; and
5. the integration of political economies in global economic structures.

On the basis of these five areas, the main part of the study examines the characteristics of China's socioeconomic order and its dynamics. Against this backdrop, Chapter 2 reconstructs the historically relevant processes that, because of the effect of the drivers of capitalism, mean we can plausibly refer to a capitalist development in China. Here, I describe how the reform process led to a new mixture of market, state, and other coordination mechanisms.

The first section in this chapter summarizes the period from 1949 to 1978. Here, I attempt to already address the phenomenon of the relative continuity of power elites after 1978. To do so I refer to the mechanisms of protocapitalism in classical Maoism, a change in the country's social structure, and the embedding of the crisis of Maoism in the global crisis of the 1970s. The latter triggered a global wave of liberalization across a broad spectrum of different political systems. To demonstrate that this also took effect in China, albeit not in the same form as in the Western world, for example, I refer, inter alia, to the role model function of the East Asian developmental states.

Applying the analytical strategy developed as part of my research framework, I use the second section in Chapter 2 to reconstruct the emergence of a variegated state-permeated capitalism from the end of the 1970s to the era of Hu Jintao and Wen Jiabao in the 2000s. First, I analyze the domestic dynamics and outline two distinct phases of the reform of the country's corporate sectors, of the political system of multilevel governance, of industrial relations, and of the financial system.[12]

I then extend the analysis to incorporate external factors, including China's integration into the global capitalist system, the evolution of an export-oriented growth model in coastal regions, the role of the overseas Chinese, and the East Asian economic region, as well as transnational production networks and the overaccumulation of capital in the North. I demonstrate how the Chinese economy benefited considerably from a combination of favorable circumstances and was able to accelerate its catch-up development so much more than other emerging economies.

Chapter 3 focuses on the current lines of development in Chinese capitalism. Although I refer back to various historical events at certain junctures in this chapter, the focus is on the period between 2008 (the start of the momentous global economic slump) and 2016. Following the assumption that my analysis must refer to the role of and interplay between three groups of actors, this chapter is divided into three sections. In the first, I discuss the corporate sector and examine socioeconomic dynamics. On the one hand, I address the issue of unity in diversity, that is, the public-private organization of the economy against the backdrop of heterogeneous business forms and production regimes. On the other hand, I analyze socioeconomic dynamics including the challenges presented by the growth slowdown in the 2010s.

Whether the government leadership has been able to meet these challenges and effect a rebalancing of the economy is the subject of the second section of this chapter. First, I further develop the themes of the state's steering capacity, distinctive policy cycles, and the prevailing significance of the CCP introduced in Chapter 2. This is all the more relevant given the role that the leadership under Xi Jinping attributes to the party. Second, I highlight the limitations of political steering in competition-driven state-permeated capitalism.

In the third section of Chapter 3, I expand the analysis to include China's restructured working class and the splintered system of industrial relations. My objective here is to illustrate the tension between the harmonious society proclaimed by the party-state leadership and the imminent limitations of the subjugation of the workers.

In the Conclusion, I summarize the key findings of the study and examine the implications for both political economy and China research.

The present work is an updated version of my book *Chinas Kapitalismus: Entstehung, Verlauf, Paradoxien* (China's Capitalism: Emergence, Trajectory, and Paradoxes) published by Campus (Frankfurt am Main, 2013). The latter was awarded a translation prize by the Börsenverein des Deutschen Buchhandels (German Publishers and Booksellers Association) in the "International Humanities" category in 2016.

For the purposes of this translation, the original German book version has been slightly modified and shortened. Although I did not include in any detail theoretical developments in China studies since 2013, I have particularly updated Chapter 3 on China's current lines of development using newer empirical work and statistical data.

CHAPTER 1

Analyzing China's Political Economy

In this chapter, I introduce an approach to analyzing China's political economy on the basis of the current state of the art. I begin with a broad outline of the relevant discourse in China studies and insights, gaps, and desiderata. In the second part of the chapter, I outline my own research framework.

Insights, Gaps, and Desiderata in China Research

This section provides an overview of relevant traditions and discourse in China research over the past few decades. These yield substantive findings but, at the same time, also exhibit gaps and desiderata. Here I focus on studies from the social sciences and only refer in passing to authors in related disciplines.

In Western social sciences, for many years, the debate about the People's Republic of China (PRC) mostly was part of the analysis of actually existing "socialist" systems. (A concise overview of the historical development of the relevant theories is provided by Stark and Nee 1989; Scharping 1988.) During the early Cold War era, China was primarily analyzed on the basis of theories of totalitarianism, whereas since the 1980s, institutionalist studies shaped the field.[1]

After World War II, approaches based on theories of totalitarianism dominated. These focused particularly on the communist ideology, on the importance of individual leaders, and on the concentration of power in the Maoist Communist Party (see, for example, Lewis 1963). China was viewed as the antithesis of Western-style liberal democracy. Reflecting this, economists depicted a stark contrast between a decentralized market economy and a centrally planned one. Their objective was to construct a clash of ideologies that was politically expedient during the Cold War era. In slightly simplified terms, the studies frequently culminated in the following elite-centric proposition: equipped with almost absolute power and having eliminated autonomous social spheres, a bureaucracy steered by a party apparatus was able to succeed in controlling Chinese society as it saw fit. However, because these assumptions threatened to hypostasize the one-party rule into a stable unchallenged regime and, to a large extent, ignored the CCP's internal conflicts or social resistance, the hypotheses based on theories of totalitarianism tended to draw rather inaccurate conclusions (for a critical account, see Dreyer 1996, 7–21; see also Shue 1988; Walder 1986).[2]

In the 1980s, institutionalist approaches took on a certain appeal.[3] These theories, which are in contrast to efficiency theory schemata, increasingly took recourse to the institutional contexts of political or economic behavior. In state socialist systems, change was found to be driven by forces beyond the control of the state. The focus here was on examining the charged relationship between state and society. The objective was to be able to define political conflicts and socioeconomic development trends (Xie 1993) or, for example, to pinpoint internal corporate negotiation processes in "communist" enterprises (Walder 1986) by refining overly simplified assumptions of the existence of fixed corporate despotism. Action taken by the state is thus seen within the context of state/society relations in order to shift the focus more toward the processes and conflicts that are inherent in state action (Derichs and Heberer 2008). Accordingly, China can be examined using similar instruments to those that have long since been widely applied to the analysis of Western societies or countries of the Global South.

From the 1990s to date, many different authors have published empirical studies that, in one form or other, picked up on these traditions. Also presented here are certain discourses that were instrumental in providing important insights but also exposed unresolved problems in research on China.

From Command to Market Economy: Discourses in Transformation Research

The transformation process in China has generally been described as a major shift from a command or planned to a market economy, with a distinction being made between liberal rationalist (Nee 1989; Sachs and

Woo 1999) and institutionalist theories (Guthrie 2002; McMillan and
Naughton 1996). Both approaches frequently refer to the debate that mate-
rialized after the collapse of the Eastern Bloc. This debate, which centered
on the question of how to transform a command economy into a market
economy, had both political and practical ramifications.

While neoliberal authors recommended that Eastern European transition economies take a "big bang" approach based on the premise that the
new cannot evolve within the framework of the old, the selfsame authors
declared China to be a special case that quite clearly did not follow these
political recommendations. For this reason, China was able to grow only
because the initial conditions there were more favorable than those in former Eastern Bloc countries. In terms of prospects, a slowdown in growth
and considerable instability was expected in China (see, for example, Sachs
and Woo 1999). In addition, the lack of clearly defined property rights and
state bureaucracies' interference in corporate processes were seen as the
main obstacles preventing the smooth transition to an efficient market
economy (D. Yang 2004, 11–12).

By way of contrast, institutionalist authors drew attention to innovative
entrepreneurship that did not necessarily manifest itself in the form of abrupt
privatization. These authors recommended linking the old with the new, proposing an institutional framework that fosters entrepreneurial risk and establishes trust. Taking into account socioeconomic points of view, authors
focused on the effectiveness of existing institutions as well as on path dependencies that affect the development of new markets in China (Guthrie 2002,
8–11, 22–23). Other authors (Wank 1999; M. Yang 2002) referred to the
tradition of frequently informal network relationships (*guanxi*).

Another slant on this can be found in comparative research on post-
communist transition countries (see Pickles and Smith 1998). King and
Szelényi, for example, employed a class theory method to develop three key
models for the formation of new capitalist systems in former "state socialist" societies. The first model uses a capitalism-from-above approach,
which is essentially the attempt by the former state and party elite, in Russia
in particular, to create a market system based on neoliberal concepts and
within the framework of large-scale privatization schemes. The second
model described by King and Szelényi is capitalism from without, as seen
in Hungary, for example, where foreign investors played a dominant role.
The third model—capitalism from below—refers to a new indigenous corporate class that emerged even before 1989 and gradually increased its

influence; this model was particularly pronounced in China. By the end of the 1970s, the technocratic staff, including managers, had reached a hegemonic position without ousting the old party officials; an alliance between these two class groups determined the country's social development from that moment on. The gradual reforms and increasing openness toward direct foreign investors then led to the development of a new type of capitalism in the PRC (King and Szelényi 2005, 220–22; see Eyal, Szelényi, and Townsley 2000).

This undirected experimental dynamic from below also formed the basis for another debate that will now be briefly outlined.

Innovative Entrepreneurship and Marketization

In order to attempt to understand the paradox of unleashing market forces amid a communist-run country, market- or corporate-centered approaches describe the advent of a new entrepreneurship as the essential catalyst for change. The prerequisite for successful growth was and still is, first and foremost, the creative entrepreneur. Accordingly, creative entrepreneurship had found a new home—particularly in parts of rural China of the 1980s—and was rapidly spreading to the cities (see, for example, Yasheng Huang 2008).

In line with this, China's rigid political system was seen as incompatible with the needs of a market system. China experienced two diametrically opposed development logics—political power and control logic versus economic growth and profit logic. With regard to the resultant development trends, either an inevitable democratization (Rowen 2007) or a collapse of the system (Pei 2006) has been and indeed continues to be predicted (for an overview of this, see Heberer and Senz 2009). In the case of democratization, this would lead to the development of a market economy with liberal characteristics akin to those found in other parts of the world. Especially in recent political economy studies, however, this forecast is justifiably challenged, as shown below.

The Debate over the Adaptive and Regulatory Capacity of the Party-State

A number of studies emphasize the need for a proactive central government and/or subnational political authorities in order to achieve a favorable growth path (see Heilmann 2008, 2009; A. Hu 2010; C. Lin 2006; Perry 2007; D. Yang 2004; Zheng 2010). The Chinese party and state elite is regarded as a pragmatically forward-thinking political power that—similar to the case in other developmental states in East Asia—acts as a driver of modernization.[4] Seen from this perspective, the authoritarian system in China, which still leaves the elites with some freedom for debate, is regarded as a highly beneficial political driver of economic development. In addition, a relationship structure developed that triggered competition between the political authorities that were subordinate to the central government, boosting economic growth (Oi 1995; see also Montinola, Qian, and Weingast 1995). According to China researchers, the post-1970s party-state had the extraordinary ability to adapt to an ever-changing environment. In the unfolding reform process, moreover, orientation toward national sovereignty was of the utmost importance, as was state control over key areas of the economy and public infrastructure planning.

For this reason, the proposition that China was seeing the emergence of a type of "crony capitalism," which, as in other developing and newly industrialized economies, encumbers economic growth, has been challenged. On balance, the political leadership's capacity for learning and adapting in fact helps stabilize the system. Accordingly, party rule is expected to remain in place, albeit by merely "muddling through" more than anything else, even as the process of market expansion continues.

In the course of the present work, repeated reference will be made to these studies. However, I believe they tend to have shortcomings that imply the existence of market/state dualism. While the policy-centered approach indicates that the Chinese government has an astute capacity for foresight—something that does not appear congruent with the anarchic reality of the Chinese reform process—the market or corporate-centered approach (introduced above) is too one-sided in its description of the forces at play in the reform processes. Moreover, the continuing legacy of elite-centered research on totalitarianism may well reinforce the abrupt juxtaposition of state and economy, and, by extension, society, where the state still is largely seen as an external regime of control and not as an actor *in* society (see Lieberthal 1995, 292–304).

Before addressing this problem in more detail, however, allow me to touch on another discourse that explores the character of the Chinese economy.

China as a Socialist Market Economy and/or Hybrid Model

Until very recently, the prevailing system in China was seen as a form of socialism known as Maoism. In the early 1990s, once even the Chinese government began officially speaking of the transition to a socialist market economy, cracks appeared in this argument. With the party continuing to play a commanding role and areas of the economy remaining in state ownership, however, some authors continue to assume the foundation of the noncapitalist society to be relatively intact (N. Lin 1995; Robins 2010). This was in line with the official position of the Chinese government. Some authors even agree with the government's belief that the policy of opening up and marketization are transitional stages toward more developed forms of a socialist society and democracy (see Itoh 2003; X. Li 2008).

However, even authors who employ theoretical tools that show a market socialist society to be conceivable in an ideal-typical scenario remain skeptical about these assumptions (Lippit 1997). One line of criticism is that in none of the existing Chinese business types do the workers have more democratic powers than those in capitalist systems. On no level of society, corporate or otherwise, are solidarity-oriented behavioral patterns of disproportionately greater significance in China than in other countries. Moreover, market allocation is not merely an appendage of a system governed mainly in the interests of needs-based production.

Or has a new hybrid form perhaps emerged in China? Does the economy have to be subdivided into capitalist private sectors and quasisocialist state sectors? Or should China be referred to as a "noncapitalist market economy"? According to Arrighi, a capitalist market economy differs from a noncapitalist market economy "in the greater power of capitalists to force their class interests onto others at the expense of national interests" (Arrighi 2008, 120, my translation). It is not the "presence of capitalist institutions and dispositions" that defines "the capitalist character of market-oriented development but the relationship between state power and capital" (Arrighi 2008, 412, my translation; see also Smith 1993). As long as the state is not subordinate to capitalist class interests, the market economy remains noncapitalist.

A stark juxtaposition between market economy and state economy or communist state is flawed, however. As state theorists have discovered, the term "national interest" used by Arrighi cannot be seen as an objective category. According to Arrighi, the state is an apparatus that is an expression of general social interests except when the capitalists impose their

restricted interests onto market development. "What this inadequate definition does not take into account is the specific organizational approach
taken by a capitalist state and definitions of state functions relating to the
safeguarding of property and ownership rights, the reproduction of relations between workforce and capital as well as the preservation of accumulation" (Panitch 2009, 20, my translation). In contradiction with the
expectation that the almost unstoppable market dynamics would undermine or even topple the bureaucratic balance of power, the bureaucracy
has, to a certain extent, proven capable of reconciling market and plan
during the reform process.

It is clearly difficult to establish a theoretical basis for the development
of a capitalist economy within the framework of a "socialist" state and
society. Consequently, it would appear that many authors are content with
continuing to describe the development in China in reference to the transition factor alone, in other words, the hybrid transformation character that
is not yet completely formed (see Meyer 2011; Hartmann 2006, 10; Taube
2001, 167–68). Without questioning the appropriateness of an approach
that seeks to represent the complexity of linking various institutional forms
in China, the term "hybrid" nonetheless appears to be an unfortunate
expression to use. After all, every social entity is hybrid or, in other words,
made up of different forms. In addition, the word "hybrid" does not reveal
which institutional forms are more dynamic than other parts of the complex whole.

It was not until the 2000s that more authors began to use the term
"capitalism" when describing China's development, albeit often more fleet-
ingly than systematically, as pointed out by McNally (McNally 2007c, 3–7).
For example, the term is often found in the titles of studies without its
being elaborated on in the work itself. Sometimes capitalism is merely
equated with a market economy (Yasheng Huang 2008), or social phenomena such as Chinese overseas networks are analyzed as "capitalist" (Guthrie
2002). Within the framework of a restrictive definition of the term "private
property," authors tentatively speak of quasicapitalism and continue to
see state property as having noncapitalist characteristics (Breslin 2007b,
79–80).

The main body of this work (Chapters 2 and 3) shows that it is plausible
to systematically examine the Chinese economy and, by extension, Chinese
society, using theories of capitalism. The political economy framework
developed for this purpose is introduced below.

Researching China from a Political Economy Perspective

Although only limited to date, political economy studies with a focus on China have provided a framework for examining the country's development. The following presents a contingency-sensitive research framework based on a synthesis of diverse theoretical approaches. Using this framework, the present work takes a holistic perspective—for "only in a panoramic view can one truly recognize the details" (Streeck 2009, 17).

Over the next few sections, I will first look at different aspects of research into capitalist dynamics, which have also been the subject of recent comparative capitalism research.

I will then outline the concept of capitalist-driven modernity, that is, the assumption that the path to modernity or modernities over the past one hundred years in various parts of the planet can be described as a process in which drivers of capitalism extensively shape the structure of social order. This will serve to introduce key characteristics of global capitalist socialization and its unstable dynamics.

Subsequently, I will present a few observations on the reality of historical institutional change and how this can impact the capacity to act on the part of social actors. I will also discuss the roles of sociocultural idiosyncrasies or past traditions and social structures that give a specific face to political economies and create various forms of coordination between economic, political and other societal actors.

Finally, five key dimensions of capitalist systems are outlined, which will largely provide the structure for the remainder of this work.

Varieties of Capitalism and Comparative Capitalisms

In order to move closer to a conceptualization of capitalism or of its different guises in the past, I will first refer to theories and concepts found in comparative political economy (CPE), in particular, but not restricted to, varieties of capitalism (VoC) theory, which has become well known in recent years.

VoC theory (Hall and Soskice 2001) includes a differentiation between liberal (US and UK) and coordinated market economies (Germany and Japan) and serves as a contrast to the notion of a (liberal) best-practice model.[5] According to this theory, market economies are composed of a cluster of functionally coordinated subsystems. Production systems, corporate governance and financing, and corporate and industrial relations, as well as training and education initiatives are examined for their institutional complementarities. Functioning complementary relationships are seen as the source of comparatively long-term institutional stability and economic growth.[6]

In addition, a number of insights have been developed in the CPE field over the past years that are relevant for research on China (see Bohle and Greskovits 2009; Coates 2005; Hancké, Rhodes, and Thatcher 2007; Streeck 2010a). These include the following:

- The knowledge that an in-depth examination must go beyond a strict market and enterprise focus. China's dynamic economic development is not only a result of resurgent entrepreneurship in parts of the mainland or among the community of overseas Chinese but is also based on, and indeed very much defined by, action taken by state actors.
- The realization that the role played by power relationships, the state, and state regulation cannot be neglected. This will be examined in further detail in the remainder of this chapter.
- The identification of different types of capitalism that cannot be aligned with liberal market or coordinated market economies (LMEs/CMEs) (for examples that attempt to do this nonetheless, see Ahrens and Jünemann 2006; Wilson 2007a; Witt 2010). In critical confrontation with and yet emerging in parallel to the VoC approach, several other models have been employed to describe further (efficient) varieties of capitalism besides LMEs and CMEs that are not limited to the West. These include state-controlled, consensus-oriented, or Asian capitalism, for instance (Coates 2000, Boyer 2005, Amable 2003). Forms of state capitalism or state-permeated capitalism lend themselves particularly well for use as templates for comparative analysis (see Crouch 2005; Fligstein and Zhang 2011; May, Nölke, and ten Brink 2013; V. Schmidt 2000).
- The recognition of the need for a dynamic, nonfunctionalist analysis of historical change that takes into account targeted human action. As illustrated below, this is of major importance, not least

when examining the strategic reform projects of state and party elites.

- A perception of institutional complementarities that goes beyond the VoC approach, where complementarity is seen as stemming from coherence or structural similarities among institutions. Höpner claims that this argument cannot be applied to every empirical case examined. Incoherent settings can also have productive consequences: "Complementarity can exist without coherence, and coherence without complementarity" (Höpner 2005, 356). Some authors thus use the concepts of positive and negative "externalities" (Streeck 2009, 93–146) or use the term "productive incoherence" to describe institutional side effects not originating from a coherent basis (Crouch, Schröder, and Voelzkow 2009).[7]

- Finally, the knowledge that studies on national economies must include a transnational focus (Bohle and Greskovits 2009; Nölke and Vliegenthart 2009; ten Brink 2014b). In the case of China, this is particularly important—here, to stay with the complementarities theme, productive transnational "cross effects" have come about over the course of reform. China has been able to benefit more than any other country from the favorable global economic conditions and advantageous circumstances in East Asia.

Taking these insights as a starting point, a more comprehensive social theoretical basis for the study of capitalist systems will be developed below.

Capitalist-Driven Modernity

In the social sciences, the latest macrotheories draw largely on the concept of "modernity" or rather "multiple modernities," with capitalism playing a lesser role. In contrast to this, in this work I argue that capitalism, as an all-encompassing social order, has sustainably and comprehensively shaped the numerous paths to modernity across several continents over the past hundred years.

Modernity is the result of a growth in human capacity for action and reflection and is characterized by a qualitatively higher degree of autonomy —or potential autonomy—than premodern or early modern societies. Modernity is a network of relations permeated by tendencies toward independence, essentially characterized by institutions for the accumulation of wealth and power, and then expanded to include dimensions such as the normative. In advanced social science theories, such a circumstance is usually gathered into a cluster of autonomous power sources including the juxtaposition of more or less independent institutions. Discussion over the diversity of modernity results in the assumption that different legacies of civilization and macroregional or national paths have come to shape the face of each individual form of modernity (see Arnason 2003a; Eisenstadt 2006; Knöbl 2007; overview: Schwinn 2009).

Studies have been conducted on the diverse dimensions of modernity that can be found in contingent combinations. The most common of these dimensions include the processes of secularization, individualization, pacification, democratization, economization, and bureaucratization. Consequently, the analytical framework developed here is clearly limited, the main focus being on processes of economization and bureaucratization, with only occasional reference to other modernization dynamics.

I argue that economization and bureaucratization processes, interpreted in the current work as driven by capitalist imperatives, are particularly important in this context. This argument is in opposition to broad contingency assumptions. The assumption here is that capitalist institutions are preeminent forms of association in modern societies. Recently, authors convincingly fleshed out this supposition by identifying various empirical characteristics of modern social orders as capitalist dimensions (Callinicos 2006; Deutschmann 2009b; Dörre, Lessenich, and Rosa 2009; Jessop 2007; Schimank 2009; Streeck 2010b).[8]

The following drivers and fundamentals of capitalism are vital to this study:

- Profit orientation and a boundless and excessive imperative to accumulate[9]—combined with legitimate greed and mythical utopian promises—which, unlike traditional, subsistence-oriented societies, help to unleash innovation dynamics and directional dependencies of institutional change
- The role of competition, logics of acceleration, and competitiveness in market *and* nonmarket social relationships, which threaten to permanently destabilize modern social orders because they prioritize competition over solidarity-oriented behavior

- Structural differences between the strategic capacity for action among the actors, which results from inequality in terms of access to resources or class positions
- The dependency on noneconomic institutions, including the modern state, which plays the predominant role (and also displays a structural interdependency with the economy)
- A fundamental tension between market expansion and social coherence, which in turn affects the social, political, and ideological conflicts in modern societies
- Finally, the drivers of capitalism including both characteristic expansion dynamics and an associated tendency among actors to subvert or bend the rules,[10] as well as the potential to integrate and restructure noncapitalist or precapitalist structures

Against the backdrop of my assumption of a universal efficacy of drivers of capitalism as well as of their divergent outcomes, the aforementioned points will function as a "heuristic checklist" (Streeck 2010b, 10) to determine whether and to what extent these can be traced back to phenomena in recent Chinese history.[11]

In order to fend off any charges of reductionism, I would like to emphasize that this study is not an attempt to describe all modernization processes currently under way in China. At the same time, it does not support the argument that all noncapitalist forms of action or independent interpretations are eliminated in the processes of capitalist-driven modernization. A modern world predominated by capitalism does not indicate in any way that all noncapitalist autonomous social practices are lost. Rather, there is evidence of recombinations of institutions and ideas, making an examination of variances in modernization processes an absolute priority. However, historical cultural traditions and interpretations are reshaped through capitalist modernization processes. Notably, it is not only the musings of Marx or the hypotheses of his apostles, but also Weber who stresses the notion of capitalism as the "most fateful power in our modern life" (Weber 1991, 12, my translation).

The overlapping of noneconomic institutions or spheres with drivers of capitalism (e.g., housework, family, cultural phenomena, natural relations, social antagonisms and oppressive relationships, which are not directly the result of capitalism) can be expressed using the term capitalist-driven society. As overarching factors linking social, political, and economic processes with one another, the drivers of capitalism exercise a long-term effect on other dimensions of society, without being subject to them to the same extent when the tables are turned.[12]

In order to understand the overarching driving forces of capitalism and their specific national and/or regional manifestations, a multistep examination into the macro-, meso-, and microdynamics of the implementation and reproduction of such forces is required. The historical varieties of capitalism are viewed as multiple outcomes of a global overarching mode of association, which also demonstrates significant variation in the different historical phases of capitalism (such as the state-interventionism phase beginning in the 1930s or the liberalization phase from the 1970s onward). National economies do not simply converge to form a homogeneous economic unit. The global system comprises a network of different yet interlinked forms of capitalism characterized by continual adjustment and differentiation processes.

In order to avoid the dangers of economic functionalism, ahistorical equilibrium models, and political voluntarism, I have integrated the following assumptions and concepts into my analytical framework:

(1) I work under the assumption of the unstable dynamics of capitalist social orders, to which many theories of capitalism rightly attach great significance—Marx's capital and circulation analysis, Rosa Luxemburg's theory of accumulation, Schumpeter's analysis of entrepreneurism, as well as Keynes's or Polanyi's theories, for example. The relevance of these theories is found in their insistence on the contradictions and conflicts of the capitalist development process and their structural susceptibility to social tensions and uncertainties.

Thus, the growing interdependencies between socioeconomic processes are just one aspect of the capitalist reproduction process. Even if the modern division of labor can be seen as the primary source of social solidarity and the basis of moral order (Durkheim 1988, 471), it will only develop its distinctive capitalist form as part of competition-driven accumulation, that is, the permanent competition between individual production units that creates an innovation dynamic rife with crises and conflicts. This is linked to the fact that capitalist modernity is an arena for social relationships where rationalization develops only in a particularist way (Adorno 1996, 231). This is precisely because the decisions taken by intentionally rational actors are often anchored in fiction or, in other words, based on unrealistic expectations (Beckert 2011). Thus, I argue for the transformation of

China's political economy to be linked with the unstable dynamics of capitalist development and the constant crisis-ridden and uncertain renewal of the system.

(2) To describe commonalities and differences between types of capitalism, I draw on the concept of an international variegated capitalist world system (see Jessop 2009; Streeck 2010a). Commonalities are based on the fact that the modern world market results from interaction between an incalculable number of different factors. The world market is thus a globally dynamic synergy of actions and exercises significant imperatives to act. The reproduction of the global economy as a whole embodies a process without a steering subject that results in innumerable unintended effects. Even when specific development paths form in a national context, they are subject to external adaptive pressure, which might be relativized through national or regional path-dependent tendencies toward inertia but which cannot be prevented altogether. The relatively simultaneous and universal nature of the great capitalist crises of the 1870s, 1930s, 1970s, and 2008–9, although occurring under different socioeconomic, political, and cultural conditions, points to this very correlation (R. Brenner 2006). This trend has grown stronger since the 1970s, as research into the transnationalization of value chains demonstrates (Gereffi, Humphrey, and Sturgeon 2005). The almost universal appearance of liberalization tendencies since the 1970s is also evidence of this.

At the same time, the differences between individual forms of capitalism have to be taken into account. Contrary to the hypothesis of the neoclassical model (for a critical account, see Kaldor 1972), global competition does not act as a force for harmony between the units of capital, leveling differences between companies, regions, and, ultimately, nations. This convergence hypothesis is based on untenable premises—such as the assumption of perfect competition and market transparency, homogeneous goods, and constant production technology and demand structures. It ignores the spatiotemporal development of companies, and the varying degrees to which institutions are embedded, as well as the reality of disparities in the development of capital due to differences in productivity levels. The expansion of capitalism thus brings about severe spatiotemporal disparities not only between but also within OECD and newly industrialized or developing countries. Global accumulation processes are implemented unevenly because the various national societies provide different conditions for the establishment and reproduction of capitalist production relationships (Block 2005).

(3) In terms of methodology, a transnational perspective is well suited to a study of this nature. Modern-day societies should not be viewed as separate entities but must be seen as a federal, overlapping nexus (Mann 1990). Capitalist-driven societies can be adequately analyzed only in the context of their integration in global economic, global political, and other intersocietal relationships. Limiting observations to national territory is insufficient. Instead, we need to examine how national, international, and transnational mechanisms overlap and engage with one another. As emphasized below, even advanced neo-institutionalist China research often fails to factor in global or macroregional economic conditions. The result is a one-sided explanation of the successful rise of the PRC, which is described as the result of inner-societal innovation and regulatory capacity (McMillan and Naughton 1996; see also the overview of China research by Perry 2007, which excludes international influences almost entirely).

(4) The unstable dynamics of capitalist social orders, specifically those in newly industrialized countries, can be explained by the notion of uneven, combined and interconnected development (Rosenberg 2006; Selwyn 2011; ten Brink 2014b). This refers, inter alia, to the combining of old and new, premodern and modern forms, and intra- and intersocietal developments, which lead to unexpected consequences, particularly in late-developing societies (Gerschenkron 1966). The fact that economic development from the late 1970s, specifically in China, would trigger such a true "leap forward," beyond the level of development determined by modernization theory, could not really have been predicted. To help overcome its backwardness, the Chinese economy was able to profit from the development advances in dominant economies: through the transfer of technological and organizational expertise, or against the backdrop of the slowdown in growth in the old centers, fueled by foreign direct investment (FDI). Also, the selective adoption of elements of advanced countries led to a combination with autochthonous structures and historical traditions, resulting in a distinctive new type of society.

(5) I also use another research assumption from economic sociologists, who explain that the reproduction of capitalist markets and the companies operating on those markets rely on noneconomic preconditions and mechanisms of cooperation (Aspers and Beckert 2008). Modern societies are coconstituted through the interaction between market-mediated and non-market social relationships. As social and political institutions have some capacity to reduce market uncertainties, they need to be included in the analysis of socioeconomic development (Fligstein 2001).

Markets themselves are permeated by a series of nonmarket coordination mechanisms (see Lütz 2003; Thompson et al. 1991). In addition to market-based coordination, the economy is also made up of other governance types such as company hierarchies, networks, associations, and bureaucracy. The production and distribution of goods and services is not merely the product of competition and price mechanisms but is also facilitated by hierarchical regulatory mechanisms (Beckert, Diaz-Bone, and Ganßmann 2007). Trust also acts as a foundation for economic action. "Only after trust has been created, are the necessarily complex transactions possible. In particular, access to capital can be eased, as illustrated by the rotating credit associations among Chinese entrepreneurial families" (Deutschmann 2009b, 21, my translation). Moreover, as with any other form of societal embedding located between market and hierarchy, we must be careful not to underestimate power as a factor in market relationships. These include the network as a form of coordination and, extending on this, communities shaped by solidarity evolving over the course of history or clans. Because of the fact that the various types of coordination can be combined in a number of ways, we must assume that many different forms of capitalism exist (Bradach and Eccles 1991; Stark 1996).

(6) The modern state represents the most important nonmarket-based institution, and not only in China. In contrast to other organizational forms, the modern state can generally rely on support from the legitimate monopoly on the use of force. It should be noted that, unlike in precapitalist societies, where the economically dominant classes normally had to resort to direct force to appropriate surplus product, in capitalist systems free contractual relationships regulated by what is at least formally an independent authority are required in both production and market activity. The state, in defining property rights, creates the main prerequisites for market activity (Bidet 1991). Any economic analysis must therefore always include politics. Without a relatively autonomous political authority with a monopoly on the use of force, establishing successful capital accumulation will prove difficult in the long term. As an ensemble of contradictory relationships, the state guarantees integration and adaptation, making the continuation of capitalist socialization possible in the first place—"they include the pacification of social life (stressed by Elias), the overall rationalization of social rules and norms (central to Weber's analyses of bureaucratization), and the institutionalization of controls needed to ensure the maintenance of legal order" (Arnason 2005, 33; see also Brand 2006; Jessop 2007;

Leibfried and Zürn 2006; Mann 1998; Offe 2006). With regard to economic policy, moreover, it it possible to distinguish between market-creating, market-regulating, and market-restricting measures.

State power can be analyzed as the product of processes mediated by both institutions and discourse within shifting societal power constellations. The objective is therefore to disaggregate the state and examine the characteristics of local government apparatuses, for instance. At the same time, the reliance of the modern "tax state" on material income results in a link between political and economic institutions. Various approaches fail to take sufficient account of the close link between the state and the economy in capitalist-driven societies, and this applies not only to the case of China. State institutions may be based on reproduction criteria that differ from those of modern companies. The latter have to assert their financial strength and hence profitability, while the state has to assert its dominance toward the populace and other countries. Generally speaking, however, the state and the economy form a nexus characterized by structural interdependencies. The paradigm of structural interdependencies "insists . . . that state action *always* plays a major role in constituting economies, so that it is not useful to posit states as lying outside of the economic activity" (Block 1994, 696).[13] Often seen as an "external" force, the government must therefore be viewed as a fundamental component of capitalist systems—despite the fact that state institutions have been able to achieve greater independence in the past than these hypotheses would initially lead us to believe.[14] The overlapping areas of responsibility of the state and its sedimented institutional properties form distinct political systems—such as liberal democracy or, in the case of China, the party-state. In a capitalist system, the state does not necessarily have to follow representative democratic principles.

(7) The contradictory development dynamics of capitalist-driven societies should also be seen as the result of the struggle between market forces or processes of commodification and the desire for social security as well as legal, political, and social recognition that continually arises in the social lifeworlds of the subordinated. According to Polanyi, capitalist dynamics as anonymously linked trade systems ("satanic mills") destroy permanent social connections and constitute a fundamental contradiction between capitalist development and the requirements for an intact lifeworld (Polanyi 2001). Should the market—in an expanded sense the production relationships—encroach on the foundations of social reproduction, this would inevitably trigger the mobilization of social forces of self-protection, either

covert or open. In the capitalist-driven modern era, this self-protection is characteristically expressed as social and political struggles within (and about the politics of) the state and in attempts to institutionalize class conflict (Wright 1997).

Consequently, in contrast to a perception of political processes in nonliberal democratic societies exclusively as a result of functional problem solving dictated from above, the present work aims to illustrate how social power structures and class conflicts played a central role also in China's past development. Class conflict, for example, could bring about market-limiting measures and improvements in labor and social standards. This illustrates the importance of examining mobilizing, societal actors here. In the case of China, a number of such phenomena can be identified. Arguments are being postulated, however, that, because of the fact that its values contradicted those of the Christian countries of Europe, Chinese history lacks the concepts of autonomy that would form the basis required for a struggle for "fair" wages or social security, for example.

As the next section shows, my research framework requires a definition of institutions that factors in the level of targeted human action over and above mere structuralism.[15]

Institutions, Historical Change, and the Sociocultural Embedding of Capitalism

The subsequent sections look at how I have approached the issue of the relationship between structure and action, on the one hand, and path-dependent and path-forming development processes, on the other hand. This is followed by an account of various concepts that will aid the examination of gradual institutional change and the introduction of historical and sociocultural traditions from China and East Asia, which I then integrate into my analysis in a nonculturalist manner.

STRUCTURES, STRATEGIC CAPACITIES, AND CHANGE

In societies where capitalism prevails, social actors are subject to external imperatives to act. Unlike orthodox liberal explanations, which postulate a balance of rational individual choices, such constraints result in practices that are not merely the result of intentional action. For this reason, relationships between structure and action (as well as their meaning) have to be looked at dialectically, as it were (Hay 2002). In addition, the different strategic capacities of social actors—the difference between Chinese migrant workers and influential entrepreneurs, for example—also have to be taken into account because such differences result in an uneven playing field for conscious or strategic intervention.

Human labor power is marked by its creative ability to recognize problems and find innovative ways of solving them. This creative ability is one of those phenomena that are difficult to capture in theory, let alone predict. Similarly, entrepreneurial innovations are difficult to comprehend rationally and, indeed, often come about as a result of spontaneous ideas, or even by chance, during search and learning processes (see Sauer and Lang 1999). Innovations require conditions that, in most cases, do not exist at the moment of innovation, which is why there is only a limited scope to calculate risks rationally. For societal dynamics under capitalism, it is important that not only the socially privileged but also the middle and lower social classes attempt to seize opportunities for advancement: "The exceptional level of commitment or motivation that capital valorization is based on can only be achieved with a strong focus on advancement" (Deutschmann 2009b, 47, my translation). Thus, to facilitate an examination of political economies, the actors' normative orientation must be factored in. An analysis of social structures must always take into account actors' options and strategies, as well as their motivation and perceptions:

> In stressing the interdependence and co-evolution of . . . interrelated semiotic (cultural) and extra-semiotic (structural) moments in complexity reduction and their consequences for meaning-making and social structuration, [one can] avoid two complementary theoretical temptations. The first is seen in different forms of structuralism and social determinism, which reduce agents and actions to passive bearers of self-reproducing, self-transforming social structures. . . . The second temptation is the sociological imperialism of radical social constructivism, according to which social reality is reducible to participants' meanings and understandings of their social world. (Jessop 2009, 8–9)

Unlike analyses where historical developments are ordered within the tight frame of reference to capitalist development logic, drivers of capitalism should generally be examined within the context of their historical change. In reality, structural dynamics and imperatives to act are shaped by social and political strategies, that is, strategies based on normative motivation, including the power elite's strategic projects. The latter may possess the power to form structures. Drivers of capitalism must not be viewed in a functionalist light as they are embedded in social, political, and other sociocultural institutions and processes.

On the one hand, specific traditions and social structures give political economies distinctive foundations for economic action. In relation to the postcommunist regimes in Russia and Central Europe, for instance, Eyal, Szelényi, and Townsley refer to path dependencies that fuel the continued existence of what they refer to as "political capitalism." This can also apply to China's recent history:

> Political capitalism is capitalism in the sense that it is oriented towards the rational acquisition of profits, but it is political because this happens under the tutelage of the state and/or in conditions of systematic political interference in the economic system. There are many reasons why managers who have become owners might feel more comfortable navigating a Weberian world of political capitalism rather than a world governed by the conditions of *laissez-faire* competition. As former socialist and post-communist managers, they know the rules of the game in a system in which economics and politics are interconnected. (Eyal, Szelényi, and Townsley 2000, 172)

With regard to institutional change, on the other hand, the creation of new paths is essential, as explained by Streeck:

> Since institutions always require a modicum of good faith on the part of their constituents, the high social legitimacy under capitalism of *creative cleverness* in relation to social obligations must give rise to a typical conflict between rule makers and rule takers in which the latter permanently test the vigilance of the former. The result is a particular direction in the evolution of capitalist institutions, in the course of which these are continuously redesigned to anticipate and adapt to a systemic bad faith of interest-seeking rule takers. . . . The typical rule *taker* that capitalist institutions must reckon with as the normal case is a rule *bender*: He reads rules entrepreneurially,

untiringly looking for ways of twisting them in his favor. (Streeck 2010b, 14–15)

Here, an understanding of path dependency and path shaping under-lines the relevance of evolutionary mechanisms of variation and selection, as well as the partial preservation of institutions. From an institutionalist point of view, the evident relevance of the past's ongoing effects on the present has long since played a role in China research (see McMillan and Naughton 1996). Nevertheless, any purported tendency toward stability in path-dependent processes ought to be called into question (Beyer 2006).

In line with this, a concept for understanding historical institutional change, which may make a valuable contribution to existing China research, is presented below.

GRADUAL INSTITUTIONAL CHANGE

More recent typologies of gradual institutional change (see Mahoney and Thelen 2010; Streeck and Thelen 2005) are helpful in facilitating an under-standing of the astonishing changes that have taken place in China since the 1970s under the continued existence of party rule. Recently, these typol-ogies have also been applied to China research (see Tsai 2006, 2007; X. Huang 2011; Young 2011).

Here, in order to factor in the transitional, adaptable, indeed, hard-fought historical character of institutions, rather than take a formalistic approach, institutions are seen as social regimes or *Herrschaftsverbände* (organizations of rule) à la Max Weber (Streeck and Thelen 2005). Specifi-cally, social power structures and class conflicts are examined—past struc-tures and struggles that led to the formation of institutions and present constellations that change the face of the institutions under the influence of the past (Mahoney and Thelen 2010, 7–8).

To avoid historical determinism, it is important to take into consider-ation the political processes behind the formation of institutions as well as the significance of social conflicts and compromises in relation to the tran-sition to a new institutional form. Institutions adapt as a result of changes in the political coalitions on which they are founded. As a rule, such changes are incremental and cumulative; sometimes, however, they can be abrupt and intermittent. The addition of new elements can bring about significant change. Generally speaking, institutional change is associated with radical historical upheaval (war, revolutions, and severe crisis in society). There is also evidence, however, of institutional change that is based on continuous incremental change but that brings about transformational results nonetheless. Thus, far-reaching change can come from small endogenous changes, not from a one-off exogenous shock (see also Lawrence and Suddaby 2006).

When exploring social change in a historical context, it is important to move beyond the scope of static institutional reproduction to examine the ramifications for and feedback loops of institutions. Throughout their development, institutions may very well call themselves into question, thus embodying quite the opposite of path-dependent reproduction. While institutional reproduction refers to phenomena where the routine processes and organizational forms within institutions prevail even in the context of historical caesura—in the PRC, on the surface, this would appear to be the Communist Party—consequences for institutions that point to evolutionary change are evident time and again. And it is this very change that the CCP is subject to. Even if the main actors in the institutions pursue very specific, goal-oriented intentions over a long period of time, the character of the actors within the institutions, as well as between the institutions and their environment, can still be subject to change. This results in discrepancies between the original goals of an institution and its function in reality.

The question arises as to how global liberalization trends observed since the 1970s mask even supposedly stable institutional ensembles in nonliberal forms of capitalism. Against this background, Streeck and Thelen (2005) conceptualize several ideal-typical modes or mechanisms of change that attempt to interpret the gradual change undergone by central institutions in developed political economies. These are used in my study as heuristic tools.

The term *displacement* refers to the dissolution of existing institutions that can be regarded as incoherent and the replacement of those institutions by new ones, for instance, when their regulatory capacity has been undermined. This term also denotes the gradual incorporation of foreign elements into the institutional system of a political economy, for example, adapting Western social security insurance schemes for use in China. As a result, institutions that were once subordinate can become significantly more important. This fact is evident in the intrastate conflicts surrounding the advancement of certain ministries. The same also applies to external influences (for instance, the role played by Western corporate practices in China, as I attempt to demonstrate below).

For Streeck and Thelen, the term institutional *layering* describes processes that result in the—albeit often informal—formation of institutions,
both alongside and in interaction with existing institutions. These processes
also trigger change within the existing institutions. Unlike displacement, no
entirely new institutions or rules are introduced here. Groups of actors
with too little power to eradicate existing institutions will induce change in
institutions from the sidelines, so to speak. As described in Chapter 2, in
China, this role was adopted by quasiprivate enterprises (township and village enterprises or TVEs) that put pressure on the entire corporate sector to
restructure. New components, or additional layers, are added to the existing
system of institutions.

The term *conversion*, in contrast, denotes processes where the actors in
an existing institution (the staff in a ministry, for instance) make an adjustment, and, from that point on, this institution serves a new purpose even
if the habitual rules officially continue to exist for the time being. "Different
from layering and drift, here institutions are not so much amended or
allowed to decay as they are redirected to new goals, functions, or purposes"
(Streeck and Thelen 2005, 26). Similarly, changes in the constellations of
social actors can affect the purpose of an institution fundamentally. Here,
the necessary pressure to adapt is created by involving new social
groups—in the PRC, this happened, among other things, in the course of
integrating entrepreneurs into the party and state apparatus, as I shall
endeavor to demonstrate in the present work.

The phenomenon of *drift* is the erosion or dissolution of institutions,
processes that are induced by what are often tentative deviations from generally accepted rules. Applied to the Federal Republic of Germany, we could
interpret the relaxing of the collective bargaining system as drift—given
that the institutions that set the tone continue to exist but protect fewer
and fewer employees. Bearing this in mind, we should probably ask our-
selves whether the gradual erosion of the strict system of registration for
residents (*hukou*) in China might also be an example of this mechanism of
institutional change.

Finally, the term *exhaustion* refers to the possibility of exhausting institutions to the point of collapse. In Chapter 2, I will examine whether the
collapse of traditional Maoist political styles and institutions in the 1970s
and 1980s might be an example of this.

It would appear that changes to the Chinese institutional system are
affected by elements of all five of the aforementioned modes of change. The

current work will now seek to ascertain whether certain modes of change have more of an impact than others.

The drivers of capitalism are always mediated by normative and historical cultural traditions. Alongside older historical traditions such as the Confucian tradition and close interpersonal network of relationships (guanxi) this also includes Sino-Marxism. Sino-Marxism's attempts from 1949 to imitate the Soviet-Marxist modernization model in fact considerably modified it, thus contributing to China's distinctive path to modernity (see Arnason 2003b).

As mentioned, historical ideational, and social cultural traditions cause path dependencies that call global convergence processes into question. In the case of China, historians, historical sociologists, and anthropologists argue, for instance, that in order to explain its extraordinary economic dynamism, older Chinese and East Asian traditions of merchant capitalism must be taken into account (Pomeranz 2000; Hamilton 2006a). This comprises a rich tradition of merchant groups operating on the basis of familial ties, which coexisted for hundreds of years with the ruling "tributary" state class without ever achieving a dominant role, until they emerged in the course of the twentieth century, under the new "tributary power" of the CCP, as a motor for economic restructuring (Gates 1996). Other authors argue that the rise of capitalism in China draws from other cultural traditions—including, particularly, those of the overseas Chinese. These include family values, network-based relationships, and paternalistic authority structures. The spirit of Chinese capitalism is also described as Confucian (see Redding 1990; M. Yang 2002). Long dominated by a Weber-inspired notion, according to which the roots of China's inability to modernize lay in the static traditional values of a culture shaped by Confucianism, the discussion now draws on opposite assumptions. Now it is precisely certain Confucian values such as diligence and thrift that are viewed as stimuli for economic growth. In a sense, then, a Confucian way of life is considered to be equivalent to the "Protestant ethic" (see Pohlmann 2002; Arnason 2003a).

In more recent historical sociological research, further arguments are propounded as to why favorable conditions for capitalist dynamics were to be found in China (and East Asia). In comparison to other regions of the world, there was a relative continuity in East Asian history, which derives from the comparative stability of Chinese culture (Arnason 2003a, 304–8). In contrast to the Indian, Islamic, or even the later Western world, what the East Asian historical region had in common during the premodern era was the more developed, more continuous existence of state structures promoting the protracted processes of nation building. "[In China] the result was . . . a more marked cultural unity than any other imperial order has achieved, and—in due course—an enduring ambition to transform this legacy into a full-fledged national identity" (Arnason 2008, 401). Finally, in comparison to other world regions, the premodern East Asian region was less affected by the influence of foreign powers. Even the colonialism of the nineteenth and (more so) the twentieth century was, for the most part, in spite of significant Western influence, an experience associated with Japanese imperialism. The relatively limited Western presence and military power allowed the region flexibility to more autonomously receive and adapt Western models.

Admittedly, far from the perspectives just outlined, research on China and Asia has long been influenced by approaches that could be described as culturalist (see Weggel 1997; Pye 1998; Jacques 2009). Abstracted in this way, Confucianism for instance is in danger of being essentialized (Dirlik 1997, 311). This reductionist "China-is-China-is-China" viewpoint (Dreyer 1996, 13) leaves no room for a comparative perspective. Rather, such approaches are frequently more concerned with emphasizing the uniqueness of China. According to Jacques, today's China should be seen as a "civilizational-state," which, unlike the Western nation-state, preserves within it an over two-thousand-year-old living tradition (Jacques 2009, chapter 2). Its most important moral point of reference is the desire for the unity of the Chinese people. While in the West the relationship between state and society is assumed to be constructed in such a way that the authority and legitimacy of a state essentially result from democratic processes, the Chinese "civilizational-state" acquires its legitimacy through its role as representative of Chinese civilization. The "Chinese," according to Jacques, experience the state as the head of the family, whereas in Western societies state power is regularly viewed as intrusive and as such to be restricted.

Furthermore, in a culturalist perspective, premodern features of life are often seamlessly subsumed under modern concepts. Prematurely drawn parallels between the emperor and CCP leaders or between Confucianism and communism are in danger of lending too much weight to the power of tradition. There is a risk, then, of neglecting to take into account the fundamental crisis experienced by imperial China from the nineteenth century onward—triggered precisely by an increase in external influence—where many traditions, previously deemed sacrosanct, were called into question. Even if recourse was and is made to certain social cultural traditions, the priority was to tackle a radical modernization and thereby overcome traditional premodern forms (less successfully in the first half of the twentieth century, but in a sustained manner following the Maoist accession to power). Moreover, a fundamental shortcoming of culturalist approaches is a failure to embed the recent historical development of China (and East Asia) in the global capitalist order. "The problem with 'Chineseness' based explanations of Chinese capitalism is that they suppress the structural context within which this capitalism has arisen. Whatever resemblances it may have in particular to past practices, this capitalism has acquired an identity of its own only in the very recent past with the success of East and Southeast Asian societies, which has empowered the projection of this newfound identity upon the more remote past and its assertion against others, in particular Euro-American capitalism" (Dirlik 1997, 315–16).

Assumptions that only emphasize a continuity of cultural factors cannot sufficiently explain China's transformation. In order not to encourage cultural determinism and exaggerated assumptions of inner-civilizational homogeneity, research must be done on the contradictory interaction between "cultures" that produced the interwoven forms of capitalist modernization.

Five Dimensions of Capitalism

To examine the proposition that the political economy of China can be understood within the scope of a broad analysis of capitalism, the research framework will now be set out more concretely on the basis of the ideas discussed so far. For this purpose, I distinguish five dimensions of capitalist systems in space and time.[16] The different proportions of these basic ingredients found in all forms of capitalism give rise to different varieties of capitalism where the three key groups of actors (companies, state actors, and workers) each play an (unequal) role. Bearing this in mind, my intention here is to determine an overarching identity of capitalist driving forces and lines of action also and particularly with respect to the real historical diversity of different types of capitalism.[17]

The first dimension of capitalist systems concerns the unstable dynamics of markets and enterprises as well as the significance of competition-driven processes. In capitalist economies the competition between enterprises renders increased accumulation and innovation a necessity. This acts as a social sanctioning mechanism subjecting each individual capital to an imperative to accumulate with a failure to comply being punishable with the enterprise's existence. In order not to let the concept of competition become too vague, it could be understood from an action theory perspective as the anticipation of a potential danger. In a field shaped by many actors, the potential exists for a competitor or new rival to participate in potential profits and/or to monopolize market segments. The relationship produces an imperative for continuous reinvestment and innovation of production processes, distribution networks, and so on.

Under conditions of competition-driven accumulation, the participating production units are coerced into selling in order to buy, buying in order to survive and reproduce, and ultimately to expand and innovate in order to at least maintain their economic position in relation to other production units (R. Brenner 2006). Under these conditions, it is necessary to produce goods for the market, rather than directly satisfy reproduction requirements and to accumulate capital, that is, to use the surplus product to expand production. The associated movement represents a specific feature of capitalism "because there is absolutely no way of measuring adequate valorization. [This] corresponds with the tendency to increase both the degree of valorization (i.e., increase in the profit rate . . .) as well as *the size of capital to be valorized* (i.e., the accumulation of the target profit, whether as investment in productive or in interest-bearing capital)" (Heinrich 2003, 314–15, my translation).

Moreover, capitalist market dynamics can be regulated only to a certain degree. At the same time, capitalist market economies are steered not only by market-based processes, but also through other coordination mechanisms: (company) hierarchies, networks or clans, associations, and state institutions. In this sense, the institutional preconditions and contexts under which the imperative to accumulate is effected determine the cooperative and competitive relations between enterprises. These can include different fractions of capital or business alliances, when specific interests of enterprises unite and become associated with one subjective interest.

THE VERTICAL AXIS OF CAPITALIST SOCIAL RELATIONS

The structure of labor relations, the associated forms of division of labor, as well as the emergence of corporatist industrial relations make up a further basic component of capitalism. The unstable dynamics of capitalist systems do not result solely from the horizontal relations between companies operating in markets. Social stratification and particularly the vertical "class polarization between those who possess wealth and those who do not and the structural social tension created by this" is a further "objective basic condition of capitalist dynamics" (Deutschmann 2009b, 38, my translation; see also Wright 1997). Capitalism as a social order rests on the particularistic appropriation of the goods produced, which, in turn, has no basis in any previously agreed social consensus.[18] The dependency of (competing) blue-collar and white-collar workers on the demand for labor and the capital owners' control over the means of utilizing labor power along with their right to appropriate the surplus product produced by the wage earners establish a specific character of dominance within the wage labor relation. This also limits the opportunities for participation in economic decision making, planning, and control processes with respect to production, distribution, and consumption.

Historically, institutional mechanisms have been established to try to moderate the polarization of the classes; these comprise diverse varieties of corporatism, that is, processes of coordination and negotiation between employers, workers, and the state. Associated with such mechanisms are prevailing, albeit contentious, norms and values (see Burawoy 1985; Wright 2000). On the other hand, class polarization can be a strong incentive for upward mobility and can foster the competition for innovation. This social tension translates into increased economic activity especially in a situation where the structural class-polarization appears to be individually surmountable (Deutschmann 2009b).

RELATIONSHIPS OF MONEY AND FINANCIAL SYSTEMS

Capitalist social orders rely on monetary and financial systems. Money mediates the exchange of goods. The circulation of industrial capital, for instance, gains its characteristic elasticity through the credit mechanism or the sale of shares. Money, however, not only mediates exchange processes, but can, in the form of financial capital, take on a life of its own (Marx 1986). Because the expansion of capital accumulation depends on credit, modern credit relationships include, in a sense, the commodification of the future. "Capitalism, in other words, is more dynamic than other economic systems because it has found ways to turn promises and expectations into presently available resources, enabling the economy at any point in time to invest and consume more than it has already produced. By creating binding obligations for individuals to devote long stretches of their future lives to working toward paying off their debts, the economy redeems the advances it continuously draws on its future production. While profit is the carrot of capitalist growth, debt is the stick" (Streeck 2010b, 25).

Additionally, in historical forms of capitalism, money, or money transformed into capital, is by no means restricted to playing an economic role; rather it embodies a source of utopian promise and can assume the function of representing the "unity" of society. "As already recognized by Simmel, money is the basis of modern, functionally differentiated association. Law, science, and politics are not possible without organizations; but organizations are not possible without money. And finally: by transforming personal dependencies into functional ones, money allows individuals to find themselves through their estrangement from the anonymity of money. Thus money is not only the basis of the organized social framework but also indirectly of the intimate one" (Deutschmann 2009b, 20, my translation).

Further, the level of state influence on the financial and banking sector becomes a central determinant of the depth of state penetration in the economy.

THE ECONOMY AND THE STATE

On the basis of the historical finding that companies and markets cannot provide continued self-regulation, that a market road to a market economy is not feasible (Polanyi 2001), and a strong state was an essential historical precondition for such a transformation and its stabilization, a central proposition of my work is that the party-state in China is not withdrawing from the tendency toward marketization, but instead is contributing to the constitution of a new form of capitalism. In this sense, the party-state must itself be understood as a central component of the new Chinese capitalism. Because the interactions between economic and political actors embody complex processes, which (not only in research on China) are discussed in very different ways, the fourth dimension of capitalist social orders will be introduced at greater length at this point. First, I will outline the basics of modern statehood, second, forms of state intervention and regulation, and, third, actions of political actors where they directly perform entrepreneurial functions. Here, I advocate going beyond abrupt juxtapositions of market and state and instead examining how economy and state are structurally linked and, to some extent, develop historically in a mutually constituting manner.

(1) The mutual dependency between state and economy can be taken as a central feature of capitalist societies. Economy and politics establish a nexus characterized by structural interdependencies (see Block 1994; Brand 2006; Hirsch 2005; Mann 1998; Offe 2006; V. Schmidt 2009). The state sanctions contractual relations, directs and/or coordinates infrastructure measures, and provides business enterprises with an educated labor force. Unlike nonhierarchical forms of regulation and decision making, the state, for its part, frequently "possesses the means for ultimately decisive intervention" (Mayntz 1996, 159, my translation), whether in the form of legal ratification or the final decision in cases of nonagreement. This is because only the state commands a monopoly on power that enables the creation and maintenance of the institutional fundaments that allow capitalist socialization in the first place. For this a functioning state requires (at least relative) independence from the social classes, associations, and so on, even if, in practice, state power is mediated by both societal institutions and discourse. Because state institutions represent an arena for social conflict, attempts are constantly made to instrumentalize them.

Certainly, it is not only the enterprises that are dependent on state institutions; conversely the existence of individual states depends on the successful activity of enterprises on its territory (and beyond). Political apparatuses are structurally dependent on successful accumulation within their territory, because this secures the basis of tax assessment. For this reason "the general and top political avoidance imperative is to forgo or prevent anything that could endanger economic prosperity. Positively formulated, the state must establish, maintain, or recreate a 'healthy investment climate' in order to prevent enterprises from making use of their 'negative rights of ownership'—the right not to invest" (Schimank 2009, 259, my translation).

Overall, then, it is not so much a case of examining the whether but rather the how of state intervention. For this I can draw from Polanyi, who, analogously to his concept of the three "fictitious commodities"—labor power, land, and money (Polanyi 2001), identified three problems of coordination that could not be solved by markets alone, but first required the assistance of state structures. First, in the course of creating a system of industrial relations, social security, educational institutions, and migration control policies, the supply of and demand for labor as well as the conflict between capital and labor are regulated. Second, private control of capital and land remains subject to the state guaranteed freedom of contract, property laws, rights of use, and other regulations. Third, even money, or at least the quantity of money, is regulated to a certain degree by central banks and other regulatory authorities. Polanyi's approach can be embellished with further coordination problems: for example, knowledge, a further fictitious commodity is coordinated to a large extent by nonmarket institutions such as universities or research institutes. Finally, to ensure continued market competition, coordination efforts such as antitrust and cartel laws are implemented (Block 2005).

(2) To be able to determine the importance of distinct political systems for the formation of different types of capitalism, different mechanisms and strategies of state intervention and coordination must be taken into account. These have increased since the late nineteenth century and include, for instance, market-creating, market-regulating, and market-restricting measures. More recent studies distinguish between market-mediated ex post coordination, hierarchically prescribed ex ante coordination, heterarchic coordination regulated by processes of self-organization mediated by networks, negotiation, and deliberation, as well as cooperation built on solidarity. State rulers do not usually limit themselves to the command hierarchy but, rather, combine forms of governance in a specific way (see Jessop 2007, 207–24, Brand 2006; V. Schmidt 2009). At the same time, we must take different territorial and administrative levels into account. To examine the local state and territorial levels below the central government, I draw on relevant literature from social-science-based geography (see N. Brenner 2004; N. Brenner and Heeg 1999; Harvey 1989).

For their economic policies, modern states have recourse to direct and indirect methods of influencing the national economy. Thus, in line with Keynesian demand policy, the state can take action to achieve economic effects by implementing (anticyclical) fiscal and monetary policy measures (Aoki, Murdock, and Okuno-Fujiwara 2005). Here, the state does not intervene in companies' investment decisions and does not plan in the strict sense, but, rather, plays a regulatory role. Indicative planning, on the other hand, goes further. The state negotiates with investors over basic principles of growth and recommends desirable behavior for the private enterprises, without, however, significantly interfering in ownership structures. By contrast, imperative planning is legally binding; the state prescribes certain modes of mandatory behavior and, when necessary, intervenes in investment decisions.

Historically, the structural interdependencies between economy and state emerge in different ways, thus constituting different forms of capitalism. From the 1930s, political authorities played a particularly important role in the various versions of state dirigism; the Keynesian intervention state in the West, the developmental state in the East and also the South. In this context, the concept of state-controlled capitalism or state capitalism was used (for early works, see Castoriadis 1988; Harris 1978; Pollock 1975; Szelényi 1982). In the more recent comparative capitalism research, Vivien Schmidt attempts to use the concept of state capitalism to distinguish countries such as France from coordinated market economies such as Germany (V. Schmidt 2000). For the analysis of East European and Central Asian transition economies, among others, the category of "political capitalism" in Weber's sense (Eyal, Szelényi, and Townsley 2000) or state capitalism as one of its variants is used (see also Schneider 2008; D. Lane and Myant 2007). Large emerging economies are, as already mentioned, also described as state-controlled or state-permeated forms of capitalism (Nölke et al. 2015).

Because, in terms of economic policy measures, a comparison of China with other East Asian countries suggests itself, I will critically draw on concepts of the developmental state. For the success of a developmental state, a particularly important question is whether the nation-state produces sufficient social coherence to create a close partnership between the local political and the corporate elites (see Gerschenkron 1966). For this it needs first to be equipped with an effective bureaucracy that obeys the rules, and within the state apparatus there must be evidence of bureaucratic rationality, that is, an appropriate distribution of power between ministries and/or between ministerial planning staffs (Evans 1995). Second, sufficient capacity to discipline the private corporate sectors is necessary. As Chibber explains, using India as an example, these corporate sectors do not automatically assume the role of a "national" bourgeoisie prioritizing the development of the nation over commercial considerations (Chibber 2003).

(3) Further, the state itself can act as an entrepreneur. With respect to the economic policies of modern states, state intervention along with state

property need not represent a negation of capitalist mechanisms but can, in fact, function as one of many forms of particularistic control over economic and political power—in the form of state capital, for instance. In this way state entities can be subject to the accumulation and competition imperative (N. Lin 2011, 70).

In China, local state actors and local public-private alliances almost act as breeding grounds for the development of productive forces. Thus the "private" owner should not be identified as the only capitalist actor. It is not only individuals or a joint-stock company comprising one or more persons, but rather also state functionaries or authorities, particularly at the local level, who can operate as exclusive controlling owners. Alongside the classic private property, there are other forms of exclusive ownership, including state-owned enterprises (SOEs). The main characteristic of property in capitalism is the separation of those who operate the means of production in exchange for a wage from the control of this means of production. Referring exclusively to the (politically defined) legal position of ownership can distract from this fact (Tamás 2007). Some authors link capitalism and private property too closely, resulting in them positioning state sectors in modern national economies outside the capitalist system (Y. Huang 2008). In the case of China, an analysis that examines state property and state action more generally against the backdrop of the power of the drivers of capitalism would seem more fitting. Thus, in the context of China, McNally speaks of "state capitalism" (McNally 2011), Nan Lin describes China as "centrally managed capitalism" (N. Lin 2011), Jessop uses the term "coordinated market state capitalism" (Jessop 2009, 18), Fligstein and Zhang see similarities with the French "dirigism" model (Fligstein and Zhang 2011, 51–52; see also Pearson 2011, who also includes a comparison with Brazil), and a short time ago, I myself referred to a "liberal market state capitalism" (ten Brink 2010; see also Nee 2005; Nee and Opper 2007; Redding and Witt 2007; Kennedy 2011a).

THE INTER- AND TRANSNATIONAL INTEGRATION
OF CAPITALIST SYSTEMS

The fifth dimension of capitalism in time and space is the integration of individual capitalist orders into global economic, international political, and other intersocietal relationships. In order to take this dimension into account, an analysis is required that explores the interaction of national, international, and transnational processes. This particularly applies to the analysis of economic instabilities and crises, the trajectories of which must ultimately also be examined in the context of the development of capitalism worldwide. Analyzing the changes in China in terms of their connection with transnational capitalist dynamics thus prevents a Sinocentric bias (Hart-Landsberg and Burkett 2006; Hamilton 2006a).

Here, as mentioned above, I follow newer concepts that refer to a variegated global capitalism. Varieties of capitalism cannot be effectively analyzed solely on the basis of methodological nationalism and using comparative statistics but rather should be seen as facets of a global capitalist socialization. This allows us to consider varying trajectories of capitalist development in an international, and by extension, intersocietal context (Rosenberg 2006; ten Brink 2012b). Unlike the global economic development phase following the major crisis in the 1930s—in which there was a balance between internationalization and nationalization tendencies—it must be assumed here that, since the 1970s, inter- and transnational integration has gained ground. The question then arises to what extent this has affected the development of China, a country that has a (potentially) extremely large domestic market and a government that, for a long time, had an interest in restricting or steering international influences.

Interim Conclusion

Finally, I will now reiterate the key points shaping the analysis that constitutes the main part of the present work. The following analytical strategy can be formulated to address the three key research questions: (1) the predominant features of China's political economy, (2) the fundamental driving forces and dynamics of the reform process and the subsequent rapid growth, and (3) the current lines of development and paradoxes inherent in the growth path.

First, I have integrated drivers of capitalist development into my research framework. In the following, I will examine to what extent these driving forces came into play in China, and in what way, and to what extent they contributed and still contribute to the country's modernization. Here, the analysis of links between state, economy, and other societal actors aims not only to provide insights into the structure of China's political economy but also explanations for the relative consistency of the political status quo and indications of its potential for destabilization. I expect to identify plausible explanations by incorporating an analysis of close alliances between

companies and government bodies as well as of the segmentation, segregation, and subordination of the working population.

My objective here is for my analysis to have a transnational focus
because varieties of capitalist development do not unfold counter to the
global market but rather with and within it. In other words, the trajectory
of reform in China's history can be adequately and convincingly described
only by taking into account its integration in inter- and transnational processes, not least because the PRC was able to profit more than any other
large country from favorable global economic circumstances.

Second, the strong assumption of universally applicable drivers of capitalism (manifested differently during different historical phases) has been
relativized using approaches from action theory. My research framework
has, to all intents and purposes, been historicized: capitalist dynamics in
China encountered and continue to encounter preexisting social arenas and
sociocultural traditions that lend the country's political economy a distinctive form. These factors are studied in the main body of the present work
and integrated into the notion of interrelated types of capitalist-driven
modernization. With a view to the conflictual interplay characterized by
power imbalances between the three key groups of actors (entrepreneurs,
state actors, and workers), I will describe the dynamics and paradoxes of
Chinese development.

Third, on the basis of these key assumptions, I have introduced a series
of tools that serve the further analyses. In an attempt to gain an insight into
the effectiveness of capitalist driving forces in specific institutions, I combine political economy analyses on the dynamic and crisis-ridden expansion of markets with empirical findings from China studies. This enables
me to identify different and, in some cases, distinctive forms of politically
integrated entrepreneurship, of competition also occurring in noneconomic institutions, and socioeconomic development trends. At the same
time, going beyond a one-sided (neo-)Schumpeterian understanding of the
individual entrepreneur's capacity for innovation, I refer to underlying
institutional and organizational conditions provided, inter alia, by the
government.

The distinction between five different dimensions of capitalist systems
is also useful for a systematic study of the drivers of capitalism in China.
With regard to the five dimensions listed—the sphere of the "horizontal"
competitive relationships between companies, the "vertical" axis of industrial relations, the interactions between economic and political actors, the

financial system, and, finally, the sphere of transnational integration—I will seek to establish whether and how capitalist dynamics emerged at these levels in China and play a dominant role. I will also explore possible complementarities between these spheres and cross effects between institutions that improve economic efficiency.

The tools for examining gradual institutional change serve in particular to provide us with an insight into the significance of informal institutions and negotiation processes in China, the reforms of the party-state, and the phenomenon of circumventing formal regulations (for instance, with regard to comprehensive enterprise reforms).

The assumption of unequal and heterogenous, combined and interlinked developments in capitalist-driven modernization processes is useful for examining unstable dynamics in China. An attempt will be made to substantiate the idea that heterogeneous production regimes, business types, and state policies were not only beneficial for economic development but simultaneously triggered unintended, paradoxical consequences.

Findings from state theory prove invaluable in my analysis of political reform strategies in China's multilevel system of governance and to explain the adaptive capacity of the party-state, and limitations of political steering. It is thus possible to distinguish between various forms of state intervention and regulation, for instance, market-creating, market-regulating, and market-restricting measures. In addition, based on the assumption of a differentiation between market and state actors in modern societies, using findings from recent China research, further specific features of the political in China's political economy can be mapped out. These features include the behavior of political actors, in which the latter directly perform entrepreneurial functions, and the relevance of local pilot projects for accelerating the reform processes.

Finally, tools from sociology facilitate an analysis of China's segmented industrial relations and the phenomenon of labor market segregation.

In the main body of the present work, I will be unable to provide a sufficiently in-depth analysis of capitalist development in China or a satisfactory examination of all the theoretical considerations introduced in this chapter. However, I also see my research framework as groundwork for further empirical research that, by focusing on the case of China, might contribute to an expanded version of a theory of capitalism.

CHAPTER 2

====

From Mao to the Hu/Wen Era

The Origins and Trajectory
of Capitalist-Driven Modernization

With the help of my research framework, I will now analyze the nature of Chinese modernization and assess to what extent and in what form drivers of capitalism can be determined in the areas examined. The focus of the present chapter is the period of reform from the 1980s into the 2000s. First, however, I will describe the background to the transition under Deng Xiaoping, that is, the key historical features of China's political economy from the 1930s to the 1970s. In contrast to more nationally oriented accounts, already at this early juncture, I also describe international factors that had a significant impact on the development and transformation of the Maoist model.

Protocapitalism: The Historical Background
to the Transition Under Deng

The beginning of the process of reform at the end of the 1970s saw the government of the PRC facing the almost herculean task of restructuring a country with a billion inhabitants without undermining its social stability. This huge challenge was further complicated by the severe social crisis faced by the party and state leadership in the aftermath of the Cultural Revolution. It was this very crisis that left the leadership no alternative but a precarious attempt at fundamental reform.

In the following section, I will summarize the key characteristics of the classical Maoist stage of development. Here I discuss continuities with

Deng's later restructuring, which is often prematurely referred to as the "new Chinese revolution" (Pei 1994). This section demonstrates that it is also essential to take into account external global economic and political developments as well as those within Chinese society. This approach allows a fruitful analysis of Maoism, which combined elements of Stalinism, Third World nationalism, and distinctive sociocultural traditions[1] to form a national modernization strategy that, in fact, resembled protocapitalist development policies (on this, see Bian 2005; Dittmer 1987; Harris 1971, 1978; Karl 2010; Leys 1972; Lieberthal and Oksenberg 1988; Naughton 2007; Osterhammel 1989; Spence 1995; Unger 2007; Walder 1986, 2015).[2]

It is still a widely held view that in China under Mao, and indeed all other real socialist countries, either noncapitalist or postcapitalist imperatives were the key structural driving forces (see D. Lane 1976). Contrary to this opinion, the present work interprets China's development trajectory as a path to modernity that was influenced by (global) capitalism from the outset. Like other underdeveloped countries classified as "capitalist," the PRC was faced with the challenge of national advancement in the context of a globalizing capitalism.[3]

As discussed in more detail elsewhere (ten Brink 2014b, chapter 6), a global analytical perspective provides us with an understanding of the different types of "real existing" socialism and state-interventionist capitalism that prevailed during the postwar period (in developing countries, frequently in a protocapitalist form). These can be understood as different versions of a common phase of global capitalist development or modernization shaped by capitalism. Global economic and geopolitical interdependencies prevented genuinely autonomous socioeconomic development. After 1945, economic competition was overlaid by the arms race to a certain extent, which not only put the defense policy of the USSR under strain but also that of Mao's China. Similarly, military-led movements that aimed to create an alternative non-capitalist form of social organization, that is, particularly the radical wings of the workers' movement and, under Mao, also peasants' movements, faced the problem of being dragged into the maelstrom of global capitalism and its power hierarchies when they assumed social and political control. The history of the Russian Revolution is, of course, an impressive example of this. Yet in China the legacy of underdevelopment came into play to an even greater extent than in Russia. The Maoists, whose primary objective was to effect radical social change, could not simply dismiss these circumstances. Bearing this in mind, the following chapter focuses predominantly on the regime's actual practices and not primarily on its ideological self-definition.

Notwithstanding its (unattained) normative objectives, to a certain degree, classical Maoism was a radical version of *instrumental reason* (Hork-heimer and Adorno), that is, of the attempt to improve the efficiency of the domination of nature and society. "The absurd Western images of Mao as some kind of utopian ruralist or twentieth-century peasant rebel have now been laid to rest: he was a super-industrializer and an empire-builder of the most ambitious kind" (Arnason 2008, 406). In contrast to using a private workforce, here Mao resorts to the "state workers" (and peasants) to obtain the surplus product required for the achievement of CCP ambitions. The existence of subordinated classes primarily facilitated the reproduction of the Chinese state class. In a sense, therefore, in Mao's post-1949 China, capitalist relations of production were imitated on the basis of a very low level of development, although modern liberal relations of distribution, consumer trends, and styles of governance were replaced by a bureaucratic form of management. A combination of preindustrial and industrial tradi-tions created a historically unique social formation. This system reached its limits, however, and was superseded by a new process of restructuring from the end of the 1970s.

Thus, in retrospect, the Maoist era constituted a kind of expedient tran-sitional phase, which both restored national integration and created certain preconditions for the subsequent growth trend: "Maoism was not madness (although some of Mao's actions were). In fact, it expressed a possible solu-tion to the fundamental problem of the Chinese Revolution: how to make China strong and independent and how to retain the power of the Commu-nists in a world dominated by Superpowers and where technological and economic development was rapidly advancing just across the China Sea" (Castells 2003, 325, my translation).

The fact that this brought in its wake considerable human suffering and repression confirms that the instrumentally rational dynamics of modernity (or modernities) are radically contradictory.

For an analysis of the reform process under Deng Xiaoping in the con-text of its historical continuity with China's pre-1978 system, we first need to examine the development of ownership structures. In contrast to the narrow notion of private ownership we are familiar with from Western industrial societies, I will conduct an analysis of ownership based on actual power of disposition. This includes the capacity to have exclusive control over access to certain resources without being legally classified as a private owner.[4] Here, China's process of reform after 1978 can be seen as a move away from one type of class society to another, which was, as yet, not clearly defined.

The separation of state-owned property stipulated by law and the actual power of disposition of government decision makers over the means of production in 1950s China constituted a class society dominated by a state bureaucracy. In this context, the disposing state class was characterized by specialized knowledge and its power was justified with the teleological argument that it was expressing a higher cause in the interests of the majority. This separation resulted in different degrees of participation in political and/or economic decision making, and differences between those in managerial and subordinate positions, as well as differences in terms of access to information and to (frequently scarce) goods. As the exclusive controlling owners, the power elites under Mao claimed their right of disposal and control, which meant that social redistribution tended to be in their favor.

Prior to 1978, surplus labor was primarily not appropriated privately but in a manner mediated by the political administration. After 1949, the state bureaucracy certainly had no immediate interest in facilitating and guaranteeing private-sector profit maximization. Instead, the political elite were far more interested in maintaining their redistributive powers. First, the subordinate classes did not exercise their democratic right of disposition over the means of production and consumption. They were denied access to strategic resources, had virtually no decision-making authority, and were subservient to the state functionaries and the party's auxiliary personnel. Second, the decisions of the bureaucracy were typically not subordinated to the material needs and normative expectations of the majority. The redistributive institutions diverted a considerable share of the country's resources to industry to meet quantitative growth targets and to withstand the pressure of competition (also militarily) from abroad. Against this backdrop, national development targets evolved into the equivalent of a compulsion to accumulate. Not least owing to the absence (or rather exodus) of a strong bourgeoisie, to a certain extent, the Communist Party leadership became the executor of a "mission" that Marx had, in fact, assigned to the bourgeoisie.

While on free markets companies attempt to link the supply (of goods) to what they expect to be lucrative demand with the intention of increasing their profits in order to survive, incentives in state redistributive economies are inherently quite different. Here, supply is determined by redistributors as part of a macroeconomic plan and demand adjusted to this accordingly. The next step is then for the redistributors' decisions to be implemented by (typically state-owned) enterprises. In China, in reality, this ideal-typical model constituted a "plan anarchy" comprising numerous particularistic disposing centers of power. I will attempt to substantiate this on the basis of the following excursus.

Excursus: The 1949 Revolution and Maoism

Historically, after 1927, the CCP evolved from a party representing the industrial working class and its struggles into a party of national modernization embedded in the peasantry.[5] In circumstances of a permanent liberation struggle and civil war, in the 1930s, the party began to create a counterelite. War was the external prerequisite for the survival of this elite, which resulted in a "party in arms" (Osterhammel 1989, 344).

The party derived its legitimacy from various sources: the successful resistance to Japanese imperialism, in particular, gave it both an anticolonialist aura and that of a national force (Selden 1993, 5). A generation of intellectuals was attracted to the party because of its consistent opposition to colonialism and its promise to provide an alternative to imperialism/capitalism. Further, compared with the policies of the Guomindang, to broad swathes of the rural population, the proposition of progressive agrarian reforms appeared to be a welcome development.

The successful national liberation of China in 1949 embodied an anticolonial revolution. Nevertheless, Mao's assumption of power did not equate to a "socialist" revolution although it was accompanied by peasant revolts and social movements in some cities prior to 1949 (Spence 1995, 575–615). Rather than a revolution where the masses strive, through their own efforts, to bring about a fundamental reorganization of society, this revolution mostly stemmed from military actions originating in rural regions. It was effectively based on the creation of a counterstate:

> A revolution can break the monopoly of the state's power by destroying the legitimacy of its rule, so that coercion cannot be exercised to repress the movement against it. . . . Alternatively, a revolution can pit an insurgent violence against the coercive apparatus of

the state, overwhelming it in a quick knock-out blow, without having secured any general legitimacy. This was the Russian pattern,
possible only against a weak opponent. Finally, a revolution can
break the state's monopoly of power, not by depriving it from the
outset of legitimacy, nor rapidly undoing its capacity for violence,
but by subtracting enough territory from it to erect a counter-state,
able in time to erode its possession of force and consent alike. This
was the Chinese pattern. (Anderson 2010b, 64; see also Osterhammel 1989, 343–47)

The struggle between two collective actors with quasi-state structures—
the CCP and the Guomindang—over the succession of the Chinese Empire
was ultimately not won by the Guomindang with its superior military
power, but by the CCP with its greater legitimacy. The result was less a
democratization of power or even a partial dissolution of domination per
se but more a transfer of power to a group of military actors and CCP
leaders who declared themselves representatives of the socialist construction yet effectively commanded a development dictatorship in an undeveloped agrarian country.

The revolution represented liberation from foreign imperial powers and
the reactionary nationalist Guomindang. In the long term, it created a
degree of nationwide unity that was unprecedented over the last century.
The Communist Party forged ahead with a land reform in which it broke
the hold of the "parasitical landlord families" (Osterhammel 1989, 357); the
CCP succeeded in halting inflation and, for the first time, reestablished a
central state authority that maintained order across China.[6]

From then on, the CCP established a bureaucratic party-state. The
party's leading staff regarded Marxism-Leninism as an ideology of national
modernization and ruthlessly forged ahead with this latter objective using
various means. "Inasmuch as the CCP came to power through a popular,
anti-imperialist revolution, the very essence of the legitimacy of the communist state was not Marxism but nationalism" (Zhao 2004, 209).[7] Of
course, the CCP's nationalism was not solely a result of a national ethos: it
was also an attempt to adapt, dictated by external circumstances, to survive
in a world that was dominated by far more developed countries.[8]

In contrast to ruling parties in postcolonial Africa and the Middle East,
for example, the CCP drew on a rich tradition of statist ideas. "The Maoists
never paid much attention to the liberal and democratic elements in the

teachings of Marx and Engels, such as those dealing with free development of the individual and the relationship between the individual and the state. In fact, it can be argued that Mao drew more inspiration about governance from Chinese classics such as *Shi Ji* (Historical Memoirs, by Sima Qian) [from around 145 BC to around 90 BC] and *Zizhi Tongjian* (Compendium on Governance, by Sima Guang) [1019 AD to 1090 AD], which he reread dozens of times" (Lam 2006, 260).[9]

Similar to other developing countries at the time, which were partially established on a foundation of "socialist" principles, partially on the basis of "capitalist" norms, this new society displayed features that were far more reminiscent of the primitive accumulation of capital discussed by Marx than socialist or communist ideals. These included the separation of manual and mental labor, a subsumption under state capital, highly pronounced hierarchies in the workplace and in everyday life, and the suppression of opposition, as well as patriarchal family structures, nationalism, and censorship of the arts and sciences.

> The key institutions of the Maoist era such as work units (*danwei*) which isolated the industrial labor force, people's communes (*renmin gongshe*) that enforced rural self-sufficiency, job allocations (*fenpei*) that rendered intellectuals dependent upon state favor, labor insurance (*laobao*) that bestowed generous welfare benefits upon permanent workers at state-owned enterprises while leaving the majority of the workforce unprotected, personnel dossiers (*dang'an*) which marked citizens with "good" or "bad" political records, household registrations (*hukou*) that separated urban and rural dwellers, class labels (*jieji chengfen*) that categorized people into "five kinds of red" (*hong wulei*) and "five kinds of black" (*hei wulei*)—all served to divide society and foster subservience to the state. (Perry 2007, 11)

In order to challenge the established perception of what has been dubbed "anti-bureaucratism," Whyte distinguishes between two distinct aspects of bureaucratization. On the one hand, he sees the term as referring to a process by which more and more elements of social life come to be governed by large hierarchical organizations (Whyte 1989). On the other hand, he draws on the finding that these organizations approximate the ideal type of bureaucratic organization based on legal-rational authority and formal rules and procedures rather than charismatic or other traditional types of authority. Because Mao and his supporters predominantly attempted to stave off this latter form of bureaucratization but effectively advocated charismatic instead of legal-rational relations, yet still overall wanted to increase state regulation of societal relationships, with the exception of the Cultural Revolution years, we cannot really describe Maoism as essentially antibureaucratic. At the same time, the Maoist concept of antibureaucratism was also the expression of an interelite conflict. The notion of a "class war" against, inter alia, "bureaucratic excesses" that formed the backbone of political campaigns was mainly devoted to attempting to oppose the old political and economic intellectual elites who still possessed cultural capital after 1949 (Andreas 2009; see also Selden 1993, 7–13). Consequently, collectivist ethics and efforts to level class differences targeted technocratic and/or bureaucratic groups.[10] However, this "Red-over-expert power structure . . . in which incumbent managers and specialists were relegated to subordinate technical positions" (Andreas 2009, 269) became less important over time. Following the peak of this interelite conflict, the Cultural Revolution, the Maoist and technocratic elites converged under Deng Xiaoping and became the new ruling elite (Andreas 2009, 269–76; also see Walder 2015).[11]

A final feature of Maoism I would like to outline here is the link between nationalism and a rural populism that led to Mao's voluntarism, that is, the attempt to "leap over" the country's material backwardness by appealing to the morality of the people (Lieberthal 1995, 62–70). In contrast to the USSR, the party-state had neither a proletarian nor a liberal legacy to deal with.

> Consistent with the absence of the class structure postulated in Marx's writings, and with the role of the intelligentsia, free from loyalty to a particular class . . . Maoism is essentially "voluntarist": that is, the aims of the leadership are seen as feasible provided they work hard, rather than provided the objective situation permits. The role of theory is thus changed from that suggested in Marx; for Mao theory is a somewhat eclectically selected element in public relations work, in the propaganda necessary to change consciousness, rather than itself a more or less accurate analysis of reality to guide practice. (Harris 1971, 174; see also Harris 1986, 170–86)

Voluntarism and its counterpart, the Mao cult, advocated hierarchical decision-making methods as well as the valorization of intuitive actions of the country's leaders. The prevailing institutionalized voluntarism found expression in the plethora of production campaigns that were conducted like military offensives, a fact reflected in the language used by the CCP ("production brigade," "grain front," etc.). Linked to this was a tradition of "socialist education" where the "educator" guided the masses who, conversely, were infantilized. This, in turn, eliminated the party cadres' individual sense of responsibility to a great extent. Under the overriding premise of acting "in the interests of the masses," these cadres were able to discard their moral scruples (Saich 2004, 219–20).[12]

Between Command Economy and "Plan Anarchy": Key Features of the Chinese Economy from the 1930s to the 1970s

To counter the myths that misrepresented the Maoist model of development as the brainchild of an insane dictator, an antibureaucratic idyll of farmers' communes, and similar, Naughton refers to China's GDP growth rates, which, compared to India, for instance, were relatively high (Naughton 2007, 140; see also Karl 2010). The average annual growth in GDP between 1952 and 1978 was around 6 percent. Industrial output increased by an average of 11.5 percent per annum between 1952 and 1978 (Naughton 2007, 56). Even as early as 1954, China had an investment rate of 26 percent of GDP, which is rather high compared to other developing countries. Particularly in the years of the Great Leap Forward and the Cultural Revolution, however, there were substantial economic downturns.[13]

During the course of its national modernization efforts, the CCP was able to build on the remnants of the prewar era (Bian 2005), including the industry that burgeoned in the early twentieth century in colonial treaty ports such as Shanghai, Tianjin, or Qingdao. Although this "enclave industrialization" was, for the most part, externally initiated and under foreign control to begin with, indigenous enterprises rapidly caught up (Hamilton 2006a). By the 1930s, Chinese-owned companies were producing two-thirds of the country's industrial output (Naughton 2007, 44). In addition, we saw the emergence of large-scale Japanese government-sponsored industrial projects in Manchuria. Thanks to their qualitative importance (heavy industry), these projects played a far more significant role than their 14 percent share of total industrial output in 1933 might suggest.[14]

From an industrial policy perspective, the precursor of the practice of substantial state intervention and the political power of disposition over companies can be found in the Guomindang government. The relocation of industrial production inland from Shanghai during the Japanese invasion and World War II, for instance, was organized by the Guomindang Planning Commission (Bian 2005, chapters 2 and 3). In the early 1940s, state-owned enterprises in the territories that were not under Japanese occupation accounted for 70 percent of China's capital. The CCP described the ruling powers at the time—almost in subconscious anticipation of their later impact—as "bureaucratic capitalists" (Au 2009).[15]

There was also evidence of path dependencies in terms of the organization of labor:

> The emergence of the Maoist system in the 1950s was itself the result of path-dependent development based on industrial arrangements that arose during the Republican era under the Nationalist government. In the 1920s and 1930s, a newly established legal framework for industrial relations, along with state-corporatist tendencies, heavy-handed state intervention, and paternalistic practices to curb a high labor turnover rate among skilled workers helped lay down the preconditions for the socialist workplace (*danwei*) system. (A. Chan and Unger 2009, 6–7; see also Bian 2005, 167–79)

Certain conditions for industrial development were therefore already in place in the form of state ownership and authoritarian collectivism. Following the Japanese occupation, the ruling CCP gradually developed these conditions further—"institutional and ideological evolution, not revolution, explains the basic structure of state-owned enterprise and its ideology in post-1949 China" (Bian 2005, 213). After 1949, the state-controlled economic sectors were largely taken over by the CCP.[16] Because large parts of (heavy) industry had already been nationalized by the Guomindang government, the subsequent expropriation policy implemented in the country's urban centers could be concentrated on light industry. Now the CCP, which at this juncture had already split internally into separate factions, assumed the role of the national power elite as a form of substitute bourgeoisie (*Ersatzbourgeoisie*). In addition, many senior members of staff from the pre-Maoist Planning Commission continued to be employed under the rule of the Communist Party.

Overall, however, after 1949, China's new elite was primarily faced with a myriad of unfavorable legacies. The years from 1937 to 1945 left the country with a desolate economic infrastructure, a financial crisis that manifested itself as hyperinflation, and an exhausted population subjected not only to fierce Japanese aggression but also repression under the Guomindang. The economy was also heavily balkanized.[17] The decades of Chinese Nationalist rule, of the Japanese occupation of parts of the country, of war, and ultimately civil war meant that the victorious CCP was confronted with an economy that was on the verge of collapse (Herrmann-Pillath 1995, 54–59).

In the first few years following the anticolonial revolution and the victory over the Guomindang, China attempted to imitate Soviet development models (Gey 1985, 15–22). Global economic crises and world war had discredited Western capitalist development policies whereas, at the time, the USSR had the highest growth rates of all major economies. This was commented on retrospectively by Justin Yifu Lin, a former Chinese chief economist and senior vice president of the World Bank: "The collapse of the New York Stock Exchange [in 1929] . . . triggered a ten-year depression accompanied by enormous mass unemployment throughout the entire Western world. Apparently completely unfazed by this, the Soviet Union under Stalin picked this of all times to fully commit itself to transitioning from a poor agricultural country into a serious industrial and military power. There was therefore great fascination about Communism's ability to do exactly as it promised" (J. Lin 2009, 56, my translation; see also Osterhammel 1989, 364–69).

China's pragmatic alignment with the Soviet Union was nevertheless adapted to the country's somewhat different conditions. It would therefore appear to be more accurate to refer to a distinctive form of Maoist industrialization based "to a certain extent, on a war communism mobilization regime with an emphasis on moral incentives," characterized by dramatic changes in direction, each of which embodied different styles to foster national development (Gey 1985, 29, my translation; see also Dittmer 1987, 12–61).[18]

Following the period of economic recovery from 1949 to 1952 and a subsequent land reform ("New Democratic Politics"), the first Five Year Plan comprising a series of command economy adjustments was implemented between 1953 and 1957. In 1955–56, China was effectively a mixed economy. Only after this did we see the start of the top-down creation of collective production units in rural areas that later entered the history books as people's communes. From then on, in the cities, companies became government-steered production plants, while the decision making took place in sector-specific ministries. Thus, individual business considerations were to be replaced by a focus on the national economy.[19]

Following a failed national campaign (the Hundred Flowers Movement), the Great Leap Forward[20] was announced in 1958. This was aimed at increasing the party's influence and accelerating industrialization but ultimately resulted in a withdrawal of human and material resources from agriculture, which culminated in a catastrophic, primarily rural, famine, further exacerbated by natural disaster. As a consequence, within the apparatus of power, the group in allegiance with Liu Shaoqi grew in strength. In contrast to the voluntarist policy of the mass lines, this group emphasized material incentives, profit as a measure of success, and the expansion of markets. This policy was later described as a version of the Soviet Union's "New Economic Policy." The group backed agricultural development and, within companies, supported the managers over the party committees. After a new growth phase, the Cultural Revolution from 1966 to 1976— with its power struggles between the different factions of the CCP and accompanying mass unrest and military mutinies—ultimately heralded a period of political instability and economic paralysis (see Leys 1972; Dittmer 1987, 77–107; Unger 2007; Walder 2015).

Because of their importance as prerequisites for the subsequent reform policy under Deng, I will now provide a more detailed description of the emphasis on industrial upgrading (1) and the structure of the Maoist command economy (2):

(1) Central to the Maoist developmental state was, in the main, a "Big Push" development strategy, which prioritized the expansion of heavy industry (including arms production) at the cost of consumption (J. Lin 2009, 82; Saich 2004, 241). The country's profitable production plants provided the central state with considerable resources, which this fiscal authority, in turn, used to advance further industrialization.[21]

As in other developing countries, this was accompanied by a transfer of the surplus product from rural areas to the cities or rather to industry, which became a catalyst for social conflict (Aoki 2011, 19). Naughton refers to a key crisis mechanism that prevailed during this period of industrialization: "Every time the system really began to accelerate, it ran into fundamental problems. The economy would overshoot and hit its head on the ceiling. What was this "ceiling"? The ceiling was the inability of agriculture to rapidly generate adequate food surpluses, combined with the weak capacity of the system to generate productive employment for its abundant labor" (Naughton 2007, 79).

Land reforms and collectivization resulted in relatively egalitarian income distribution in the countryside (at the lowest level), which, at the same time, was juxtaposed with a privileged cadre group that had amassed all political power. The urban-rural divide was consolidated with the establishment of the *hukou* system in the 1960s: a strict system of household registration that ascribed people with a rural or urban residency status.[22]

As in the countryside, the CCP also promoted social homogenization in the cities. This was, however, in contrast with the privileges of the party cadres.[23] The emerging *danwei* system, which involved the creation of an urban work and life unit encompassing place of employment, hospital, school, administration, and cultural services, at the same time also guaranteed bonuses for sections of the industrial working class. However, the significance of the danwei could not be reduced to an instrument of control: it also had economic, political, and social functions including a paternalistic role (acting as a type of substitute family), and, in addition, it provided identity (Heberer 2008, 94–98).[24] At the same time, the All-China Federation of Trade Unions (ACFTU) was ascribed the role of an arm of the party within companies. The ACFTU was subordinate to the national goal of development of productive forces: "The general direction was definitively established in a 1948 report by Chen Yun in which he proclaimed a policy of 'developing production, making the economy prosper, caring for both public and private, benefiting labor and capital' for trade unions in liberated areas. . . . In order to do this, union leadership exhorted the working class to distinguish between 'short term' and 'long term' interests, i.e. to sacrifice immediate economic and political advancement for the good of the nation" (Friedman 2011, 48).

In 1950–51 and 1956–57, for example, labor disputes and worker discontent resulted in factions of the ACFTU distancing themselves from this position politically. However, these disputes were suppressed by the party and state leadership as "economistic" or "syndicalist" tendencies.[25]

Some authors have compared the industrial system during this period with the authoritarian structures of the twentieth-century war economies in the capitalist West: "Individuals were asked to sacrifice for the common national cause during speed-up-production mass mobilization campaigns that swept the nation one after another" (A. Chan and Unger 2009, 7; see also Walder 1986, 85–122). The country's limited material development combined with Mao's collectivist practices created a factory regime that can be referred to as a type of "bureaucratic despotism" (Burawoy 1985, 12). In terms of ensuring particular levels of performance, as in the early capitalist period of "market despotism," coercion predominated over consensus. This resulted in workplace conflicts, even before the Cultural Revolution (Unger 2007).

However, certain segments of the working class profited from the focus on industrial development: in key sectors, the industrial labor force in state-owned enterprises[26] in particular benefited from social security systems, unlike workers in the collective enterprises (C. Lee and Selden 2007).[27] Anita Chan thus sees similarities between the Chinese danwei work unit system and the lifetime guarantee of employment in Japan's bureaucratic-paternalistic postwar system (A. Chan 2006, 93).[28]

(2) To a large extent, the structure of the command economy was based on China's regionalized national economy. After 1949, there was frequent friction between the provinces and/or between the provinces and the central state. In the 1950s, the central state leadership deemed it feasible to make the country's individual regions into autonomous economies ("running on their own steam" as it were).[29] This position in favor of a regional autonomy was also fed by fears of serious geopolitical clashes on China's external borders as well as by the Maoist voluntarist tradition of making a virtue of necessity. The ultimate result of all this was a plan anarchy.

On the one hand, we had the state's attempt, using the tool of "material balance planning" (Naughton 2007, 61), to issue commands assigning specific production targets to companies and allocating resources and goods among the different economic entities. Within the national planning organization, the allocation of planning responsibilities among the various sectoral ministries was fundamental, and the Coal Ministry (and indeed other sectoral ministries) had its own planning office. In order to ensure coordination both between the sectoral ministries and the provinces and to draw up a national plan (based on the orchestration of regional and national plans), the State Planning Commission, which was under formal control of the Chinese State Council, was assigned a key role (Lieberthal and Oksenberg 1988, 63–72, 137–45). Consequently, prices lost the function of regulating supply and demand. Furthermore, the monetary and financial system served primarily to develop the command economy, not to finance private investment (Jinglian Wu 2005, 217–19).

On the other hand, unlike the USSR but, to some extent, similar to its Eastern European vassal states, the planning system in China was less centralized and less tightly controlled, however (see Lieberthal and Oksenberg 1988; Lyons 1990).[30] What Kornai referred to as "plan bargaining," which prevailed in the countries of the Eastern Bloc, was a particularly apt description of the system in China (Kornai 1992, 121–24), where it evolved into competition between state-owned enterprises, (sectoral) ministries, subnational power elites, and collective enterprises, and within the army. Among themselves and in the struggle for the support of the higher-level authorities, these actors bargained over investment resources. Here, the fulfillment of planning targets was not always the decisive factor, but political maneuvers, bribery, and lobbying representatives of specific branches of industry were of equal importance.[31] In China's command economy, planners were not the only ones determining production, distribution, or consumption.

A vital component of the Maoist planning system, therefore, was the central-state efforts to coordinate the main subnational units, that is, the provinces. In reality, however, this resulted in a checkered history of decentralization and recentralization implemented in an attempt to get a grip on the macroeconomic losses of control (Lyons 1990, 40). From this, a regime emerged that essentially constituted a combination of local/regional and national planning. During this period, the command economy was therefore simultaneously controlled in both a "cellular" and "centralized" manner (Herrmann-Pillath 1995, 112).[32]

Two parallel systems existed. Roughly described, the key components of these systems are: a national ministerial planning organization, which supervised the centrally controlled economic units within the provinces, and a regional provincial planning organization, which, with the exception of the above-mentioned centrally controlled economic units, incorporated all other areas of responsibility in its plan. This planning logic was also flanked by other economic units with overlapping jurisdictions:

> Abstracting from the sub-branches and tiers within each ministerial and provincial branch, there are four types of planned agents: provincial, provincial/central, central/provincial and central. . . . The two mixed cases are those subject to dual leadership, with either the province or the centre (i.e. a ministry) predominant. In the case of a provincial/central enterprise, the province is responsible for the

production and financial plans, and the enterprise is accommodated in provincial balances. In operating its provincial/central enterprises, a province must comply with national plans and, in particular, must ensure any required "exports" from the province. The relevant ministries provide "guidance and support" and may supply some key inputs. In the case of a central/provincial . . . enterprise, a branch ministry is responsible for the production and financial plans, for providing most inputs and for distributing outputs. The province in which the enterprise is located handles political and ideological work, arranges "co-operative assistance" and supplies of locally controlled inputs, and receives in return a fixed share of the output or the right to have materials worked up after completion of ministry orders. (Lyons 1990, 41–43)

In the second half of the 1970s, only ten thousand enterprises were central or "central/provincial." Both the overwhelming majority of state-owned enterprises (over seventy thousand) and the even larger number of collective enterprises were controlled by regional or local institutions.[33] Many provinces therefore had considerable room for maneuver and a level of financial leeway that should not be underestimated. While the development of a heavy industry core and the distribution of important industrial goods were still centrally controlled in the 1950s, over time, the central power apparatus delegated the authority for numerous industrial enterprises to regional governments. Consequently, the Maoist era was characterized by a disparate economy, which also applied to the situation in the provinces themselves:

It was possible for a company to be located in a specific city and for it to be assigned to the municipal authorities and yet for that company to actually manufacture goods for a second enterprise which, although situated in the very same city, was in fact under the jurisdiction of the provincial authorities. Neither company had the power to directly decide their own supply relationships but both were required to first seek approval for their respective plans from the relevant—but different—administrative bodies. This of course had an impact on production. Where necessary, the manufactured goods still had to be delivered to the state supply office, which also maintained a branch in the city. It was possible for the input requirements of the second company to first need to be processed by the entire hierarchy of the State Bureau of Material Reserve until the enterprise possibly—but certainly not as a matter of course—was allocated the product by the local office of the State Bureau of Material Reserve, which, in turn, was produced by the other company located in the very same city. (Herrmann-Pillath 1995, 113–14, my translation)

This system of local and regional state ownership rights and the principle of different jurisdictions—according to which a company could be assigned to a subnational authority and yet functionally still be under the control of the central government—differed from the ideal type of command economy. Complex processes of negotiation between the different units resulted in economic plans with roughly formulated targets that generally gave the companies a certain degree of leeway in terms of their production decisions. The conflicting interests at different levels within the government apparatus could be understood as an expression of a "quasi market" in which those responsible were trapped in permanent barter activities and procurement efforts, although prices were still officially fixed and in fact only performed a limited allocative function (Herrmann-Pillath 1995, 116).

Accordingly, national planning also manifested itself as a competitive process—as a plan anarchy that was reflected in discrepancies between the central and regional plans as well as higher-level plan targets and the political considerations of local authorities and managers. The administrative command center's attempt to unite a multitude of partially competing economic subunits using an overarching accumulation strategy failed (Lyons 1990, 53).

In order to establish a more detailed explanation of the radical change at the end of the 1970s, we now need to outline the main reasons for the turnaround under Deng.

The Crisis After the Crisis: The Erosion of Maoism in the 1970s

In the mid-1970s, it appeared that the nation was gradually recovering from the trauma of the Cultural Revolution. However, the escalating political conflicts within the party leadership from 1975–76 onward expressed social tensions that had only temporarily faded into the background. They reflected a weakening of Maoist self-definition, development policies, and the systems of the danwei and the rural people's communes that had underpinned the daily and working life of the population (Dittmer 1987, 207–9).

The reorientation of certain sections of the power elite from the late 1970s was an expression of this predicament. However, Deng Xiaoping's policies did not represent a complete break with the country's economic history. Deng belonged to a camp within the CCP that advocated a pragmatic economic policy, unlike Mao's model. In the 1950s, a fierce debate erupted between this right-leaning wing of the party supporting Liu Shaoqi and the left-leaning, or more precisely, voluntarist wing allied with Mao about the pace at which agriculture was to be collectivized.[34] While Maoist voluntarism primarily (if not at all times) relied on the rural population and the party, the pragmatism of Liu and others developed a popularity among industrial workers and intellectuals that should not be underestimated. The Great Leap Forward campaign from 1958 and the establishment of people's communes could therefore be implemented only in the face of significant internal party resistance (Kosta 1985). After 1961, on the instruction of Liu Shaoqi, aspects of collectivization were temporarily reversed, which meant, for instance, that plots of land were made available for private use. The agricultural policy implemented in the province of Anhui in 1962–63 created foundations for the subsequent strategy of land leasing.

China has never had a monolithic unified development model. This is another reason why it is inaccurate to describe the post-1978 reform period as a genuine break with the past. Deng himself, like Mao, attached great importance to national development. Communist policies and the CCP were vehicles for creating a prosperous and powerful China in a competitive global environment. Similarly, the wing of the party with an allegiance to Deng also saw the CCP as having an undeniably essential role as an instrument of modernization. The internal factions within the CCP were therefore ultimately proponents of different responses to one and the same national development issue. In this respect, the gradual change in party ideology after 1978 comprising a transformation of the CCP from a "class-based" to a "people's" party was belated recognition of the nationalistic development policies targeting the entire "people."[35]

To answer the question as to why the wing of the party with allegiance to Deng was able to prevail, it is essential that we first acquire an understanding of the severe crisis of the 1970s and the weakening of Maoist institutions and that second, we consider global economic and political processes of restructuring.

The slowdown in industrial growth between 1970 and 1979 marked a crisis in the success of the Maoist development process in China's urban centers. Similarly, the rural population's standard of living also stagnated (Selden 1993, 60). From the 1970s, the combination of slow industrial growth, the crisis in agriculture, supply shortages, and the resultant political and social discontent constituted a somewhat volatile set of circumstances (Lieberthal 1995, 297).[36]

The crisis among the country's political leadership linked to this situation was, however, not yet sufficient to bring about significant change. After Mao's death in 1976, the coalition of market-oriented reformers in the party and the rural periphery allied with Deng Xiaoping—based, inter alia, on a technocratic intellectual class—faced "Maoism without Mao" under Hua Guofeng (chairman of the Communist Party from 1976). The latter in particular insisted on reviving the command economy using traditional Soviet methods (D. Yang 1996, 441). Only the rise in social opposition created sufficient impetus to tip the balance of power within the political leadership in favor of the reformers.

The years from 1976 up until the Chinese democracy movement in 1978–79—the call for, among other things, the Fifth Modernization, in other words, democratization—and isolated worker protests in 1980 was a period of diverse social protest (Spence 1995, 774–83; Wenten 2011, 33–34). The root causes of the change in political direction can, therefore, be identified using a conflict model where the farmers and the working class forced the power elite to change course (Bernstein 1999, 204–5; Heberer 2008, 37–40). The April Fifth Movement (Tiananmen Incident) in 1976—mass protests triggered by the death of the beacon of hope, Premier Zhou Enlai—already illustrated this. The protests that took place during what was dubbed the Beijing Spring convinced the wing of the party allied with Deng Xiaoping that a change of course was a matter of urgency (Eifler 2007, 102–7; Xie 1993, 323). The rural population played a particularly active role in this. Food shortages coinciding with a crisis of confidence in the CCP consequently forced the party and the state apparatus under its control to authorize spontaneous land distribution. This paved the way for a return to family-centered methods of farming.

At the end of 1978, there was finally a breakthrough on the political level: during the Plenary Session of the Eleventh CCP Central Committee, Deng and his allies established themselves as the new ruling group. One year later saw the tentative, and, to a great extent, still unfocused, implementation of modified economic policy concepts. In order to overcome the resistance from the senior cadres within the party and the army (in Beijing, but also and particularly in the northern provinces), the group in allegiance with Deng endeavored to win the support of the subnational governments. The prospect of fiscal decentralization gave many local leaders hope that their existing room for maneuver would be expanded. In addition, productivity increases in the provinces of Anhui and Sichuan were linked to the reforms, bolstering the institutional strength of the reformers (Goldman and MacFarquhar 1999a, 7–8).[37]

As a look at global trends of this era reveals, it is no coincidence that the group of leaders allied with Deng Xiaoping advocating "institutionalized revisionism" (Dittmer 1987, 266) favored a partial liberalization route and, a little later, the controlled policy of opening up—although they still classified this as an increase in the efficiency of the command economy.

THE GLOBAL REFORM MOVEMENT OF THE 1970S AND NEW DEVELOPMENT POLICY MODELS

The Chinese leadership's change of direction coincided with an unprecedented global economic situation—characterized by the end of a long period of growth after 1945 and the transition to the neoliberal phase of global capitalism. The propensity toward state-controlled economies that had prevailed from the 1930s had run its course (Altvater and Mahnkopf 1996; R. Brenner 2006; Harris 1986; ten Brink 2014b).

Worldwide, the changes observed in the 1970s—the end of the "economic miracle," the crisis of Western Fordism, and a tendency toward stagnation on the "periphery"—created ideal conditions for neoliberal discourse. This also applied to developing and newly industrialized countries. If the West believed that Keynesianism had failed, then certain versions of development theory and Stalinist command methods would also be perceived as doomed in many less developed countries. Instead, Third World elites increasingly considered more liberal development models to be a viable alternative (Hurtienne 1988; Chibber 2003). Elites who, to a greater or lesser extent, had followed a policy of state planning and "import substitution" (Fröbel, Heinrichs, and Kreye 1988) now attempted to liberalize the economy, facilitate deeper integration into the global market, and increase the country's focus on exports.[38] Here, reference could be made to various positive role models: particularly in East Asia, there were a number of export-oriented economies, primarily Japan and what later became known as the "Tiger states," on a successful growth path that served as the basis for creating a new development policy model.

Against this backdrop, socialist planning concepts were also increasingly beset by crisis. Since the 1930s, to an extent, the Eastern Bloc countries and China had represented the most extreme form of state intervention.[39] However, the pace of their economic development continued to be influenced by the tempo of the global economy and the balance of power within the system of states. In the national context, the state-capitalist period that commenced in the 1930s permitted the model of catch-up industrialization with import substitution to embark on a relatively efficient catch-up process. With the increasing integration of the global market from the 1960s, this strategy reached its limits, however. Over the course of time, China's autarkic ambitions lost momentum. The development of the forces of production, which was accompanied by close links between companies and individual states during the first half of the twentieth century, now evolved into a trend toward surpassing national economies. Endeavors in state socialist countries to circumvent the accompanying new international division of labor, as it transpires, increasingly hampered the efficient accumulation of capital. More recent research shows that the failure to adapt to the internationalization of capital flows is one of the key causes of the demise of these regimes (see Dale 2004; Haynes 2002). A flawed technology transfer as a result of isolation from the global market is one example of the dilemma created by an economy geared toward self-sufficiency. The closer a sector moved toward global product development, as was the case with the microelectronics sector, for instance, the more apparent the deficiencies of the model became. Here, the transition from Fordist to post-Fordist forms of production and employment was the least efficient.

The crisis of state interventionism and of command economies also hit the most populous Asian countries. For instance, even the power elites in India, who in the immediate postindependence period were still proposing to implement economic policy through development plans (the Bombay Plan), declared the end of Nehruvian socialism and, against a backdrop of economic stagnation, began to search for alternative accumulation strategies (Chibber 2003, 248–53).

Ultimately, the PRC underwent a similar development (Harris 1986, 163–69). As well as the inefficiencies in the state-controlled economy, the erratic foreign economic relations that prevailed during the Mao era were subject to criticism, particularly because global economic integration had effectively already become more relevant.[40] The model of successful development exemplified by some East Asian economies, particularly Japan's, which stimulated a wave of industrialization in East Asia, became a template here, which, of course still had to be given its own national form. Deng expressed this at the National Congress of the CCP in 1982: "[We should] learn from foreign countries and draw on their experience. But the mechanical copying and application of foreign experiences and models will get us nowhere" (quoted in Hartig 2008, 43). Making an implicit reference to the adoption of Soviet industrialization strategies, which had been fraught with problems, Deng pointed out that China had already "learnt many lessons in this respect."

Particularly the economic dynamism of the neighboring countries was a role model for China, although it did not really admit to this (Goldman and MacFarquhar 1999a, 5). The proximity of Japan, whose economy was still in tatters around 1945 as a result of World War II and yet from the 1950s broke numerous growth records and in addition to competitive export industries also managed to create a modern consumer society, caused Mao's achievements to pale in comparison. In China's historical vassal states, growth was virtually unstoppable: "By the late 70s, South Korea had industrialized at a break-neck pace under Park Chung Hee and, most galling of all, the GMD [Guomindang] regime in Taiwan was not far behind. The pressure of this setting on the PRC was inescapable" (Anderson 2010b, 79). Although the city-state of Singapore could not really be compared with China, developments under the state capitalist, de facto one-party rule of Lee Kuan Yew after 1955 and the changes in political ideology from socialism to anticommunism and ultimately Confucianism suggested a possible path to economic modernization (E. Lee 1997, 54–71). Further, the economic stagnation in other state socialist countries weakened arguments in the Chinese party-state for blocking a transition.

A further development provided the pragmatic factions within the Communist Party leadership with the opportunity to drive the reforms forward and open up the economy: geopolitically, the position the People's

Republic found itself in after the Cultural Revolution made it easier for the country to change direction and move away from the Soviet Marxist path. From the early 1970s, diplomatic relations with the United States were resumed, and a bilateral strategic partnership was formed, which, from 1978, resulted in stronger foreign trade relations. It is also important to bear in mind that this gradual integration of China took place at the beginning of a global economic period of extensive free trade, which was accompanied by an increase in global economic activity. In this respect, the ramifications of the international crises occurring during the 1970s created favorable circumstances for the PRC, which prevailed over the coming decades. It was only in this context and in combination with the relocation of commodity and production chains toward East Asia and an increase in demand for consumer goods from the North that the country's growth was able to succeed.

EXCURSUS: THE EAST ASIAN DEVELOPMENTAL STATE AS A ROLE MODEL

In fall 1978, Deng Xiaoping visited Japan. Impressed by the country's level of development, he conceded: "I understand what modernisation is at last" (quoted in D. Guo 2009, 12). In the PRC, Japan, and other East Asian "late developers" in particular were (and still are) seen as role models, although this was initially virtually unacknowledged.

In analyses of East Asian capitalisms, the focus of attention (not only of the Chinese government) is the (authoritarian) developmental state (see Deyo 1993; Evans 1995; Wade 1990). However, we can really speak of an "East Asian capitalism" only at a high level of abstraction (Amable 2003, 102–4). Country analyses refer to stark differences between the various forms of capitalism in East Asia, despite the fact that virtually all the countries underwent a process of state-led, export-oriented industrialization. However, certain parallels cannot be denied, primarily as a result of similar historical experiences and similar geopolitical and global economic conditions.

A key catalyst for state dirigiste industrialization outside Japan were conditions of profound social crisis in the aftermath of World War II. This enabled the state bureaucracies to establish legitimate rule—a prerequisite for which was the submission of the traditional, now disorganized, ruling classes similar to the subservience of the subordinate groups—and to formulate and implement economic development strategies (Hamilton and Biggart 1997). Later, by focusing on external markets, various countries occupied trade niches in a comparable way, if at different points in time, and also achieved success in the field of export of more sophisticated industrial goods. As well as profiting from the expansion of world trade, this undoubtedly also benefited from the geopolitical order of the Cold War. The geopolitical architecture of the Cold War—particularly the inclusion of Japan, Taiwan, South Korea, Hong Kong, and Singapore in the U.S.-dominated bloc—created a type of safety net and made it easier for these countries to integrate into the global market well into the 1970s. The economic growth of East Asia resulted in close intraregional economic ties, which developed into an inner hierarchy with Japan at the helm.

From the 1970s, certain segments of China's power elite became increasingly aware of the success of these regimes and the extent of the state's regulatory capacity also in more market-based economies. This was the case despite the fact that mainland China was distinct from its development policy role models in various ways.

Interim Conclusion

This work represents an attempt to elucidate an interpretation of the modernization of China where the transition that took place from the 1970s is not seen as a complete break with the past but rather a gradual, if ultimately comprehensive, process of restructuring.

Contrary to the assumption of a transition from a command to a market economy, which is perceived as a systemic break, the transition that actually took place was from one form of national modernization, already imitating capitalist mechanisms—although this did not primarily draw on market forms (protocapitalism)—to a distinctive new variety of capitalist-driven modernization. Contrary to popular belief, the Maoist economy had a polycentric structure and created uncontrollable internal dynamics. At the same time, as opposed to the myth of cooperation and planning, the system was repeatedly fueled by irrationalities (plan anarchy). Just as in capitalist economies, where anonymous markets are not the sole factors determining which goods are to be produced and how they are to be manufactured, in China's command economy, planners were not the only ones controlling production, distribution, or consumption. The Maoist period of the PRC was characterized by fragmented, anarchic attempts at coordination rather than comprehensive, forward-thinking, calculated steering and yet still served as a suitable foundation for later market reforms and for the drivers of capitalism to increase their impact. However, comparatively speaking, the country's attempt at national development was an overall success according to quantitative economic efficiency criteria.

We can therefore not assume a sudden transition from plan to market. In reality, China's social institutions underwent a process of change that culminated in a distinctive mixture of plan, market, and other forms of coordination. Old and new, internal and external traditions came together to form a unique synthesis of social change. Both the decentralized system (in comparison with the Soviet Union) and the lower level of industrialization created favorable conditions for gradual institutional changes. At the same time, this change was based on the emergence of a modern social structure: land reform and Maoist economic policies had disposed of China's relatively unproductive, quasi-feudal system. The average level of education of the overall population was comparatively high.[41]

The root causes behind the transition under Deng were the deep social crisis after the Cultural Revolution and the gradual exhaustion of Maoist institutions and self-definition. The reality of a ruling system that exhibited characteristics of an intermittently random and contradictory complex of power with overlapping spheres of responsibility and whose government had been repeatedly shaken to its foundations since 1949 led segments of the power elite to the conclusion that they needed to explore new avenues. From a sociostructural perspective, this was facilitated by the convergence of Maoist collectivist and technocratic elites: "The new CCP leadership . . . insisted they were not abandoning egalitarian Communist ideals, only the destructive approach of class levelling. In the future, everyone would get rich, but some would get rich first" (Andreas 2009, 274; see also King and Szelényi 2005, 220–22).

It is also necessary—as assumed in my research framework with reference to an extended analysis of capitalism and to the power of the drivers of global capitalist development—to embed the global organic crises of the 1970s in this process. China's path to liberalization is indeed part of a profound global change, although the country's restructuring or, more precisely, the transformation of the relationship between policy and economy was quite distinctive.

The ambitious attempt, linked to China's historical heritage, of national development with a transregional impact after Mao ultimately, paradoxically, combined aspects that had previously been ascribed to competing projects of the modern age—marketization and the party-state. This combination advanced a process during which Sino-Marxism fostered a transformation into a new variety of capitalist-driven modernity. The following chapters focus on the developments that China's new ruling class set in motion from the late 1970s onward in order to secure their position of power by implementing gradual reforms, molecular processes of change, and model experiments.

The Emergence of State-Permeated Capitalism (1): Two Phases of Reform

With my historical account of China's modernization process from an extended political economy perspective, I aim to prove that a key driving force behind the transformation of China's economic and political institutions was the dynamics of a boundless and excessive process of accumulation. My analysis examines the role of competition in market-based and nonmarket-based types of coordination and presents a detailed account of how crisis-ridden market dynamics advanced the transformation of the state and, conversely, how state reregulation became a determinant of market expansion.

As described in the previous section of this chapter, China's economic and political transition was triggered by the various crises in the 1970s. The trend toward the decentralization of economic decision making that was accelerated by this process by no means represented any form of targeted policy implemented by the party leadership under Deng. It would be far more accurate to see it as a result of a crisis-induced form of restructuring, which, over the course of time, led to permanent tensions between the process of market expansion and the problems of social integration. This was accompanied by external shocks such as the radical changes between 1989 and 1991 or the Asian financial crisis.

Although political decision makers implemented certain shifts in focus—from promoting the development of the country's interior to favoring that of the coastal regions, for instance—initially, the transformation was certainly not a planned process, neither in an imperative sense nor in accordance with gradual reforms. What was, in retrospect, a reform process characterized by gradual change should not blind us to the fact that by no means did the CCP carry out well-engineered political and institutional reforms, particularly during the first phase of reform. This is especially valid considering that the term "gradualism" suggests calm and forward-looking steering capacity. In reality, the reform decades were permanently accompanied by social conflict, which, in turn, had an impact on how these reforms were implemented in practice. At times, there were also various internal ideological clashes between the power elites.[42] Different factions within the apparatus of power demanded that the right "line" be toed. To a certain extent, reform years (1979, 1984, and 1987–88, for instance) were thwarted by antireform policies (in 1981–82, 1986, and from 1989 to 1991, for example). If at all, the course of events was defined by a transformation that had been characterized by successful experiments, that is, those that resulted in economic growth, in accordance with Deng's maxim "to cross the river by feeling the stones."[43]

The Four Modernizations, called for from the 1970s in the fields of agriculture, industry, science and technology, and national defense, functioned only as general cardinal principles and remained open to interpretation and local adaptations. Consequently, written political decisions cannot really contribute to an adequate understanding of the process of reform:

> Party policies, usually in the form of "Document No. 1 of Year 19XX," consisted mainly of vague statements. . . . If the documents had been taken seriously, no reform would have happened. The famous Resolution of the 1978 Third Plenum of the Eleventh Central Committee, for example, did not mention institutional reform in the agricultural sector. Rather, it reaffirmed that the production team "should remain unchanged" . . .—only for the whole commune system to be completely dismantled immediately afterwards. Like many other reform "policies," the document itself was as remarkable for what it did not say as for what it did, as it was open to interpretations, negotiations and reversals. (Z. Zhu 2007, 1504)

The key institutional innovations were not inaugurated in the chambers of the Politburo but introduced by countless nameless local actors, frequently in the form of informal strategies that circumvented the rules.[44] The unintended consequences of the policy of opening up were also of fundamental importance: for example, the state leadership under Deng Xiaoping actually regarded the creation of a series of Special Economic Zones as just a limited experiment. However, over the course of time, the party and government leadership developed the ability to harness the benefits of positive local experiences nationwide. The majority of the pivotal reform initiatives were first tested in the form of pilot projects in local trial runs before they were rolled out across the country.

The following section focuses on the key developments of the reform period that, in China research, is usually subdivided into two phases. Because the process of reform achieved its first successes in the agricultural sector, that is, higher growth rates, profits, and productivity gains, I will begin with the reform of rural areas. Next I will present the institutional change in the urban commercial sector, with particular reference to the interplay between economic and political actors. Finally, by describing the restructuring of the state apparatus, the transformations of the financial market, and industrial relations I outline other institutional spheres that I presented in Chapter 1 as key dimensions of capitalist social orders.

As described above, China's pre-1980s economy was structured in the form of a national sectoral and regional system. While, in the sectoral system, the national ministries, which maintained branch offices in the relevant regional authorities, were at the top of the hierarchy, the regional system had a decentralized structure. Here, the relevant regional authorities were entrusted with the regulation of state-owned enterprises and other economic units. The coexistence of these two systems resulted in an unstable relationship between them and disputes over issues concerning the national chain of command (plan anarchy).

The administrative reforms implemented from 1979 onward resulted in a shift in power toward local authorities. The group allied with Deng was partly able to prevail over the conservative forces supporting Hua Guofeng because it "[bought] support from local cadres by granting them more control over resources as well as positions in the bureaucracy, enabling the cadres to participate in the economic success of the enterprises in their area of responsibility without having to bear the corresponding risk in the event of economic losses (caused by the reform)" (Krug 1993, 72; see also Shirk 1993, 208).[45]

During the first phase of reform from 1978, the extent of the central state's influence declined, but the second phase of reform, from the 1990s onward, in contrast, was characterized by extensive attempts to create more freedom to act for the central state. Overall, the processes of capital utilization became more important determinants of state policy than previously.

Reform of the Agricultural Sector, Market Expansion,
and the Rise of Township and Village Enterprises

Between 1978 and 1984, China's collective agricultural production units
were effectively replaced by small-scale family farms. The "household
responsibility system" allowed the long-term leasing of land, which was,
over time, increased to fifty (and later seventy) years.[46] This, in turn, provided individuals with an opportunity to produce autonomously: "With
the elimination of the workpoint system in most units after 1982, the
household replaced the collective as the primary agricultural production,
income-generating, and distribution unit" (Selden and Lu 1993, 192–93).
A downward transfer of authority from the old "production teams" (typically thirty to forty households) to individual households marked a trend
toward informal privatization that required tough physical labor from the
farmers.

The local CCP decision makers were heavily involved in the restructuring, despite the fact that local party cadres repeatedly opposed it for fear of
losing power (Shirk 1989, 341–42). In the meantime, the central government eased the sales conditions for farmers: "Procurement targets were
stabilized and slightly reduced; procurement prices were raised; and, most
importantly, prices for farm deliveries above the procurement target were
raised dramatically. . . . In order to pay for the policies, planners in 1979
had to reduce investment, double grain imports in three years, and chop
back the ambitious technology import program" (Naughton 2007, 89).

After the share that had to be transferred to the authorities had been
deducted, the crop surpluses that exceeded the plan targets could be sold at
a profit in newly emerging markets. By 1983, this system had been adopted
throughout China, almost without exception. In 1984, boosted by increased
use of synthetic fertilizers, the grain production output was one-third
higher than in 1978. This represented a breakthrough in terms of eliminat-
ing food shortages.[47]

Overall, the hours of labor required to cultivate grain decreased, and
many farmers used the additional time to diversify their crops or to work
outside the agricultural sector. The result was social differentiation of the
farmers. After the people's communes collapsed and consequently ceased
to attract investment, the resources that were freed up were channeled into
rural small and medium-sized enterprises (SMEs). The rise of collectively
owned enterprises (COEs), or, to be more precise, township and village

enterprises (TVEs) began at the time. These enjoyed a golden age up until 1996 and played a catalytic role in the elimination of the plan anarchy. They operated outside the national plans and, in the 1980s, became an engine for growth in the coastal provinces of Jiangsu and Zhejiang, for example (Naughton 2007, 271–93; Saich 2004, 251–53; Shirk 1989, 355). Their influence also extended to urban areas, where they presented considerable competition for state-owned enterprises. The number of people employed by TVEs grew from 28 million to 135 million between 1978 and 1996, and TVE managers were frequently the heads of village or township administrations.

The key reasons for the rapid growth of TVEs until the mid-1990s were:

- an exceptionally high labor supply and the commensurate low wages that are correlated with labor-intensive production;
- remarkably high profitability—profit rates of 30 percent were the norm in the 1980s, a phase where TVEs often filled demand niches;
- a supportive institutional framework, that is, local village governments, initially the de facto owners of many TVEs, who were also their enthusiastic proponents. This still continued during the second phase of reform when the TVEs formally became private enterprises. This situation ensured that rural enterprises paid very low taxes and, indeed, were frequently also exempt from national taxation. Local governments acted as investors funding the development of production infrastructures. In addition, a certain proportion of Chinese rural household savings, which skyrocketed during the 1980s, was invested in TVEs, partly via informal credit institutions (Cho 2005, 38);
- a revival of traditions of merchant capitalism in the coastal provinces of Jiangsu and Zhejiang, for instance;
- competition linked to the country's regionalized structure: although, to a certain extent, individual townships operated miniature command economies, ultimately they still competed with thousands of other villages to become attractive business locations. This competition also fostered hard "budget constraints" (Kornai 1992): in contrast to the higher levels of government, the village governments did not really have the option of introducing safeguards in the interests of their companies. For example, they

very rarely had access to sufficient funds to sustain local enterprises in the event of an economic crisis (Montinola, Qian, and
Weingast 1995, 68).
• international factors: in coastal provinces such as Guangdong or
  Fujian, foreign direct investment or FDI (initially, largely from
  overseas Chinese from and via Hong Kong) stimulated the growth
  of TVEs and the emergence of tens of thousands of producers of
  consumer goods.

From the 1980s, this entailed an evolutionary transformation with
adaptive institutions taking center stage: de facto private companies were
established in the guise of collective enterprises (COEs and TVEs). Prior to
1988, it was prohibited to run a private company with more than eight
employees. One solution enabling the establishment of larger private enterprises was to register the company as a COE or TVE.[48] The rule-breaking
practice of "wearing a red hat" (*dai hong maozi*), which was a commonly
used phrase in everyday language, demonstrates an informal adaptive institutionalization that gradually altered the institutional framework of company management (see ten Brink 2011a). The success of this practice of
creating de facto private companies was increasingly accepted by both the
local political authorities, which had an interest in local economic development, and by proreform leaders within the national power elite (Tsai 2006,
2007; see also Holbig 2004).
    These processes of layering formal institutions with innovative informal
practices resulted in an institutional conversion: the party leadership
responded with an official change in their attitude toward the private sector
and institutional adjustments. As early as 1988, the State Council implemented a reform of company law with the new Private Enterprise Law and
"a subsequent constitutional amendment acknowledged the private sector
as a supplement to the socialist public sector" (W. Chen 2007, 60). From
then on, we increasingly saw the creation of legitimate private companies
(Walder 1995, 268).
    The new enterprises soon presented serious competition for the SOEs
as described by Naughton in his summary of the first phase of reform:
"Entry of new firms combined with adoption of market prices on the margin led to enhanced competition and began to get state-sector managers
accustomed to responding to the marketplace. Gradual price decontrol was
essential. Competition eroded initially high profit margins for state firms

and induced the government, as owner of the firms, to become more concerned with profitability. . . . The economy gradually grew out of the plan" (Naughton 2007, 97).

Overall, the reform measures initially restricted the capabilities of the political authorities to directly siphon off the newly created surplus product. Command economy mechanisms were replaced by market mechanisms, and this redefined the relationship between political and economic actors: the way was paved for an "entrepreneurial" society where not only SOEs operated but also private and other "collective" enterprises. Unlike black markets in other command economies, market-regulated sectors grew out of the plan (see Naughton 1995).

The second phase of reform, from the 1990s, saw another transformation of TVEs. Growing problems acquiring investment loans from the credit institutions increased the pressure to restructure: "In a nutshell, TVEs . . . could develop speedily in particular once they received support by local governments to get access to credit. This privileged position was lost in the first credit crunch in the early Nineties. . . . This resulted in a strong pressure for restructuring. The most famous case is the so-called "Sunan model" [an industrial model primarily controlled by local political actors] which was silently and stepwisely dismantled after the crunch" (Herrmann-Pillath 2009, 129).

Additionally, especially after 1996, a more competitive environment put the TVEs under pressure and reduced their profit and growth rates. Larger urban enterprises in particular were now increasingly operating in the fields that were once dominated by the TVEs. A significant wave of TVE privatization followed.

As the section on the transformation of industrial relations below shows, this trend toward privatization was promoted by granting formally private enterprises more leeway in terms of the regulation and remuneration of employees than SOEs or COEs. At the same time, even following privatization, the managers of the TVEs were frequently still able to retain their positions of power (for an account of insider privatization, see H. Li and Rozelle 2003).

The Transformation of Urban Centers and Industrial Sectors

In contrast to the agricultural sector, the process of restructuring in the urban sectors had to overcome more significant hurdles. Unlike agriculture, which was only marginally mechanized, the organization of industrial production was regulated by more complex dependencies that made it more difficult to introduce market mechanisms (Saich 2004, 253–63; Shirk 1989, 332–40). The transformation can be divided into two phases: the phase from 1979 to 1993 and the phase after 1993.

THE FIRST PHASE

Against a backdrop of growing competition created by rural non-state-owned companies, the first phase of the transformation, commencing in 1979, is characterized by limited opportunities for private economic activity and free product marketing as well as decentralization through the transfer of economic power to the local political level. The new concepts followed on from previous reform initiatives within the party.[49]

At the company level, distinctive new performance incentives advanced the transformation of industry. However, curtailing the economic planning system did not immediately result in the company management having more decision-making authority. Generally speaking, it was initially the local governments that were able to expand their powers of intervention. Although the grip of the central state authorities was loosened, close ties between local political authorities and companies guaranteed a high level of nonmarket allocation, despite the fact that these alliances were in competition with other alliances (Nee and Su 1996, 116–24; Nee 2005). Local governments became the holders of residual interests, even if they were not directly involved in business activities themselves. This meant that they were entitled to shares of ownership and profit. Up until 1992, local governments were able to substantially increase the proportion of industrial output under their control. At the same time, between 1985 and 1992, the share of locally controlled foreign investment, which had, in many cases, previously been handled by the central government ministries, increased dramatically (Montinola, Qian, and Weingast 1995, 62).

The reform of state-owned enterprises can be subdivided into three stages from 1983 to roughly 1993. During the first stage, the central government increased the authority of SOEs, and the separation of sectoral ministries and companies was gradually driven forward. This meant that a share of the companies' profits could be retained and reinvested as that company saw fit. As part of enterprise reforms, in a second stage, the "management responsibility system" was introduced for managers, and a new definition of an enterprise as a relatively independent producer with autonomous management was codified.[50] Thus, the separation of government property and managers' power of disposition could be accelerated.

A third stage saw additional restructuring of SOE corporate governance, by, inter alia, further loosening the government's grip on management. In the 1980s, the majority of SOEs were still subject to a fixed plan for the lion's share of their production. However, by the early 1990s, they were able to use more and more of their capacity for the production of goods to be sold on the market. This resulted in a two-pronged price system where command economy price setting and market-regulated prices coexisted. As a rule, goods had both a (frequently low) price set by the state and a (normally higher) market price.

The juxtaposition of the two price systems was reflected in how the financial revenues were distributed. Whereas in the past, these revenues had to be transferred to the government, initially, the local political authorities in particular now agreed to collect only a predetermined share of the profit—thus tacitly limiting their rights of disposal over the relevant company. This allocation of the rights of disposal and control increased operational autonomy: the management, previously obliged to fulfill public production targets, now became more focused on maximizing company profits (Nee and Su 1996). SOEs now had to pay taxes of around 50 percent of their surplus. The profit that remained with the company acted as an incentive for higher industrial growth. The management had the power of disposition over "internal resource allocation, the residual profit from market production, and also the right to capital utilization. The latter included the right to make investments as well as the right to transfer capital" (Krug 1993, 202, my translation).

SOE managers were increasingly motivated to act in a more market-oriented fashion. After 1984, they successively replaced the CCP functionaries as company decision makers. State Council directives further relaxed the regulation of corporate industrial relations—the system of the "iron rice bowl," for instance, which entailed life employment for industrial workers—by transferring authority to plant managers to dismiss staff and, at the same time, to reward employees with promotions or bonuses.

However, overall, these developments did not result in the "transition from redistributive to market coordination [shifting] sources of power and privilege to favor direct producers relative to redistributors" (Nee 1989, 663) as liberal theories had anticipated. This was because, ultimately, it was also the forces of "redistributive" power, that is, state actors, who knew how to make the most of the new opportunities offered by the market (Szelényi and Kostello 1996).

This situation explains why the political decision makers relinquished some of their control over the wealth created. First, against a backdrop of years of instability and hardship, a large number of local political leaders were already inclined toward testing new approaches to development. Second, changes in tax legislation introduced in the 1980s offered greater financial flexibility. This compensated for possible losses incurred during the course of local economic reforms: local governments were able to profit substantially, increasing their income through levying taxes such as land transfer fees when industrial parks were developed or land was leased. The relative loss of influence was offset by growth in tax revenue. Third, the consequences of transferring decision-making powers to the managers exerted significant pressure to move toward further marketization, which even the antireform cadres were not really able to oppose. Fourth, informal, and later formal, privatization provided many political actors with an opportunity to increase their own personal wealth. Fifth, the dynamic growth in local political economies improved the financial levying potential of the central state, which, overall, contributed to a weakening of antireform factions (Wank 1999, 228).

CRISIS-INDUCED TRANSITION TO THE SECOND PHASE
OF RESTRUCTURING

In the 1980s, the tendency toward decentralization resulted in macroeconomic targets being repeatedly undermined by overlaps in areas of responsibility and divergent local interests. At the same time, central government policies were not consistently implemented. This resulted in an implementation gap, that is, a discrepancy between the objectives set by the central government and their implementation at the subnational level. The increase in the decision-making powers of the provinces as well as the cities and districts led to a complex conflict between the implementation of targets and local variations.

Far from creating a stable configuration, the first phase of transformation led to a social crisis that was signaled by economic destabilization as early as 1988. In addition, the removal of further price controls resulted in inflation. In 1989, around three million TVEs went bankrupt or were taken over by other TVEs while a large number of SOEs, on the other hand, were subsidized (Montinola, Qian, and Weingast 1995, 68). The crisis culminated in the Tiananmen Square protests of 1989, which was far more than a student movement and signified a serious threat to social integration, particularly in China's urban centers. In retrospect, the 1988–89 period can be "seen as a crisis in the relations of production, which almost brought about regime change because of its impact on the accumulation regime (early signs of hyperinflation in 1988) and which, with the 1989 civic movement, also jeopardized social consensus" (Herrmann-Pillath 2001, 196–97, my translation). The Tiananmen intermezzo[51] led to a conservative rollback between 1989 and 1991 that was eventually brought to an end by the party's reform wing in early 1992.[52] On the one hand, the brutal suppression of the protest boosted the determination of the regime to use everything within their powers to avoid a collapse on a par with that of the Eastern Bloc. At the same time, however, after a period of stagnation, there was a growing perception that the reform process had to be driven forward by hook or by crook, even if it meant the regime paying with its own demise. The transition to a market economy had now become an explicit objective of the reformers.

THE SECOND PHASE

From the 1980s, indicators such as business competitiveness and profitability successively replaced the fulfillment of the plan as criteria for success. At the same time, significant demand for modern consumer goods had developed. The CCP responded to this at its Fourteenth National Congress, in October 1992, by expressing an official commitment to a "socialist market economy." Combined with Deng Xiaoping's famous visit to the flourishing southern coastal regions (*nan xun*), which set the agenda for the National Congress, this can be seen as symbolizing the start of the second phase of transformation.

Admittedly, economic development still had its own unexpected dynamics. From the central government's perspective, the first phase of reform resulted in a quickly growing, if regionally splintered, economy. Because the Beijing state leadership was reluctant to give decentralization a radical new organizational framework, its relationship with the local and regional authorities was frequently based on agreements that were negotiated individually. Further, while the domestic economy remained fragmented, at the same time, the coastal regions became increasingly transnationalized (Herrmann-Pillath 1995).

I will now outline key factors in the second phase of transformation: (1) a new level of corporate restructuring, culminating in the privatization of SOEs and a successive increase in non-state-run enterprises; (2) the de facto end of the two-tier pricing system[53] and an increase in regional competition to attract business and investment; (3) an increase in the rate of investment; and (4) the establishment of (local) public-private growth regimes that were often based on close interpersonal alliances. Additional factors included the restructuring of the political system and reform of the financial system and of industrial relations and social policy.

(1) *Corporate restructuring.* In 1978, the local and central government SOEs produced 77 percent of total industrial output. COEs, nominally in the hands of the workers, but in real terms actually under the jurisdiction of the local governments and party cadres, accounted for the remaining 23 percent of industrial output. By 1996, the SOEs were producing only 33 percent of total industrial output. Collectively owned enterprises (primarily the TVEs) accounted for 36 percent, private firms (particularly smaller businesses) produced 19 percent, and foreign-invested enterprises (FIEs) achieved 12 percent (Naughton 2007, 300; Nee 2005, 66).

During the second phase of reform, the private sector grew more rapidly than all other sectors. The Company Law of the People's Republic of China, which entered into effect in 1994, and the replacement of direct party and state controls with more autonomous company boards were a milestone on the path toward a more market-oriented industrial structure, which led to the creation of new private enterprises and a decline in the number of SOEs (Jinglian Wu 2005, 198–204). The step toward de facto privatization, which the government had prevented up until that point, now became possible for certain areas of the economy.[54]

Previously, increased competition, not only created by the entry of TVEs and privately owned enterprises (POEs), but more and more frequently also by international investors, resulted in a drop in profit margins, particularly for the local SOEs (Naughton 2007, 304–5; Nee 2005, 68; see also Gallagher and Ma 2011; D. Yang 2004), whose debt levels had also risen. At this point, the government's economic policy strategists developed a plan to address the situation that went down in the annals of history as "grasping the large, releasing the small" (*zhuada fangxiao*). From 1995 to 2000, three-quarters of all local SOEs had been subject to restructuring measures ranging from rationalization to formal privatization. At the same time, this process showed considerable regional differences, and/or more comprehensive restructuring measures were carried out only with a time delay (Oi and Han 2011; Zeng and Tsai 2011). Between 1995 and 2006, the number of SOEs was halved (J. Chen and Wang 2010, 44) with thirty to forty million employees laid off (Andreas 2009, 251; Y. Cai 2011, 84–87).

The remaining state-owned enterprises obtained the right to sell company shares. The increase in joint-stock corporations after 1994 thus had the greatest impact on the SOEs themselves. At the same time, from 1995 onward, the majority of SOEs were ultimately transformed into tax-paying companies, which meant that their corporate budgets were separated from the public budget. The board and management of the companies that had restructured to become joint-stock corporations were frequently recruited from among the previous management staff.

However, by no means did this result in a transition to a liberal market economy. Because companies continued to be closely linked to government actors and to rely on government assistance for their reproduction, the state authorities maintained a key role, particularly at the local level. Further, the government pursued a strategy of privatizing smaller SOEs while maintaining control over state-owned enterprises that were categorized as strategically important. As part of this concept, in 2003, control of the largest SOEs was transferred to a new organization, the State Asset Supervision and Administration Commission (SASAC). This commission was founded by consolidating an enterprises working committee from within the CCP's Central Committee, parts of the Ministry of Finance, and the Bureau for State-Owned Enterprises of the State Economic and Trade Commission (SETC): "[SASAC] was designated as the agency responsible for exercising the central government's rights of ownership of nonfinancial firms. Subsequently, during 2004 and 2005, local SASACs were set up at the provincial and municipal level as well" (Naughton 2007, 303).

(2) *Regional competition to attract business and investment.* Regarding the effectiveness of capitalist driving forces in the PRC, the increasing competition on expanding markets during the process of reform appears to have dictated the pace. This competition stimulated economic growth. Through targeted industrial and fiscal policies, subnational governments used their relative autonomy to attract (domestic and foreign) investment and compete with other regions.

During the first phase of reform, domestic competition displayed strong protectionist characteristics (Shirk 1993, 185–87; Wedeman 2011), but this was tackled relatively successfully during the second phase.[55] Instead, we saw the development of economic competition between the regions to attract industry and investment projects. As the following example illustrates, this applied (and applies) in particular to municipal and township governments:

> Worried that Xiqiao [a township within the Nanhai district of the city of Foshan, in the province of Guangdong] might lose its standing in the national textile market, they [the township leaders] keep a watchful eye on the major centres elsewhere in China that produce chemical-fibre cloth. In 1995 a group of township officials led by the township head took an investigative trip to the textile centres in Zhejiang, Xiqiao's major competitors, and returned with warnings that these were gaining on Xiqiao. Anxious for Xiqiao to strengthen its competitive edge, the township authorities decided to subsidize purchases by Xiqiao factory owners of a new generation of looms that cost some Y120,000 apiece. The Xiqiao government now provides a low-interest soft loan of Y20,000 for each new machine. In this and other programs to provide support to the private sector, the township administration (similar to the village governments) generally favours the more prosperous, larger entrepreneurs, feeling that they have the best chance of expanding local production against outside competition. (Unger and Chan 1999, 65)

The increase in competition during the course of economic and political decentralization and selective liberalization of the trade and investment regime—particularly in the coastal regions, less so in the western and northeastern provinces—was described by economists in the mid-1990s using the model of "market-preserving federalism" (Montinola, Qian, and Weingast 1995). According to some experts at the time, from then on, particularly in terms of the decentralized delegation of authority over economic, fiscal, and financial policy, the People's Republic of China essentially had more of a "federal" structure. Although local governments often had extensive control over the local economy, companies were still subject to hard budget constraints (Montinola, Qian, and Weingast 1995; see also Zheng 2007). Despite the fact that the central state occasionally intervened in local economies' monetary and regulatory affairs, they largely confined their interventions to the prevention of protectionist measures, however. Below the central government level, there were now virtually no constraints that could reduce the powerful incentives to improve competitiveness. However, as will be shown, this finding should not be overextended, as has been revealed by recent recentralization efforts, in particular.[56]

(3) *Increase in the rate of investment.* During the second phase of reform, growth was increasingly stimulated by a rise in the rate of investment: "In essence, China subordinated most institutional issues to the quest for a high and adequate investment effort. . . . The leadership was alarmed at the under-investment of the early 1990s. . . . As a result, they focused institutional development on measures that would strengthen the government and restore its ability to lead investment programs" (Naughton 2009, 11).

Investment-driven growth was based, first and foremost, on infrastructure modernization: "As late as 1990–1992, China was investing only 4 percent of GDP on physical infrastructure (narrowly defined as transport, communications and electricity). The extra-ordinary saver and investor we know today only emerged after the mid-1990s, after almost 20 years of successful reforms" (Naughton 2009, 11). The construction of the Three Gorges Dam was just one of many such infrastructure projects.

The following steps contributed to a higher propensity to invest among both private and state actors: a reform of the tax system increased the central government's resource base; the retention of after tax profits increased SOEs' willingness to invest; a few, primarily state-owned, enterprises were subject to pressure of competition in key infrastructure sectors (telecommunications, power, and aviation, for instance) and therefore compelled to invest constantly;[57] establishment of new actors in the financial sector, such as the policy banks, systematically channeled resources into the infrastructure sector; and, the competition-driven propensity to invest of local governments and businesses also made a significant contribution to ensuring that profits were reinvested. The expansion of investment came at a price, however: regular overheating of the economy.

(4) *Public-private growth alliances and* guanxi *networks.* During the second phase of reform, the development of public-private alliances between government institutions and companies as well as close interpersonal networks (*guanxi*) became cornerstones of the new Chinese capitalism. To illustrate their relevance and particularly the development of an "entrepreneurial state" (including the founding of companies by government actors)[58] requires an examination of the broader institutional framework within which these actors develop and use their entrepreneurial resources.

In China studies, the term "local state corporatism" is used to describe this development (see Duckett 2001; Holbig 2004; Howell 2006; Oi 1995; Walder 1995).

As already intimated, over the course of the reforms, the subnational political units frequently adopted the role of a local developmental state. In addition to the functions linked to this role—promoting market reforms and local development, primarily indirectly via subsidies and the creation of infrastructures, and so on—some state authorities intervened directly in the economy. The entrepreneurial state at local level founded companies and/or subjected state-owned or collective companies to restructuring measures and thus played a central part in the country's economic growth. Here, in some instances, individual state institutions and local government officials were not acting in pursuance of a broader local government project but rather in the interests of generating personal profit: "Indeed this activity is best termed "entrepreneurial" because it involves individual departments investing directly, to generate income, in businesses that operate in a market environment. In these cases, individual departments invest their own finance in businesses, which therefore differ from traditional state enterprises that receive budgetary funding as designated in state plans. Moreover, they do so to employ some of their own staff and to generate profits for themselves rather than for local or central government" (Duckett 2001, 28).

In order to explain why, in the Chinese context, it was not only private businesspeople who assumed an entrepreneurial role, but also local governments, I combine several arguments. First, as mentioned above, informal (and later formal) privatization provided many political decision makers and public officials with an opportunity to increase their own personal wealth. For this reason, the TVEs, for instance, which were de jure collective enterprises, were run like private businesses. As typified by the "wearing a red hat" phenomenon, profitability considerations served as incentives for investment and innovation activity, particularly in the lower echelons of government: "the private incentives are larger as one moves down the hierarchy of government, to the point where in many rural townships and villages local officials have something functionally equivalent to an 'equity share' in public firms that ties their personal and family income directly to the growth and prosperity of local industry" (Walder 1995, 292).

Second, an increase in market mechanisms and competitive imperatives increased competition to attract business and investment among local governments (Naughton 1995). The presence of a large number of competing government bodies at different levels removed an important basis for the assumption that soft budget constraints persist in state-controlled economies (see Kornai 1992). These soft budget constraints usually result in paralysis of economic activities: "The analysis of soft budget constraints usually proceeds *as if there is only one owner* in the economy, 'the state,' *although in fact* [in China] there potentially are as *many owners* of public enterprises as there are government jurisdictions" (Walder 1995, 268; my emphasis). There was, therefore, an extremely large number of competing companies and subnational governments, all of which were striving to improve the economic performance in their territory. Here, government officials often substituted entrepreneurial activity. Additionally, at the lowest administrative levels, another assumption of the theory of soft budget constraints was relativized: unlike the higher echelons of government, which had to manage an unimaginable number of companies, there were fewer businesses to be regulated at the lower levels of the hierarchy. This increased the likelihood of efficient corporate management running a profitable company. In the early 1990s, the central government's ministries and bureaus were still responsible for the management of around four thousand SOEs in a wide range of sectors. The average number of companies the provincial and municipal governments had to manage was considerably lower (Walder 1995, 273–76). At the district level, the corresponding figure was only thirty companies on average, while in villages and townships, it was just four.[59]

Third, within the public-private networks of probusiness government officials and their partly private, partly parastatal business partners there were further incentives for the local governments to promote entrepreneurial activity. This included the leasing of land to companies that promised to generate good profits, particularly in China's coastal regions.[60] As a result of the reform of the tax system, there was also an increase in local revenues, particularly through business taxation and other extrabudgetary items (Oi 1995, 1137–41). On the one hand, the likelihood of being able to access resources from the higher level regional authorities decreased, particularly as a result of central government public sector cuts. This meant that, from that point on, local economic areas were subject to hard budget constraints in this field, too (Burawoy 1996, 1107; see also Walder 1995, 280, 292).[61] On the other hand, local governments systematically invested their own resources into promoting the development of their territory. In this context, Burawoy refers to significant differences between development in China and in Russia:

In China regional and local governments strategize how to generate more resources from below whereas in Russia they strategize how to extract resources from above. . . . Social ownership is a decentralized property relation but not yet privatized. Managers cannot freely dispose the capital they use but they may control income flows, use of capital, and production. . . . The local state, can both monitor enterprise managers and apply sanctions for malfeasance. *Indicative planning can actually work quite effectively at this level.* Even where enterprises are nominally private they are dependent upon public enterprises, often in the urban areas, for orders and supplies, and on the local government for loans, subsidies, licenses and so forth. *The distinction between social and private ownership loses its significance.* In Russia, on the other hand, property relations have been privatized so that the state lost control over local resources. (Burawoy 1996, 1108; my emphasis)

Overall, it can be said that the lower subnational levels not only contributed to economic efficiency and/or profit increases but also created close alliances with parastatal and increasingly private companies for this purpose. A situation arose in which the economic behavior of "government" decision makers as well as managers of SOEs or COEs could be viewed as analogous to "private" actors.

The public-private regimes were and are still based on close interpersonal and frequently informal relationships (guanxi) between companies, local government officials, and party cadres. This is illustrated by the following example:

According to Ms. A [proprietor of the furniture company *AB Furniture*], the rapid growth of AB Furniture in the late 1980s endeared her to top government officials in the township where AB was located. Therefore, starting with strong political contacts at the local level, Ms. A became a representative in D city's PCC and a member of one of D city's district-level People's Congresses in 1993. In 1996 Ms. A moved up a further step and became a representative in the D City People's Congress. Finally, in 1998 Ms. A was invited to serve on the D City Quality Inspection Association. . . . Despite Ms. A's

refusal to acknowledge direct links between AB Furniture's development and her political activities, . . . her political standing has
yielded a standing in China's political system for AB Furniture. AB
thus enjoys greater respect from government officials and the
bureaucracy works faster, better, and with less trouble. . . . Specifically, AB Furniture has benefited in the following rather direct ways
from Ms. A's political guanxi networks. First, the granting of official
awards, such as the "famous brand name" award on the provincial
level, has generated free advertising and public relations for AB Furniture. . . . Second, Ms. A's political status has made it easier for AB
to access credit, especially in the early 1990s as it was very difficult
for privately run enterprises . . . to take out big loans. Third, Ms.
A's political stature facilitated access to crucial market information.
. . . Finally, Ms. A's position on the D City Quality Inspection Association gives her indirect influence over the implementation of government policies in the furniture sector. (McNally, Guo, and Hu
2007, 9–10)

The entrepreneurs' networking gave them access to political support,
from the district municipal authorities, for instance. In addition, the
companies were also privy to information regarding planned political
reforms. A study by He provides a somewhat less sober summary of this
situation: "In some coastal cities [in the 1990s] job advertisements
appeared that openly stated employers' preferences for applicants with
connections in governmental agencies! . . . Companies attempting to
comply with normal standards of business conduct will often realize that
they are participating in an environment of unfair competition" (Q. He
2006, 158, my translation).

The findings of empirical studies conducted in Xiamen (province of
Fujian) support the assumption that close connections exist between private companies and political decision makers, referred to as "backstage
bosses" (*houtai laoban*) (Wank 1996, 821). In Xiamen, cooperation between
the municipal government and private companies developed and expanded
to such an extent that the municipal authorities urged the local governments in the surrounding areas to favor companies from Xiamen in terms
of taxation and other concessions (Wank 1999, 217).

The Political System during the Process of Market Expansion:
Decentralization and Recentralization

The assumption of China's state-permeated capitalism developed within my research framework requires a more detailed examination of the continuities and changes within the political system of the PRC and the reciprocal relationships between politics and the economy. What began as a process of trial and error at the start of the reforms evolved, over the last few decades, into systematic state capitalist advancement and regulation of market processes.

Over the course of the reforms, government interventions were initially increasingly transferred to the subnational political levels, that is, decentralized to local government authorities. While the extent of the central state's influence declined during the first phase of reform, the second phase of reform was characterized by political efforts to provide the central state with more room to maneuver. Predictions of an erosion of the state in the medium term (see Goldman and MacFarquhar 1999a) were not borne out. In actual fact, following a period of instability, it was precisely the partial erosion of the state during the first phase of reform that lent the central government and the rule of the CCP new legitimacy. Overall, the state management successfully created internal unity and was able to weather times of crisis.

Why were China's political decision makers in a position to be able to do this? Although the present work primarily attributes this to the favorable domestic and international economic conditions, at this juncture it would still appear useful to briefly outline certain additional political reasons why the CCP, unlike the Communist Party of the Soviet Union (CPSU), was able to safeguard and, in fact, during the second phase of reform, even expand its power, despite all the difficulties it faced.

Because large segments of the power elite acknowledged the need to reform Maoism and modify its guiding ideology and practice, it was possible to create a relatively high level of political-ideological homogeneity at an early stage despite the centrifugal forces at work within the power bloc.[62] As mentioned above, from a sociological perspective, this homogeneity was based on the recomposition of a technocratic class comprising former Maoists, bureaucrats, and intellectuals, which was expressed by Deng as the need to be "red" and to be "expert." Notably, from the 1980s, this homogeneity guaranteed the triumph of the "red engineers" (Andreas 2009). In 2002, all nine members of the Standing Committee of the Politburo were engineers.[63] The relative homogeneity and autonomy of the political class created scope for initiating and implementing new policies—although many of the reform measures triggered fierce ideological controversy. One difference between China and other transition and emerging countries was, therefore, the homogeneity of the country's political decision makers (D. Yang 2004, 295–96).

At the same time, the power elite developed the capacity to create an authoritarian model of legitimation. One illustration of this is how the party and state leadership handled the collapse of the Eastern Bloc and particularly the dissolution of the USSR: a factional dispute about the reasons for the collapse rapidly erupted within the elite, which was partly played out in the semipublic arena of specialist journals. The conflict comprised two opposing groups: first, a hegemonial group in alliance with Deng, who interpreted the analysis of the collapse as an instruction to continue the reform path, and second, a marginalized group supporting the "left-leaning" and/or "Maoist" wing of the party. The latter blamed the collapse of the USSR on Gorbachev's "revisionism" and feared that, should China continue along its reform path, it would see similarly destabilizing results. However, the reformists who dominated the discourse referred to a phase of economic stagnation under Brezhnev, which, from a structural perspective, condemned Gorbachev's reform path from the very outset (Wilson 2007b, 275; see also Shambaugh 2009b, 42–48, 54–67). According to the reformists, the overextension of Soviet military power led to economic exhaustion. In summary, the Deng group, which was effectively oriented toward excessive and boundless accumulation of capital, asserted that the gradual reform path must be codified. This argument had also been used to legitimize the violent suppression of the protest movement in 1989.[64]

In the years that followed, the modernized avant-garde thinking under Deng merged almost seamlessly with meritocratic principles of promoting the "best and the brightest," traditional Confucian virtues, and also liberal traditions. A belief in progress ensued that was reminiscent of the heydays of modern industrial capitalism in Europe and the United States at the end of the nineteenth century, and, simultaneously, took advantage of the benefits of economic planning and entrepreneurial creativity.

In the following sections, I will describe a number of structural political reforms supporting the establishment of variegated state-permeated capitalism, particularly those implemented during the second phase of reform from the 1990s. Two examples are the government's fiscal policy and the restructuring of state institutions.

Up until the early 1980s, the subnational political authorities, that is, principally the provinces, were still transferring a significant share of their revenue to the central government, which, in turn, redistributed these funds based on a system of prioritization. A reform of the financial constitution granted the provinces the right to retain the lion's share of their revenue. Only a marginal share of their tax revenues was still transferred to Beijing. This presented the poorer provinces in particular with a serious challenge as they had previously profited from the system of financial equalization. In 1993, the subnational authorities accounted for 78 percent of state revenue (see Table 1).

Until 1993, the central state's revenue plummeted. This was primarily due to decreasing transfers from the lower-level regional authorities and also a drop in income from the state-owned sectors of the economy. By then, the central government's share of total revenues was as low as 22 percent. Poor organization exacerbated the government's dilemma: although it had a monopoly over taxation, Beijing still lacked a uniform national tax administration system. For tax collection, the central government remained dependent on the local administrative units and the provinces, the latter acting as "intermediaries" between the local authorities and the central government.

The minister of Finance at the time, Liu Zhongli, bluntly described the ensuing central government fears—"when the [central] government does not have money, its words no longer count" (quoted in D. Yang 2004, 72). A fundamental financial reform was designed to remedy the situation. This aimed at changing the ratio of national to subnational revenues as well as increasing tax receipts. The whole budget planning cycle was reformed, from formulation to decision-making powers, from implementation to bookkeeping and accounting systems. The central government endeavored to counteract fears of a united front, particularly of antireform provincial governments: "the central leadership marshaled its organizational and other resources and adopted a divide-and-rule strategy vis-à-vis local officials. A special working group . . . travelled 17 provinces one by one to hammer

Table 1. Division of State Revenue

	Central government	Local governments
1980	24.5%	75.5%
1990	33.8%	66.2%
1993	22.0%	78.0%
2000	52.2%	47.8%
2009	52.4%	47.6%
2010	51.1%	48.9%

Source: NBS 2011, table 8–3.

out the base revenue figures for each province and readjust the fiscal relations between the central government and the provinces" (D. Yang 2004,
72).

The upshot was that following years of fiscal leanness, the central state
was able to increase its revenues again. By the year 2000, the central government commanded over 50 percent of total state revenue again (see Table 1).
Between 1994 and 2009, the local governments' share of total government
revenue had fallen to around 47 percent. The 50/50 ratio between central
and local authorities stabilized, although tax policy remained contested terrain (Shiyu Li and Lin 2011, 529; see also Wong 2009).

Although the introduction of budgetary management by department
meant that fees and duties that had previously been disregarded were integrated into the official budget, extrabudgetary posts continued to account
for a considerable share of state revenues (and expenditures), particularly
at subnational levels (see Saich 2004, 168–70; NBS 2010, table 8–10). These
included certain fees and duties, subsidies, and SOE spending on training
and social services, as well as income from leasing land (Wong 2007, 15).[65]
Overall, the assumptions of authors who saw China as being on its way to
becoming a lean state were relativized not least by these large extrabudgetary items (see Steinherr 2008, 833). Strictly speaking, public finances also
include the extra-budgetary items of state-owned enterprises and banks,
particularly at the local level.

The recentralization of revenues was not accompanied by the recentralization of expenditures, however. Quite the contrary in fact: the tendency
toward decentralization in this area prevailed, through an intergovernmen-
tal fiscal transfer system (Duan and Zhan 2011, 59). Over the course of

Table 2. Division of State Spending

	Central government	*Local governments*
1980	54.3%	45.7%
1990	32.6%	67.4%
1993	28.3%	71.7%
2000	34.7%	65.3%
2009	20.0%	80.0%
2010	17.8%	82.2%

Source: NBS 2011, table 8–4.

history, an increase in the disparity between central state spending and that of the subnational authorities can be determined: in the 1960s, the central government's share of expenditures still outweighed the local governments', and by the 1970s, the levels of spending by the two authorities were roughly equal, but, by the mid-1980s, there had been a trend reversal. In 1990, subnational spending was twice as high as that of the central government, and in 2007 it was three times higher (Shiyu Li and Lin 2011, 529). This meant that, in the 2000s, local governments controlled two-thirds of total public spending (see Table 2).

By international standards, China's spending has, to a large extent, been decentralized:

> By comparison, sub-national governments account on average for only 14 percent of total budgetary expenditures in developing countries, and 32 percent in developed countries. This decentralisation is even more notable because China is virtually unique among countries in the world in assigning responsibilities to local governments for providing vital social services such as social security, basic education, health care and public safety. Cities at the third and fourth tiers account for all expenditures for social security: pensions, unemployment insurance, and other income support and welfare schemes. Counties and townships (fourth and fifth tiers) are together responsible for providing basic education and public health for the rural populace; these two tiers account for 70 percent of budgetary expenditures on education, and 55–60 percent of expenditures on health. (Wong 2007, 17)

In general, the high degree of decentralization of the budgetary system has become permanent. The division into five basic tiers of government—central government, the provinces, prefectures, counties, and townships—gave rise to a decentralized structure. This situation is in line with the assumption that local government spending was largely responsible for advancing the country's economic growth.

At the same time, entrepreneurial activities of state actors were also promoted by the fact that the majority of public bodies were (and still are) only partially financed from the public budget: "On average, budget allocations account for roughly one-half of their total funding, and they raise the other half from fees and 'other incomes.' The budgetary portion varies across sectors and types of institution, though none is 100 percent budget-financed, not even the police or fire departments" (Wong 2009, 94). In some regions, they even charged fees for police services, thus insidiously commercializing public services.

MEETING THE CHALLENGES OF MARKET COMPETITION:
BUREAUCRATIC RESTRUCTURING OF THE (CENTRAL) STATE

During the second phase of reform, a whole series of restructuring measures were undertaken with the objective of dealing with the effects of capitalist modernization and developing an effective crisis management strategy (for a detailed account, see Heilmann 2004; D. Yang 2004; Saich 2004). This strengthened the central government apparatus with the result that it was able to regulate the market expansion that took place in the 2000s to a greater extent than governments in other newly industrialized countries.

In the late 1990s, there was an increase in the number of restructuring measures commissioned by the central government.[66] The Asian financial crisis had provided the final impetus for this development (D. Yang 2004, 63), bringing significant revenue losses and an increase in corruption in its wake; there was a rise in goods smuggling by members of the military and police force from 1997 onward, for instance (see D. Yang 2004, 110–49).[67] In order to avert the looming crisis of legitimacy, the state leadership acted swiftly, with its anticorruption campaign ultimately evolving into a campaign for the restructuring of public authorities.[68]

The central government took the opportunity presented by the economic destabilization and associated corruption to undertake comprehensive restructuring. This was in keeping with the trend toward economization and marketization.

In 1998, under Zhu Rongji and Jiang Zemin, the number of central government ministries was reduced from forty to twenty-nine (and subsequently twenty-seven), and their administrative apparatus was cut by half. The restructuring plan particularly had an impact on the successor authorities of the industrial sectoral ministries. The Ministries of the Coal Industry, Machine Building, and the Chemical Industry were incorporated into the State Economic and Trade Commission (SETC) (D. Yang 2004, 37–41). The official end of the system of sectoral ministries strengthened the Chinese delegation's position during negotiations on its entry into the World Trade Organization (WTO).

In 1998, the government also launched an administrative reform process across the entire public service, which, by mid-2002, had resulted in substantial cuts in the number of staff. Even the lower level authorities were strongly encouraged to rationalize.

In 2003, now under the Hu Jintao and Wen Jiabao administration, there was another wave of restructuring. The government decided to put a previous proposal into practice by establishing an agency resembling Japan's MITI (Ministry of International Trade and Industry, known today as METI). Departments of the SETC and the State Development Planning Commission (SDPC) were merged to create a center for controlling and organizing industrial development in the form of a restructured National Development and Reform Commission (NDRC).

From 2003, the largest SOEs were covered by the new State Asset Supervision and Administration Commission (SASAC). The SASAC, which was not really a traditional planning authority (to which companies pay money), primarily controlled the oil, metallurgy, energy, and defense industries, as well as telecommunications. Unlike in the past, enterprises were now left to their own devices in terms of their operational business, and they faced competition from other companies as a result. Moreover, state authorities assumed a steering function in the process of privatization: empirical studies show that, in 60 percent of cases, government authorities initiated the privatization of SOEs. Even if managers initiated the process, this still required the approval of (primarily local) government bodies (Oi and Han 2011, 28).

In addition, the Ministry of Commerce (MOFCOM), which had been reorganized in 2003 by merging various governmental agencies for foreign and domestic trade, played a key role in the process of market expansion, in helping to overcome internal trade barriers that distorted competition, and in establishing a single domestic market (D. Yang 2004, 62–63). MOFCOM exemplifies the internal and external foundations of gradual change in Chinese government institutions. Its institutional precursors in particular played the role of an intragovernmental avant-garde driving the development of export-driven growth and transferring the high hopes for successful integration into the world market to other state authorities (Chin 2007).[69]

Finally, significant steps were taken toward the development of an auditing authority. The National Audit Office (NAO), established in 1983, a ministerial authority (with local offices), was upgraded. It now audited government authorities more effectively and was also authorized to impose sanctions where necessary. This form of "horizontal accountability" (D. Yang 2004, 259) suggests that modern bookkeeping and accountability can also be implemented in nonliberal contexts.

The aforementioned ministries and commissions as well as other committees, agencies, and bodies with special status that were responsible for economic regulation were under the control of the State Council. This meant that central ministries and commissions were covered by the departments of the State Council, each of which was coordinated by a vice premier.

REDEFINING THE RELATIONSHIP BETWEEN THE STATE AND THE PARTY

From the mid-1980s, both government and party leadership advocated a stricter separation of the state and the party. In this context, Heberer argues that, to a certain extent, China was undergoing a transition from a "traditional" to a "rational" bureaucracy (in a Weberian sense) (Heberer 2008, 72–76).

As a result, China's political system had a dual structure where (from an ideal-typical perspective) the party establishes the policy objectives that the government's administrative bodies are then required to implement.[70] In other words, there is a distinction between the executive authorities (the state) and the supervisory or control apparatus (the party).

In the 1990s, decision-making authority in economic policy was effectively transferred to government agencies, and many former parallel structures were dissolved or reorganized. "The party apparatus responsible for economic affairs was . . . cut to around five hundred thousand positions, which, compared with China's almost forty million government officials . . . is not a particularly high number" (Heilmann 2004, 92, my translation).

The CCP also partially withdrew from the legislative process and daily administrative activities. To some extent, the increasing importance of the National People's Congress at the provincial level (and the levels below that) reflected a process of social pluralization and a certain degree of local autonomy associated with the economic regionalization of the country. Consequently, the CCP could increasingly be referred to as a "reactively constitutive" party, which secured its survival in an authoritarian, consultative manner (Hartig 2008, 29; Saich 2004, 183–212).[71]

However, the notion that the cadres,[72] government bodies, and state-owned enterprises might exert too much autonomy was not accepted: thus, party control was maintained through the heads of government authorities or through the directors of SOEs remaining members of party committees, for example. The latter had the power of veto, sometimes the authority to issue directives, and, finally, the capacity to report to higher authorities or to publicly discredit any behavior classified as detrimental. Further, since the 1990s, a series of measures have been implemented to address a crisis in the influence of the party (see Shambaugh 2009b, 38, 161–70; Brodsgaard and Zheng 2004; Zheng 2010).

On balance, this resulted in a process, not at all remarkable in the history of capitalist-driven modernizations, of rationalization and mechanization of state action. During the course of the reforms, the dominance of the administration that emerged arguably created a higher level of conformity than the inconsistent inspections and appeals to revolutionary morale during the period of primitive accumulation of capital under Mao.

EXCURSUS: CHINESE LAW AND REGULATION OF THE ECONOMY

After 1949, the importance of a legal system was disparaged. Although the CCP's leading role in both government and society was enshrined in the constitution, the party itself was founded and established its legitimacy pre-legally. It justified its claim to power by referring to its privileged knowledge about the path of the historical process leading to communism. The dual structure comprising the party and state apparatus still reflects this situation to this day, although what is now the fourth Constitution of the People's Republic of China, adopted in 1982, played down the significance of the party (Saich 2004, 122).

With China's reform and its new policy of openness, the legal system was adapted significantly. Analogous to the gradual valorization of rational-bureaucratic authority, more formalized procedural rules were introduced

—following internationally recognized legal principles (Pissler 2009, 1423; see also Bu 2009). The discussion on and drafting of a comprehensive code of law, initiated in 1979 and completed in 1986, was accompanied by the expansion of law faculties. Numerous provisions concerning implementation were adopted, particularly with respect to economic issues (Spence 1995, 824–25).

The development of the legal system primarily served to facilitate the efficient regulation of the economy. The history of the last decades is reflected in the retrospectively enshrined legislative amendments, as a result of the change in focus of the country's economic policy (Tsai 2006, 136). Consequently, along with labor law, commercial law, the development of which frequently drew on models from other countries and guidance from foreign advisors, is the most modern field of Chinese law.

In light of the comprehensive reforms, a Company Law was passed in 1993 and then revised twice by 2007, a Contract Law was adopted by the National People's Congress in 1999, the constitution was amended to guarantee private ownership in 2004, and, in 2007, ownership rights (Property Law) were codified, private property was recognized and protected, and compensation was guaranteed in the event of expropriation. The codification of property law dominated the debate on civil law for many years (Bu 2009, 126–52).

In addition, the Labor Law was modified and expanded several times to regulate industrial relations, and in 2010, a new Social Insurance Law was adopted:

> The imperative of accumulation has to be balanced with one of legitimation, or the creation of consent among the subordinated classes, and of some means of conflict resolution so that stability can be maintained for accumulation to proceed on a peaceful and expanded basis. More fundamentally, the enforcement of labour contract[s] requires the promulgation of the National Labour Law and institutionalization of a bureaucratic apparatus of regulating labour relations. This brings us to the strategy of "rule by law," that is the attempt to channel conflicts into the bureaucratic and judicial apparatus controlled by the Chinese state. Unfolding concomitantly with economic reform in the past 30 years, Chinese legal reform entails a remarkable and momentous increase in

law-making activities by the central authority and the professionalization of the judiciary and the legal workforce. (Friedman and Lee
2010, 515)

At the same time, the central government endeavored to combat corruption, demonstrated by its efforts to establish administrative jurisdiction
and new criminal offences (Heberer 2008, 112–19). The anticorruption
measures (which went as far as the death penalty for senior officials) of
course also had the symbolic function of responding to popular discontent
and presenting the state as a champion in successfully combating individual
criminal machinations. In order to be able to enforce the new laws and
decrees and to monitor compliance, the number of employees working for
the judiciary was increased dramatically, to over ten million. Linked to this,
a new legal culture has developed: young Chinese people in particular no
longer shy away from lawsuits and legal action in a bid to exercise their
rights.

There is still evidence of considerable differences between the Chinese
system and that of developed capitalist democracies. In the latter, from an
ideal-typical perspective, the law embodies autonomous terrain where legal
dogmatics and mechanisms can develop independently and where, at most,
mediated intervention by political and/or economic decision makers is possible. Conversely, in China, historical elements of "socialist legality" are
evident: further, the preamble of the constitution reflects the autocratic rule
of the CCP, which, in principle, allows a political instrumentalization of the
law. The Supreme People's Court (there are also courts at the provincial,
district, and county levels) is the highest judicial body.[73] However, when it
comes to interpreting the law, it is not the Supreme Court but rather the
Standing Committee of the National People's Congress that is authoritative.
One fundamental difference between the Chinese and liberal democratic
legal systems is the absence of a body with the power to resolve conflicts
between public authorities (like the Federal Constitutional Court in West
Germany). Although the constitution guarantees the independence of the
courts, they are permanently subject to political interference (see Kroymann 2009, 17–19, 31–32).[74]

This leads us to the following conclusion regarding the nature of the
Chinese legal system: it is questionable whether the idiosyncrasies mentioned above "continue to justify us referring to an area of 'socialist legality'
since influences from continental European law and common law are now

at least equally evident in Chinese law" (Pissler 2009, 1424). At the same time, China's legal norms are frequently vague and are generally less stringent and more open to interpretation than in Europe, for instance. This makes it possible to avoid sensitive issues using vaguely formulated regulations and to solve these problems with ad hoc political decisions. The (still prevailing) configuration where the party-state strives to rule the country with the aid of the law (*yifa zhiguo*) with the objective of efficiently regulating the economy but is not aspiring to the rule *of* law itself—this would be applied irrespective of the government's view—can be seen as another specific feature of Chinese society during the phase of capitalist modernization.[75]

Transformation of the Financial System

A comprehensive analysis of the financial system would go beyond the scope of this work (see Allen et al. 2012; Gruin 2016; IMF 2011; Lardy 1998; V. Shih 2008; Walter and Howie 2011; Jinglian Wu 2005, 217–53). At this juncture, therefore, I will provide only a brief history of the crisis-driven restructuring measures implemented in the financial sector and an overview of the key institutions. I will highlight the main features of China's financial system and raise the question as to the compatibility of this system with the needs of the "real economy."

Because of the strategic role of the state, the situation in the financial sector worked against the advent of a liberal model. The logic of a finance-driven accumulation regime has not taken hold in China although the development of stock markets, bond markets, and real estate markets as well as an increase in consumer credit have all created the necessary preconditions. Even in the late 2000s, financing through bank loans exceeded financing through the capital markets. To a certain extent, government steering enabled money to be efficiently exchanged, but it also generated specific problems. At the same time, the financial system was supplemented by an informal and nonstandard credit regime.

During the first phase of reform, market expansion forces brought about considerable change in the financial sector. The end of the people's communes and the emergence of agricultural markets and TVEs increased the level of financial transactions and the demand for credit. This also applied to urban enterprises that were becoming increasingly independent. Political decision makers were therefore forced to adjust, all the more so because of the sudden rise in informal credit relationships. In the 1980s, this was followed by a reform of the former state banking complex and the central bank (People's Bank of China, PBOC), and the establishment of bond markets (from 1987) and stock markets (from 1990), as well as the revival of Rural Credit Cooperatives (Jinglian Wu 2005, 219–22). Credit-financed investment increasingly prevailed over direct investment from the government. The associated interest payments heightened pressure on companies, which, it was assumed, would make them more aware of the consequences of their investment decisions and, from a business perspective, make them more focused on profitability. The key decision makers were able to benefit from, inter alia, experience on Hong Kong's financial market, where the PBOC and its subsidiaries had already been active for many years prior to 1978. Chinese financial market actors had already accessed Western knowledge of financial markets and become familiar with modern standards in the finance sector—"even before economic reforms in 1978, China's bankers had a very good understanding of how capitalism functioned" (Tobin 2011, 707).

The banking reforms carried out in the 1980s promoted industrial development. As a result, loans were brokered (frequently informally) between the local branches of banks and enterprises as well as the relevant local authorities. The decentralization of the country's economy led to a decentralization of the financial system. Local government influence over the allocation of credits increased: "Ex ante, the local governments were directly involved in the credit-plan formulation and might impose loans on specialized banks. Ex post, the local governments had the authority to decide whether the enterprise should pay back the loan" (Montinola, Qian, and Weingast 1995, 67; see also Honohan 2008). The exertion of influence over the local branches of the PBOC even occasionally undermined the overarching functions of a central bank (D. Yang 2004, 81–82).

Also starting during the first phase of reform, China's long-term land leasing system evolved into a form of "enclosure movement," where land was centralized in favor of influential political and economic actors (Q. He 2006, 76–79). A primary market in land use rights subject to political control was supplemented by a secondary land market where third parties with land use rights were able to trade. As noted in a number of studies, there are parallels between the strategy of using partial land marketization as a driver for capitalist development and the enclosure movements in early modern England or the expropriation of ancestral lands in the United

States (Walker and Buck 2008, 45).[76] Further, the process of dismantling the danwei system, which included the sale of property, was accompanied by the emergence of a real estate market that also attracted capital from overseas Chinese. Many of the wealthiest Chinese owe their fortunes to property trading.

The transformation of the financial sector was characterized by increased competition. This competition between the local actors and locations to restructure the credit regime in an innovative way, particularly pronounced on the capital markets, was exploited by the central government through integrating the competition between the regions into a distinctive policy cycle. The latter could and still can be described as a mechanism of experimental innovation. This was sustained by pilot projects, normally in local test runs conducted in the Special Economic Zones, for instance. If successful, these projects were then rolled out by the government nationwide: "Stock market history in China overall is marked by a series of experimental schemes. Most important are the repackaging of SOEs into listed shareholding companies (early 1990s), selected transfers of legal person shares to new owners (1992), Hong Kong listings of SOEs (1993), the creation of 'national champions' (from the second half of the 1990s), and several attempts at reducing the holdings of state shares (1999, 2001, and 2005)" (Heilmann 2008, 18).

Although the competition-driven course of reform was shaped by central government institutions and state-affiliated groups, in no way was this steered by an almighty master plan, however. Moreover, crises in the banking and capital market sectors regularly created an unanticipated pressure to restructure (Gruin 2016):

- In the late 1980s and 1990s, many state-owned banks were on the brink of bankruptcy, and the number of nonperforming loans reached massive dimensions; the banks were then bailed out, recapitalized, and restructured (Walter and Howie 2011, 25–27, 46).
- In 1993–94, economic instability and speculative booms forced the government to carry out adjustments, such as the creation of policy banks (intended to help relieve the four biggest state banks of some of the burden of financing government projects) and asset management companies acting as government liquidating companies (Jinglian Wu 2005, 222).

- The Asian financial crisis and the insolvency of an important investment bank (GITIC) brought even more far-reaching adjustments in their wake (Jessop and Sum 2006, 204–5; D. Yang 2004, 81–94). At the end of 1998, the PBOC was further centralized to enable it to carry out the functions of a central bank more effectively. The government also established various national regulatory authorities, such as the China Securities Regulatory Commission (1993) and the China Insurance Regulatory Commission (1998), as well as the forerunner of the China Banking Regulatory Commission (CBRC), which was not created until 2003 (Jinglian Wu 2005, 228–29). The banks also tightened their lending criteria. Because the Asian financial crisis was partly attributed to tensions associated with the liberalization of the financial sector, the Chinese government also took action in the area of capital market access and monetary policy. The general opinion was that the global trend toward liberalization had to be kept in check through state intervention.

Another factor impacted the course of reform: conflicts between rival factions and authorities. A "generalist faction," backed by the provincial authorities and aiming to stimulate local development by decentralizing lending, regularly had to face a "technocratic faction," aspiring toward an efficient centralization of the financial sector (V. Shih 2008). At the same time, there were frequent (power) struggles between the various relevant central authorities, between the Ministry of Finance and the PBOC, for instance.

THREE SEGMENTS OF THE FINANCIAL SYSTEM

For a long time, unlike more liberalized monetary systems, China's financial system was not characterized by a strict focus on interest revenue. It financed loss-making SOEs and their social security systems, for instance (Herr and Tober 1999). Lending was also rationed. As part of its credit plan, the PBOC set the banks' lending and deposit rates and the maximum credit volume (Herr 2002, 40). Yet the state-owned banks repeatedly exceeded the prescribed credit quota. Ultimately, in 1998, the credit plan was replaced by a "credit recommendation," which gave the commercial banks more leeway without impacting substantially on the political authority of the central bank.

Over the course of the reforms, diverse financial institutions, such as commercial banks or insurance companies, and various financial markets (money, bond, and stock markets and other informal credit relationships) evolved in China. Alongside FDI, government budgets, bank loans, and the stock markets, another important source of investment financing is equity financing (Allen et al. 2012). This highlights the structure of the financial system, which can be crudely divided into three segments.

(1) The government-controlled banking system plays a key role. According to official data, in the 2000s, three-quarters of investment was financed by bank loans and shares, while other bonds accounted for just under 15 percent.[77] Bank credits became the preferred source of financing particularly for state-owned and large enterprises.

The banking system comprises a broad range of state-owned commercial banks and state-affiliated city banks, as well as local banks and credit cooperatives. At the core of the system is the People's Bank of China, which determines monetary policy, controls the exchange rate, and grants credit to the commercial banks.

The four biggest banks, which all operate as state-owned publicly listed commercial banks, descended from subdivisions of the former state banking complex (V. Shih 2008, 31). These four banks dominated the credit system: "The Big Four state-owned commercial banks are still the most important part of the entire financial system, accounting for 53% of total banking system assets in 2005" (Naughton 2007, 456). The largest of these four banks, the Industrial and Commercial Bank of China (ICBC), concentrates on lending and deposit taking in the cities. The Agricultural Bank of China (ABC) has the same functions in the countryside. The China Construction Bank (CCB) specializes in financing real estate and infrastructure projects. The Bank of China (BOC) handles foreign trade and foreign-exchange transactions. The Big Four—since 2007 referred to as the Big Five because the four biggest banks were joined by the Bank of Communications (BoCom)—are among the biggest financial institutions in the world.

As well as the Big Five, there are also a number of significant policy banks that were set up in 1994: the China Development Bank, the Agricultural Development Bank of China, and the Export-Import Bank of China. These took over certain responsibilities related to financing government projects from the Big Four (although the latter were not fully relieved of this responsibility; see V. Shih 2008, 32). This also applies to international projects: the China Development Bank and the Export-Import Bank of

China (since 2007 via the China-Africa Development Fund, for instance) played a key role in supporting and financing (also private) FDI.

Further, since the 1980s, the banks that have thrived have increasingly almost exclusively been those originating from regional power structures and with close links to subnational governments and enterprises. In the 2000s, these banks were frequently listed. More than a dozen transregional banks (joint-stock commercial banks such as the China Everbright Bank [Pang 2005, 57–86]), over 115 city banks, the establishment of a very large postal savings bank, and thousands of (both urban and rural) credit cooperatives all increased competition in the banking sector. In addition, private banks were permitted in the 2000s, and foreign financial market actors were also able to increase their influence. The opening up of the market to foreign banks, which was negotiated as part of China's WTO accession process (Lardy 2002, 133), resulted in a rise in foreign investment in Chinese financial institutions.

However, competition was restricted by the fact that banks were allowed to enter only into interest rate competition, that is, to charge different interest rates for loans and deposits, to a limited extent (G. Yeung 2009, 291). National policies also restricted the impact of foreign investors. Investment required approval from the regulatory authorities, which was granted strategically and with a view to stemming conflicts of interest: shareholdings in banks were not to exceed 20 percent (for individual investors) or 25 percent (for joint investors) (Hansakul 2007, 4).

Another group of key actors were the Chinese sovereign wealth funds. Because the central bank did not generate very high returns on interest by holding foreign government securities, the high foreign exchange reserves were invested in the form of sovereign wealth funds, which utilized a wider investment spectrum (Lim 2010, 681–82). The Central Huijin sovereign wealth fund was one of the driving forces behind China's financial reforms and became the investment arm of the China Investment Corporation (CIC). In 2007, the CIC took over Central Huijin.[78]

(2) The capital markets were (and still are) also determined by state or state-affiliated actors whose investment behavior is not fundamentally different to that of private financial market actors. Admittedly, Western financial experts regularly claim that the Chinese capital markets are inefficient owing to pronounced insider trading dominated by government actors and a tendency toward speculative bubbles (see Walter and Howie 2011; IMF 2011). However, whether there is any evidence of actual qualitative differences

between Chinese and Western insider trading or speculative bubbles seems to be questionable, not least in light of the series of Western financial scandals and the global financial crisis of 2008.

The development of capital markets was initiated by local actors. The cities of Shanghai and Shenzhen had already begun to invest in establishing stock markets in the late 1980s, in other words prior to formal central government consent (Naughton 2007, 467–68). The original intention was only for the capital markets to increase opportunities for capital procurement. However, trade in securities was also permitted in the second phase of reform.

Despite their more limited significance compared to the banking sector, the mainland Chinese stock markets have caught up with the largest in Asia (Tokyo and Hong Kong).[79] The stock markets were (and still are) characterized by two path dependencies, however: a substantial proportion of the shares were not tradable, and largely SOEs were listed. The majority of the companies listed on the stock exchange were still under state control, and state institutions remained the largest shareholders (the Huijin state fund, for instance). However, by 2010, the proportion of tradable shares had been increased to around 50 percent. Over the 2000s, it has also become easier for non-state-owned enterprises to organize stock market flotation, and a number of joint ventures were also listed (in Shenzhen, for instance). Deep-rooted integration in the global financial markets still has to occur, however.

As well as the stock markets, the bond and/or investment markets also play an important role. In the mid-2000s, Chinese government securities and bonds primarily traded on the bond markets accounted for approximately 20 percent of the country's GDP. In addition, the policy banks issued securities and/or bonds totaling a further 10 percent of GDP. The market for corporate bonds remains relatively underdeveloped (Allen et al. 2012, 24–25).

Finally, the real estate market continued to grow in the 2000s leading to the emergence of large-scale mortgage lending in which the banks participated. "Not surprisingly, bank loans are the most important source of real estate financing" (Allen et al. 2012, 29; Honohan 2008, 116–18; see also Sum 2011).

(3) A frequently neglected segment of the financial system is an informal and nonstandard credit regime. Even in the 2000s, non-state-owned and small and/or medium-sized businesses have found it particularly

difficult to secure loans from state-owned banks (see Allen, Qian, and Qian 2003). It was, and still is, easier for banks to lend large sums of money to a smaller number of big companies than to grant numerous small loans to SMEs; large companies can also use real estate as collateral and often appear to be more creditworthy. In addition, for SMEs, flotation was often associated with unrealistically high costs.

As mentioned above, over the course of the reform process, a mixed economy evolved comprising state-owned, quasi-state, and private enterprises, frequently based on informal connections between government and private actors. The various forms of public-private alliances found their counterpart in informal and nonstandard credit relationships. These included funds from family estates used during the set-up phase of enterprises and financing through private and frequently informal credit agencies and money lenders, as well as extending credit based on trust, reputation, and good connections—with local governments, for example, which extended loans without recording them in their budgets (Allen et al. 2012). Even companies such as Huawei had to borrow money from larger enterprises at an earlier stage in their development (into the 1990s) (Fan 2011, 835). To this day, the third segment of the Chinese financial system has not been eliminated, despite the repeated calls from political decision makers to improve banks' lending to SMEs.

CHINA'S DISTINCTIVE FINANCIAL SYSTEM

Finally, I will summarize key dimensions of the Chinese financial system from the late 2000s that are important to bear in mind in the context of market expansion and competition- and crisis-induced adjustments.

First, the central state endeavors to consistently maintain a steering role with a view to implementing a macroeconomic regulatory policy. In a number of cases, this has been successful: the state proved its capacity to conduct bank bailouts and roll out nationally what it classified as local innovations in the financial system. By way of preferential treatment for SOEs, the government succeeded in maintaining the importance of the state enterprise sector and ensuring credit flow into "strategic" sectors of the economy. The government's macroeconomic steering function is particularly evident in matters of international integration although this is a rather difficult objective to achieve in a transnationalized global economy. The strict regulation of foreign trade in certain sectors during the Chinese process of transformation, limited integration into the global financial markets, the regulation of cross-border movement of capital, or restrictions on borrowing by Chinese companies abroad speak volumes here. A similar situation prevails with regard to monetary policy: Beijing learned some important lessons from the 1997–98 Asian financial crisis: State control over the movement of capital and the rate of exchange needs to be maintained. Indeed an undervaluation of the RMB because it was pegged to the US dollar rate resulted in many years of positive demand effects in the export business. Overall, the Chinese financial system weathered the 2007 financial and banking crisis, which began in the United States and spread rapidly, far better than the Western monetary systems. This appears to be because government control over movement of capital and rates of exchange in the years preceding the crises prevented deep-rooted integration into the global financial markets, thus limiting spillover of the crisis tendencies.

Second, the political steering function of the government is repeatedly called into question, however. Attempts to introduce overarching government steering were hindered by competition between a number of state, quasi-state, and private actors, as well as between central and local actors. Although the organization department of the Central Committee of the CCP is in a position, through its *nomenklatura* system, to recruit and dismiss key decision makers in the financial system, this does not produce any kind of comprehensive conformity (Pistor 2012). This is evidenced by the power struggles between the PBOC and the Ministry of Finance and substantive differences between factions and also by the high number of (different) government owners of banks whose interests are not always compatible.[80] Particularly at the levels below the most important financial committees, actors carry out partly divergent operations even if these have a negative impact on the country's overall economic development. This is an aspect that will be discussed in more detail in Chapter 3.

Third, although there are certain similarities with coordinated market economies (Germany and Japan), the financial system in China can by no means be seen as congruent with these other economies. Similar to Germany or Japan, large companies in China frequently have long-term links with a bank. Overall, the banks in China play a marginal role in the practice of corporate governance and control, however.[81] It appears that, for an analysis of the financial system, the efficiency criteria developed on the basis of the U.S. and German financial sectors and presented in CPE as ideal-typical models of efficient support for economic growth (Hall and Soskice

2001) will not suffice in the case of China: "Despite its poor legal and financial systems measured by existing standards, it has one of the fastest growing economies in the world" (Allen, Qian, and Oian 2003, 35). A combination of different elements that do not correspond to the standard approach in the West and are therefore frequently the subject of criticism (see Walter and Howie 2011) have generated institutional compatibilities: "China has found very non-standard institutions to support its growth" (Ahrens and Jünemann 2006, 29; see also Herr 2011, 21–23). Therefore, the financial system was able to particularly effectively support the investment-driven growth that occurred during the second phase of reform.

Chapter 3 will examine in more detail the question as to whether the financial system continued to ensure a successful allocation of credit even after 2008–9 and thus contributed to maintaining socioeconomic stability.

Changes in China's Social Policy and System of Industrial Relations

The following section focuses on the development of "vertical" social relations. China's capitalist modernization required historical changes in the country's labor, social security, and employment systems. These, in turn, triggered processes of commodification and precarization of employment (Friedman and Lee 2010).

During the first phase of the reform, or more precisely, in 1984, a liberalization of the labor market was initiated on the basis of a policy of optimizing labor utilization, which rescinded certain regulations such as the provision of secure employment and gave company management the authority to select employees according to performance criteria. Attaching more importance to economic criteria made it easier for companies to lay workers off. In 1986, the government introduced new rules for recruitment in SOEs as part of an employment contract system—from that point onward, employment relationships were successively converted to individual labor contracts. Analogously, since the 1980s, the urban system of work units (danwei) with its substantial impact on an individual's life was gradually eroded (Jinglian Wu 2005, 327–53).[82]

During the second phase of reform, from 1992, justified by the need to modernize state-owned enterprises, the number of employees was cut, contributing to a further flexibilization of the labor markets. The establishment of new forms of ownership brought a diversification of employment relationships in its wake—"private enterprise employment relationships therefore became . . . the norm. . . . The 14th National Congress of the Communist Party of China [1992] decided to introduce performance-related remuneration, which resulted in the emergence of a multitude of different wage systems" (K. Chang, Lüthje and Luo 2008, 7, my translation). The restructuring of the corporate sector, which was stepped up from the mid-1990s—the transformation of SOEs and the substantial increase in the number of POEs and in the activities of foreign companies—further strengthened the aforementioned tendencies. Soon, over 90 percent of SOE employees had new employment contracts. At the same time, informal forms of employment thrived in China.

Over the course of the second phase of reform, flexible labor markets took root. Particularly the growing number of migrants relocating within China—over two hundred million people surged from the countryside to the new industrial zones—resulted in a development that has been referred to by economists as an increase in "factor mobility" (Montinola, Qian, and Weingast 1995, 65). This influx was controlled by the authoritarian hukou system, which brought about labor market segregation. The competitiveness of the Chinese economy repeatedly highlighted by economists was principally based on an "incremental and managed transfer of the world's largest primary industry (agricultural) labor force into tertiary and secondary industries, made possible through the rigid agricultural/non-agricultural and local/non-local divisions of the hukou institution" (Young 2011, 135).

On the whole, the transformation of industrial relations was a result of selective state regulation that manifested itself in the inadequate enforcement of legal standards and/or the absence of effective institutions to achieve social equity between labor and (state) capital. The country's heterogeneous multilevel structure was reflected in a fragmentation of industrial relations.

Although the balance of power in industrial relations was clearly tilted toward employers and government actors, these actors did not unilaterally define these relations. At an early stage, they were affected by the collective resistance of some groups of workers.[83] A cycle of social conflict that began in the 1980s was broken by the discontent of segments of the urban population, who had little to gain from the restructuring at the time and, to a certain extent, suffered as a result of work intensification, unemployment, and inflation.[84] Although the Tiananmen Movement of 1989 itself was

initiated and led by students, a significant proportion of the urban population provided the social mainstay for the movement. Against the backdrop
of privatization of the state sector, China experienced a second wave of
conflict in the mid-1990s. Through petitions, strikes, factory occupations,
and street demonstrations, the workers forced the government to pay out
compensation and, to a certain extent, delay the dismantlement of industrial combines. Ultimately, the massive wave of redundancies could not be
stopped, however.

In 2003, a new cycle of company disputes commenced. This time, labor
migrants were at the eye of the storm. Their struggles against inhumane
working conditions were fought by means of petitions, rallies, and (often
militant) demonstrations as well as slowdowns and strikes (C. Chan and
Pun 2009; Wenten 2011, 42–43). These events formed a backdrop for the
government's efforts to establish labor law standards and social welfare
institutions.

SOCIAL POLICY

At the same time, the liberalization of the labor markets, the erosion of the
danwei system,[85] and the dismantling of public sectors created major social
policy challenges. A fundamental function of the state under capitalism is
illustrated by China's social policy. The Chinese welfare state should therefore not be perceived as solely a result of social struggles—despite the fact
that the quantity and quality of welfare benefits are determined by these
struggles. It is equally an expression of the interest of the political class in
social equity and thus the sustainable reproduction of social relations.
Social welfare institutions are key factors in the maintenance of the legitimacy of the party-state.[86]

Particularly during the second phase of reform, the objective of the
state leadership or the Ministry of Human Resources and Social Security
(MOHRSS) and other social security authorities, was to transform the old
social security system (the danwei system in the cities and the communes
in the countryside) into a social system partially based on Western and East
Asian models and administered by public institutions (Frazier 2010; Gao,
Yang, and Li 2013). Over time, the aim was increasingly to implement a
universal insurance system based on principles of security and equality.
Some of the key components of social policy were:

- the creation of a pension system from the mid-1990s—"a basic
  public pension funded on a pay-as-you-go basis, a fully funded

pension funded by mandatory contributions, and voluntary personal savings. The first two of these three elements are funded by contributions from the enterprises and the employees" (Naughton 2007, 203). At the same time, beyond the state-owned enterprises, there was a trend toward the establishment of company pensions, in foreign companies, for instance;

- unemployment benefits and a (low) basic social assistance (*dibao*), the level of which varied across China (with the maximum payments in the country's metropolises);
- development of the rural areas driven forward under the Hu/Wen government, with the objective of reducing the glaring urban-rural differences: taxes were cut and ultimately abolished; the government improved rural health care and promoted primary education;[87] from 2006, a campaign promoting "socialist villages" was conducted in different parts of the country (Ahlers and Schubert 2009; J. Lin 2009, 182–89);
- government increase in efforts to establish a universal health insurance scheme; shortly before the onset of the 2008 crisis, as a few years previously, only two-thirds of urban workers had guaranteed access to health care; the intention behind health care reforms was to develop a standardized universal system of basic services (Tong 2010);
- partial delivery of various improvements promised by the government; with regard to the precarious position of labor migrants, however, it continued to be the case that very few labor migrants and workers in the informal sector received state transfer payments.

Because social welfare responsibilities were transferred from companies to local governments (particularly county and township governments) (see Table 3), the development of social security systems was an uneven and slow process in practice (see Wong 2007, 17). Political prioritization, which, in reality, often paid scant attention to redistributive measures, and intra-state rivalries delayed the reforms (Smuthkalin 2011). Because the fiscal treatment of employer and employee contributions to pension insurance were the remit of the subnational governments, the management of this varied. By 2005, only 17 percent of the total working population and 48 percent of the urban working population were covered by the pension insurance scheme (F. Cai 2010, 111). However, there were also significant

Table 3. Division of Public Spending in Selected Areas, by Central
and Local Governments, 2010

	Central government	Local governments
Total government spending	17.79%	82.21%
General public services	8.97%	91.03%
Education	5.74%	94.26%
Social welfare and employment	4.93%	95.07%
Housing subsidies	16.26%	83.74%
Health care	1.53%	98.47%
Environmental protection	2.85%	97.15%
Public security	15.86%	84.14%
Transport	27.14%	72.86%

Source: NBS 2011, table 8–6.

delays at central government level: the codification of social security legislation was already planned in 1994 but failed owing to internal party conflict
"regarding the urgency and affordability of the development of a social
security system" (Brückner 2011, 1, my translation). The Law on Social
Insurance was ultimately not passed until October 2010.

Moreover, many local governments were driven to implement social
policy measures only by protests held during the course of the privatization
of SOEs in the 1990s (in Shenyang, for instance) (Smuthkalin 2011, 194).
Admittedly, social spending by the regional authorities had increased since
the 1990s from around 3 percent of GDP to 4 percent by 2004. In the same
year, the local governments contributed a further 2.8 percent (Frazier 2011,
95).[88] On the whole, however, the country's social welfare budgets were still
low by international standards, partly because of the absence of civil society
organizations, that is, effective independent groups representing the interests of citizens and workers that would be able to place pressure on the
government to shift its priorities.

Interim Conclusion

During the reform period, there was clear evidence of drivers of capitalism
in China: in the key institutional spheres of the country's political
economy—in the corporate sector, industrial relations, (economic) policy,
and the financial system—these driving forces became the primary engine

for social change. During the reforms, China saw the emergence of an imperative to accumulate, maximize profits, and compete, which is typical of capitalist development, as well as new relationships between the market, state, and other types of coordination—mostly in the form of close connections between enterprises and local authorities. Here, the three key groups of actors in capitalist development—companies, government decision makers, and workers—played the following role:

(1) After the late 1970s, China's new entrepreneurialism developed unforeseen momentum. Against this backdrop, the transformation of economic institutions was initially largely defined by a trend toward informal privatization with adaptive entrepreneurs taking center stage ("wearing a red hat"). These processes of layering formal institutions from below, through innovative informal practices, culminated in an institutional conversion. Yet over time, the corporate sector was increasingly also reformed from above, through innovative new performance incentives, a focus on company profit maximization in state-owned enterprises, and more (goal-) instrumental organizational forms. At the same time, during the second phase of reform, the state-permeated financial system increasingly supported investment-driven growth.

However, by no means did this result in a transition to a textbook liberal market economy. This is demonstrated with reference to the assumption (developed within my research framework) of a relativization of the global trend of liberalization by different historical traditions and path dependencies. Because companies continued to be closely linked to government actors and to rely on government assistance for their reproduction, the state authorities maintained a key role in markets, particularly at the local level. Close and informal public-private links between companies and subnational political authorities also resulted in a high level of nonmarket allocation, although these alliances were, in turn, in competition with other local growth alliances. A setting evolved where the economic behavior of both political decision makers and the owners of state or collective enterprises could be understood as analogous to "private" owners. The decisive factor here is not their legal status but rather their economic function. In China, the legal form (de facto private ownership versus collective/state ownership) does not determine the power of budgetary constraints in the customarily assumed dichotomy of soft budget constraints for state-owned enterprises and hard budget constraints for private enterprises. It is rather the wider institutional framework of enterprises that determines the effectiveness of budget constraints. Here, the juxtaposed concepts of private and collective/state-owned enterprises, frequently referred to in analyses of state socialist economies, do not really help to clarify the situation in China.[89]

(2) The reform processes did not substantially weaken the political power elites as had still been anticipated by many authors in the early 1990s. Initially through using processes of trial and error, the party-state decision makers managed to relatively successfully maneuver their way through the vagaries of the reform process. From a state theory perspective, this suggests a transformation of statehood where state actors develop capitalist entrepreneurial skills. While former managers of state enterprises became managers of private or hybrid enterprises who were closely connected with the political sphere, many local government officials, particularly in the coastal areas, were able to maintain their positions of power and even to strengthen them. In the process, as part of their accumulation strategies, local government officials developed skills that were comparable with those of private capitalist managers. This was in contrast to other varieties of capitalism where political institutions concentrated on classical government functions and also to the period under Mao where local governments were not primarily concerned with corporate profitability but rather focused more on output, that is, production yield. Nevertheless, comparable with the transformation and reterritorialization of the local state in Western industrialized societies, the Chinese reform process mobilized competition between the regions, and this influenced the behavior of local decision makers, who, from then on, automatically behaved as though they were running a business. Much as the "cutting free from the local state activities from the welfare state and the Keynesian compromise" (Harvey 1989, 15) was a prerequisite for this development in Europe and North America, the process in China was initially accompanied by cuts in the state's redistributive programs.

After the first phase of reform when the central state tended to be seen as "reactive" and its influence declined, the second phase, from the 1990s, was characterized by the party-state's proactive approach and far-reaching attempts to provide the government with more freedom to act in order to guarantee the regulation of the market. This is illustrated by the recentralization of public revenues for instance. In the process, the central state and party apparatus gradually developed its economic capacity to roll out positive local experiences across the country. The emergence of a relatively homogenous technocratic power elite was the sociostructural prerequisite for this development. Moreover, the reorganized processes of capital utilization as a central determinant of government policy initiated a series of bureaucratic restructuring measures. These included establishing new supraministerial organizations (such as the NDRC) as well as striving toward a stricter separation of state and party. Although a fragile multilevel competition-driven system and a juxtaposition of re- and decentralization tendencies was developing in China, against a backdrop of virtually uninterrupted growth in national income, the central government was able to relatively easily maintain its power well into the 2000s. It achieved this through controlling the financial system, which at the same time allowed room for informal credit relationships, through large companies, and with the help of indicative plan policies.

(3) The workers were unable to have the same level of impact as enterprises and government institutions on the reforms discussed in this chapter—the social balance of power did not change to the benefit of the working population. However, on the whole, regulating industrial relations and securing social integration presented a major challenge for the management of capitalist modernization. Fundamental changes in China's labor, social security, and employment systems led to processes of commodification and precarization from the 1980s, which also occurred in liberal, coordinated, and other state-controlled market economies. Urban enterprise restructuring undermined the welfare institutions that were linked with the company. Private companies in particular now had more freedom regarding the regulation and remuneration of their workers than SOEs. This resulted in social imbalances. During certain phases of the state-permeated market expansion, social movements became a public expression of the latent loss of legitimacy: for example, the Tiananmen Movement in 1989, supported by broad swathes of the urban population, a second outbreak of social conflict triggered by a massive wave of privatization from the mid-1990s, and another cycle of social movements around 2003, where, for the first time, labor migrants were at the heart of the conflict. These movements were an important background to the government efforts to create labor law standards and social welfare institutions.

Last but not least, capitalist modernization triggered the largest internal migration in the history of the Middle Kingdom and initiated another period of primitive accumulation of capital. Over two hundred million people surged from the countryside to the new industrial zones. Whereas the first generation of labor migrants in particular could be handed over to the underdeveloped (state and enterprise) social administration, the second generation, however, developed forms of collective resistance and articulated social demands.

Overall, a variegated state-permeated fabric of power did emerge in China. Because of its heterogeneity, it can be referred to as a fragmented multilevel structure. As I will attempt to substantiate in Chapter 3, within this structure, national plan policies are repeatedly thwarted by the actions of subnational governments that are contrary to the plan. Similarly, the attempt to improve the effectiveness of regulatory capacity by recentralizing resources resulted in adaptive difficulties and, despite remarkable GDP growth rates, macroeconomic developments are rife with contradictions. Thus, a conflict of interests emerged between the need to establish social equity and to remain internationally competitive.

As suggested in the following section on China's global integration—the fifth dimension of analysis of capitalist systems introduced in Chapter 1—the emergence of variegated state capitalism should not be reduced to its internal restructuring. If we fail to take into account the favorable international conditions that drove the country's economic growth and, to a certain extent, underpinned the regulatory capacity of the government institutions, we risk subjecting the concept of the success story of (partial) liberalization or that of the far-reaching state regulatory capacity to biased generalization.

The Emergence of State-Permeated Capitalism (2): China's Integration into the Global Economy

As outlined in my research framework, China's political economy cannot be adequately explained without taking the country's global integration into consideration. Although China studies have produced an abundance of relevant literature focusing on changes within China over the last few decades, an analysis of the country's global and regional integration does not have a comparable body of research to draw on (for some exceptions, see Arrighi et al. 2003; Breslin 2007b; X. Chen 2005; Hung 2009a, b; Hürtgen et al. 2009; ten Brink 2011b; Zweig and Chen 2007; Zweig 2002).

The literature examining the sources of Chinese economic growth frequently emphasizes domestic factors—particularly the "advantages of catch-up development" (see Holz 2008; Lardy 1998; Taube 2009). According to these studies, China's economy was able to profit from high productivity gains accompanied by industrial development in a country, which, at the end of the 1970s, had still been far from industrialized—in contrast to the USSR and other command economies: "The fact that socialism fell when world manufacturing already suffered from excess capacity contributed to the destruction of the productive capacities of former socialist economies. This is much less the case in China . . . , where the agrarian sector remained dominant through the whole socialist epoch" (King and Szelényi 2005, 209). An argument linked to this stresses the importance of a virtually unlimited supply of labor.[90]

Nevertheless, neither the country's dynamic growth nor its socio-economic transformation was based solely on domestic factors. To supplement this line of argument, in the following sections, I will describe three levels. First, from the 1980s onward, export of goods and selective integration into transregional and global economic processes during the implementation of the policy of opening up and the creation of Special Economic Zones (SEZs) had a massive impact on the country's economic growth and the transformation of the domestic economy.

Second, there was far-reaching integration, particularly between China's coastal regions, Hong Kong and Taiwan (the China Circle), and other East Asian economies. Here, the overseas Chinese played an important role as "patriotic" entrepreneurs.

Third, the Chinese economy was heavily influenced by shifts in global value chains from the 1980s onward: while Chinese producers integrated themselves into global production networks, direct investment from developed countries drove growth and access to technologies and contemporary forms of corporate governance.

On the whole, it is evident that the country was able to benefit substantially from a series of favorable circumstances and consequently moved forward with catch-up development far more than other large emerging countries.

Focus on Export and Opening Up

By global standards, China's development appears to be so exceptional partly because the country survived the major crises of the non-Western world from the 1970s onward virtually unscathed. These include the "lost decade" of the 1980s debt crisis in the Global South, the catastrophic economic slumps in the former Eastern Bloc countries in the 1990s (with ramifications for the South), and the Asian crisis from 1997, which shook other newly industrialized countries in East Asia as well as Argentina, Brazil, Russia, and India. One of the main reasons for its resilience, along with internal dynamics, is China's policy of reform and opening up, which transformed the coastal regions into competitive production platforms for domestic and foreign companies and made export-oriented growth possible against the backdrop of increasing foreign investment.

Since the early days of its (undeniably selective) policy of reform and opening up, China has developed into a trade power (Naughton 2007, 377–99). In terms of export volume, the country has even taken over the lead from Germany. In the past few decades, the factions of the power elites who stress the benefits of cooperation for economic development have prevailed over those who fear China has been depending too heavily on foreign countries. To all intents and purposes, the prospects of positive external effects of foreign capital inflow outweighed the risk of crowding-out effects harming domestic industry.

A historical milestone for the intensification of the country's global economic integration and the partial authorization of FDI was marked by the resuming of diplomatic relations with the United States in the early 1970s and the subsequent formation of a bilateral strategic partnership. Moreover, there was already a long-established link to the trade hub and financial center of Hong Kong (Tobin 2011).

The emergence of a labor-intensive export regime in coastal China from the 1980s onward coincided with a phase of extensive global free trade, which was triggered and driven by a massive expansion of transnational economic activity. The beginning of a new international division of labor, also as a result of the major crisis in the OECD economies in the 1970s, and the associated restructuring provided favorable conditions for mainland China, surrounded by extremely dynamic economies and innovative enterprise groups run by ethnic Chinese entrepreneurs, and this continued into the following decades. All this occurred in parallel to a shift in focus of economic actors toward East Asia: although the US-American GDP was still three times as high as that of East and Southeast Asia in 1950, this balanced out over the following fifty years. In the new millennium, the GNP of East and Southeast Asia reached a level that almost equaled that of the United States (and of Europe).

A particular role in China's partial opening up was played by the SEZs. These initially clearly demarcated zones were created in four waves.[91] Of course, these new economic areas extended beyond their specified boundaries over time and contributed to the reorganization of the entire economy.

After the opening of the first SEZs in the provinces of Guangdong (for instance, in Shenzhen), Fujian (in Xiamen), and Hainan from the early 1980s, it was possible to attract foreign investment from Hong Kong in particular. Investors benefited from low tax rates, low land rents, and minimal red tape. As a result, much needed foreign currency was channeled into the Chinese state coffers.

After fourteen cities were given a status similar to that of the SEZs in 1984 (for instance, Guangzhou, Shanghai, Tianjin, and Wenzhou), the second wave of opening up commenced. As a result of the policy of the "22 regulations," there was an increase in the level of FDI predominantly from overseas Chinese nationals. As well as the formation of joint ventures, there was also now the option of founding wholly foreign-owned enterprises (WFOEs) (see Gallagher and Ma 2011, 138–39).

In the first phase of reform, FDI's share of GDP never exceeded 1 percent. It was only the second phase that facilitated a qualitative change. Deng Xiaoping's trip to the prospering southern coastal regions in 1992 marked a turning point. The share of FDI increased now to 5 to 6 percent of GDP. Individual coastal provinces such as Guangdong, Fujian, and Shanghai even reached levels of between 9 and 13 percent. This third wave was a result of several developments. First, from the perspective of international investors, sufficient institutional foundations, that is, production infrastructures, had been laid. Second, the positive experience of overseas Chinese capital paved the way for other foreign investors. Finally, the central government initiated the selective opening up of the Chinese domestic market and the real estate sector.

China's accession to the WTO in 2001 initiated the fourth wave of opening up. (Partially) foreign takeovers of Chinese companies were now permitted. In 2004, total FDI in China accumulated over the years surpassed the half-a-trillion-USD mark. In 2007 alone, another 140 billion USD was invested in mainland China, particularly in the manufacturing industry (World Bank 2009, 144).

Following a settlement reform in 2003, the Chinese central government controlled approximately two hundred "development zones," which extended deep into the interior of the country. The successors of the SEZs were divided into economic and technological development zones, high-tech industrial development zones (frequently located close to universities), free trade zones (near seaports), and export processing zones. Development zones are frequently subdivided into several development parks. There are also up to two thousand regionally or locally controlled development zones, which are not subject to direct central government control (Saich 2008, 182). Increasingly, over the course of time, the special zones merged with the rest of the economy.[92]

The policy of opening up also had consequences for monetary policy and in terms of increasing the international economic activities of domestic companies: in 1981, the government established a dual exchange rate system.[93] In addition to the fixed official exchange rate, a second exchange rate was introduced for commercial transactions (Herr 2008, 27). Other steps included the dissolution of the foreign trade monopoly—around ten thousand companies were given import and export rights—and the establishment of national customs barriers and nontariff barriers to trade (Cho 2005, 138–45). Companies engaged in foreign trade were now permitted to deal directly with buyers and suppliers and also given the opportunity, with the approval of the foreign exchange authority, "to be allowed to retain some of the foreign currency themselves" (Hagemann 1990, 120, my translation). In 1994, the centralized planning of imports and exports was abolished de facto. More and more Chinese companies now made use of foreign financing.

In the second phase of reform, the government created a standardized foreign trade system. "China formally switched to a system of flexible exchange rates with interventions by the People's Bank of China" (Herr 2008, 28, my translation). The exchange rate was, however, linked de facto to that of the USD. Moreover, import duties were reduced in the course of WTO accession (IMF 2004, 83).

In a reverse movement, the injection of capital, technical know-how, and modern forms of corporate governance all supported the formation of Chinese companies engaged in transnational operations. At the same time, the central government developed an export drive strategy that includes active involvement in the international, or rather, transnational division of labor, exploitation of comparative cost advantages, the objective of a competitive export industry, and improvement in the level of technology of the exported goods. The advent of a first generation of Chinese transnational corporations (including Lenovo, Haier, and Huawei) sent a strong signal to the rest of the world that the country was leaving behind its role as "workshop of the world." Ultimately, the opening up of the economy led to a significant dependence on exports and an increase in competitive pressure within China. Back in the crisis years from 1988 to 1991, the almost doubling of the export rate, supported by a devaluation of the RMB, simultaneously contributed to overcoming economic instability (A. Zhu and Kotz 2011, 20). In the 2000s, the Chinese economy owed its exceptionally high growth rates partly to an average annual increase in exports of around 25 percent. The share of GDP accounted for by exports rose from 25 percent to almost 30 percent after 2000 (Edmonds, La Croix, and Li 2007). In 2005, 21 percent of exports went to the United States, 22 percent to Europe, and 48 percent to Asia (Holz 2008, 1683).

The FDI inflows (a total of just under six hundred thousand projects were financed by this form of investment between 1979 and 2006 [Yuan 2008, 97]), increasing exports of finished products to markets in developed economies, and growing imports of intermediate products predominantly from East Asia formed a "virtuous cycle" and transformed China into the new hub and growth platform for international trade. This resulted in trade surpluses with the United States and European countries as well as trade deficits with East Asian countries. From the 1990s onward, the volume of inner-Asian trade surpassed the similarly increasing interregional trade with Europe or North America (Gaulier, Lemoine, and Ünal-Kesenci 2007, 54–58; ADB 2011, 77).

This is how China's economy became irrevocably integrated into the global economy—with the support of its national government. Critical voices were powerless to halt the momentum. This was also partly because, unlike other developing countries in the past, no one-sided economic dependencies and restrictions on the government's freedom to act in the field of economic policy resulted from the extensive, yet selective, integration.[94] A strategy of dynamic and flexible protectionism and selective market deregulation insulated local companies to a certain extent. Also in the financial sector, we saw only limited global market integration. Moreover, China had enough leverage to impose conditions on foreign actors, if deemed necessary, and to facilitate technology transfer. Even WTO accession in 2001, considered to be high-risk by many commentators in China, did not fundamentally change this situation.

A special role in the internationalization of the Chinese economy was played by what is known as the China Circle, which the following section will focus on.

Hong Kong, Taiwan, and the Overseas Chinese

A decisive factor in China's global market integration was its macroregional environment, namely, the East Asian growth process and the interlinking of the economies in the region after 1945. Consequently, China's development must be evaluated in the context of interconnected "economic miracles" in East Asia, frequently simplistically described as the result of a powerful snowball effect. A renaissance of East Asia as a center of the global economy was observed. This started with Japan's rise in the 1950s and 1960s and continued with the growth spurts in Hong Kong, South Korea, Singapore, and Taiwan from the mid-1960s and in the ASEAN-4 (Indonesia, Malaysia, Philippines, and Thailand) from the 1970s. This development created a transregional setting that facilitated the shift in economic policy in China and the country's integration into capitalist networks.

The ethnic Chinese business community played a prominent role in this process. Because the "overseas Chinese" (*huaqiao*),[95] or the ethnic Chinese entrepreneurs I will focus on here, contributed to China's distinctive form of capitalism, I will now first explore the significance of their trade and production networks. Second, I will describe the role played by Hong Kong and Taiwan (also see Naughton 1997).

While the business communities in the West and in Japan were still criticizing the investment climate in China in the 1980s, as mentioned above, overseas Chinese entrepreneurs became the most important source of FDI. Between 1980 and 1994, 70 percent of FDI flowing into China was from overseas Chinese entrepreneurs (Hsing 1998, 147). "The overseas Chinese . . . could bypass most regulations, thanks to familiarity with local customs, habits, and language, to the manipulation of kinship and community ties (which they strengthened through generous donations to local institutions), and to the preferential treatment that they received from CCP officials" (Arrighi 2008, 436, my translation).

Because investment from overseas Chinese contributed to industrialization, particularly of the coastal regions, in the late 1980s, the government granted many privileges to the Taiwanese that had previously only benefited Hong Kong residents. From then on, the government classified Taiwanese investment as "patriotic ethnic Chinese" or "special domestic capital," with preferential regulations on entry and residence for Taiwanese investors as opposed to other sources of FDI. At least in the commercial sector, all this compensated for the shattered confidence in the past. In many cases, the patriotic overseas entrepreneurs have since acted as consultants for local party cadres and assumed a teaching role for the mainland Chinese business community (Lam 2006, 238; Taube 2009, 121).

Transnational integration further accelerated during the second phase of reform (H. Yeung and Olds 2000) when the networks of overseas Chinese frequently merged with mainland Chinese business operations. For some time now, people have referred to the emergence of the China Circle or of Greater China for this reason. In terms of economic policy, the China Circle describes a geographical area comprising the southern and southeastern Chinese coastal provinces (Guangdong, Fujian, Jiangsu, Zhejiang, and Shanghai), Macao, Hong Kong, and Taiwan. Singapore and other Southeast Asian states maintaining significant economic ties with the "core area" are also frequently included. The term *Greater China* on the other hand is used to denote a political area that is becoming increasingly homogenous; it often describes a new epicenter of international politics led by the PRC (*Pax Sinica*). Because this regional economic area is still barely integrated politically, however, the term *China Circle* will be used in the present study.

The structure of the China Circle has specific features that contradict key assumptions of the diverging poles in the discourse regarding the consequences of globalization—on the one hand, the theory of the blurring of national borders and the declining importance of the state, and, on the other hand, a skepticism about the reach of transnationalization processes (Sum 1999). For instance, state intervention, particularly in mainland China, retains its key significance, although processes of transnationalization certainly fostered change. A distinctive new balance of power between policy makers—on the level of the central government, the provinces, and the lower-level authorities (the central interface was the Ministry of Commerce and its subdivisions)—and mainland and overseas Chinese and other foreign enterprises resulted in distinctive local public-private networks:

> The networks . . . involve municipal authorities specializing in Hong Kong/ Taiwan investment, county-township cadre entrepreneurs, as well as small- and medium-sized firms from Hong Kong and Taiwan. They draw on pre-existing guanxi to build a flexible and open system of networking relations which allows them to build trust, obtain advice, communicate demand, and gain resources at below-market prices. The form of interaction tends to be group- and not firm-based: . . . However, this . . . involves power asymmetries

between actors and institutions. . . . For example, local party-state officials still control resources such as land, labour, capital and regulations; semi-public enterprises command information and contacts; and private firms control capital, managerial skills and market outlets. (Sum 1999, 133–34)

As, over the course of time, the Western and Japanese production networks also increasingly saw themselves compelled to shift their manufacturing to China, companies owned by ethnic Chinese entrepreneurs were able to hold their own against the powerful large corporations: multinational corporations thus became dependent on the predominantly overseas Chinese production networks, which became the key mediators between these and the local Chinese companies. Overseas Chinese capital was thus ideally positioned to benefit from the expansion of the complex Japanese system of subcontractors beyond Japan's borders and the growing demand from U.S. companies for business partners in the region (Arrighi 2008, 434). This led, for example, to the development of a transnational triangular relationship in the IT industry between the business hubs of California's Silicon Valley, the Taiwanese city of Hsinchu, and Shanghai in China (Saxenian 2005).

As well as the role of overseas Chinese entrepreneurs, that of Hong Kong was of exceptional importance for China's integration into global capitalism. Even before the 1980s, the metropolis became the interface between global capitalism and the Chinese economy.[96] This was consolidated through a close coalition of interests between influential Hong Kong Chinese and the mainland Chinese power elite.

The rise of Hong Kong is frequently attributed to its laissez-faire system (Yasheng Huang 2008, 3). But certain aspects of its history and older traditions of trade capitalism were more important contributory factors here (Hamilton 2006b). Also in this case, state institutions laid the foundations for the functioning and the subsequent competitiveness of the economy, in the area of labor-intensive export goods, for instance (McNally and Chu 2006, 56). Unlike in Taiwan, however, we did not see the emergence of a developmental state in Hong Kong after 1949; neither British business interests nor the initially cautious Chinese refugees supported a policy of a strong state.

From the 1980s, private companies from Hong Kong made a key contribution to the industrialization of southern China. At the time, relocation of production to the Pearl River delta was in line with Hong Kong's expanding role as a global financial and service center (Deyo 1993, 13–15). Between 1988 and 1998, half of Chinese exports were routed via Hong Kong. Moreover, mainland Chinese companies used the city-state for (temporary) investment, in order to ultimately benefit from advantages normally granted only to foreign companies by reinvesting in China ("round-tripping," see Breslin 2007b, 110).

From the early negotiations with the British on the reintegration of the city in 1981, the Chinese government's primary strategic interest was to establish close links with the ethnic Chinese entrepreneurial class. Up until 1997, these had been suppressed by British business leaders:

> Keen to maintain Hong Kong's economic vitality throughout the transition period, Beijing cultivated the goodwill of the business elite, and increasingly prioritized their views. The PRC's dependence on foreign direct investment from Hong Kong in the 1980s only increased the CCP's sensitivity to these business interests, which feared that the introduction of universal suffrage would bring high taxes and a measure of redistribution. Consequently, Beijing sided with the business elite on practically all controversial issues during the drafting of the Basic Law, vetoing all the Democrats' proposals for articles on social rights . . . and on thoroughgoing political reform. (Hung 2010, 61)

The more dependent ethnic Chinese entrepreneurs from Hong Kong became on China as a business location and on the country's domestic market over time, the more reliable they became as partners of the Chinese power elites.

The geographical proximity to Taiwan and its policy of export-oriented import substitution that was regarded as successful on the mainland, combined with the close ties of many Taiwanese with China, provided another favorable circumstance, which resulted in a close economic connection despite all the (geo)political differences (Hsing 1998).

Historically, Taiwan's political economy was characterized by a tight-knit network of relationships between the leading party, government, administration, and business activities and was therefore referred to as "party-state capitalism" (Pohlmann 2002, 206–9, 306–18). After 1949, against the backdrop of Cold War confrontation, the party elite of the newly founded Republic of China (Taiwan) developed a strong interest in the formation of independent infrastructures and in industrial development. Like the CCP, the bourgeois nationalist Guomindang, displaced from the mainland, aimed at national modernization by all available means. After 1949, to a certain extent resembling the mainland, a developmental state with an all-powerful party at the helm shaped the contours of industrial upgrading (Evans 1995, 54–60). And just like in China, the original accumulation of capital in Taiwan (despite a comprehensive land reform) was at the expense of the rural population because the state transferred a high share of the rural surplus product to the industrial sector (Kay 2002, 1081–84; Selden and Ka 1993, 114, 116–21).

As in Hong Kong, historically, Taiwanese companies were able to benefit from the "retail revolution," that is, a rising demand for (initially often simple) consumer goods in Western consumer societies (Hamilton 2006b, 141–43; Hamilton, Petrovic, and Feenstra 2006). Over time, a large number of private companies merged to become enterprise groups, which increasingly invested in mainland China from the 1990s. These frequently operated as original equipment manufacturers (OEM); in other words, they produced goods for export that were then sold on the global market under another (for instance, American) brand name. One well-known example is the company Foxconn, which now carries out the assembly of cell phones and laptops (for Apple, inter alia) as the world's largest contract manufacturing company in China. In one business park alone, north of the city center of Shenzhen, the company employed approximately three hundred thousand (largely migrant) workers in 2008. A basis for the Foxconn industrial park (Foxconn City) with its huge production halls was solid political relations with the provincial and municipal government, without which, for instance, the internal customs clearance (which minimizes transaction costs) would not have been possible.

Through the relocation particularly of labor-intensive segments of production to mainland China, strong ties developed between Taiwanese and Chinese companies and frequently subnational political authorities.[97] As in the case of Hong Kong, close coalitions of interests formed a solid foundation for economic integration. Since as early as the 1990s, at the level of the functional representation of interests, we have even started to see the "creation of Taiwanese business associations on the mainland that are endeavoring to establish close cooperation with their local semiofficial parallel organizations and with the Chinese authorities" (Meyer-Clement and Schubert 2004, 13, my translation).

The Role of Global Production Networks and
the Overaccumulation of Capital in the North

The development of the China Circle accelerated China's selective integration into global capitalism to a significant extent. However, there are further variables to take into account: first, the global production networks, led by Western brand companies, in which ethnic and mainland Chinese companies were frequently integrated as strong partners, and, second, the massive shift of production sites toward East Asia, supported by an overaccumulation of capital in the North.

It was not until the 1990s that FDI in China from OECD countries rose sharply. Although foreign corporations had already been contributing to industrial value added through regional partners earlier than this, now, to a far greater extent, "foreign capital jumped on the bandwagon of an economic expansion that it neither started nor led" (Arrighi 2008, 437, my translation; see also McNally 2007b, 116).

Yet how did this shift of capital from the leading industrial nations of the world come about in the first place? One of the prerequisites was technological and organizational developments that increased the opportunities for outsourcing relevant work processes. An advanced technological stage of development allowed large corporations to restructure and become transnational production networks and, as part of the new international division of labor, to delegate parts of complex production processes to subcontractors in underdeveloped regions (contract manufacturing). Producers of industrial goods hereby took advantage of uneven conditions for accumulation (Hart-Landsberg and Burkett 2006). A qualitative difference between this situation and the internationalization processes at the turn of the twentieth century is that the formation of supranational value chains, no longer only product chains, led to a rapid recombination of economic areas (Gereffi, Humphrey, and Sturgeon 2005). Because East Asia demonstrated a relatively high level of internationalization at an early stage—under the direction of Japanese companies, from the 1960s onward, a close interlinking of transregional production networks was observed (including overseas Chinese networks)—this area provided an exceptionally favorable framework for transnational production processes (ADB 2011).

The opening up of the Chinese economy meant that there was more scope for transnational capital and that Chinese production sites (and China's domestic market) could successfully be integrated into the business

strategies of the multinational corporations (MNCs) with the highest turnover in the world (Hürtgen et al. 2009; also see Herrigel, Voskamp, and
Wittke 2017). At the same time, the form of investment also changed: "In
the mid-1990s, roughly three-quarters of investments were joint ventures
with Chinese partners. By the mid-2000s, three-quarters were wholly
foreign-owned subsidiaries of MNCs" (Kennedy 2007, 182–83). Calculations show that FIEs in China exported more than all other companies
combined. Between 2000 and 2004, their share of exports was over 50 percent, followed by Chinese SOEs at around 25 percent. In production segments with more advanced technology, the distribution was even more
unequal (Ernst and Naughton 2007).

From the 1990s, China's economy profited in particular from the trends
toward economic stagnation in the North. Unlike in the "golden" postwar
period, the old centers of capitalism showed a lower investment rate and
weaker GDP growth. The underlying causes were a stagnation phase in
Europe, Japan, and North America that had been ongoing for a long time,
a drop in productive investment, which drove the internationalization of
production, and, to a large extent, "financialization" (see R. Brenner 2006;
Glyn 2006; Harman 2009; Hung 2009b; Sablowski 2009). The relatively low
GDP growth in the North and what economists referred to as an "investment crisis," that is, a lack of profitable investment options, found their
counterpart in the trend toward overaccumulation of capital, in other
words, capital surpluses that cannot be put to profitable use, and a slack
labor market.

The possibility of tying up capital to alleviate the overaccumulation
problem could, however, be localized in East Asia and, increasingly, also in
China (Glyn 2006, 86–87). More so than in other large emerging countries
such as India, Brazil, Mexico, and Russia, developed infrastructures and
prospering "supply chain cities" offered stability, and the positive experience of the overseas Chinese provided reasons for investing in China (Gereffi 2009). This trend of capitalist colonization, of seeking out new "spatiotemporal fixes" for the problem of "surplus capital" (Harvey 2010) affected
not only companies from Europe and North America.[98] Japanese companies, too—against a backdrop of domestic growth stagnation—shifted the
focus of their investment regime more onto East Asia and China. The transfer of capital promoted the further development of the growth trend in East
Asia by fixing surplus productive capital and labor in a new way. China was
able to take full advantage of these processes, even in periods of crisis: in

1997–98, the consequences of the Asian crisis, incisive according to many economists, further accelerated the process of relocation to mainland China (ADB 2011, 65). The same applies to the bursting of the "dotcom bubble" in 2000–2001, which triggered a rapid transfer of mass production capacities to the new Chinese contract manufacturing sites in the style of a herd mentality.

This historic shift of capital toward China initially helped to counteract the trend of stagnation of the global economy: the U.S. and Chinese economies achieved growth from the 1990s in two different but interdependent ways. While in the United States GDP growth could be largely attributed to (debt-fueled) consumption and less to investment, the course of the Chinese upswing was in a sense the reverse of the process in the United States—it was based on a very high investment rate. Large quantities of available liquid assets in the North ensured the supply of equity investment and continued to fuel the boom. Meanwhile, the old centers served as end consumers of export goods from China. However, by 2007–8, as the analysis in Chapter 3 shows, this win-win situation was drawing to an end.

Interim Conclusion

As assumed in my research framework, the roots of the Chinese "economic miracle" from the 1980s can be explained only by taking into account external variables. Both geographical and temporal factors facilitated the success of China's selective policy of reform and opening up and provided the PRC with an edge over other emerging countries, which had to shoulder a greater tendency toward disintegration in the phase of liberalization from the 1970s on. In terms of geographical factors, the Chinese investment location was close to the East Asian growth region with its (often authoritarian) developing states—whose economic policies served as role models for China—and to the overseas Chinese investors who contributed to the reorganization of the coastal regions of the PRC. In terms of temporal factors, particularly from the 1990s onward, China was able to profit from the advanced transnationalization of production, which helped bring about international production sharing and thus transnational production networks, and from weak economic growth in the old centers of global capitalism, including Japan. From the 1990s on, the latter led to a larger-scale shift of capital to mainland China. In the process, the PRC developed into the new economic center of East Asia. A Sinocentric constellation was superimposed on the former Japan-centric regionalism.

In order to define Chinese capitalism more precisely, the PRC's comprehensive integration into the global economy must be factored into the analysis. Another feature of variegated state-permeated capitalism is its competition-driven integration into transnational economic networks and its reliance on patriotic ethnic Chinese and other foreign companies. This also substantiates the criticism voiced regarding the limiting of research on capitalism to the national context: the specific form of "ethnic Chinese capitalism" is difficult to classify according to national varieties of capitalism.

This section has also illustrated that many of the factors that have shaped the face of the Chinese economy and facilitated its growth are not under the control of the Chinese leadership and are far from easy to steer. As I will demonstrate in Chapter 3, this complex inter- and transnational integration has recently created dependencies and negative externalities that have made it difficult for the party-state to maintain the country's socioeconomic dynamism.

CHAPTER 3

======

Current Developments in Chinese Capitalism

In general, the literature refers to two key actors in China's process of modernization: companies and party-state decision makers. The analysis presented in the next two sections focuses on these groups, while also taking international factors into consideration. However, a third group of actors, previously neglected in research on China, has also come into play—namely, the workers. The third section of this chapter is therefore devoted to industrial relations. This takes into account the assumption of my research that a more comprehensive analysis of the new Chinese capitalism and its lines of development is possible only if we examine the role of and interplay between these three groups of actors.

For an analysis of the drivers of capitalism, the five aforementioned dimensions of capitalism once again play a central role. My objective is to identify the key dynamics and paradoxes of variegated state-permeated capitalism. The focus is on the period between 2008 and 2016 although at numerous junctures I make reference to the longer-lasting development trends and path dependencies introduced in Chapter 2. This includes sections on economic policymaking and on the relationship between local pilot projects and centralized coordination, which, although established before 2008, are still key to an understanding of China.

The Corporate Sector and Socioeconomic Dynamics

In this section, I first describe the business forms and production regimes that emerged over the course of gradual institutional transformation in mainland China. The business sector is governed by a "mixed economy" characterized by both formal and informal relationships that is neither "free" nor "planned."

The heterogeneous corporate landscape is layered with close ties between political and economic actors, that is, public-private regimes embodying the central economic coordination mechanisms of the Chinese system. Second, I describe how the interdependencies between economic institutions and political power have reconfigured. At the same time, trust-based relationships (*guanxi*) or social capital are additional elements and important factors in explaining the fundaments of growth.

Third, I come to the conclusion that the dynamics of the corporate sector and the close alliances between companies and government institutions have, to date, contributed to stabilizing the status quo.

Fourth and finally, this brings me to more recent socioeconomic developments, which I argue are shaped by dynamics that make it difficult for the party-state leadership to maintain rapid growth via rebalancing the economy for instance.

Unity in Diversity? Heterogeneous Business Forms and Production Regimes

If industrial value creation is differentiated by company type, the official statistics indicate a substantial increase in the contribution made by privately run companies in the past twenty years. Private domestic businesses (among them, of course, a number of hybrid companies) and a smaller share of foreign-invested enterprises (including those from Hong Kong, Macao, and Taiwan) currently account for the majority of industrial production (Lardy 2014). However, state-owned enterprises (SOEs) still account for approximately 25 percent of industrial production, despite the gradual decline in their share over the last decades. From the 2000s, once the massive wave of privatization had abated, the state leadership was keen to see the SOE sector endure.

BUSINESS FORMS

To be able to further differentiate between Chinese and foreign private enterprises, collective enterprises, and state-owned enterprises, unless stated otherwise, I use data and definitions from the National Bureau of Statistics of China (NBS). According to this, *private enterprises* are further subdivided into three groups:

- *Domestic privately owned enterprises (POEs).* As explained in Chapter 2, during the second phase of reform, the private sector was primarily bolstered by the establishment of new private enterprises, and also, to a certain extent, by reforms to the collectively owned and state-owned enterprises. According to estimates provided by the All-China Federation of Industry and Commerce (ACFIC) and the Chinese Academy of Sciences, only 25 percent of officially registered private companies had formerly been part of the state-owned enterprise sector (B. J. Dickson 2007, 832). Today there are numerous ways for private companies to be entered in the commercial register. If the foreign capital share is below 25 percent, the company is classified as a domestically financed enterprise. In 2015, POEs employed around 99 million workers, compared to approximately 55 million in 2009 and 12.7 million in 2000 (NBS 2015b, table 4–2).
- *Companies from Hong Kong, Macao, and Taiwan.* Under this heading, the statistics cover enterprises from the two Special Administrative Regions and Taiwan. A distinction is made between four different types: "Enterprises with Funds from Hong Kong, Macao and Taiwan refer to all industrial enterprises registered as the joint-venture, cooperative, sole (exclusive) investment industrial enterprises and limited liability corporations with funds from Hong Kong, Macao and Taiwan" (NBS 2010, appendix).
- *Other foreign enterprises.* These are referred to as foreign-owned enterprises (FOEs) or foreign-invested enterprises (FIEs).[1] Notably, there has been a decline in the share of joint ventures compared to wholly foreign-owned enterprises (WFOEs): between 2000 and 2012, the share of foreign direct investment (FDI) in joint ventures fell from over 50 to around 20 percent, while investment in WFOEs increased from 47 to 77 percent during the same period (Davies 2013, 71).

Compared to private companies, the importance of collectively owned enterprises (COEs) declined significantly. Currently, for example, they include township and village enterprises (TVEs) that have not yet been privatized. By 2014, COEs employed only 5.4 million people in Chinese cities (NBS 2015b, table 4–2). As mentioned previously, in the 1990s, the path to the "cadre capitalist" class was opened up to many political cadres.

This was the result, inter alia, of a clause in the 1994 Company Law, which enabled COEs to be restructured as limited liability companies. In these enterprises, which are companies with diverse shareholders of limited partner status, government bodies frequently continue to hold ownership shares. Although they are registered as POEs, they remain embedded in local politics.[2]

According to popular neoclassical theory, unlike private companies, SOEs tend to perform badly and, in the medium term, would be expected to disappear in China, too. State-owned enterprises, however, continue to play a key role here to this day. Nevertheless, there are considerable differences between sectors, also with regard to the performance of SOEs. In various industries, such as the steel, petrochemical, and other generative sectors (the transport and energy sector, for instance), the telecommunications sector, public utilities, and the finance and banking sector, SOEs are still going strong. In other branches, they attempt to maintain their influence through equity investment, in the automobile or chemical industries, for instance. The aim here is to achieve learning effects in "nonstrategic" fields with the objective of comprehensive import substitution. At the same time, SOEs in traditional fields such as heavy industry have also lost out against POEs in terms of competitiveness, despite them enjoying more government support. However, to some extent, this is because SOEs tend to respect compliance standards more. A large state-owned steel plant would therefore normally purify waste water in the surrounding districts whereas a private company would not be prepared to do this.[3]

SOEs frequently behave in a similar way to private companies but, on average, have better access to government support than other enterprises (Shaomin Li and Xia 2008). At the same time, they can be expected to conform more closely to policy guidance. From 2000 to 2009, the number of people employed by SOEs fell from 81 to 64 million, and has stabilized since then (2014: 63.1 million; NBS 2015b, table 4–2).[4] Between 2006 and 2016, the number of big national SOEs under the control of the SASAC was cut from 161 to 102 (SASAC 2016).

Because of efficiency considerations, the restructuring of the state sector led to the creation of large state-owned enterprise groups (*qije jituan*). Strategically important SOEs were reorganized as follows: "the best portions of their assets were spun off to form new, financially attractive entities. The new firms would then be listed on the stock market, while the parent firms remained state-owned entities. The latter is referred to as an enterprise group" (Oi and Han 2011, 31). The form of enterprise groups such as the Baosteel Group or the Donglian Petrochemical Group lies somewhere between a highly integrated conglomerate and the loose grouping of companies within a Japanese *keiretsu*. At the same time, the enterprise groups no longer concentrate on one branch of industry but are now also moving into sectors where, because of their influence over the administration and the accompanying favorable access to resources, they are in a position to make considerable profit. This is something that is usually quite difficult in their core business. It is often rather awkward for power producers and petrochemical companies that their margin is tied to purchasing prices fixed by the state. They therefore invest in real estate, public utilities, or retail. As SOEs, they are able to take out bank loans with favorable terms and then issue loans to, inter alia, other companies in the group. The profits generated by these transactions are frequently used to cross subsidize the company's actual core business. The fascinating thing about this is that, through profit-driven lateral diversification, the SOEs become involved in sectors from which they had previously withdrawn, also for reasons of profit maximization. In isolated cases, the sheer power of these vast SOEs hampers the work of the state regulatory and competition authorities (Naughton 2011a, 73).

Moreover, a large number of major SOEs are publicly listed. At the end of 2016, about one-third of the 3,008 enterprises listed at the two Chinese stock exchanges in Shanghai and Shenzhen were SOEs or their subsidiaries. Although the boards of directors of the companies converted into joint-stock corporations also endowed the state with certain powers, SOEs are nevertheless exposed to competition—at least temporarily. Even in the sectors that used to be more or less monopolies, there are always at least two competing companies; and even in the defense sector, where the government is the only customer, companies were dismantled and exposed to competition (the North Industries Group Corp and the South Industries Group Corp, for instance). In civil aviation, companies under the control of the central government (Air China, China Southern, and China Eastern) compete with private and/or quasistate concerns (such as Hainan Airlines or Dragonair). However, in recent years, a countertrend has also been observed—SOE megamergers such as between China North and China South Locomotive forming China Railway Rolling Stock Corp in 2015 were intended to create world-class competitive firms. Now that the Chinese market has become more saturated, this should make it easier for companies like this to acquire international contracts.

On the whole, the continued existence of many of the SOEs calls into question the assumption of an inefficient state economy (on this see, for example, Yergin and Stanislaw 1999, 282–84). The Fortune Global 500 for 2011, an annual ranking of the top five hundred corporations worldwide in terms of revenue, included sixty-one mainland Chinese companies. Almost without exception, these corporations were state-owned, and forty-one of them had headquarters in Beijing. In 2016, the list included as many as 103 Chinese companies, about two-thirds of which were state-owned, with a clear majority of them still headquartered in Beijing.

The assumption that state-owned enterprises have a debilitating impact on the non-state-owned sectors of the economy (see Yasheng Huang 2008, 6) should also be qualified. SOEs ensure stable demand for many private manufacturers, for instance. A case in point is the telecommunications market, where private enterprises meet growing demand for equipment from the SOEs. Conversely, close business ties with private companies can also be observed.

Yet an important change in recent years has been the shift away from the notion that SOEs have to provide all that is essential for China's economy and society. The SOEs are not flying the Chinese flag alone. This responsibility is borne by a diverse "National Team." On the whole, the reform process has created a heterogeneous corporate landscape, a mixed economy, where national capital predominates. Finally, it is also important to bear in mind the following circumstances: the demarcation of a diverse range of types of ownership, including private forms, should not cause us to neglect the overlapping of these types of ownership with party-state actors. It therefore seems plausible to refer to unity in diversity, that is, a heterogeneous ensemble of business forms and production regimes, which, to a certain extent, is embedded in a state capitalist *dispositif.*

HETEROGENEOUS PRODUCTION REGIMES

In industrialized China, there are different types of regional and sectoral production regimes, where POEs, FIEs, or SOEs predominate. In the majority of cases, however, the production regime is a combination of private and state enterprises, as Tsai already argued some time ago: "Most localities . . . have a hybrid economic structure that lies somewhere in the middle of the private-to-state sector spectrum, with an ambiguous mix . . . that may be quasi private, deeply embedded in the local political economy, or both" (Tsai 2005, 1144; see also Conlé 2011).

One example of a regional economy dominated by Chinese private companies is Wenzhou (in the province of Zhejiang). This is a metropolis with a population that has now grown to over nine million and that already produced a flourishing private sector (of mostly small and medium-sized enterprises or SMEs) during the first phase of reforms. In contrast to private enterprises, the share of industrial output contributed by SOEs was considerably below the national average as early as the mid-1980s. Their share then fell from 19.4 percent in 1985 to 3 percent in the 2000s (Zeng and Tsai 2011, 50; see also Friedman 2011, 94–97). It was not an early wave of privatization but rather the competition-driven growth of the private enterprises that caused this shift.[5] The basis for this was that the region had no traditional strong economic planning with a focus on heavy industry. The regional economy around Wenzhou always concentrated on light industry. Here, there was very little evidence of any legacy of the command economy. Further, it was primarily local entrepreneurs who drove the increase in economic efficiency by learning how to manufacture and market lighters, buttons, and biros. However, in 2011, Wenzhou experienced a profound debt crisis, which it did not manage to recover from until 2015–16.

Xiamen in the coastal province of Fujian, which was declared a Special Economic Zone (SEZ) during the first phase of China's policy of openness, is one example of an economy dominated by FIEs. Here, the share of industrial output accounted for by the public and quasipublic sector declined from almost 90 percent (1983) to less than 12 percent (2014) (Xiamen Municipal Statistics Office 2015). Foreign companies produce more than two-thirds of all the goods in this city. In contrast, although the gigantic industrial center in the Pearl River delta (in the province of Guangdong) is also dominated by private enterprises, here Chinese firms occupy a considerably more important position (NBS 2015a).

However, in the former centers of heavy industry in northeast China, there are still some areas where state-owned enterprises play a significant role—the province of Liaoning is one example of this. Yet even here, important changes took place. In this province, it was the government institutions themselves rather than the pressure of the market that initiated the reforms. Hundreds of SOE managers who had previously been government officials became owners of private companies in the process but still maintained close contact with the party-state ("red capitalists"). Another relevant factor was the establishment of private companies as service providers for major SOEs in the steel or mining sector. As a result of the "plan legacy," the spirit of entrepreneurship was very underdeveloped, and this had to be changed.

Although it is not possible to provide a detailed sectoral analysis at this juncture, it is important to bear in mind that various studies also determine sector-specific paths of restructuring:

> On the one side, the steel and to a lesser extent the petrochemical industry are still dominated by SOE, however, under strictly market-oriented management. . . . In the chemical industry, a rapidly expanding private sector exists and joint ventures and foreign companies are playing a bigger role, such as Germany's chemical giants BASF and Bayer, which operate some of the largest petrochemical complexes in China. . . . The auto industry occupies the middle ground between state-dominated and privately dominated industries. It is led by Joint Ventures of multinationals with the three large Chinese auto holdings, FAW, Shanghai Automotive, and Dongfeng. Smaller private and local-government-owned automakers or auto holding companies are competitors. . . . On the other hand, the electronics and the textile and garment industries, China's two largest single manufacturing industries by employment, are mostly privately owned, industry structures are dominated by subcontractors or subsidiaries of foreign multinationals. (Lüthje 2009, 7; for a more detailed account, see Lüthje, Luo, and Zhang 2013)

According to both regional and sectoral criteria, China's economy has a heterogeneous structure, which is an advantage for businesses. Chinese and foreign enterprises benefit from the fragmented development, and particularly from the unequal production conditions and wage systems. The uneven levels of development across the country—ultramodern urban centers, second-and/or third-tier cities, suburban areas, and backward agrarian regions—also foster internal competition to attract business and investment. All in all, this initially calls my proposition of unity in diversity into question. However, in the following sections, additional dimensions of Chinese capitalism will be analyzed, enabling me to refer to the diversity aspect without ignoring the crosscutting characteristics.

First, however, we should examine the nature of Chinese production regimes in more detail, starting with the example of the exceptionally important IT sector.

The hardware segment of the IT sector is one of the most technologically advanced industries in China. With regard to the performance of Chinese enterprises in this sector, certain companies (including some that were nominally state owned but in practice had operational autonomy) managed to acquire new market shares and become globally competitive.

From the 1980s, companies operating in the IT sector began to increase their autonomy. Perhaps the most well-known example is the computer company Legend, now privately owned and rebranded as Lenovo: "Legend became . . . what is arguably the first government-sanctioned management buy-out (MBO) of a state firm. Technically, Legend was an SOE, 'owned' by the Chinese Academy of Sciences, which provided the initial personnel and modest financing for its creation. Along with other SOEs after the mid-1990s, Legend was to be 'corporatized,' which involved explicitly demarcating the corporation's formerly vague and ambiguous ownership stakes" (Ernst and Naughton 2007, 41).

The type of change in ownership where company management acquires the majority of the capital from the firm's former state owners was periodically a key vehicle for the transformation of SOEs in the IT industry. Since then, a three-tier structure has developed. The first tier involves state-owned enterprises, primarily in the telecommunications industry (China Mobile and China Telecom, for instance) controlled by the SASAC. "The head of SASAC, Li Rongrong, has repeatedly made it clear that he sees SASAC's mission as increasing the value of government assets. While the central government will share ownership stakes with strategic investors and the public by floating some of the companies on stock markets, the government intends to maintain substantial control. Ironically, SASAC's interpretation of its mandate has increasingly followed a well-known business school logic: focus on core competencies, spin off non-core businesses" (Ernst and Naughton 2007, 43).[6]

The second tier comprises large companies such as Lenovo, TCL, Founder, Huawei, and ZTE. Apart from foreign IT firms, this tier is the most innovative: "Second-tier firms have diverse origins: they may come from the state sector, from foreign investment, or, increasingly, may be domestic Chinese start-ups. . . . These firms are . . . creating one of the seed-beds of the new production forces and new interest groups shaping China's emergent capitalism" (Ernst and Naughton 2007, 45). Shares in these companies are frequently owned by local governments. Further, these corporations network with foreign producers, are geared toward major transnationals, and outsource the lion's share of their production to contract manufacturers (for an account of more recent developments, see L. Shih 2015).[7]

The third tier is primarily smaller private manufacturers that focus on the production of specific and no longer solely low-technology products, create industry clusters, and develop close ties with local authorities. In the industry clusters, hundreds of companies compete and cooperate with the aim of selling their products on domestic and global markets.

The Public-Private Organization of China's Economy

As has been outlined above, even in a highly technologically developed branch of industry, such as IT hardware, there is evidence of a close interrelationship between the economy and the state. This illustrates a general feature of Chinese production regimes that I will turn to in the following section. As has already been established in Chapter 2, the close ties between state, quasistate, and private actors are just as much a distinctive characteristic of Chinese capitalism as the entrepreneurial activities of the local authorities. The links between the party, the state, and the business community, sometimes described as symbiotic, continued to exist even after formal privatizations.

To further substantiate the assumption that the public-private organization of the Chinese economy is durable, I will now examine the impact of companies on state institutions and the social ties between the business elite and the political class. Finally, the guanxi networks are interpreted as being a perpetual nonmarket-based type of coordination within variegated state capitalism.

THE IMPACT OF COMPANIES ON STATE INSTITUTIONS

Since the start of the reforms, companies have established a wide range of channels for influencing state institutions. The need to constantly have an impact is a result of the structure of China's political economy, which encourages the dependence of entrepreneurial activities on state institutions: "Every sector, from mining to computers, is highly regulated at every stage of business, including acquiring a business license; obtaining financing; engaging in research and development, production, sales, and distribution; distributing profits; and paying taxes. Because these regulations directly affect the profitability of MNCs and local industry alike, there is a strong incentive for firms to pay attention to and influence the policy process" (Kennedy 2007, 183).

With this in mind, first, businesses employ the medium of consultation. Second, through petitions, proposals are made to (local) consultative conferences to revise existing regulations. These are filed by members of parliament who are also part of the business community. Even more important, however, is active lobbying (Heberer 2002; Holbig and Reichenbach 2005; Kennedy 2011b).

To exert collective influence, employers have recourse to a range of associations and similar organizations. As well as local chambers of commerce, there are large federations such as the ACFIC, representing private companies, and a plethora of smaller, regional business associations. There are around seven hundred national business associations and thousands of regional organizations.

Although these associations are registered as nongovernmental organizations (NGOs), generally speaking, they are still under state control. The ACFIC, for instance, is affiliated to the United Front Department of the Central Committee of the CCP (for an account of the history of the ACFIC, see Holbig and Reichenbach 2005). This does not mean that they are ineffective, however. On the contrary, the existing links with the state apparatus are used to represent specific interests at every political level. The ACFIC also grants loans and has a long-standing cooperative relationship with the state banks in order to help lobby for an increase in the credit volume for the private sector.[8] Indeed, it has already made numerous contributions to furthering reforms benefiting private companies, also at the national level, such as the constitutional change guaranteeing private property in 2004 and the codification of ownership rights (Property Law) in 2007.

On closer examination, unsurprisingly, the role played by business associations varies from industry to industry and region to region, and there are also different methods of exerting influence (see Friedman 2011, 101–6; Fewsmith 2011, 284–86). When they play a more significant role, the associations fulfill a valuable function by enabling industries to self-regulate and relieving state authorities of this responsibility. For the administration, associations are a valuable source of information for policy formation and also play an important supervisory role for policy implementation. Moreover, they can protect decision makers from anticorruption procedures and business disputes. In the past, transactions (purchase agreements etc.)

would have been carried out directly between government authorities and companies. Nowadays, as intermediaries, associations insulate each side from one another. Associations receive money and distribute it, for instance, through R&D competitions. They also carry out technical inspections and duties related to formulating norms—these are responsibilities that the government authorities are only too happy to outsource to qualified partners. The wire rope association in Nantong, for instance, sends inspection teams into individual companies to conduct on-site checks of compliance with product quality, occupational safety standards, and so on.

Within the network of associations, foreign enterprises are also calling for changes in legislation and are making the most of the opportunities arising from collective influence. Various trade groups also play a relevant role here,

> established without any Chinese government involvement, and thus, they fall outside the standard state-corporatist framework that governs local bodies. There are dozens of nationally based chambers of commerce, all of which have offices in the capital, and a few also have offices in Shanghai and Guangzhou. Some, such as the American Chamber of Commerce, were created by industry, and membership is limited to those who voluntary join. Others, such as the German Chamber of Commerce and the European Union Chamber of Commerce in China, were founded by their home governments, and all companies in China from their region are members. (Kennedy 2007, 187; see also GM 2010, 34–50)

The chambers of commerce make a concerted effort to point out "further need for optimization" in selected areas. Their position papers are often very comprehensive, extremely well researched, and detailed. Thus, the European Chamber of Commerce in China provides extensive input into the policy process, for example. Moreover, the foreign enterprises are involved in sectoral interest groups and consult with global lobbying and public relations firms. Some of them are also members of Chinese associations. In the event that these channels prove ineffective, they can always use their link to the governments in the countries where they are headquartered to indirectly exert additional pressure on the Chinese authorities.

In addition, businesspeople seek direct, face-to-face contact with political decision makers. Apart from SOEs, where informal meetings were always preferred, this form of influence is significant among private and foreign enterprises as well. The tradition of reciprocal personal connections plays an important role here. Even in the most developed coastal regions (also in terms of legislation), such as the Pearl River delta, entrepreneurs cultivate close connections with government officials. For the very same reason, the largest foreign companies frequently have a representative office in the capital of Beijing to maintain direct contact with central government staff. During over twenty-five visits to China, Microsoft CEO Bill Gates regularly met with members of the Politburo Standing Committee of the CCP with the objective of building confidence.

Employers as a whole are not a homogeneous entity. For example, domestic POEs have frequently expressed their resentment of the preferential conditions offered to state-owned enterprises, and the SOEs, in turn, conducted successful lobbying activities to abolish tax breaks for foreign companies (Gallagher and Ma 2011, 140). Ultimately, however, cross border coalitions of interests or transnational alliances did develop. Foreign companies cooperate with Chinese ones when there are close relationships owing to joint ventures, for instance:[9] "Having Chinese allies has substantially increased their chances of changing regulations to suit their interests. When foreign companies have economically important and politically powerful Chinese firms on their side, it has been difficult for the Chinese government to adopt blatantly protectionist economic policies, because such regulations would hurt the Chinese partners as much as they would the foreign targets" (Kennedy 2007, 189).

These transnational alliances have already proven to be effective on many levels. Common interests shared by domestic and foreign companies had an impact on the outcome of international trade disputes. At the start of the 2000s, a coalition of interests from the domestic automobile and foreign steel industries managed to block a joint initiative by the Chinese government and major government-owned steel corporations to introduce antidumping duties on steel imports (Kennedy 2007, 192–93).

Overall, the close links between businesses and state authorities lend the socioeconomic system a relatively high level of coherence. These ties by far outweigh the horizontal cooperation between companies, which is the norm in other varieties of capitalism. Because companies (including foreign enterprises) can generally count on support, at least at the local level (we will come back to exceptions in the current discussion), on the whole, they have no economic reason to question China's institutional context and political system. It is more a case of the business community contributing to the state's ability to maintain this distinctive form of capitalism with no democratic participation rights.

The unique structure of the Chinese economy is not the only evidence of the strong links between companies and state institutions. There are also close social ties between the country's business and political leaders.

The *Hurun Rich List*—the Chinese equivalent of *Forbes Magazine*—confirms this assumption: of the 1,363 individuals classified as "yuan billionaires" in 2010, 12 percent had "significant government advisory posts, handing them a powerful platform in a business climate that values official contacts" (www.hurun.net/listreleaseen512.aspx).[10] Until 2016, the number of yuan billionaires had grown so fast that editors found it necessary to list only individuals with a net worth exceeding thirty billion RMB: 1,903 at that time (http://www.hurun.net/en/HuList.aspx, last accessed December 12, 2016).

It is estimated that one in three billionaires in China is a party member, and almost all have good to very good informal links with the political system. The heads of large companies are often delegates from the People's Congresses (at various levels). Similarly, business representatives also frequently sit on local CCP committees and their standing committees. This means that business leaders sometimes simultaneously hold different positions within the public administration and the party. After having held a position in a company, some entrepreneurs become mayors or party secretaries. The same applies to wealthy Chinese who have family ties with political decision makers and/or occupy positions as representatives in local People's Congresses, consultative conferences, and business associations, as well as chambers of commerce (M. Chen 2015).

Aside from influential foreign and overseas Chinese entrepreneurs, China's business leaders come from several areas. They include, first, SOE and state bank managers, second, managers of large and medium-sized private enterprises, and, third, the owners of large and medium-sized enterprises. In the first and second segments of the business elite, close social ties with the political functionary elite are evident. Those concerned often previously occupied senior administrative positions in the state apparatus or state-owned enterprises. The third segment of the business elite also comprises, to a certain extent, families with an "official background," who frequently operate on the principle of "one family, two systems"—the husband or parents occupy senior positions in the (local) administration, for instance, and the wife or children are business owners (for a number of examples, see McGregor 2010, 194–228).

Another group was able to climb the social ladder albeit from a disadvantaged position. However, even this group, "which had no official background, gradually advanced through a clever exchange of extrasystemic material values for 'insider' power resources. [Members of this group are] linked to the political elite through institutional channels rather than personal ties and use these contacts with functionaries to maximize their personal interests"(Q. He 2006, 422, my translation).

Recently, another group, one particularly active in high-tech sectors (resembling modern prototypes of the Schumpeterian entrepreneur), has used the new freedom to act for their own social advancement. The final group included here, municipal civil servants, has a direct political function and has also used its position to successfully become involved in business activities.

The use of the terms "red capitalist" or "cadre entrepreneur" convey that China's processes of transformation are based on extraordinarily close alliances (albeit not always free from conflict) between economic and political power elites, also reflected in individuals occupying dual roles.[11] As Bruce J. Dickson argues on the basis of extensive field research in four provinces (Hebei, Hunan, Shandong, and Zhejiang), no significant countertrends are evident over the course of China's fundamental process of privatization and the emergence of its private sector (see B. J. Dickson 2003, 2007). On the contrary, the number of private businesspeople with party membership rose from around 20 percent to approximately 35 percent between the late 1990s and 2006 (see Heberer 2008, 55; Tsai 2007, 72–104). While this number has only continued to rise as the CCP has asserted its dominance in managing the economy, the representation of private business in the organization's top ranks has remained modest. Only 24 of the 2,270 delegates to the Eighteenth National Party Congress are private businesspeople.[12]

Because the majority of employers, or at least those affiliated with the party, are generally happy with the government's work and with the reforms being carried out, it can by no means be assumed—as analyses continued to do until recently (see Rowen 2007 and also the special issue of the *Journal of Democracy* 9 [1], 1998, "Will China Democratize?")—that the business community harbors an interest in significant political change: "In contrast to the popular perception that privatization is leading inexorably to democratization, and by extension that China's capitalists are democrats at heart, the most recent survey data suggest that they are increasingly integrated into the current political system. They are part of the status quo, not challengers on the outside looking in. On a variety of political questions, the views of entrepreneurs are remarkably similar to local Party and government officials" (B. J. Dickson 2007, 852; also see B. Dickson 2016; Goodman 2016).[13]

It is more likely to be the small entrepreneurs who express reservations about the political system and policies implemented, but they then ultimately tend toward political indifference.

PUBLIC-PRIVATE BUSINESS ALLIANCES AND GUANXI NETWORKS: MICROSTRUCTURES OF VARIEGATED STATE-PERMEATED CAPITALISM

An extended analysis of capitalist development assumes that modern economies are permeated by a series of nonmarket-based forms of coordination. This chapter examines the role of associations and the links between the business elite and the political class. In the sections that follow, I will also incorporate the factors of trust and social capital.

In China, close ties between individuals and small groups are generally referred to using the term *guanxi*. China is often seen as a guanxi society where extremely personalized and calculated modes of interaction govern behavior. As a reciprocal system (based on a balance between services rendered and services received by individuals over long periods of time), guanxi are an essential part of the interaction between firms and between bureaucratic institutions, as well as between these two groups. Studies on the subject also refer to "human feelings credit cards" (*renqing xinyongka*) (Heberer 2008, 93). Guanxi are developed and nurtured by private individuals, and they have a decisive effect on the actions of the organizations these individuals are involved in.

As already mentioned, China's economic history shows a rich tradition of network-based business activities and close family ties (M. Yang 2002). Its continued existence, however, is only superficially a premodern form of socialization. A closer look shows that it is precisely these patterns of social interaction, which, when viewed from a modern perspective, support the capitalist allocation of resources. The term *guanxi* should therefore not be understood as an essentialist typification but should be analyzed as a form of marginally legislated, nonmarket-based cooperation, from a comparative perspective.[14]

From a political economy perspective, guanxi interactions are seen as compensation for a lack of foundations creating a regulatory structure for the market economy (Wank 1999; Jieh-Min Wu 2001). In the absence of clearly defined, and thus legally enforceable, claims with a basis in legislation, guanxi provide a certain degree of morally founded legal security. The risk minimization created by this structure in business contexts facilitates a more rapid reaction to market signals and provides important preconditions for the involvement of family and friends in business activities. The latter are also important sources of investment capital, essential for tapping into new areas of business. As a means of building confidence, guanxi therefore provide a level of protection that the anonymous market does not. Notably, contrary to most media coverage, the overall setting in China also is not predominately corrupted. Local governments in prosperous regions in particular share the overall goals of development with their business partners to such an extent that corruption detrimental to economic growth is kept below rates of corruption in other large emerging countries (Bai 2015). The competition among (local) state-business alliances is an important corrective against economically harmful types of corruption and state-capturing. To be sure, recognized guanxi practices and corruption that is punishable by law are located on a continuum and subject to constant revaluation, as demonstrated by the Xi Jinping government's anticorruption campaigns after 2013.

Foreign investors are able to adapt to these circumstances, as the following example from the automobile industry illustrates. The case shows that by employing nonmarket-based strategies, the VW group was able to gain a competitive edge over its rival Peugeot. Both companies had been involved in joint ventures in the Chinese market since 1985. However, while VW became one of the biggest foreign automobile manufacturers over the next decades, by and large, Peugeot's attempts failed: "VW's success lies in its market and nonmarket strategies, its amicable relationship with Chinese officials, . . . its use of local management, and its quick response to challenges with strong local manufacturing and distribution networks. Peugeot, on the other hand, used . . . approaches developed in France. It developed only narrow networks . . . , and depended too much on French expatriate managers" (GM 2010, 54).

A specific function of these social connections is that, as politicized networks, they link private businesspeople with decision makers and, thus, create a basis for the country's economic growth: "In a sense, the practice of guanxi is being adapted to the structural needs of China's emerging capitalism. . . . Guanxi are melded with newly established formal institutions and serve as a key mechanism through which wealth is accumulated. In the future, the penetration of guanxi networks into all aspects of business-industrial activities might even be perceived to lend the emerging institutions of Chinese capitalism their competitive advantage" (McNally, Guo, and Hu 2007, 2).

Bourdieu referred to this as a form of "social capital" resulting from the use of networks of more or less institutionalized relationships based on mutual knowledge and recognition (Bourdieu 1992). These are microstructures of variegated state-permeated capitalism where state and private actors (ultimately defined by the state) are connected at various levels. The guanxi networks lend the Chinese economy a high degree of particularistic coordination, yet they still occur within the confines of competition with other networks. These public-private alliances thus do not represent a gradual transition to the "pure" market but rather should be viewed as a form of nonliberal marketization themselves. This situation simultaneously reflects a form, albeit a distinctive one, of the structural interdependence between political and economic actors that is characteristic of capitalist systems. In this context, commercial rationality is based on the continued cultivation of personal connections with administrative bodies, and vice versa.

The Corporate Sector as a Means of Safeguarding the Status Quo: Initial Conclusions

In China, we have seen the development of a heterogeneous business landscape with different production regimes. In order to understand this institutional bricolage, we need to take into account party-state behavior as well as other nonmarket forms of cooperation, which are layered with the corporate sector in a distinctive way and thus give rise to unity in diversity. The same applies to China's figure of the risk-taking (private) entrepreneur. The activities of these businesspeople, focused on pursuing narrow individual interests, must be analyzed in the context of their institutional embedding. Despite the recurring disruptions to the public-private growth alliances of Chinese capitalism, on the whole, the relationships between domestic enterprises and state institutions, flanked by informal guanxi networks, continue to work in the interests of capitalist-driven modernization.[15] They have been less prone to economically harmful forms of corruption than commonly assumed. Overall, the public-private alliances also outweigh the (purely private) horizontal cooperation between businesses and their associations. If we borrow the wording employed by research on comparative capitalism, here, what at first glance appears to be an incoherent setting produces institutional complementarities, that is, productive consequences for economic development.

Thus, the corporate sector has provided an impetus for China's capitalist modernization and contributed to safeguarding the status quo. This particularly applies to companies with especially close connections with state authorities: "Red capitalists operate the largest firms and are the most likely to be involved in the political arena. Indeed, most of them . . . are more likely to support the . . . existing authoritarian political system rather than pose a direct challenge to it. This is a key element of the CCP's strategy for survival, and so far it is working" (B. J. Dickson 2007, 852; see also B. Dickson 2016).

Another feature of the Chinese economy can be identified by drawing on the notion of uneven, combined and interconnected development: the different levels of regional economic development and the country's heterogeneous production regimes foster intensive competition, which, in turn, enables companies to exploit the inequality of production conditions and wage systems to maximize profits. Further, this heterogeneity hampers efforts to harmonize employment standards. Domestic and foreign enterprises benefit considerably from the regional differences in development—implicitly turning a blind eye to the resulting social costs. Because, to date, social concerns have not really taken priority over market forces and the processes of commodification (and precarization), the range of options open to business initiatives is correspondingly wide. The combined development aspect also serves to explain how modern forms of corporate management were and continue to be linked to autochthonous traditions (such as guanxi) to guarantee relatively efficient commercial activities beyond familiar liberal coordination mechanisms.

On balance, the public-private business alliances have acted as an anchor of stability for China's social development to date. However, some of the trends of Chinese capitalism are threatening to undermine the country's growth path, which had been comparatively stable for such a long time. Moreover, the question arises as to whether the continued absence of an autonomous civil society may be an obstacle to growth, suggesting that "subordination" has its limits. The following sections attempt to substantiate this.

Paradoxes of Prosperity: Economic Development After 2008

Up until 2016, China's public-private economy exhibited exceptional accumulation dynamics. However, for some time now, there has also been evidence of factors that threaten the country's high growth.

To illustrate this, first I will outline some fundamental economic data, such as GDP growth rates, investment rates, and company profits. I will then examine the consequences of China's global economic integration. I will show that the dependence of the Chinese economy on global economic developments partially jeopardizes the growth dynamics. However, so far, this problem has been mitigated, particularly by the dynamism of the country's domestic markets.

GROWTH RATES, INVESTMENT RATES, AND PROFITS

The average annual gains in industrial value added of 14.6 percent observed from 1980 to 2014 was nothing more than a historically exceptional process of industrialization. In 2016, around 20 percent of global industrial production takes place in China, a figure that surpasses the United States, the most important industrial location of the last century. Further, the world's largest infrastructure investments have accelerated the process of urbanization: in 2011, 51 percent of China's total population officially resided in the cities. In reality, however, the urban population is likely to have crossed the 50 percent line some years before. This is first and foremost due to the millions of migrant workers who are not registered as city residents, and, second, it is because areas officially declared to be "rural" are in fact more (sub)urban in reality.

The GDP growth rates reached record levels during the period of reform. Between 1978 and 2015, GDP increased by an annual average of 9.9 percent (at purchasing power parity).[16] Statistically, Chinese economic growth since 1978 exceeds every other long upturn in the entire history of capitalism. Between 2000 and 2015 alone, the average per capita income grew by 12.8 percent per annum (NBS 2015b). Even Japan, during its period of intense economic growth, was unable to attain long-term growth comparable with these figures. Relative to the Japanese role model, China's achievements appear all the more impressive if we consider the population differences. Unsurprisingly, there are significant regional discrepancies: while the coastal provinces recorded growth rates of more than 11 percent over long periods, the poorer inland provinces were able to achieve growth of only 6 to 8 percent. As pioneers of modernization, in 2015, the Pearl River delta (PRD) and the Yangtze River delta (YRD) together made a 25 percent contribution to national economic output. This enabled them to maintain the prominent positions as economic centers (in the YRD, this also applied to the financial sector) they had occupied previously (Jiaxing City 2016; Guangdong Province 2016). As early as 2008, these two large regions accounted for one-quarter of China's GDP. Also within the individual provinces, economic development was uneven. Average income, per capita GDP, foreign trade, and other economic indicators are considerably better in the provincial capitals and other cities than in more rural regions.

The basis of the development of modern industry in China is an investment rate that, by international standards, is exceptionally high. This investment rate is defined as the share of capital investment of the economy's GDP. Because of the need to create a modern infrastructure, to accommodate rural-urban migration, and to develop the industrial sector, investment rates in developing and emerging countries are typically higher than in industrialized countries. In the case of China, the investment rate was consistently high from the beginning of the reform era, and values in fact even increased over time—from over 30 percent in the 1990s to 40 percent after 2000. From 2008 into the early 2010s, historical highs of up to 45.5 percent of GDP have even been reached, which, in turn, resulted in the development of overcapacity in many sectors of the economy (World Bank 2016). These values surpass those of other newly industrialized countries.

Over recent years, the slow transition from primarily labor-intensive to increasingly capital-intensive production has accelerated. Since the start of the policy of reform and opening up, the Chinese accumulation regime has been heavily based on extensive use of wage labor and natural resources. Since the mid-1990s, the focus on light industrial production sectors has increasingly been replaced by the growth of technology-intensive sectors, particularly in medium-tech industries. At the same time, from the 1990s to around 2010, we have seen a high rate of labor productivity growth. Chinese workers were not only comparably cheap, but very productive.

Increases in productivity in fact offset wage rises during the 2000s. Growth in labor productivity surpassed the rise in unit labor costs, that is, the average cost of labor per unit of output. China's labor productivity has been increasing much faster than that in Brazil, South Africa, India, or any OECD country since the 1990s (Herr 2011). This trend has been thanks to more efficient employment of labor by companies (particularly by enterprises with foreign capital shares), positive infrastructure and transportation network externalities, new management systems, and a rise in more technology- and capital-intensive forms of production. Only since the early 2010s has labor productivity no longer outpaced the increase in wages. Moreover, although 2015 still saw a 6.6 percent increase in labor productivity (calculated as output per worker), observers have warned that China requires further and higher productivity gains in order to successfully catch up with developed countries. Researchers have calculated that productivity in 2015 was still 15–30 percent below the OECD average (Woetzel et al. 2016).

With regard to returns on invested capital, experts distinguish between a period of falling profit rates (not only among SOEs) in the 1990s and an increase in the profit margins from the late 1990s to 2007, a peak phase of GDP growth (Felipe, Laviña, and Fan 2008, 748–53; Lo and Zhang 2011, 48–49; Ma and Yi 2010, 12; Naughton 2011a, 74–75). The share of total industrial profits accounted for by the private sector doubled in the 2000s. During the "crisis years" of 2008–9, the high level of profitability could not be sustained, however (Liang 2010, 65). Between 2009 and 2014, profitability of industrial enterprises remained within a rather high corridor of 6 to 8 percent. A review of the financial performance of enterprises of various ownership types has revealed only minor deviations from average profitability (during that period, SOEs underperformed compared with the overall industrial sector by at least one percentage point every year; conversely, companies with overseas investment beat the sector average in most years, albeit by less than a percentage point: NBS 2015a, 2015b).

Overall, as in other capitalist economies, GDP growth in China was cyclical: periods of particularly high growth rates of 11 percent and above in 1978, 1984–85, 1992–94, or 2006–7 were interspersed with weaker phases with growth of 3 to 4 percent (1989–90) and 7 to 8 percent (1998–99). The global crisis of 2008–9 certainly hit the Chinese economy. But growth recovered quickly: Initially after the global crises, a major economic stimulus program was established in China. Measured against GDP, this government program was the biggest in the world. Indeed, the program has effectively orchestrated a fast recovery by extending economic infrastructure (railway and highway networks, for instance) and upgrading technology in several strategic industries (D. Schmidt and Heilmann 2010). Local governments and state banks played an active part in this. While Chinese and international observers had initially welcomed the Chinese government's resolve and rapid action, attention had shifted toward fear of structural imbalances and financial risks toward the end, however. Many infrastructure projects, planned with great haste, were struggling with cost overruns or shoddy construction or simply failed to produce the expected investment returns. Heavy industries, such as steel or nonferrous metals had benefited from increased demand and plant utilization thanks to government-initiated construction schemes. As their effects began to ebb in mid-2011, excess capacity developed and profitability dropped.[17] Here, the competing subnational authorities contributed to the continuation of investment-driven growth. Extremely high investment rates fostered the trend toward overinvestment and, consequently, overproduction.

Thus, following a peak of 10.6 percent in 2010, growth settled into a gradual decline—although, again, on a comparatively high level. In 2015 and 2016, the economy grew by 6.9 and 6.7 percent, respectively. Chinese authorities have dubbed the expected period of slower growth the "new normal" (*xin changtai*). Official statements about an L-shaped recovery pattern suggest that slower but less volatile growth is indeed regarded as the new long-term trend. The term "new normal" combines the acceptance of slower economic growth with a stronger focus on more equitable and green growth. In order to put a positive spin on the faltering economy and stress its strategic nature, the term "high quality growth" was introduced. In order to reassure a populace accustomed to double-digit growth rates, government media posited the "new normal" as an entirely acceptable side effect of controlled economic reform. Officially, it was not to be regarded as a cause for concern or something undesirable but rather as an opportunity to address development gaps and weaknesses.

OPPORTUNITIES AND LIMITATIONS OF CHINA'S GLOBAL INTEGRATION

As has already been outlined in Chapter 2, not all sectors of the Chinese economy were opened up to the same extent to foreign commercial activity: while, in many cases, barriers to FDI and foreign trade, as well as technology and knowledge transfer, have been removed, international capital transactions and access to the Chinese financial market are still subject to strict controls. The Chinese authorities use fiscal, monetary, and currency policies as tools to intervene to a significant extent in the process of international integration. The consequences of these developments over the past few years can be summarized as follows:

(1) *FDI.* The inflow of foreign direct investment has made an important contribution to China's dynamic economic growth. As significant employers and taxpayers, FIEs have become key actors in the Chinese economic system. At the same time, FDI promoted the enhancement of the country's export goods profile—from simple, labor-intensive goods to technologically more sophisticated and capital-intensive ones (electronics, for instance).[18] Also, through technology transfer, FDI contributed to the further development of domestic companies and facilitated their transformation into internationally competitive corporations (Fu 2015). The transfer of know-how from foreign-invested companies to domestic enterprises, or what are known as spillover effects, promote, on the recipient side, the further development of production technology and product portfolios and facilitate quality improvements and cost reductions.

We have particularly seen an increase in FDI since China joined the World Trade Organization (WTO) in 2001. The global crisis in 2008–9 caused FDI to only temporarily subside—in the years that followed, the strong upward trend continued. By the end of 2014, China's FDI stock had increased to US$2,678 billion (OECD 2016). The most important provenance of investment continues to be Hong Kong as this Special Administrative Region serves as a starting point for FDI from numerous foreign companies.[19] Since 2005, FDI from EU countries has surpassed investment from the United States. Of the East Asian countries of origin, Japan, South Korea, and Singapore are the leading players. In the northern provinces of Shandong, Liaoning, and Jilin, South Korean and Japanese FDI predominates and is driving the integration of China into transnational networks of Northeast Asian companies.

(2) *Foreign trade.* The China discourse generally portrays the reliance on the consumer markets of the North as an Achilles heel for the country's economic growth. The loss of demand as a result of the global financial crisis and the continued weak demand due to the European debt crisis have made this export dependence painfully apparent.

These dependencies prevail to this day. In 2015, the export of Chinese goods and services to the United States represented the largest international trade flow. US imports accounted for a total value of US$659 billion, whereas Chinese imports were worth only US$162 billion (Office of the United States Trade Representative 2016). The European Union member states are also exceptionally important export markets for China.

Interestingly, the degree of dependence has declined slightly since 2008, however. The export share of GDP initially increased from 20 percent in 2001 to 35 percent in 2007, the year before the crisis, and then gradually dropped back to its initial level by 2015. As I will describe below, this is linked to the incredible dynamism of the internal market and to rising domestic consumption as a growth driver. Partially, the government's efforts play a role here too: extensive infrastructure measures and purchasing incentives for environmentally friendly products, such as household appliances and cars, had already led to a rise in domestic demand by early 2009.

Additionally, the reliance on exports to a small number of OECD markets was reduced through an accelerated expansion of exports to other developing and newly industrialized countries. The growing importance of the markets in the Global South is evidence of a countertrend to the assumption of extreme dependence on the markets in the North. In contrast to the former world economic centers, certain emerging markets show a stronger growth dynamic: "The share of the South in world GDP rose from about 25 percent in 1980 to 45 percent in 2010, of which developing Asia alone contributed two-thirds" (ADB 2011, 39, 47). There has been a rise in "South-South trade" and China is playing a prominent role. In the event that the East and Southeast Asian regions (particularly India) were to continue to record higher GDP growth rates than the former centers of capitalism, according to a not entirely unfounded assumption we may see a situation where not only global industrial production but increasingly also global demand will be concentrated in these regions in the future. Because the demand structure in these regions, that is, the composition of household consumption, will initially be focused on the cheaper product segments, Chinese (and also Indian and other Asian) companies have an advantage over their Western competitors: the product markets below the premium sectors frequently have only low entry costs, and equally companies from the South are able to build on greater experience in their domestic markets.

(3) *Technology/knowledge transfer and the large domestic market.* Throughout the reform era, China became increasingly integrated into the

international technology and knowledge exchange. Until around 2010, China's domestic industry was effectively largely a recipient of international best practice in the fields of production technology and management know-how. This phenomenon made a significant contribution to improving the performance and competitiveness of Chinese companies.[20] The large and still growing number of Chinese students studying abroad, at elite universities in the United States, for instance, should also be seen as an important instrument for the transfer of knowledge and technology. In order to avoid a brain drain, the government lured highly qualified professionals back to China with lucrative job offers.

Notably, by the 2010s, integration in global production networks provides more opportunities for technological upgrading. The relocation of R&D from the West to China, generally driven (and rewarded financially) by the Chinese government, fosters the regional concentration of intellectual property in China (Fu 2015; for early evidence, see Ernst 2006). As a consequence of these measures, particularly since the global financial crisis, Chinese producers have managed to strengthen their influence on the primarily Western brand companies and their product technologies. This is partly because of China's exceptional circumstances, due, inter alia, to the special role played by the state, which (in contrast to other contract manufacturing locations in Eastern Europe or Mexico) also pursues an active industry and technology policy supporting the development of independent technologies and standards (also see Herrigel, Voskamp, and Wittke 2017).

The Chinese authorities are able to place international corporations under pressure to accelerate the technology and knowledge transfer. In the past, foreign investors have been and indeed are still today frequently forced to trade the intellectual property rights to their production processes for access to the Chinese market. In sectors such as automobile manufacturing, where international companies are obliged to cooperate with local partners (under the auspices of joint ventures), the authorities insist on disclosure of key technologies. They also demand the formal legal transfer of intellectual property rights to local companies, as well as the relocation of R&D for future technologies.[21]

Apart from technology transfer supported by the state, a voluntary exchange takes place, particularly between companies with comparable skills and resources. Intellectual property protection has also improved in the last few years, and now, for Chinese companies, too, it is an important prerequisite for safeguarding their development activities.

When China joined the WTO, there were still major concerns among the Chinese that foreign competition might be the downfall of domestic producers. However, one factor, previously often overlooked, enabled Chinese companies, which, at the time, were often still technologically backward, not only to survive but even to catch up: the demand structure of the large domestic market (Woetzel and Towson 2015). Although foreign companies continued to dominate the premium segments, domestic producers were able to command the lower price segments and, in many sectors, increasingly also the midprice segments where demand was fastest growing (Brandt and Thun 2010). Empirical studies on the automobile industry and the mechanical engineering and construction machinery sectors show that Chinese companies benefit both from the advantages of "deep experience with a particular product range" and "policy support" (Brandt and Thun 2010, 1570).[22] Moreover, domestic producers prefer to recruit employees who have been trained in foreign companies or joint ventures. The consequences of this are apparent when we look at the international market for construction machinery. Chinese enterprises such as Sany, Xugong, and Liugong have managed to bring the technical features of their products up to a global market level. Their integration in China's high-volume mass market enabled them to finance substantial R&D activities and to become frontrunners in the international construction machinery industry. Thanks to its commercial success, in 2013, Sany even managed to acquire the German company Putzmeister, the world market leader for concrete pumps.

(4) *Going global—international activities of Chinese enterprises.* Not long ago, some authors referred to the emergence of an extremely dependent and compliant "comprador class" in China (Breslin 2007a, 31). However, the increasing international activities of domestic companies recently point in quite the opposite direction. In the last few years, there has been a significant increase in FDI by state-invested, hybrid, and private firms from China, with a focus on Asia and other emerging economies. At the same time, these companies have also increasingly been investing in developed economies, however (for more detailed analyses, see ten Brink 2014a and 2015). Striving to tap into a rich base of markets, technology, and brands, large Chinese firms are now among the leading global investors. Although this is far from being an absolute unmitigated success, paradoxically, companies in developed economies have contributed to creating a powerful new competitor through, largely unintended technology transfers during their

expansion into China. The result is a restructuring of competitive relationships in international markets, where a whole range of Chinese companies have been able to catch up with the major established corporations.

Chinese outward foreign investment comprises a variety of elements, from international contracts, joint ventures, or foreign subsidiaries to mergers and acquisitions and the purchase of equity. Chinese investment thereby reflects the development stage of its domestic economy in that foreign investment largely concentrates on the manufacturing sector, mining, and wholesale and retail trade. Firms often follow the path to economic development laid down by other companies from emerging economies that went global. These latter companies can be grouped into at least three relevant types: First, focused export firms such as Midea use a single market sector to gain footing. Midea has become a leading manufacturer of medium-tech products (in this case, microwaves and air conditioning appliances). Second, technological leaders are enterprises that have become internationally competitive in high-tech sectors (Lenovo in the computer industry, and Huawei and ZTE in telecommunications, for instance). Third, resource-oriented corporations such as the three big oil companies Sinopec, Petrochina, and CNOOC, whose objective of which is to secure raw materials and which are often active in geopolitically sensitive states such as Iraq and Iran (see Jiang and Sinton 2011; ten Brink 2015).

Although some resource-based investments are complemented by geopolitical motives, economic motives prevail over geopolitical considerations in the internationalization drive of Chinese firms. On the whole, from the perspective of Chinese policy makers, encouraging foreign investment can be best understood as an economic development strategy with the primary objective of advancing the domestic economy. The principal goal is not to gain more influence over host economies but to move up the value chain and to facilitate industrial upgrading. Collectively, close connections between private and state actors in China, a pronounced orientation toward growth, and an emphatic focus on foreign economic policy lead to dynamic internationalization efforts.

REBALANCING THE ECONOMY AND THE LARGE DOMESTIC MARKET

In the wake of the global economic crisis, the Chinese government attempted to modulate its traditional economic policy overemphasis on capital investment and foreign trade in favor of "rebalancing the economy," that is, focusing more on the domestic market and domestic consumption

(P. Li 2011; Naughton 2010). Studies have indicated a comparatively low level of consumption relative to investment in the 2000s, structurally weak demand and low wages among employees (particularly migrant workers), and, by international standards, very high savings rates (ADB 2011; Akyüz 2011; J. He and Kuijs 2007). A high savings rate was a necessity because Chinese households largely had to finance their own health care, pension provisions, and children's education.

However, various interest groups existed that attempted to stop the economy from being rebalanced and had a stake in the continuation of the low-wage model (ten Brink 2013). There were three main interest groups. First, indigenous and foreign companies keen to see the low-wage model continue. Major foreign corporations or their local contract manufacturers relocated parts of their production to the northern, central, and western provinces in order to profit from the competitive advantages there (low wage costs and taxes, and cheap land). To a significant extent, this applies to the IT industry, which the local governments in the inland provinces are wooing to encourage them to relocate their labor-intensive manufacturing processes. For the same reasons, in the most highly developed coastal provinces such as Guangdong, production sites were moved to nearby less developed regions in the province.

Second, because domestic and international companies were still keen to utilize the competitive advantages linked to low wages, local governments generally accommodated their needs. In this respect, the competition between political authorities below the central government level led to the perpetuation of the low-wage model. This competition between the subnational authorities also contributed to the continuation of investment-driven growth.

Third, notably the central government itself also preserved the status quo to a certain extent. This was evidenced by the hesitant approach of the party-state toward reforming the labor unions and the system of wage determination, for instance. In other words, the government was unwilling or unable to exacerbate the conflict of interests between social equity and the maintenance of "international competitiveness."

However, on closer examination, there is evidence of another trend, one that becomes more pronounced over time: the growth of China's large domestic markets. Perhaps somewhat surprisingly if we consider standard economic analyses, which mostly focus on China's opening up efforts and its achievements in export, domestic industrial firms sell, on average, three to four times more goods on the domestic market than abroad. Given the distinctive demand structure of China's domestic markets, it increasingly entails producing medium-tech goods to meet domestic consumer needs. This is a segment where domestic firms enjoy strategic advantages thanks to their proximity to home markets, knowledge about consumer preferences, and state support. In earlier periods, it was principally low-tech industries that contributed to Chinese GDP growth. However, since the 2000s, an increasing number of medium-tech segments of the market have emerged as growth drivers (see Nölke et al. 2018).

The political class made the notion of strengthening the country's domestic markets a subject of public discussion around the late 2000s (ten Brink 2013). Since the introduction of the Twelfth Five Year Plan (2011–15) in March 2011, strengthening domestic consumption has been one of their key political objectives (Wen 2011). The plan stipulated, inter alia, an annual 13 percent increase in the minimum wage and considerable improvements in social security. Officially, the disposable income of China's urban population increased by an average of 7.7 percent per year between 2011 and 2015 (the target was a 7 percent increase) (National People's Congress 2016, 3). The government has announced a further increase of more than 6.5 percent per annum for the period covered by the Thirteenth Five Year Plan (2016–20).

Indeed, as Figures 1 and 2 show, the long-term growth in disposable income had already resulted in a sustainable increase in private consumer demand, even before these government measures were introduced.

As shown in Figure 1, retail sales have maintained very strong growth that even allowed for a tripling of sales figures between 2007 and 2016. Despite a surge in spending, retail sales growth rates have leveled out in recent years, dropping from values in excess of 20 percent in 2008 to roughly half that currently. During the same time frame, monthly fluctuations eased, and the growth rate settled into a more stable trend. Figure 2 illustrates that the rapid expansion in household consumption expenditures (measured in absolute numbers) has coincided with a decrease in its share of overall economic performance. The time line does, however, show a trend reversal.

But where is this demand located? Certainly, the Chinese luxury markets are rapidly becoming the world's largest. However, what is more relevant is the rise in mass consumerism, which resembles consumption patterns in the Fordist era of the 1950s and 1960s in the West. Consumption in China grew from around US$650 billion to almost US$1.4 trillion between 2000 and 2010. Irrespective of its relative percentage of GDP and

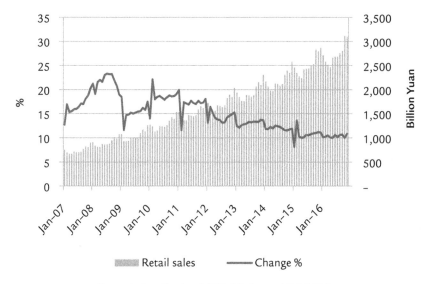

Figure 1. Retail sales, 2007–16. *Source*: NBS 2016.

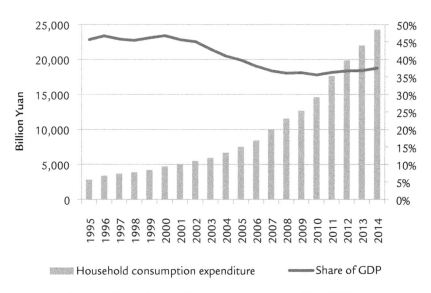

Figure 2. Rise in household consumption. *Source*: NBS 2015b.

despite huge inequality gaps in all rural and urban regions, China's consumption has thus been growing faster than any other large economy in absolute terms. In addition, China's household income is huge: currently over US$5 trillion a year with substantial unreported income (Woetzel and Towson 2015). A key driver of domestic demand is the new middle class. This results in a vast need for durable goods, ranging from textiles to white goods and mobile phones, and the desire to travel (tourism has become a multibillion RMB business in recent years). Alongside end consumer demand, the very high demand for intermediate goods, that is, goods consumed as production inputs, including office equipment, computers, motor vehicles, and machinery, has played an important role. Thanks to the investment boom, domestic manufacturing firms are among the most important producers of intermediate goods. Construction is an equally essential activity. This sector contributed the single biggest share of GDP growth in the late 2000s. Intermediate goods are also often obtained locally.

As demonstrated above, the problem of underconsumption has declined somewhat since 2010 because both the increase in disposable income and improvements in social security systems have resulted in an improved consumer climate. Accordingly, the International Monetary Fund (IMF) expects a drop in the savings rate from 48 percent to 42 percent between 2016 and 2021 (IMF 2016, 12).

Interim Conclusion

This chapter revealed that the public-private organization of the Chinese economy created, into the 2010s, fertile ground for implementing efficient corporate strategies. At the same time, over a long period, this also contributed to social cohesion. The process of capitalist modernization could be regulated in the interests of the prevailing alliance of economic and political elites—here the notion of "regulation for competition" (Obinger et al. 2010) via state institutions, a concept we are also familiar with from Western societies, applies.

However, this stability has been called into question. Although the public-private networks underlying the Chinese economy facilitate a high degree of particularistic coordination, the growth model has its limitations (also see L. Chen and Naughton 2017). In the PRC, we can identify paradoxes of prosperity that serve to undermine the stability of Chinese-style development.

In order to attenuate the effects of capitalist modernization, the Chinese central government has been pushing for a comprehensive rebalancing of the economy. However, various factors have presented major hurdles along the way: first, owing to the persisting dependency on an unstable global economy and transnational value chains, the low-wage regime was upheld. Domestic and international companies had and continue to have a significant interest in the competitive edge associated with low wages and taxes, and local governments are all too often prepared to accommodate this interest. Second, there used to be and still is a clear propensity to overinvest. Moreover, an expansive monetary policy enabled borrowers to purchase land and property, as well as shares and other types of financial product. The acquisition of assets like this created speculative bubbles. Although monetary policy decision makers are attempting to prevent the economy from overheating, here the limitations of national interventions in volatile markets are obvious. Inflationary trends could, in turn, undermine the government's social policy measures because an increase in food prices generally has a more negative impact on poorer families than on wealthier ones.

A countertrend that is advantageous for the government is that the thriving domestic markets have so far prevented a more serious downturn in China. However, as will also be shown in the following section, despite its extensive regulatory capacity, the Chinese government has failed to gain full control over the country's domestic competition and the associated high-risk growth and finance policies pursued by companies and local governments. To a certain extent, the interests of key groups within the local government apparatus, in the corporate sector, and in the financial system undermine the central government's efforts. The country's overinvestment tendencies initially appear to resemble a typical capitalist crisis mechanism. However, the policies of competing local governments are also thrown into the equation, and these then exacerbate the problems to some extent. The next section will therefore comprise an analysis of the role of state institutions in creating socioeconomic stability and simultaneously causing paradoxical developments.

Planning for and with the Market(s):
The Heterogeneous Party-State

State institutions play a key and enduring role in Chinese capitalism. In this section, I will provide a more detailed analysis of the party-state, in order to highlight additional characteristics and particularities, as well as problematic features.

In recent decades, a series of informative analyses have been published on the transformation of China's political system. These studies depict, with impressive rigor, the transition from a totalitarian to a consultative authoritarian system of governance (see, for instance, Fewsmith 2008; Heilmann and Perry 2011b; Saich 2004; Shambaugh 2009b; Jinglian Wu 2005; D. Yang 2004; Zheng 2010). The authors of these works frequently attest to the brilliant command of governance practices of the Chinese elite (unlike the *nomenklatura* in the Soviet Union), which is partly attributed to their exceptional willingness to learn and adapt. Note, however, that some of these authors have had a change of opinion after the coming to power of Xi Jinping who was seen to significantly reduce state adaptability and willingness to reform through a recentralization of power (see Heilmann and Stepan 2016; Shambaugh 2016).

I would now like to make a number of additions regarding the transformation of political intervention and regulation using the language of political economy. As introduced in my research framework, I argue that large parts of the political system are subject to imperatives of capitalism and this is reflected in the modus operandi of the central government and its local counterparts. The party-state is not retreating from market expansion but instead has itself become a key actor in Chinese capitalism. To a great extent, state actors have assumed the role of institutional entrepreneur. Notably, this calls into question one prevailing interpretation of the reform process: on the basis of a definition of capitalism that equates it with a liberal market economy, this interpretation sees the second phase of reform as a type of bureaucratic backlash due to the persistent and indeed increasing intervention of state actors (Yasheng Huang 2008). The capitalist transformation process, however, is not advancing in accordance with the predicted transition to a liberal market economy. At the same time, China's variegated state-permeated capitalism also exhibits differences with coordinated and other state-led forms of capitalism.

Sinologists rightly argue that the drivers of competition and the imperative to increase economic efficiency have already been evident for some time now. Elements of a "commercialization" and "economization" of the state apparatus can be identified, which are reminiscent of the restructuring measures conducted in Western industrial societies. These measures, introduced in the last few decades, saw state bureaucracies begin to use cost-benefit calculations as part of a process of internal rationalization. Additionally, competition between party-state decision makers has increased, also at the top level.

This certainly does not mean that state institutions are now subject to the same incentive mechanisms and criteria for reproduction as companies. For example, political institutions are still geared toward fulfilling a diverse range of tasks that make a crucial contribution to social integration: these include economic and political regulatory functions, as well as providing political stability (by creating social consensus and arenas for conflict resolution and opinion formation, for instance). In China, specific political incentive mechanisms for political actors at different levels, "generated by the cadre responsibility system, the political contracting system, and the performance contracts" (Saich 2008, 186), also remain in place. However, particularly at local government level, the latter is now interspersed with considerations related to capitalist revenue growth.

I will now first discuss the regulatory capacity of the (central) state in the field of economic policy, providing evidence of a transformation of the party-state organization, as opposed to its dismantling. In the next section, I will examine in more detail China's distinctive policy cycles (established already in the 2000s as mentioned in the following section) with a view to contributing to an explanation of the regulatory capacity of state institutions. This is followed by a discussion about the ongoing role of the CCP in the political process, as a "People's Party" of modernization. I will then describe a number of guiding principles that serve to legitimate the rule of the party-state—and exhibit certain features of ideological acrobatics.

Finally, I will summarize factors evidencing that the strong state of the People's Republic of China has its regulatory limits, even under Xi Jinping. The background to my analysis in this section is the power of local authorities and the impact of different social forces on the state, which turns the authoritarian party-state into an arena for social conflict. Taking into account the findings of the previous section of this chapter, I will describe the paradoxes of the Chinese multilevel system of governance that also prevent the economy from being substantially rebalanced and hamper sustainable development, for instance.

The Regulatory Capacity of the Entrepreneurial Party-State

As already highlighted in Chapter 2, since the 1990s, a whole series of restructuring measures have been implemented to strengthen the central government apparatus. The result is that the central state apparatus of power has been able to increase its steering capacity in the area of economic policy and regulate market expansion to a greater extent than governments in other newly industrialized countries.

Particularly since the second phase of reform, the central government has created institutions of market control and regulation with the intention of facilitating development planning based on the estimated growth potential of both local and international markets. In contrast to the trends of the 1990s, economic policy concepts since then have increasingly been focused on the micromanagement of policy again. By the same token, the importance of the party's role in this process is also emphasized. When President Xi Jinping and Premier Li Keqiang assumed power, many observers expected more economic liberalization and a palpable retreat of state actors from market regulation. The Final Communiqué of the Third Plenum of the Eighteenth Central Committee in November 2013 then did indeed promise to strengthen free competition and to view the market mechanism as having a decision-making function. This apparent change in official terminology was received particularly enthusiastically by Western analysts and the media. Three years later, however, it is evident that the current political leaders are just as unwilling to abandon their discretionary structural economic policy as their predecessors were.

In contrast to a bureaucratic allocation of resources, China's more recent development planning system is already accepting and integrating the market as an important allocation mechanism that enhances efficiency. Because, according to China's highest level of government, market forces can develop unwelcome internal dynamics, they must be kept in check through "macroregulation" (*hongguan tiaokong*) as well as microregulation at the local level. The often chaotic competition-driven development of the economy should be coupled with an economic policy based on the concept of "intelligent design." Here, in addition to modified, primarily indicative planning elements, fiscal and monetary policy measures are used. In contrast to the liberal market projects in Western societies, in China, the prevailing guiding principles are state-centric, and there is a very deliberate focus on political steering. Even in branches of the economy where liberalization tendencies win though, concerted efforts are made to avoid losing instruments of control and regulation: "Further liberalization of certain sectors of the economy will proceed, such as for some service industries, parts of the financial system, and the *hukou* (residency) system. But this is '*strategic liberalization*' contained in key sectors. Overall, statist tools will be front and center to affect reforms in areas such as public housing, infrastructure, industrial policy, social welfare system reforms, and . . . the CCP controlled cadre incentive system" (McNally 2011, 25; my emphasis).

Since 2008, against a backdrop of liberalized economies confronting quite obvious problems around the globe, this position has been defended even more vehemently. Conversely, voices within the party in favor of forging ahead with more radical liberalization have lost ground for the time being.

ECONOMIC POLICY

One of China's long-term strategic economic policy goals is the creation of a knowledge and innovation economy, promoted and shaped by the central state. Here we can identify similarities with other East Asian developing nations, which are undergoing a transition to neodirigiste, "Schumpeterian," competition states (see Jessop 2002, 95–139). One characteristic of the Schumpeterian state is its attempts to make innovative capability a central element of the government's economic policy. Technology, structural, and innovation policy initiatives emphasize the expansion and localization of technological knowledge and innovative capacity within China's borders in order to ensure competitiveness in the face of global competition.

The PRC remains some way from reaching this goal, however. In order to gain an overview of the economic policy measures currently being implemented by the (central) government, which work toward achieving this objective, we can differentiate between market-creating, market-regulating, and market-restricting policies. The following are some of the key elements of China's current economic policy (although some have been revised after 2013).

State institutions continue to provide basic infrastructures for accumulation. There is also still considerable support for the generative sectors of the economy, such as telecommunications, transport, and energy as well as natural resources. With respect to logistics performance, such as the quality of the transport infrastructure, the processing of international shipments, and customs clearance, China has worked its way to the top of the emerging countries group.

Market-creating measures have become increasingly important but are supplemented by elements of indicative planning: one example of this is the organization of public tenders by the National Development and Reform Commission (NDRC). The manner in which these tenders are conducted is no longer remotely similar to the process carried out by a planning authority. Admittedly, the NDRC initially sets general development goals and prepares a budget for promoting wind energy, for instance. In a second step, however, an invitation to tender is issued, and a diverse range of both state and nonstate companies compete. A small number of companies are then selected—in a chain of (sometimes corrupt) negotiation processes—and financed. Ultimately, it falls to the relevant authorities to use operative adjustments to (further) open up the market for wind energy to foreign bidders, who, to date, have only had very limited chances of success in these procedures. This enables the authorities to create tougher competitive conditions. Market creation and market regulation go hand in hand here.

The market for factors of production (labor, land, and capital, and, in a wider sense, also energy and environmental resources) remains highly regulated. The opening of the market that has occurred over the last few decades is thus twofold: while the markets for end and consumer products have been partially deregulated, the markets for basic production inputs remain subject to state control. This provides state actors with a broad range of instruments to selectively promote and shape the cost structure of finished products in downstream industries. For the Chinese leadership, a universal reduction in the price of all intermediate products to lower production costs across all areas of manufacturing is of less importance here. Instead, economic policy is implemented more selectively to ensure that the "desired"[23] products and processes profit from the lower-cost inputs and are able to exploit the competitive advantage. Conversely, and equally rigorously, this government steering function ensures an increase in the production costs of "undesired" products and processes. State control and intervention continue to play a central role in the markets for factors of production and serve to steer the development of markets for finished products (Taube and in der Heiden 2015). Moreover, market restriction is employed in the form of sector-specific reregulations (Hsueh 2011; Pearson 2010). Branches of industry that are classed as being strategically important, such as renewable energy, electromobility, and biotechnology, profit from easier and cheaper access to resources than other sectors. This crude classification is layered with and influenced by issues of employment security, regional development, and the special treatment of state-owned and very large private enterprises.

The relatively liberal foreign trade regime is supplemented by a nonliberal domestic investment regime. Here, the instrument of market regulation is employed again. To counter the increasing import competition, in retail for instance, the Chinese government makes more use of a practice that had already been established for some time: investment control. An extensive catalog stipulates in detail in which branches of the economy, production technologies, and production areas foreign investment is to be encouraged, tolerated, restricted, or forbidden. One of the objectives of this targeted control of FDI is to encourage spillover effects. The catalog stipulates the areas in which international investors are permitted to operate in China only in the context of joint ventures with local partners. The catalog is adapted to the changed circumstances every three to five years in order to optimize the effectiveness of government steering (see Bu 2009, 190–97; Kroymann 2009, 41–56, Taube and in der Heiden 2015). On the whole, there is evidence that this has improved opportunities for foreign investors to access the Chinese markets. At the same time, the government's intention is to regulate the different categories of market. What is remarkable here is the manner in which dynamic adjustments are made to the catalogs to take into account the new needs and requirements of the domestic industry: individual products and technologies that used to be listed as "encouraged" have been downgraded to the "tolerated" or even "restricted" categories. Automobile production is a case in point. As the Chinese auto market has gradually been approaching the point of saturation in recent years, in 2015, the final assembly of cars was removed from the list of "encouraged" products and technologies. Instead, the "encouraged" category has been amended to now include other highly specific and advanced car components that, at that point in time, were still not produced inside China (or by Chinese companies) in sufficiently high quality or quantity (NDRC and MOFCOM 2015).

As my analysis of the reciprocal relationships between the state and the business community has already shown in detail, state actors are endeavoring to maintain their influence in the expanding private economy. Frequently, the "privatization" of state-owned enterprises does not follow the pattern of a complete transfer of ownership to private hands. During the process of organizational privatization that predominates in China, as former owners, state administrative bodies maintain an equity stake in the relevant company, though this firm is subject to the new rules of competition. Alternatively, the state transfers public services to private providers, but, during this privatization of tasks, it retains responsibility for those tasks. Additionally, the concept of "public-private partnership" has become increasingly important in recent years: a large number of private actors are involved in urban planning and infrastructure projects for instance. The government thereby strives to improve efficiency and contain costs. Additionally, the SASAC, which reports directly to the State Council, can relatively effectively fulfill its official function as a regulatory authority for major SOEs. The SASAC thus functions simultaneously as both owner and regulator (Jung 2011, 131–32). Here, it is important to reiterate that state institutions promote not only state-owned enterprises but also private companies. The general rule of thumb is: the larger the company, the keener the state institutions are to maintain a close relationship.

The central government traditionally responds to economic downturns with quasi-Keynesian crisis and stimulus programs. During the international financial crisis of 2008–9, as with the Asian crisis ten years previously, stimulus packages costing several trillion RMB were unveiled to compensate for the slump in demand. Measured according to GDP, these relief measures exceeded the equivalent programs implemented in every other major industrial nation. The stimulus package passed by the State Council in November 2008, directly after the outbreak of the crisis, comprised measures costing forty-six hundred billion RMB (the equivalent of around 460 billion euros based on the exchange rate at the time). The program was primarily focused on expanding the infrastructure by extending and modernizing roads and promoting research, for instance. The government leadership adopted programs for "recovery and structural adjustment" in key industries (the IT, automobile, steel, mechanical engineering, and shipbuilding industries). The aim was to ensure that, in line with its industrial policy concept, the extensive financial assistance provided by the state would be invested in technological upgrading and, by extension, in sustainably strengthening the international competitive position of these sectors (see D. Schmidt and Heilmann 2010). The lower levels of government and the state banks were heavily involved in this process (Tong 2010, 50–58). In addition, the local governments drew up local development plans that were purportedly worth the equivalent of around eighteen hundred billion euros in total.

Fiscal policy is also employed as an important instrument of economic regulation. Through selective use of tax breaks, the government creates investment incentives for key industries, environmental protection, and other economic policy priorities. Already in January 2008, the preferential tax treatment of foreign companies was abandoned, and the corporate tax rate was decoupled from owner status (Bai, Lu, and Tao 2009). At the same time, firms have the option of registering as high-tech enterprises, enabling them to profit from a lower tax rate (15 percent instead of 25 percent). The approval procedure is regulated through a strict set of requirements and extensive obligations to provide supporting documents. Even companies in economically underdeveloped provinces, particularly in western China, can expect to pay lower corporation tax, provided that their business falls in the areas that are considered beneficial to economic policy. Individual sectors (such as the software industry) also profit from sales tax refunds.

As the following section illustrates, state institutions also play a key role in the education sector and in the promotion of technological development.

THE EDUCATION SECTOR AND THE PROMOTION OF TECHNOLOGY

Following the technologically determinist spirit of the three-pole dynamics comprising education, research, and innovation, in the education sector and the field of technology promotion, the power elite is endeavoring to catch up with the world's most developed economies. Given the real wage increases since the 2000s, the focus here is more and more on boosting productivity. Because the competitive advantage of low-wage production methods has, to a certain extent, been lost to other developing and newly industrialized countries, the Chinese government is increasingly pushing for the expansion of technology- and knowledge-intensive production branches of industry.

Because of China's education system, which was relatively advanced compared to other large developing countries such as India, the average level of education of the total population was not particularly low at the end of the Mao era. However, reconstructing the educational institutions, in ruins after the Cultural Revolution, presented a major challenge. In order to create first-class and internationally renowned educational and research institutions, an authoritarian centralized education system was established by learning from other East Asian countries such as Japan and South Korea. The main features of this system are a lack of egalitarian principles and a focus on supporting gifted students as well as continuous learning and a heavy emphasis on the system of elite schools, that is, specialist schools and institutes of higher education.[24]

Once they have completed lower secondary schooling, generally at the age of sixteen, students progress to a technical college (vocational college) or a high school. While a technical college leads students directly into the world of work and whole cohorts following this (mainly three-year) educational path are placed in companies, after three years at high school, students can embark on a university course (Woronov 2011). In order to fulfill its objective of technological upgrading using well-trained technical experts, the Chinese government has introduced certain elements of the "dual" education system based on the German model. Here, the practice of individual German companies is used as a precedent. Trainees at a leading German lighting manufacturer in Foshan (Guangdong province) undergo a two-year in-house training program followed by a year at a technical college. This scheme has been publicized as the government's pioneer model in Guangdong. However, nationwide, there appears to be only a small number of functioning interest coalitions promoting "vocational training." Simultaneously, there is a rising demand for well-trained employees with more of a focus on practical than academic skills (see Benson et al. 2013).

With a view to strengthening China's position in the face of global competition, the Chinese government has given the promotion of technology high priority: in 2015, R&D expenditure amounted to 2.1 percent of GDP. This places China at the top of the emerging nations group, while gradually approaching the top ten worldwide.[25] The People's Republic is now also a leading player in terms of the number of experts working in the research field. Numerous universities and other state research institutions employ scientists and engineers to work on product and process innovations. Establishments like these have produced companies with strong technological capabilities—Legend (later Lenovo) was founded as long ago as 1984 as a spin-off of the Institute for Computer Technology at the Chinese Academy of Sciences (under the State Council). Foreign investment is also a crucial source of innovation (Herrigel, Wittke, and Voskamp 2013). In return for transferring important know-how, foreign companies are granted privileged market access.

The different programs launched since the end of the 1980s to stimulate innovation (the National Torch Plan, the 863 Program, and the National Medium- to Long-Term Plan for the Development of Science and Technology 2006–2020, for instance) have produced a range of instruments to promote innovation and high technology (Fu 2015; Di Guo et al. 2016; Werner 2010). On the one hand, research institutes are more exposed to competition than previously. On the other hand, a new governance system was introduced in the field of research and technology to "facilitate more rapid commercialization of new ideas" (X. Liu, Lüthje, and Pawlicki 2007, 226, my translation). The government no longer views intellectual property as inalienable state property, and, consequently, patent rights are transferred to research institutes or universities.

Today, projects conducted by research institutes to promote innovation are no longer exclusively funded by the state budget. Here, as in other countries, more importance is now attached to increased cooperation with industry and business-oriented contract research. The result is competition for "limited funding from government coffers or industrial funds. This, in turn, has led to increased pressure on researchers, forcing them to conduct shorter-term research projects promising greater economic value" (X. Liu, Lüthje, and Pawlicki 2007, 227, my translation).

The focus of R&D expenditure has increasingly shifted to companies, and there has been significant growth in spending by companies as a share of total science and technology expenditure. This trend is particularly pronounced in state-owned and foreign enterprises. Government-funded high-tech experimental zones, which provide local companies with financial and nonmonetary support, form a vital infrastructure for commercially funded R&D activity. Dozens of high-tech zones at the national level, such as Zhongguancun in Beijing or Zhangjiang in Shanghai, as well as national incubators supporting high-tech start-ups, form the backbone of the country's innovation promotion. Many of these zones follow the shining example of Silicon Valley.

In recent years, efforts have been stepped up in this area. These have focused on "indigenous innovation" (*zizhu chuangxin*), for instance, that is, the subsidization of "strategic industries" and large-scale projects in various areas including civil aviation and the military sector, as well as other projects to promote indigenous innovation (Prud'homme 2016). There is increasing evidence that China has now gone beyond imitative innovation and moved into real innovation. Highly innovative companies such as Alibaba, Tencent, Didi Kuaidi, Baidu, Huawei, and Xiaomi have steadily improved their competitive position in the past few years. At the same time, the majority of Chinese technology companies are geared toward "incremental," rather than "radical" innovation. Moreover, many of today's internationally successful Chinese companies were originally established by imitating foreign technology and cultivating collaborative partnerships with transnational corporations.

How Does the State Regulate? The Relationship Between Local Pilot Projects and Centralized Coordination

There are certain regulatory tasks anchored in the party-state that serve to ensure the smooth running of the markets. For now, this appears to substantiate the assumption of a "learning" or "adaptive" state: the state restructures without substantially losing control, it exposes itself and other actors to increased competitive pressure without allowing the anarchic effects of marketization to have the upper hand, and it seeks nonstate partners to (partially) carry out state responsibilities. Yet it still maintains ultimate responsibility for monitoring and regulating this.

Here, the Chinese power elite has, in many ways, borrowed from Western states, as well as from East Asian developmental states. It has learned from the concept of state dirigism, urban planning models from Japan, and forms of human resource management from South Korea and Singapore. Continental European social security systems were used as reference models. The Chinese government is resolutely pursuing a policy of selectively adopting Western or East Asian models (but not complete systems) in individual, narrowly defined areas. These serve as complementary elements in a distinctive ensemble of institutions with the intention of taking the specific features and requirements of Chinese development into account. One of the particularities of the political system is also the increased centralization of decision-making processes in crisis situations (economic crises, social unrest, or natural disaster) with the aim of curtailing the time-consuming process of consensus building.

Further, a distinct policy cycle has developed, which is still relevant in the 2010s. It can be divided into three parts: plan formulation, plan implementation, and plan adjustment (see Heilmann 2010; Heilmann and Melton 2013).

(1) Plan formulation, or the formulation of development programs, was gradually modernized over the course of the reform era. In this process, imperative planning was superseded by indicative planning, which was geared more toward market signals than previously (Naughton 2011b, 318). The focus of the plan also shifted from quantified targets to general guidelines. With the Eleventh Five Year Plan (2006–11), the term "plan" was

replaced with "program." At the same time, despite opposition from market liberal officials, new binding targets were introduced in the fields of environmental and resource protection.

We can distinguish between a number of different methods of coordination here. First, within a framework of binding targets, large-scale projects are implemented, such as in the infrastructure sector (the construction of the world's biggest high-speed rail system, for instance). Imperative planning is limited to a small number of select key sectors, however. Second, there are more flexible methods of coordination, based on contractual agreements between the central and provincial governments, for example, and also between public authorities and companies. These come into play in the field of technology policy, for instance. Third, there are more open forms of indicative planning that attempt to use incentives to stimulate market activities. These include the tax breaks indicated in the (central and regional) development programs and other plans as well as the incentive of privileged access to bank credits and/or foreign markets.

As described by Heilmann, consultation already plays an important role in the process of plan preparation: "In addition to the high-profile year-end planning conferences, there are frequent central, provincial or joint work meetings which officials from both administrative levels attend. Moreover, communication through phone calls and personal visits between provincial-level and central planning bodies to deal with *ad hoc* policy or investment adjustments belong to the daily administrative routines" (Heilmann 2010, 10).

Leading figures in the highest echelons of the party, various departments at the NDRC, and government-affiliated and independent research institutes, as well as influential economists and select business representatives, all participate in this process of consultation. As a result of a scientification of politics, policy advice is playing an increasingly significant role, particularly with regard to consensus building in the planning process (see S. Wang 2009).

However, the coordination of project goals appears to be a harmonious and cooperative interelite process only at first glance. In fact, there is frequent (rarely documented) conflict between different state bodies and business interests about, inter alia, the content of development programs and the allocation of subsidies (Heilmann 2010, 10–12). However—and this signifies a high degree of state autonomy vis-à-vis particularistic, sectoral interest groups—these result in pull effects that should not be underestimated. This especially applies to programs below the level of the national and regional Five Year Plans,[26] including plans for the promotion of technology and innovation, for the creation of technological development zones, and transregional development programs with longer timescales (such as the Western Development Program and the Plan for the Reform and Development of the Pearl River Delta). These latter programs in particular have gained in importance and are seen as slightly more flexible steering instruments by the relevant actors.

(2) Plan implementation or the achievement of plan targets presents a dilemma also experienced in Western countries, that is, the hierarchical mode of governance or how to address the difficulties of putting hierarchical control into practice. In China, the latter is also always a result of negotiations. Plan implementation was traditionally conducted in a highly personalized manner through informal networks. In principle, this modus operandi continues to this day and also applies to the freedom to deviate from the plan at local level. In the 1990s, as part of the reform of cadre evaluation, the system was modernized: the regular and mandatory performance evaluations of all party and state employees are linked to the fulfillment of economic and social indicators derived from the plan targets. Apart from preventing social unrest, which is imperative, the main focus continues to be on other economic aspects: "Cadres are subject to annual evaluations, in which they can score up to 100 points, of which more than 70 are awarded for outcomes that are directly linked to economic growth" (Naughton 2011a, 81).

The provincial and municipal authorities play a particularly important role in the implementation of economic policy initiatives. The lower administrative levels are responsible for creating detailed plans and regulatory mechanisms for specific projects based on what are often very general national plan targets. The relationships between upstream and downstream regional governments are critical interfaces for the exchange of information, financial management, implementation control, and project success. In addition, the regional offshoots of the NDRC in the intrastate hierarchy consequently had their status upgraded, although, when interviewed, employees in these regional development and reform commissions refer to a lack of staff to launch and efficiently monitor projects (Heilmann 2010, 16).

(3) Particularly when it comes to plan adjustment, the distinctive nature of the political system stands out: plans with medium- and long-term

timescales are regularly adjusted in order to take account of experiences acquired in decentralized pilot projects (J. Chen and Wang 2010; Naughton 2009). Because the local pilot projects, known as "experimental points" (*shidian*), result in the creation of new institutions alongside and in interaction with already existing ones, they can also be seen as examples of institutional change through layering.

The central state defines the objectives and boundaries of this "experimentation under hierarchy." Pilot projects that prove to be successful *and* have the potential to be rolled out are adopted nationwide and modify established institutions: "Despite the fact that experimentation procedures have been delegated to local authorities, the central administration in Beijing plays an indispensable role in universalizing local innovations, thereby injecting coordination into the Chinese policy cycle" (ten Brink 2011a, 17).

This mechanism was used in the process of reform in a number of different areas, such as in the creation of stock markets, the transformation of SOEs, and the recent reforms of the social security system. Among the experimental regions, particular importance is attached to the Special Economic Zones. Local pilot projects such as the introduction of land auctions, the registration of foreign companies, or the liberalization of the labor market were initiated in the SEZs and from there were rolled out across the country (J. Chen and Wang 2010, 77). Since the mid-2000s, select inland regions have also become testing grounds for experiments: Chongqing and Chengdu for the reform of the hukou system and the promotion of technology, for instance (McNally 2011, 9).

The rigid, authoritarian policy context and the absence of a formally organized political opposition (which manifests itself more as informal political rivalry) resulted in the emergence of a distinctive policy cycle: in contrast to a practice where problems are analyzed and laws are then drafted, in China, the process is reversed. Policy innovation occurs by way of the (initially) geographically limited implementation of new projects, which, if successful, are then rolled out and ultimately declared to be the norm or even written into national law.[27]

These distinctive policy cycles are based on historical Maoist traditions: "In China, proceeding from experimental programs to national policy is shaped by a policy terminology and methodology that stem from the formative revolution-era experience of the Chinese Communist Party, which legitimated developing policy by 'proceeding from point to surface' and implementing policy in accordance with local circumstances" (Heilmann 2008, 5; see also Heilmann and Perry 2011b).

This is what also distinguishes the Chinese approach from a federal system (see Ehlert, Hennl, and Kaiser 2007). The experimentation "from below" requires the patronage of higher-level public authorities, which are also important for marketing innovative pilot projects: for example, central authorities promote a veritable form of "policy tourism" in the zones declared as successful in order to effectively familiarize political decision makers from other regions with new policies and to stem the bureaucratic forces of inertia.

The Power of the CCP

In this section, I will shed light on the importance of the Chinese Communist Party and its strategies of legitimation. Unlike in other state-led forms of capitalism, the party provides the Chinese power elite with access to another channel of vertical political intervention in the administration and the economy.

The role and influence of the CCP in China is far greater than that of other major parties in liberal democracies. As the central and only legally legitimate representative of the interests of the Chinese people, the CCP is positioned above the state whose administration it permeates and steers. The only similarities that can be identified are with other authoritarian regimes that, for the most part, comprise one party dictating the process of nation building (Zheng 2010). According to the official line, the CCP epitomizes society as a whole and, for the people of China, serves as a guarantor of stability, prosperity, and development (Shambaugh 2009b). During the course of the reform era, the party's ideological self-definition underwent a fundamental transformation. As early as 1993, the class struggle—the key sociopolitical contradiction to be resolved—was replaced by the primacy of improving the quality of life of the Chinese people, against a backdrop of limited resources. This means that the CCP is no longer restricted to being the political representative of the working class and the farmers but has opened up to companies and other social groups. At the helm of the "People's State," the party's aim is to create a system of cross class rule by experts to contribute to national development and modernization (Dingping Guo 2009). Critical Chinese authors classify this as a characteristic of the "state-party system," in which the CCP itself is an integral and overarching component of the state apparatus (H. Wang 2008, 467).

In response to the political and ideological crises of the 1990s, far-reaching reforms were implemented in the following years (see Shambaugh 2009b; Brodsgaard and Zheng 2004; Zheng 2010) with the aim of elevating the party (with currently over eighty-five million members) to the position of pacesetter for the process of modernization. In fact, campaigns led by the party had an extraordinary political reserve capacity even before the advent of Xi Jinping. In the post-Maoist era, a "revolutionary" authoritarianism has been reinvented that is still laced with elements of voluntarism:

> How has the current regime held onto power for three decades now, weathering a series of potentially destabilizing leadership successions . . . while presiding over what may well be the fastest sustained economic and socio-cultural transformation that any nation has ever undergone? A large part of the complex answer to this question lies in the retention—and reinvention—of many elements of China's revolutionary heritage. In moving from Maoist Communism to post-Mao authoritarianism, China has not simply jettisoned its revolutionary past as it "transits" toward a democratic future. Rather, a succession of post-Mao leaders have managed to fashion a surprisingly durable brand of "revolutionary authoritarianism" capable of withstanding challenges, including grievous and growing social and spatial inequalities, which would surely have undone less hardy regimes. (Perry 2007, 7; see also Anderson 2010b; Heilmann and Perry 2011b)

In short, the party leadership transfers older Maoist virtues to present-day China. This is why millions of party cadres attending party schools continue to commit to the guiding principles of "socialism with Chinese characteristics". The party's mass organizations have also retained their significance, particularly the labor unions, the Communist Youth League, and the All China Women's Federation.

While the CCP should be referred to as a *People's Party of capitalist modernization* (as described below), it also performs the function of a conduit to the power elite. The share of party members with a higher level of education has increased dramatically compared to those who are workers and farmers (Heberer 2008, 63). From 2002 to 2007, the party admitted thirteen million new members, and the majority were highly skilled (Zheng 2010, 5).

As is recounted in Chapter 2, in the past thirty years, the relationship between the state and the party has been adjusted in line with the rationalization of rule (on recent efforts to strengthen the party vis-à-vis the state administration under Xi Jinping, see Heilmann and Stepan 2016, also see the subchapter on "The Limitations of Political Regulation" below). A form of intrabureaucratic consensus building and a type of bureaucratic "self-control" have gained ground. Yet the transfer of control and decision-making responsibilities to public bodies, private actors, and NGOs is only permitted to a limited extent.[28]

With the aim of facilitating thorough preparation for the decision-making process and rapid problem solving, leading small groups (LSGs) at different administrative levels are entrusted with the task of coordinating planning and policy measures across departments and policy fields. The hierarchical structure of the party organization mirrors that of the state administration (national, provincial, city, etc.), and this parallel structure ensures that all regional authorities are assigned a suitable counterpart within the party. Personnel and functional overlaps between the two hierarchies are both frequent and intentional. One example at the provincial level illustrates this: the provincial governor is the highest-ranking decision maker in the provincial administration. The party organization is led by the CCP's Provincial Committee secretary. Traditionally, the party secretary has the highest decision-making powers, and the provincial governor is one of his deputies. Consequently, there are efficient channels for the vertical (central government ⮕ local governments) and horizontal (party ⮕ state) conveyance of information and directives. This administrative system, which requires considerable human resources, serves to ensure the implementation of national policies and simultaneously allows flexible adjustments to local circumstances. At the same time, the party maintains control over the staffing of key positions through a comprehensive list of the authorized number of personnel (*bianzhi*) and the nomenklatura system. The party controls the civil security agencies and the armed forces (People's Liberation Army) in the same way.

After 2013, far-reaching reforms of the system have been carried out with the aim of making the work of the administration more efficiency and qualification based. With this in mind, an expanded anticorruption campaign was launched to curtail informal network building and to strengthen the public image of the party as a legitimate representative of the people's interests. While anticorruption campaigns have been a recurring theme in Chinese politics, the ongoing campaign under Xi Jinping is the largest and most comprehensive by any measure. During the four years since the campaign was launched, a total of ninety-one thousand cadres have been punished for violations, thirty-four thousand in 2015 alone (Xinhuanet 2016). Although the campaign has been underway for some time and has gradually increased in intensity, it still turns up remarkable cases of corruption. One example is a vote-buying scheme that was uncovered in the summer of 2016 in the province of Liaoning. As a consequence, 523 of the 619 delegates of the Provincial People's Congress who were linked to the vote-buying scandal have been removed from their posts and put under investigation. In addition, half of the delegates representing the province at the National People's Congress (NPC) (forty-five individuals) have been stripped of their status. Further, five senior provincial officials, including Li Feng, party secretary and vice chairman of the Standing Committee of the Provincial People's Congress, have been arrested. *Caixin*, a prominent Chinese economics magazine, reported that "in the wake of the housecleaning, all provincial legislative operations have ground to a halt. The NPC Standing Committee has assigned a special committee to sort out the mess" (S. Hu 2016).

The party's control over the economy is maintained by encouraging firms to create company party committees where the members of the firm's management boards have a prominent presence. Through the organization departments of the party at national, provincial, city, and county levels, the CCP also exercises the right of appointment for management positions within state-owned enterprises. The organization departments appoint, evaluate, promote, dismiss, or transfer administrative staff across the entire party and government and within SOEs. In 2004, for instance, they reshuffled the boards of the three largest telecommunications companies and did the same in the three largest oil companies in 2010.

Within the CCP, there is a clear dominance of the public-private growth alliances that are distributed throughout the country. However, the party is by no means a monolithic bloc. In both discourse and institutions, the party reflects social power relations—because it is the sole relevant and, at the same time, the largest decision-making platform in the country. Looking at a highly simplified picture of the 2000s, we can identify two key groups that struggled for dominance in a process of reciprocal checks and balances (see C. Li 2009; Fewsmith 2008). A "populist" coalition allied with Hu Jintao and Wen Jiabao united individuals who had achieved significant social advancement, who frequently occupied high-level positions in the poorer provinces, and/or who had pursued careers in the Communist Youth League.

A second, "elitist" group comprised the descendants of former party leaders (princelings), what is also known as the Shanghai Group allied with the former president Jiang Zemin, and professionals who gained their training and qualifications abroad. Their power is concentrated in the wealthier coastal regions, and they dominated the higher echelons of the party in the 1990s, in particular. While there are no fundamental differences between these two camps in terms of their basic political strategies and philosophies, conflict frequently arises when it comes to tactical questions of realpolitik. By the end of the 2000s, a system of checks and balances had evolved between the two groups that was fraught with tension (de Haan 2010, 91). The populist faction allied with Hu Jintao and Wen Jiabao accentuated the need for state-controlled social equity, while the elitist group called for a natural dissemination of the profits of modernization to the less developed hinterland regions ("trickle-down effect").

The administration under Xi Jingping, while putting more emphasis on recentralizing power by strengthening the party, has largely continued the previous government's attempt to even out regional development gaps (Lam 2015). In order to facilitate an orderly urbanization process and ensure a more equitable pattern of development, a series of programs were introduced. One of the most prominent, alongside social policy reforms (see Ngok and Chan 2016), is probably the planned increase in the integration of the two cities of Beijing and Tianjin with the province of Hebei (Jingjinji) to create an economic rival to the Pearl River and Yangtze River delta megaregions.

Ideological Acrobatics: Concepts of Development
and Leadership Legitimacy

The present work is based on the assumption that China has undergone a distinctive process of capitalist-driven modernization. This also applies to the tendencies within the party, as is highlighted by the following, somewhat older, example: "It is not necessarily true that the Party will influence decisions that contravene the efforts of governance reform; as pointed out by John Thornton (who among many hats, is board member of one of China's largest telecom firms, China Netcom), 'The chairman of Netcom likes to say that he does not see a contradiction between Party influence and the protection of (non-party) minority shareholders because the goals of the two are the same—namely, Netcom's success as a business'" (Pearson 2011, 30).

Yet how can this situation be reconciled with the power elite's interpretation of socialist ideology? The answer is by equating "socialism" first and foremost with economic development and national modernization. For this purpose, Maoist avant-garde thinking and a strong belief in progress is combined with principles of meritocracy. Consequently, a form of populist pragmatism has emerged in circumstances where the fourth and fifth generations of CCP leaders do not possess legitimacy comparable with earlier generations in terms of anti-imperialism and antifeudalism (Lam 2006 and 2015). At the same time, Sino-Marxism unites a belief in the advantages of state-coordinated economic organization with the creativity of the entrepreneur. Chen Yuan—the son of Chen Yun, one of the first-generation leaders of the CCP, and, himself, a member of the Central Committee of the CCP and former chairman of the China Development Bank—captured the pragmatic essence of the state-party in a nutshell: "We are the Communist Party and we will decide what communism means" (quoted in McGregor 2010, 34).

Since the start of reform and opening up, the CCP's legitimacy to rule has largely depended on a comprehensive improvement in standards of living. However, this factor alone is not enough to achieve normative integration (Holbig and Gilley 2010, also see Zhao 2017). The CCP's monopoly position has enabled it to perform ideological acrobatics in the last few decades. A syncretistic combination of concepts of a strong state and Confucian and (cultural) nationalist ideas emerged, which turned "Sinosized" Marxism into a distinctive non-Western program of capitalist modernization.

(1) On the one hand, Sino-Marxism as a philosophy of state interventionism and of the uncompromising development of productive forces was effectively given center stage. A short look back over the history of the reform process illustrates this: in the course of introducing more elements of a market economy, in the early 1980s, the power elite allied with Deng Xiaoping initially attempted to introduce new social conditions based on the concept of "socialism with Chinese characteristics." This would have been vehemently attacked just a few years previously as a challenge to Mao's concept of socialism. The vague content of the concept created more leeway for the further development of the reform agenda. Deng's motto, reminiscent of one of Mao's maxims, to "make practice the sole criterion of truth," was meant to nip unnecessary discussions in the bud, because, in reality, the reform policy ultimately proved successful (see Cho 2005, 210–18).

With the "socialist market economy" formula, from 1992, the de facto coexistence of market and state control was conceptually merged. The market economy was reinterpreted as a system-neutral means of control that is not synonymous with capitalism. As an accompanying instrument for unleashing productive economic forces, the market mechanism (within narrow confines) was to support the state's development planning. This was supposed to foster and accelerate the achievement of the appropriate material requirements for the transition to socialism. The transformation of state-owned enterprises in the 1990s meant that "mixed ownership" concepts were presented as an extension of public ownership. Here, partly in reference to traditional cultural beliefs, a dichotomous separation of "private" and "public" was contested. At the same time, the influential proposition that a further decline in state capacity could curb the country's development potential consolidated the continuing significance of a state-centered development policy (Herrmann-Pillath 2001, 184). It also became popular to take a pragmatic approach to dealing with selected Marxist concepts that were taken out of context to suit the Chinese situation. In reference to Marx and Mao, Communist Party intellectuals called for the country to adapt to new historical circumstances, and the role of entrepreneurs was thus legitimized: "They noted that in the age of traditional manufacturing, when Marx wrote . . . , workers were indeed at the forefront of productivity. However, in the information technology (IT) epoch, businessmen and professionals had displaced relatively less educated workers, not to mention farmers, as society's vanguard" (Lam 2006, 66).

According to the concept of the "Three Represents" introduced in the year 2000 by Jiang Zemin, the CCP represented "advanced productive forces," "advanced culture," and the "fundamental interests of the majority." Jiang himself argued:

> Since the start of the reforms, China's social class structure has changed. For example, there are entrepreneurs and technical personnel working for companies in the nonstate sector; administrative employees and technical staff; employees in joint venture firms; the self-employed; private companies. They are all working to build socialism with Chinese characteristics. The grand . . . task of building socialism with Chinese characteristics requires outstanding elements from all areas that are loyal to the motherland and to socialism. (quoted in Hartig 2008, 123, my translation)

In the search for a renewed "mandate of heaven," under Hu Jintao and Wen Jiabao after 2002, against a backdrop of social polarization, further substantive changes in emphasis were observed. With the "scientific development concept" and, in particular, the objective of a "harmonious socialist society," aspects of social justice and—more than previously—also traditional elements of Confucianism increasingly became the focus of discussion (see Holbig 2005, 2009). The Eleventh Five Year Plan (2006–11) then also promised that the state would intervene to eradicate social and regional disparities, in other words, to bring about a far-reaching improvement in the population's standard of living.

(2) A second concept that has gained ground since the Hu/Wen government, and continued with the Xi administration, draws on authoritarian traditions of Confucianism and harmonious thinking resembling ideas of social partnership. Elements of Confucianism were evident in the campaign for the creation of a harmonious society, for instance. Wen Jiabao, for example, adorned his speeches with quotes from various works of Chinese philosophers and teachers (from Confucius to Sima Qian).[29] A common feature of Confucian and post-Maoist traditions is that they both view China's nonstate elites as more of an appendage to the state than independent groups.

The return to Confucian values (not only in the sense of an ideological campaign ordered by decree but manifestly underpinned by a renewed recognition of Confucianism in certain segments of the population) serves, first, to fill the moral vacuum created by modernization by referring to the ethics of social responsibility and the cultivation of interpersonal relationships.[30] Second, focusing on these values once more serves to legitimate the regime by emphasizing norms such as forbearance, subsumption, and subordination, as well as hierarchical thinking. The government's reference to "rule by virtue," which should be combined with "rule by law," is also evidence of reverting to old Chinese traditions of authoritarian rule (N. Lin 2011).

(3) Another strand of discourse, intended to provide normative orientation and engender identity, is "new nationalism" (Schubert 2001b; Zhao 2004), which follows older concepts of patriotism. The aim of drawing on this source of political legitimacy in a post-Maoist era is for China—after a long phase of weakness and oppression—to take up its rightful place among the leading nations once again. The advent of nationalism accompanied China's policy of opening up—the nationalist discourse supported this

development with the practical intention of gaining maximum benefit from the country's integration into the global economy.

There are various versions of this new nationalism. "Techno-nationalism" (Amelung 2009) is based on the conviction that scientific and technological successes, such as the space program, for instance, would have the direct result of improving China's global position. "Cultural nationalism," however, refers to China's "formidable" history and asserts the nation's continuous progress. In the media, this was implemented by reminiscing about imperial China or presenting today's aspiring People's Republic (Holbig and Gilley 2010, 20–23; Schmidt-Glintzer 2008, 253).[31] Although the People's Liberation Army is one of the main pillars of cultural nationalism (Saich 2004, 154), intellectual factions also contribute to its effectiveness.

Soon after coming into office, the administration under Xi Jinping refreshed the "new nationalism" by cultivating the concept of the "Chinese Dream" (Lam 2015). The concept takes up the older promise of building a "moderately prosperous society" by 2020. However, it goes beyond earlier concepts and touches on domestic and international factors. The official *China Daily* published the following outline:

> The Chinese Dream integrates national and personal aspirations, with the twin goals of reclaiming national pride and achieving personal well-being. It requires sustained economic growth, expanded equality and an infusion of cultural values to balance materialism. Dreams are powerful. In advancing the Chinese Dream the government is uniting people around a shared mission and driving change, especially people in lower-tier cities and rural areas, as they experience increased affluence and opportunity. Externally, the Chinese Dream can improve the image of China as a fast-growing nation striving to improve the welfare of its people and secure its place as a respected leader of the international community. (*China Daily* 2014)

For a long time now, the new versions of nationalism have also been reflected in different ideological currents. In the debate about market reforms, roughly three currents took the limelight: neoconservative, liberal, and new left. All three factions share an essentially affirmative position on

China's system.[32] The distinction between the new left and the liberals con-
ceals the fact that the academic protagonists in the former faction typically
do not turn toward civil society actors (as the term "left" would suggest
because of its traditional association with the working class, the labor union
movement, or other social movements), but rather represent different positions within the power elite, all of which are geared toward the rise of the
nation. Cho eloquently summarized this (still largely prevailing) intellectual
terrain some years ago:

> In the intellectual discourse of the reform era, there was a ten-
> dency to conform with the official party line, although there is evi-
> dence that the political and ideological framework was transcended
> at the margins of the spectrum of opinions. In the center of this
> spectrum were the etatist and culturally traditionalist conservatives
> whose discourse did not diverge from the official state ideology. The
> strands of discourse that were critical of the government represent
> differing radicalized concepts of the official ideology. They are thus
> either much more nationalist or have a much stronger faith in the
> market. (Cho 2005, 274, my translation; see also Fewsmith 2008,
> 83–162; Schubert 2001b, 67–74)

The different factions are supported by various groups of economic
actors in the ruling power bloc:

> The New Liberals enjoyed greater resonance in the 1990s, when
> the government launched the policy of completely embracing for-
> eign capital. After ten years of dependent growth, the danger of eco-
> nomic recolonization has become real and the New Left's discourse
> of national rebirth appeals to the bureaucracy. Neither the bureau-
> cratic capitalists nor the private capitalists are homogenous. Because
> of their specific position in the economy there is always a faction
> seeing closer partnership with foreign capital as a choice, or, in con-
> tradistinction, another faction want more state intervention. The
> former is therefore more receptive to the New Liberals' perspective,
> while the latter more inclined to the New Left. (Au 2008)

It is of little importance whether we refer to state interventionism in the
interests of an uncompromising development of productive forces, proclamations of Sino-Marxism (supplemented with fragments of Confucianism)

that strives to achieve state-administered social equity, the attempt to create an "imagined community" through nationalist discourse, or certain measures (not outlined in detail here) that accommodate, to a limited extent, calls for democratic participation.[33] The state-centric guiding principles strive, without exception, toward maintaining party rule—in a way that (in an authoritarian manner) also takes into account the realities of increasing social pluralism (for an update on this, see Zhao 2017).

The Limitations of Political Regulation

So did it prove possible for the party-state, through its regulatory capacity, its financial resources, and increased bureaucratic and organizational abilities—enhanced by a range of effective strategies of legitimation—to tackle the challenges of capitalist modernization? For the period between 1995 and 2016, there are indications that it did: for instance, the recentralization of fiscal resources in the mid-1990s laid the foundations for a socially acceptable mode of coping with the wave of privatization where millions of workers were awarded (admittedly low) state compensation payments. The trend toward disintegration that emerged during the course of the Asian crisis from 1997—and again in the course of the global crises in 2008–9—was addressed by the central state using macroeconomic measures (reminiscent of Keynesian crisis and stimulus programs) and improved access to bank credit. The expansive debt-financed public spending in the fields of residential construction, infrastructure development, and social security reform between 1998 and the early 2010s—combined with international factors, particularly increasing foreign capital inflows—ensured that economic growth and social stability were maintained. Further, the reform of governmental institutions resulted in a more efficient regulation of the market.

However, overall, the limitations of political regulation that were previously latently perceptible have become more visible in recent years (ten Brink 2013). This is connected with the specific characteristics of the political system that were outlined earlier and the resulting competition between the political authorities below the central government level (and within the government itself). The large number of political decision makers in China as well as the uneven levels of development and the varying production regimes across the country frequently translate into competing political interests that undermine the coherence of the central government's development program—in all probability, this is also still a challenge for the government under Xi Jinping, despite its recentralization efforts.

Consequently, political institutions in China do not always act in line with the plan, which is regularly counteracted, and rules are contravened or turned on their head. Despite the professionalization of bureaucratic processes, individuals in senior posts have enormous authority to circumvent rules or to interpret them in a specific way. The transfer of responsibilities from the central to the provincial and lower levels, already described in Chapter 2, and the associated emergence of multiple coalitions of interests, frequently result in regulatory anarchy. Where national and local development interests diverge, state institutions and/or individual administrative cadres sometimes act for the benefit of particularistic interests. This does not necessarily go hand in hand with corrupt behavior. It is more likely that the conduct referred to here simply fulfills local development objectives (and contributes to a positive performance assessment for the authorities and cadres concerned) but runs counter to national policy strategies. Until recently, a classic example was the weak enforcement of environmental protection standards in industrial projects that were deemed important for the local economy and employment. Motivated by personal career objectives and local patriotism, innumerable political decision makers prioritized strengthening local economic growth over meeting the increasingly stringent standards of national climate policy. The protectionist isolation of local procurement markets for the benefit of local manufacturing companies is also common practice although nondiscriminatory trading in goods in the national market is officially stipulated.

In numerous fields, local growth alliances undermine the national policy designed to produce coherence and efficiency. Here, "plan anarchy" or plan regionalism was replaced by an anarchic market regionalism (for earlier evidence, see Heberer 2008, 107–12). Thus, subnational deviations from the centrally prescribed directives can be interpreted as a consequence of divergent local competition and development strategies. One example of this is the attempt by provinces to pursue an independent foreign trade policy because the central government's policy fails to ensure tight control of exports. The provinces are also keen to minimize the transfer of resources to the central government. Moreover, what is happening between the provinces and the central government in terms of market regionalism is also taking place within the provinces in the form of cities' and counties' tendency toward greater autonomy. In actual fact, local units frequently act as a form of holding company and also exhibit internal tendencies toward greater independence.

The vast industrial region in the Yangtze River delta with its ninety-five million inhabitants illustrates the effects of this competition-driven regulatory anarchy. The city of Shanghai and the two neighboring provinces of Zhejiang and Jiangsu are not really incorporated into regional cooperative networks. Because of a lack of transregional coordination, already over the course of the 2000s, there was a buildup of excess capacity in numerous branches of industry and a duplication of public infrastructure for business development. Early on, this resulted in inefficient cutthroat competition between companies, on the one hand, and between industrial parks, on the other (Yu 2010). In particular, the competitive relationships between the larger cities and the districts and counties under their authority were and remain the subject of political interventions that were fraught with conflict:

> The conflict between prefecture-level city and county (county-level city) became sharper. In order to deal with regional internal and external cut-throat competition, accelerating the growth of prefecture-level cities . . . became more urgent. In 2000, the goal of making the central cities "stronger" and "bigger" was put forward in both Jiangsu Province and Zhejiang Province. Therefore, since 2000, a large-scale adjustment has begun in the Yangtze River Delta. Prefecture-level cities have annexed counties or county-level cities and transformed the latter into the urban districts of the former. (Zhang and Wu 2006, 9)

At the higher levels, attempts were made to resolve the problem of the administrative divisions by way of administrative annexation. The example of the municipal government of Hangzhou illustrates this: the county-level city of Xiaoshan (a subdivision of the city of Hangzhou) had its own bureaucratic apparatus and acted as an independent region in competition with Hangzhou. Yet even after administrative annexation, these competitive relations continue to exist, and, for example, industrial parks continue to be built without consultation with other administrative divisions in order to attract capital to the location concerned.

Overall, neither the central government nor the subnational governments are able to practice refined micromanagement against a backdrop of heterogeneity of the country's political economy. For instance, the long-term development program for the Pearl River delta (NDRC 2008) specifies the approximate direction of the region's development, but potential plan implementers, local governments, and companies compete for the associated state funding in a manner that fosters economic instability and corruption.

Even the sectoral regulatory authorities, which were mostly established in the 2000s, exhibit weaknesses: some are unable to retain their position vis-à-vis the NDRC and therefore fail to have an impact. On the other hand, some sectors of the economy have such a large number of regulators they are either unable to have any effect, or each side paralyzes the other: "The telecom sector provides the most egregious example, with at least ten other government bodies . . . retaining a say over telecom decisions" (Pearson 2011, 31). A similar development can be identified in the financial system: "The trouble is that in China, the different regulators have over the past few years created so-called 'independent kingdoms'; effective coordination across these fiefdoms has been difficult" (Walter and Howie 2011, 198; see Naughton 2017 on recent attempts at reregulating the financial sector).

Even the SASAC has, in reality, not proven to be an omnipotent steering body: many of the companies overseen by the SASAC are massive conglomerates controlling huge resources and thus representing independent poles of power. Although, together with the organization department of the Central Committee of the CCP, the SASAC appoints the key members of staff in the companies under their control, they are unable to comprehensively influence their business orientation. This situation also calls the sometimes mystifying assumption of overarching party control into question. The CCP's control over the management staff of SOEs is frequently not enough to prevent companies from unilaterally pursing their particularistic business interests. Even the wide reach of company party organs has made only a limited contribution to coherent regulation of the national economy.[34]

The problem of micromanagement also affects the central government ministries: certain ministries have quite considerable leeway to make decisions, and there is scope for different interpretations of new regulations. The NDRC, for example, prioritizes technological upgrading (NDRC 2011) over sociopolitical elements of modernization such as those propagated by the Ministry of Human Resources and Social Security (MOHRSS). In practice, the NDRC concepts predominated into the second decade of this century. The country's fiscal policy is evidence of this: for a long time, corporate taxation made only a limited contribution to the cost of social security. Tax incentives, investment grants, and low-cost loans remained important instruments for supporting the economy.[35] To promote research and high technology, the authorities, particularly at the local level, attempted to attract investors with substantial incentives to establish businesses, which included comprehensive exemptions from taxes and duties, a special infrastructure, and the provision of services (such as personnel recruitment) at the state's expense.

The most recent economic policy realignment, what are known as "supply-side structural reforms" (*gongjice jiegouxing gaige*), inter alia to reduce overinvestment, also continue this trend: the supply-side reforms, which were first enshrined in Chinese regulations from spring 2016, further reduced corporate tax burdens. The Work Plan for Lowering the Cost of Enterprises in the Real Economy,[36] published by the State Council in early August 2016, called for the evaluation and elimination of taxes and fees in order to reduce corporate costs across a wide range of fields including financial services, energy supply, and logistics (State Council 2016). Following the central government's initiative and instructions, subnational governments were quick to publish their own work plans outlining the benefits to be made available to local companies. Naughton (2016) elaborates on the scope and scale of such documents and points out that within a month of the State Council initiative being released, twenty provincial governments had launched corresponding plans: "The leader is almost certainly Guangdong. . . . It has set a target of reducing firm costs by 400 billion RMB by the end of 2016: over 5 percent of provincial GDP, a substantial number. More than half of this would come from reduced taxes; further reductions would be achieved through partial elimination of administrative fees and by decreasing contributions to various social security and welfare funds" (Naughton 2016, 5–6).

Notably, this trend was counteracted to a certain extent, as a look at the payment of dividends in the state-owned sector shows. Here, for a long time, the retention of profits improved the capital situation and enabled extensive investment in capacity increases, technological development, and international expansion. In order to avoid wastage and misallocation by companies, the Chinese government opted for a gradual reintroduction of a system of dividend distribution. The intention was to use these resources to plug the funding gap in China's social security systems. From 2007, companies in particularly profitable industries, such as petrochemicals and tobacco, had to pay 10 percent—increasing to 15 percent from 2011—of their net profit to the Ministry of Finance. For those in competition-driven sectors, such as steel, a reduced rate of 5 percent applied—increasing to 19 percent from 2011. Companies operating in the research and military sectors, however, remained exempt from the dividend payment. SOEs that had issued shares on the Chinese stock exchanges in 2006 or later were forced to pay 10 percent of their revenue, with retroactive effect. In November 2012, the Central Committee of the CCP approved a 30 percent hike in the dividend payment by 2020 (CPC Central Committee 2013). As a result of these measures, the provinces and downstream administrative bodies also successively increased their payment demands.

As has already been mentioned, centralization measures and steering initiatives implemented by the party and the government sometimes have only limited impact. The vertical control structures branching out from the capital to the local bureaucracies do not automatically guarantee the central government direct powers of intervention. These vertical structures are overgrown with horizontal branch structures at the relevant administrative levels. Even the regular rotation of administrative cadres has not been able to prevent the emergence of (sometimes corrupt) local interest coalitions (Tang et al. 2015).

Since the government under President Xi Jinping and Premier Li Keqiang assumed office, we have observed aggressive measures to break up these coalitions. Through closer monitoring and tighter sanctioning of local economic policy, the central government is attempting to counter initiatives that run contrary to national development strategies. In sectors with significant overcapacity, substantially more vigorous measures are being taken to close smaller, outdated, and polluting industrial plants than was the case under the previous government. A more resolute approach can also be observed in the field of environmental protection. The rigorous implementation of the polluter pays principle, more stringent sanctions for violating regulations, and a higher risk of detection owing to an increase in the number of on-site inspections have all meant that local governments are less willing to tolerate environmental offences—even if this threatens the survival of the companies affected and risks job losses.

At the same time, by creating and/or strengthening parallel advisory and decision-making party committees—the leading small groups (LSGs)—the CCP has attempted to improve its control and regulatory capacity. Shortly after the new government came into office, existing LSGs were already given more responsibility, and senior cadres were appointed to staff these groups. The LSG for Financial and Economic Affairs, already in existence since the early 1980s, was strengthened and became a key policy organ under the direct leadership of President Xi. The same applies to the LSG for the Comprehensive Deepening of Reform and the recently established LSG for Network Security and Information Technology. While, in the past, policy initiatives were developed by the ministries, discussed by the State Council, and adopted by the Standing Committee of the Politburo of the CCP, it is now increasingly the case that policy plans are initiated by the LSGs, further developed by that same group, and then presented directly to the Standing Committee for a decision (and then returned to the state committees for implementation). Because the central LSGs are staffed by members of the Standing Committee of the party or even report directly to the general secretary, the formal policy process (with the participation of state ministries) is shortened and thus accelerated. This did not result in government bodies losing all their authority. In fact, in the majority of areas, the same individuals are involved in drafting policy plans—albeit in different capacities. However, this development is notable because it proves the determination of the party leadership to secure direct and unrestricted control over the policy process.

Whether the recent centralization efforts under Xi will significantly increase regulatory capacity and ultimately also economic stability in the long term, however, is a question to be addressed by future studies. One is inclined to approach this situation with a certain amount of skepticism because these measures are being implemented against the dynamically unstable backdrop of China's competition-driven process of modernization. The competition between local state administrations, for instance, continues to have undesirable side effects: the problems of overinvestment as well as the duplication of infrastructure and other investment projects has increased in recent years, for example. Admittedly, the economic stimulus measures implemented in the early 2010s have triggered a veritable wave of investment. However, numerous investment projects and development programs have neglected to conduct careful demand analysis and also, again, failed to comply with the required approval procedures. A drop in the development of demand leading it to revert to its "natural" growth path (which in China still tends to be on more of an upward trajectory than in other major economies) and procedural flaws due to a rushed approach to planning and implementation have, since 2013, increasingly revealed the less positive sides of development. These excesses are reflected in the huge shopping malls with everything except customers and in the factories working substantially below maximum capacity and pushing their overproduction onto the market at cutthroat prices.

To refer to one final example, the limitations of regulation are also evident in the growing dilemma of state finances: public debt is one of the most sensitive policy areas in China. When disclosing relevant information, the government is always extremely cautious and strategic in order to prevent any pessimistic assessments and doubts as to its conduct. However, the ostentatiously optimistic presentation of information has aroused doubts regarding the quality of published data. Independent investigations are significantly less confident than the Chinese government as far as the country's long-term debt sustainability is concerned. However, the validity of analyses like this is undermined because these are based only on more or less well-founded estimates because of limited access to primary data (Shiyu Li and Lin 2011).

According to official government data, China's sovereign debt doubled between 2010 and 2015 (NBS 2015b). The total debt stock relative to GDP rose during this period from 35.1 percent to 43.9 percent. This still places the country's annual budget deficits (2.3 percent in 2015) substantially below the average of most Western industrial countries. Further, China's public debt differs from that of many Western states and particularly other countries of the Global South in that by far the majority of liabilities are held by domestic creditors. This makes China less exposed to international creditors and organizations. Another advantage of this is that exchange rate effects have only a marginal impact on the debt and its sustainability. Here, to a certain extent, China follows the Japanese example: for some years now, Japan (with its far higher debt level) has profited from the predominance of domestic creditors.

However, it is not entirely clear whether the central government itself has a complete overview of all, particularly indirect, public liabilities. It was not until 2010 that any kind of serious analysis of the indebtedness of local governments and of the financial institutions under their control was first conducted. Because, as a result of administrative regulations, the provinces and their subordinate administrative units have been blocked from direct borrowing from banks and are also forbidden from issuing securities, they established what are known as local government financing vehicles (LGFVs). Because they have the legal status of a company, these LGFVs are not subject to the same stringent financing provisions and controls as their state owners. Moreover, their favored position as state-owned enterprises, which, through the explicit guarantees of state shareholders, means they have a relatively low risk of nonpayment, has resulted in privileged access to capital. The identity and number of these companies, as well as their outstanding liabilities, have been recorded centrally only since Xi Jinping's government took office.

As outlined in Chapter 2, in 1994, as a consequence of far-reaching tax reforms, a major process of recentralization of state revenues was initiated. At the same time, however, a process of decentralization of expenditures ran parallel. In 2010, a total of 82.2 percent of all government spending was incurred by subnational governments, which resulted in increasing budget deficits at local level. Whether this situation, facilitated by an intrastate transfer system (Duan and Zhan 2011, 59; NBS 2015b), is reversible appears doubtful. One of the primary causes of this concentration of financial obligations at the lower government levels is the delegation of costly social expenditure (particularly for welfare, education, and job creation) to precisely these authorities. Although this may contradict the proclamations about strengthening domestic consumption and creating social equity, this arrangement enables the central government to save money and deflect social discontent to the regional authorities.[37]

The increase in the financial obligations of local governments benefited the "creative entrepreneurial" activities of the cities and counties that have already been mentioned at various junctures in the present work. Because the government authorities below the provincial level were no longer able to meet financial needs through "regular" revenues from taxes, fees, and transfers from the higher authorities, they were increasingly forced to generate additional revenue from company profits and land sales. The growing importance of the local government's commercial interests tied up the staffing and financial resources that were needed to fulfill their original administrative duties.

In this context, the disparity between central government spending and that of the local authorities rose from a ratio of 1:3 in 2007 to a ratio of 1:5.7 in 2014 (Figure 3).

Figure 3 indicates a substantial rise in (debt-financed) expenditures resulting from the global economic downturn and the subsequent economic stimulus packages. Because the central state has failed to effect a marked reduction in this increase (and the persistently high extrabudgetary

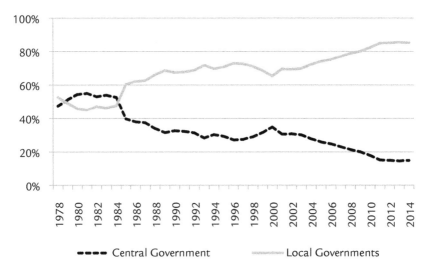

Figure 3. Distribution of budgetary expenditures by central and local
governments. *Source*: NBS 2015b, table 7-1.

posts of the subnational governments), a crisis of the fiscal system has
become more likely. In fact, we cannot assume that it will be possible to
reverse this trend within the space of a few years—particularly in view of
the unfavorable demographic development. The redistribution of tax revenues in favor of the central government has not been accompanied by a
corresponding redistribution of spending responsibilities.

Admittedly, to compensate for financial deficits and to be able to fulfill
the responsibilities transferred to them, as mentioned, local governments
have developed a number of entrepreneurial initiatives. For example, city
administrations have attempted to generate revenue from corporate profits
by founding or buying shares in companies. At the same time, they have
managed to cover a large proportion of their costs by selling land use rights
(and other levies linked to the construction and sale of real estate). As the
sole owners and monopolists in the allocation of land, they are in an ideal
position (Tian 2014; Lockett 2016). According to unofficial estimates, city
governments obtain up to 35 percent of their income from transactions like
this.

However, the additional local revenue acquired through the sale of land
use rights is fraught with risk. First, the supply of suitable land is limited

and, to a great extent, already depleted. Second, because of the burden on disposable income due to higher mortgage debt, price buoyancy on the real estate market has a negative impact on private consumption. This contradicts national "rebalancing" schemes. Price increases may enable municipal governments to plug budget deficits. At the same time, they can undermine a central pillar of the country's current economic growth. Falling prices would lead to the loss of major revenue items and cause substantial budget deficits. At the same time, the market values of a lot of real estate would fall below the mortgage value. For property owners and debtors, this development has a doubly disastrous impact. On the one hand, they would be forced to service loans, which, in part, no longer have any value, or they would have to anticipate losses on the sale of their real estate. On the other hand, as mortgage issuers, the banks would have to demand an increase in the loan collateral deposited by borrowers. This really would be fatal because the majority of households will already have borrowed heavily to purchase their property and it is unlikely that they would be able to deposit more financial assets. In this case, consumption could suffer a severe blow, which would have a direct impact on the country's overall economic growth.

Interim Conclusion

In this chapter, I have referred to a range of evidence for the proposition that large parts of the political system are subject to the driving forces of capitalism. Here, the holistic strategy established in my research framework proved useful, according to which the interdependencies and tensions between economic dynamics and the transformation of the party-state should be taken into account.

China's restructured state and party institutions now recognize the market mechanism as a cornerstone of social order. They create and regulate the markets in which they themselves conduct business—also within the public administration. The pressure to adjust, stemming from extremely dynamic regional development, exposes participating (market) actors to cutthroat competition. Pursuing a neodirigiste, Schumpeterian strategy, supplemented by elements of indicative planning, the Chinese government is striving to catch up with the most developed economies in the world. This is evidenced by looking at the fields of economic policy and technology promotion.

The aim is for the state to regulate market activity, a regulation for competition. Market-limiting measures do not present a challenge to the system but are mostly aimed at party-state regulation and control of market expansion. The ruthlessness seen here has "certain affinities with the 'business as warfare' theme that permeates recent writing on market competition by today's captains of global capitalism" (Heilmann and Perry 2011a, 13).

Particularly with regard to economic policy, the state leadership appears to have excellent mastery of methods of governance. In fact—admittedly from an instrumentally rational perspective—China's political system was effectively reorganized to facilitate institutional learning and through processes of institutional layering and conversion. At the same time, distinct forms of governance have been adapted, as perfectly exemplified by the central coordination of local pilot projects. In the policy cycles of Chinese state-permeated capitalism, where binding requirements, both contractual and informal agreements, processes of learning, and indicative steering methods converge, the heterarchic, networked negotiations and market intermediation coexist alongside hierarchical directives. This also substantiates my research proposition that, in China, we should not assume a strict separation but more of a differentiation between state and market activity.

Some Western observers consider the party-state to be at an advantage in terms of its implementation capacity solely on the basis that it is able to pursue longer-term and more sustainable political strategies than liberal democracies, which are subject to the temporal constraints of electoral periods (see Meerwaldt 2010). The CCP also has a largely intact monopoly on power, and campaigns led by the party have an extraordinary political reserve capacity. Inherent in the CCP's leadership legitimacy (before and under Xi Jinping) is syncretism, that is, the linking of various different traditions of thought, even ostensibly anti-capitalist ones, to form a pragmatic Sino-Marxist canon, which should be more accurately described as a non-Western program of capitalist-driven modernization. Here, philosophies of state interventionism and the development of productive forces combine with harmonious thinking (partially derived from Confucianism and resembling social partnership) and nationalist discourse.

However, the current dominance of the party and the guiding principles of the regime do not by any means make it possible to eradicate all the contradictions of China's modernization through conflict regulation based on a combination of coercion and negotiation. Although the central state and the CCP have, in many respects, managed to successfully contain the centrifugal forces of market expansion, political fragmentation, and regionalization, this has not resulted in a union that is free of conflict. Against a backdrop of economic instability, regional development disparities, and competing coalitions of interests, China's multilevel system, which, by international standards, possesses considerable steering capacity, comes up against the limits of regulation.

Of the pitfalls described in this chapter, a number of points stand out: it is evident that the local authorities do not follow directives blindly and unquestioningly. Even at the central level, government actors do not determine and carry out public functions autonomously. This tends to occur in a consensus-oriented informal association of various different groups of actors, driven by the imperatives of capital accumulation. This invariably leads to problems. The horizontal and vertical consensus- and decision-making structures give rise to political deadlocks, implementation gaps, and also adjustment difficulties and miscalculations in the financial sector, for example. Because it seems virtually impossible to disentangle China's multilevel system, this constitutes a distinctive form of the joint-decision trap (Scharpf 1985). However, in line with the research framework of the present work, the latter is not primarily attributed to political organizational weaknesses but is linked to the effects of capitalist catch-up development.

Local economic policy then is not structured according to a cooperative, coherent approach geared toward the national economy but is driven more by particularistic business interests. This has fueled competition between locations to attract business and investment but ultimately led to overinvestment, and an increase in public debt. Linked to this, spending was decentralized, which further exacerbated the debt problem. Figuratively speaking, China's political economy is less of a supertanker navigated by an omnipotent captain and more of a group of different-sized ships, each motivated by their own individual interests, traveling at full speed in different directions with no concern for the impact on the fleet as a whole. The heterogeneity and complexity inherent in this multilevel framework calls the successful continuation of modernization into question. There is reason to expect that, should instability increase, there would be a rise in intra-elite conflict and, as a consequence, more political stalemates.

The Limits of Chinese-Style Subordination?
Developments in Labor Relations

In the first two sections of this chapter, the workers were treated more as passive objects of corporate and state policies than active subjects. In practice, however, the new working class actively influences the social fabric of the PRC. Based on my assumption of the significance of the social balance of power and class conflict in capitalist-driven processes of modernization, in the next few sections, I will proceed as follows. First, I will describe the idea that wage earners constitute the backbone of economic development. Here, I will illustrate the importance for "efficient" economic development of a segmentation and segregation of the working class and of a decentralization of labor regulation to the company level. Second, in my analysis of the features of the labor system, I will outline in detail how the central government has introduced quasicorporatist consultation mechanisms and is promoting the juridification of industrial relations. However, these measures, which aim to resolve conflict, do not take full effect because the workers have inadequate institutional representation in the system of industrial relations.

This is evident from the tens of thousands of social protests both within and outside companies since the 2000s, which are viewed by the government as "unofficial mass events" (these include demonstrations, violent protest actions, and workplace conflict; see CLB 2009 and 2016). Workers' participation in these events is huge: "The strikes in the new booming capitalist industries . . . have been . . . increasing in scale and extent, so that 'collective bargaining by riot' . . . has become the normal method by which workers defend their rights and interests. Workers have developed a very good idea of what they can get away with and how far they can go" (Clarke and Pringle 2009, 93; see also CLB 2016).

Urban areas appear to have become the main terrain for social protest— this is in contrast to the 1990s, when it was primarily the rural areas that were the arena for numerous protests, mainly directed against the local authorities (Heberer 2007, 165). The labor disputes over working conditions, the violation of labor standards, or delayed wage payments were also accompanied by various forms of protest and violent riots outside the work environment.

A wave of strikes in the province of Guangdong in early summer 2010 attracted particular attention—according to official reports from labor union representatives, in the city of Guangzhou alone, there were over sixty strikes during this period. These took place in the context of the tragic spate of suicides at Foxconn, the largest Taiwanese contract manufacturer of Western brand products in consumer electronics. As a result of a spontaneous strike at a Honda supplier in Nanhai (Foshan), a movement developed that caused a media furor both in China and abroad for a number of weeks (see Butollo and ten Brink 2012; Hui 2011). Triggered by the unsatisfactory implementation of the statutory minimum wage, the movement propelled corporate power structures into the limelight—a breach of taboo. Compared to previous campaigns, this movement's wage demands were high and were largely successfully pushed through. Unlike with earlier protests, the unrest spread rapidly in this case. Moreover, while the mobilization of workers had previously almost exclusively been directed at local governments, the disputes now resembled classical forms of collective wage bargaining. Finally, the strike wave was characterized by a high level of participation and democratic principles. Some workers claimed the right to independent interest representation in the company. In the case of Honda Nanhai, the confrontation with the company union (which itself had proven to be ineffective) resulted in the election of a strike committee.

The volume of social protests and labor disputes against a backdrop of unusually high GDP growth rates by global standards combined with government efforts to rebalance the economy suggest that the increase in prosperity had not benefited all segments of the population equally. This applies to migrant workers in particular: "During the eight years after the Chinese central government began making . . . moves towards class compromise in 2002, migrant worker insurgency grew rapidly. While there are a number of factors behind this, the overarching reason is that while the country experienced an economic boom of historic proportions things did not significantly improve for migrant workers" (Friedman 2011, 151; see also C. Chan and Pun 2009).

At the same time, it became clear to the ruling elite that it was not going to be possible to secure the socioeconomic (and ultimately also political) stability of the system without strengthening institutionalized rights and conflict resolution mechanisms within and across companies. Hence,

> the unprecedented wave of labour legislation . . . was no accident. It was a direct response to the pressure exerted by the workers' movement over [the 2000s]. A government committed to maintaining social order and harmony could no longer afford to ignore the strikes and protests staged by workers on an almost daily basis across the country. It sought to create a comprehensive legislative framework that could help mitigate labour conflicts and better protect the legal rights of individual workers. This legislative approach has made workers much more aware of their rights. (CLB 2009, 13)

In the following sections, I will outline the key features of the Chinese labor system and attempt to answer the question as to why, despite the establishment of quasicorporatist consultation mechanisms, there was so little progress made toward "harmonizing" industrial relations. In the final part of the chapter, I will elaborate on the shortcomings of Chinese corporatism.

Characteristics of the Chinese Labor System

Despite regional differences, it is possible to identify some key characteristics of the urban labor system in the context of the historical transformation of the labor force from a largely agricultural to primarily industrial one. First, I will outline the structure of the labor force and the production regimes. I will then introduce the system of industrial relations. (Note that neither the large informal sectors in the cities, frequently in the service industry, nor rural labor relations are considered in any detail here.)

(1) *The segregated labor force.* China's working population increased from 779 million in 2009 to 797 million in 2014 (NBS 2015b, table 4–1). The number of people working in agriculture declined from 297 to 228 million during the same period. As a result of urbanization, only 20 percent of the working population in coastal provinces was now employed in agriculture, in contrast to the 45 percent in the country's inland provinces. The number of people working in the secondary sector increased from 216 to 231 million between 2009 and 2014. Three-quarters of this number were employed in manufacturing and one-quarter in the construction industry (NBS 2015b, table 4–1). In the tertiary sector, which has employed more people than the secondary sector since the mid-1990s, 314 million people were employed in 2014 compared to 266 million people five years previously. In the 2000s, the working age population grew by an average of ten million people per year (Herd, Koen, and Reutersward 2010, 6). The unemployment rate in urban areas has periodically been around 4 percent since 2011, though estimates (from Chinese university studies) frequently indicate higher values, including for (temporary) youth unemployment, for instance.

Migrant workers now constitute the largest segment of the urban labor force. Between 2000 and 2015, their share of the urban working population increased from 36 percent to over 60 percent (C. Lee 2016).[38] The country's largest group of workers only have precarious residence permits in the cities and essentially "guest worker" status. In contrast to the first generation of these "peasant workers" (*nongmingong*), the second and third generations of migrant workers have gravitated toward the cities, despite the fact that they still frequently move house and switch jobs (Wenten 2011).

Labor market segregation is a result of preserving the hukou system, which brought about substantial wage differentials between migrant and local workers. This restrictive household registration system, which assigns a person rural or urban resident status, perpetuates the disparities between urban and rural incomes, standards of living, and social safety nets. Migrant workers in cities still have inferior entitlements and rights (with respect to children's education and hospital charges, for instance). The capital still views this migration control regime as an indispensable pillar of stability and the foundation of the country's economic growth, and the Ministry of Public Security responsible has gone to great lengths to coordinate the regime (Ngok and Chan 2016).

The internal migration flows have admittedly made some holes in the hukou system and gradually changed it in line with a conversion process (Young 2011, 148–51). The household registration system was decentralized and modified, but, overall, its function was preserved (K. Chan and Buckingham 2008; F. Wang 2011). Although it has been made easier to acquire permanent local hukou, it is primarily the affluent and more highly qualified migrant workers who are granted permanent urban registration. Moreover, the less wealthy individuals gaining a local hukou lose their land rights the moment they register: "In most cases, those people are included in the city's social welfare system in exchange for their loss of land permanently, an asset which usually can derive far greater present and future financial benefits in the urbanizing region. Some critics have considered this 'equalization' an indirect pillaging of peasants' property" (Chan and Buckingham 2008, 598–99).

(2) *Segmented production regimes.* Only at first glance does China's huge army of workers give the impression of a homogenous mass. In fact, over the course of the reforms, the labor force has been segmented. Boy Lüthje differentiates between five generic types of production regimes among companies in the country's core industries (Lüthje 2009, 2010; see also Butollo and Lüthje 2012; Lüthje, Luo, and Zhang 2013).[39]

- *State-bureaucratic.* This regime can be found in the steel industry, for instance, and is characterized by a relatively stable core workforce, for the most part with medium or high skills, a comparatively limited share of migrant workers, low base wages, and a correspondingly high proportion of allowances (up to 50 percent of the base wage). Traditionally, the labor union plays an important role in the comanagement of the company.

- *Corporate-bureaucratic.* This regime is similar to the state-bureaucratic one in terms of the relative stability of the conditions of the workforce and primarily employs urban workers who receive better pay and legal protection than migrant workers. This results in higher base wages, more regulated working hours, and a tendency toward workforce skilling and education. Examples of this regime can be found in the automobile and chemical industries, for instance. The labor unions are co-opted into factory management.

- *Corporate high-performance.* This production regime is characterized by a strong performance orientation, a flexible workforce, lower base wages, and weak labor unions. It can be found in American and European, as well as Chinese and other East Asian IT companies.

- *Flexibilized mass-production.* This production regime is based on the exploitation of low-paid migrant workers and can be found in the (overseas) Chinese contract manufacturers and large suppliers for Western electronics companies, for instance. The regime is defined by its long, flexible working hours and low base wages, pronounced wage differentials between production workers and engineers, and labor union structures (if these exist) dominated by the company management.

- The *low-wage classic* model in the textile industry, for example, is at the bottom end of the production regime hierarchy. SMEs and also numerous large companies of this type primarily employ migrant workers. Labor unions are rarely to be found in such workplaces.

A series of other factors foster segmentation: on the whole, for example, there is a strong hierarchization of wage systems—within the production regimes outlined above and along the supply chain—and significant systems of personnel leasing or temporary labor. By law, how temporary labor is used should have become substantially more restrictive from mid-2013.

However, strong protests, particularly from large SOEs, led to the adoption of the law being postponed until 2016. There is also a pronounced gender gap: women's wages are around 20 to 30 percent lower than their male counterparts with comparable work experience and qualifications. As already described, further discrimination is evident as a result of the unfavorable position of migrant workers.

Certain groups of urban workers nurtured aggressive ambitions for professional advancement that are incompatible with solidarity-oriented behavior among work colleagues. However, certain similarities between the different production regimes and employment relationships can be identified. Because of the limited influence that workers have over a company's performance policy or restructuring and the relocation of production, they are, on the whole, very dependent on their employers' decisions. Further, in the majority of industry sectors, base wages comprise only around 50 percent of the total wage. Overtime and bonuses as nonwage benefits exemplify the weak bargaining position of employees. This is accompanied by fierce in-house competition for better pay and allowances. Serious collective bargaining over wages and working conditions is just as rare as industry-wide collective wage agreements (Friedman and Kuruvilla 2015). Therefore, "the absence of effective collective regulations on base wages, bonuses, working hours, and working conditions can be viewed as a common characteristic of industrial relations, both in state-owned and private companies. The high level of wage flexibility is effectively the lowest common denominator between the labor regimes at the top and bottom ends of the hierarchy, often associated with extensive overtime. Thus, the proverbial dedication of Chinese workers seems in no way to be a 'natural' characteristic" (Butollo and Lüthje 2012, 8, my translation).

The segregated and segmented structure of the labor force described in this section forms the foundation of an undeveloped, quasicorporatist nexus where four key players interact.

The "Four Parties" in the System of Industrial Relations

Comparative political economy (CPE) and industrial sociology approaches refer to concepts of corporatism to depict the trilateral network of relations between employers, employees, and the state that is typical of capitalist-driven societies. Here, a stable corporatist structure has been identified as a functional complement of successful capital accumulation (see Wright 2000).

In normative terms, corporatist relations are also seen as favorable in China, particularly to defuse vertical social conflicts. From the point of view of the state authorities, corporatism has the additional advantage of safeguarding their influence over institutional pluralization and relieving them of regulatory functions. The Chinese authorities have gone to great lengths to establish institutions of this type. Trilateral consultative conferences were introduced at all relevant administrative levels to harmonize industrial relations (K. Chang, Lüthje, and Luo 2008; Shao, Nyland, and Zhu 2011). Here, the Ministry of Human Resources and Social Security (MOHRSS) represented the central government, the All-China Federation of Trade Unions (ACFTU) represented the workers, and the China Enterprise Confederation represented employers, primarily from state-owned enterprises. The association of private businesses, the ACFIC, also joined. The conferences address a diverse range of labor law issues and develop guidelines for drawing up employment contracts. They particularly aim to prevent and contain labor disputes and also set minimum wages (which differ from region to region). According to statements from conference delegates, despite the occasional uncertainty as to whether or not their decisions are binding, these meetings have, in fact, already successfully resolved some regional labor conflicts (Shao, Nyland, and Zhu 2011, 368).

Different studies have taken different positions on industrial relations. Some authors refer to a transformation of "state-corporatist" regulation of the labor system into a "social corporatism," where the state no longer imposes diktats but instead allows the different groups to reach a temporary consensus in negotiations (A. Chan 2008). However, only an incomplete form of corporatism has evolved to date, which has a striking lack of one typical feature of corporatism in developed capitalist systems, namely, representation of the collective interests of the workforce. Because unions have not managed to achieve independence from the state-party and act more as intermediaries, in China, a fourth actor has effectively joined the conventionally tripartite corporatism—the labor force, which is inadequately represented by the unions. A brief look at the four key actors gives us a general impression of this configuration.

(1) *State institutions.* Analogous with the changing relations at the corporate level, at the labor system level, it can be said that the withdrawal of direct or imperative government intervention is accompanied by a tendency toward more mediated political influence—specifically the juridification of industrial relations. The aim is to strengthen legal and regulatory

norms for employment contracts. China's Labour Law, which entered into force in 1994; a series of provisions that followed; and the Labour Contract Law adopted in 2008 (and amended again in 2012) serve as the foundation: "The Labour Contract Law makes major steps in improving the ability of workers to ensure that they are actually paid for work that has been undertaken. One of the most important improvements concerns underpayment of wages. . . . If no contract has been signed (as is the case for most private sector employees), the law specifies that after working for one month the person is deemed to have been employed on an indefinite contract" (Herd, Koen, and Reutersward 2010, 26).

Because no collective labor rights (such as the right to collective wage agreements or industrial dispute) are guaranteed, individual lawsuits, arbitration proceedings, and court cases have all increased (CLB 2011, 11, 46).

However, there continues to be a sizable gap between theory and reality as far as labor policy is concerned: a number of provisions, even those that have entered into legislation, are not adequately implemented and are more or less freely interpreted in practice (Herd, Koen, and Reutersward 2010, 24–29; Friedman and Lee 2010, 513–14; also see Gallagher 2017 for recent developments). Here, both the employers and the local authorities have proven to be unreliable partners. Although, by law, the weekly working hours should not exceed forty, employees often work sixty hours or more (with overtime). Despite the changes in legislation, for migrant workers, the employment relationship is still frequently based on verbal agreement. According to the results of a survey conducted by the Chinese National Bureau of Statistics, in 2014, this applied to over half of all migrant workers (C. Lee 2016, 320). This results in a very high turnover of workers.

Collective industrial action continues to fall in a legal gray area. Moreover, although labor regulation at the company level is formally undergoing a transformation from individually to collectively negotiated contracts, these remain underinstitutionalized or ineffective. Luo illustrates: "Millions of collective contracts have been signed in the last few years, but in reality, wages and other labor standards remain low and unstable. . . . Many collective contracts contain only general principles or legal terms, instead of any substantial statements or quantitative figures on labor standards. . . . In practice, workers are usually excluded from the process, enterprise unions are unwilling or unable to make any resistance, and consequently collective contracts are virtually in the hands of employers" (Luo 2011, 67).

Until 2016, no serious attempts have been made to regulate labor standards at a cross company level, let alone to conduct industry-wide collective bargaining.[40] Against this backdrop, the ACFTU's five-year plan for strengthening the country's wage policy attracted even more attention. In contrast to the previous three-year work plan, which ran until 2013, the reform agenda for the period from 2014 to 2018 resolutely moved away from the customary ritual of quantitative targets and instead formulated unusually clear qualitative core objectives for strengthening and modernizing wage policy. The focus of the reform agenda was the expansion of a cross-company sector-specific wage policy as well as an increase in the legitimacy of collective bargaining provisions. According to the agenda, wage policy was supposed to be a top priority in the future. However, when it came to practical implementation, there was considerable opposition. The position of the party and the employers on the project ranged from critical to openly hostile. In 2016, in his activity report presented to the National People's Congress, Premier Li Keqiang was tellingly silent on the subject of wage policy. Only shortly after the ACFTU had announced its reform agenda, in 2015, did the State Council and the Central Committee of the CCP publish a position paper on the development of "harmonious" industrial relations. This could be seen as a counterproject to the ACFTU's wage policy plans. The position paper emphasizes "collective consultation" instead of collective bargaining.[41]

Perhaps more significant, however, is the fact that employers have so far been neither willing nor able to act as collective bargaining partners at cross company level. Some observers see the decisive opposition to wage policy as currently coming less from the political leadership and far more from the employers.

On the whole, labor law to date still appears to be more of an individual labor law, supplemented by local, in parts sector-specific, guidelines often deviating from national provisions. Significant implementation deficits, different local interpretations of the law, and self-imposed obligations are evidence that Chinese labor law continues to be perceived as soft law (Friedman and Kuruvilla 2015).

Simultaneously, as already mentioned in Chapter 2, for some time now, the Chinese central government has been attempting to cushion social polarization by developing a social security system, and through employment agencies and retraining measures. Particularly since 2008, there has been significant development of social policy in the PRC, especially in terms of extending geographical coverage and inclusion (Ngok and Chan 2016). The sociopolitical measures implemented by the government, frequently (partially) based on Western universalistic models, are, inter alia, the central state's response to its legitimacy deficits. Accordingly, China's Social Security Act 2010 awards *all* Chinese citizens the right to access social insurance. Although there are still considerable shortcomings in terms of implementation, these measures have contributed to some extent to stabilizing precarious employment relations "from the outside."

(2) *Labor unions.* With its over 270 million members, the ACFTU is formally the largest labor union organization in the world.[42] After the ACFTU declared migrant workers to be members of the proletariat in 2003, its membership officially rose substantially. It is not recognized by the International Confederation of Free Trade Unions (ICFTU) as an independent labor union, however, because it is still largely under the control of the party-state, or, to be precise, the CCP.

As the sole national labor union organization, with its subdivisions, the ACFTU is represented at almost all administrative levels. Recently, urban district unions were introduced as new tiers in the system between the company-level units and the higher echelons of the ACFTU. For the most part, these are closely linked to the local party-state apparatus. On the whole, company labor unions have precedence over the sectoral unions. The latter still play only a marginal role in China, which makes for a difficult starting point for establishing collective wage bargaining and wage agreements.

To this day, the status of the ACFTU is disputed in academic debate because it does not function as an autonomous representative of workers' interests (see Feng 2003). In fact, the guiding principle of the ACFTU should be viewed as "cross class" and primarily committed to "national" modernization—"the interests of the working class were always seen as a particular subset of the general interests of the nation, a formula that persists to this day" (Friedman 2011, 154). This organizational philosophy contributes to the very pronounced conservative stance of the ACFTU.[43]

Nevertheless, as a result of competition-driven modernization and (limited) social pluralization, the role of the ACFTU has been partially transformed. It is no longer solely responsible for maintaining discipline in the workplace and administering certain aspects of the social services. Nowadays, first, it is proactive in labor policy lobbying, although this lobbying is rather limited. Currently, the main aim of the ACFTU is to provide legal representation for workers and, if necessary, it also organizes legal assistance for its members. In labor disputes, however, the ACFTU generally plays only a defensive, intermediary role. Second, it takes steps to strengthen labor union structures at company level, particularly in private enterprises. This enables it to help establish collective regulations, although, as described earlier, these provisions either are rarely binding or are just insubstantial shells (CLB 2011, 39–40). Since 2008, company labor union structures have been successfully established in over 80 percent of the Fortune Global 500 companies located in China. Third, the ACFTU also conducts workplace inspections. It is therefore plausible to see labor unions as intermediary organizations between employers, the party-state, and workers (or ordinary union members).

From the perspective of the party-state leadership, the highly fragmented production sector in the PRC demands a modern union representation of interests. The effective institutionalization of industrial relations, however, requires the ACFTU's capacity to be strengthened (Luo 2011). Of course, the latter should take place within the confines of the party and state leadership's concepts of harmonious industrial relations through corporate comanagement and the settlement of labor disputes. The criteria for assessing "harmonious" industrial relations include the company's competitiveness, the working environment, and the successful resolution of labor disputes. For this reason, in individual disputes, cooperative relations with the company generally take precedence over the determined and consistent defense of workers' interests. A number of union officials also use their positions as a springboard for a corporate career or advancement into public administration. These officials, including company union leaders, earn substantially more than skilled workers. This undermines the union's power of mobilization and cohesion.

At enterprise level, there is frequently close cooperation between the (personnel) management and the company union structures. The personnel departments of large enterprises often participate in establishing unions. Executive positions in the union are frequently held by members and/or representatives of the management. "Thus, while much of the criticism of Chinese unions focuses on their lack of independence from the Party-state, lack of independence from capital is an equally vexing problem" (Friedman 2011, 62).[44]

China also has what are known as Staff and Workers' Representative Congresses (SWRCs). Although there are some similarities, these workers' congresses cannot really be compared with (German) works councils, however (see A. Chan 2008). The company union leader is often the central authority in the SWRCs. Their legal rights of control and codetermination, such as the right to propose a candidate during the recruitment of management staff, are not normally used in the interests of the workforce. The frequently long intervals (often a year) between the meetings of the congresses prevent them from operating like works councils (according to the German model, for instance), which are ideally dedicated to addressing day-to-day staff problems. The congresses participate in the negotiation of employment contracts, but these more closely resemble works agreements than collective wage agreements. Wage levels are not generally mentioned in these contracts, which, instead, focus primarily on issues of workers' welfare and overtime regulations.

Alongside employee representation, many large companies also have party cells. The party plays an intermediary role and takes on a conciliatory role in conflicts. As well as in SOEs, some domestic and foreign private companies also have company party committees. As soon as a company has a minimum of three employees who are party members, they are required to create a company party committee. Workers frequently first address their complaints to the company party cell (CLB 2009, 37–38). In a Honda joint venture in Guangdong, the party cell even decides on the "employee of the month." According to the company union, party membership extends from the ordinary workers right up to managerial level.

Overall, the unions (and also the workers' congresses and party committees) still are doubly dysfunctional: they neither pursue a strategy (used in other countries at sectoral level) to curb competition between employees, nor are they in a position or willing to represent interests at company level. Their self-definition as a moderator of workplace relations and their dependence on employers and the CCP limits their ability to act as independent representatives of the workers' interests.

(3) *Employers.* Employers control the most important economic resources and often also have political influence. The employer associations discussed in the first section of Chapter 3 (such as the ACFIC) and the lobbying functions exercised in consultative processes for labor laws and local regulation, for instance, have represented the formal framework of Chinese quasicorporatism for some time now. These associations have been able to augment their influence driven by their own momentum.

Thus, already many years ago, employers became a "strategic group" (Heberer 2002). On many issues, they developed "a remarkable awareness of common interests and positions" and act, "beyond the myriad differences in worldview and mentality . . . 'collectively,' in the practical sense" (K. Chang, Lüthje, and Luo 2008, 11, my translation). In the official trilateral consultative conferences, the employers generally refrain from going on the offensive against the unions. At the same time, within the company, they frequently circumvent labor standards and sabotage the implementation of new labor rights. Moreover, Chinese *and* foreign lobby groups already contributed to mitigating the 2008 Labor Contract Law during the consultation phase for the draft law (Friedman and Lee 2010, 526; GM 2010, 87–96). Even once the law had come into force, large companies such as Huawei and Lenovo publicly voiced their criticism.

Frequently, Chinese companies' incentive and motivation systems prove to be resistant to legal obligations. In parallel, these companies attempt, within the framework of the international concept of corporate social responsibility, to declare themselves as the actual representatives of the workers' interests. In many cases, this method enables the company to increase management control over the employees, to circumvent the PRC's legal directives, and to outmaneuver the company union (for a critical general account, see Beckert 2009).

(4) *Workers.* In sharp contrast to the position of the employers, workers in the "socialist market economy with Chinese characteristics" are assigned only the position of powerlessness, objects with no independent interest representation. "Labor remains entirely excluded or at least entirely subservient to the CCP's monopoly on labor organization" (Frazier 2011, 109). Though the constitution provides for a range of citizens' rights, the reality of the modernization process significantly curtails these: "China's constitution provides for a wide range of citizens' rights, including the rights to freedom of information, free speech, freedom of association and the right to demonstrate. The reality for China's workers is that information is monopolised by managements, freedom of speech is curtailed by internet censorship and the official media, the ACFTU monopolises the right of association, and the local police decide who can demonstrate and when" (CLB 2009, 22).

Because the ACFTU acts as only a weak negotiator for the workers, if at all, they are frequently not even aware of the existence of a (company) union. Further, because of a lack of confidence, these workers are often reluctant to approach the union (for earlier evidence, see Blecher 2008, 265; CLB 2011, 25).

On the whole, despite having social power, the segmented labor force remains institutionally underrepresented. Here, the production and market power of a diverse range of categories of workers is in stark contrast to their limited organizational power (see Wright 2000). As well as options for legal action in individual cases, new forms of collective resistance have emerged—for example, more or less loose associations of workers from specific towns and provinces and other nongovernmental organizations (NGOs) acting as self-help groups. Here, labor law serves as an important base. The options for collective industrial action open to workers are outlined in more detail below. Paradoxically, on the one hand, they reveal the shortcomings of Chinese corporatism, and, on the other hand, they could serve as starting points for autonomous representation of employee interests.

"Tripartism with Four Parties": Initial Conclusions

We are able to draw some initial conclusions from the analysis above. First, we can now be more specific about the importance of the large supply of labor as the backbone of Chinese economic development. It was particularly the segmentation and segregation of the labor force that proved to be a source of value added and an engine for accumulation. Thus, labor not only remained "cost effective" for a long time but simultaneously, workers were fragmented both geographically and within companies. Precarious employment continues to be the norm for the vast majority of workers (Gallagher 2017; C. Lee 2016). This means that wages are regulated at the level of the individual company, and there is a lack of collective and cross sector regulation of labor standards. The local environment has become the key arena for the management of industrial relations, comparable with developments in other industrial nations since the 1980s, which resulted in "increased flexibility in managerial strategies in geographically segmented labour markets" (Harvey 1989, 11). However, on the whole, the current system of industrial relations in China is less reminiscent of the forms of corporatism that can be found in Western Europe and more closely resembles East Asian models of corporate paternalism that strive to create an effective corporate community.

Second, the central government introduced quasicorporate consultation mechanisms with the aim of regulating conflict, and legislation for industrial relations is being enacted. The latter includes a large number of soft regulations, however. Yet this strategy of authoritarian social partnership is not entirely effective because workers have virtually no institutional representation in the system of industrial relations and consultation (Lee 2016). There is still no evidence of genuine "social" corporatism. Despite their new areas of responsibility, the unions have still not gained any real independence from the state-party *and* the employers, and, as a result, in China, a fourth actor has come into play—the labor force, which is barely represented by the ACFTU. Consequently, here we can refer to "tripartism with four parties," because, although the workers are largely excluded from the formalized system of consultation, they are still able to influence it through their own initiatives and resistance.

Third, however, the fragmented representation of employees' interests is still not incompatible with the party-state and local public-private economic alliances that have a vested interest in the "competitiveness" of their location. When it comes to monitoring labor rights, the Chinese state has exercised and continues to exercise restraint in an almost "neoliberal" manner if this looks likely to disrupt the unbridled capital accumulation. At the same time, in some locations (such as the Pearl River delta), this has resulted in a tacit understanding between wealthy farmers, local governments, and foreign investors that perpetuates the hukou system:

> Large portions of agricultural land in the Pearl River Delta region have become industrial, and in most areas the land use rights still rest with the collectives, which have been actively constructing and renting out factory buildings to foreign investors for the past twenty-some years. Villagers, as a group, have become a rentier class. The very direct personal gains that can be made from foreign investors using migrant workers from poorer provinces contribute to the villagers' unconscionable disregard for the exploitation of the migrant workers. . . . There is an unspoken alliance between the local village governments (and the levels of government immediately above them) and foreign-invested enterprises with regard to keeping the migrant production-line workers in line. (A. Chan 2011, 41)

Under increasing pressure to prove its legitimacy, the central state has taken on a partially conciliatory role (as predicted in my research framework), also with regard to particularistic business interests. This has resulted in China's labor policy presenting a fundamental problem: on the

one hand, at least the central state has an interest in functioning consultation mechanisms and a balance of interests. On the other hand, "cost-
effective" labor continues to give China a competitive edge in the global
economy. At the same time, the shift of industrial relations to the company
level and the segmentation of production regimes makes the standardiza-
tion of wages, working hours, and so on much more difficult.

An important question to be addressed at this juncture is whether there
have been any recent development trends that change this basis for industrial relations.

Incomplete Corporatism and Volatile Social Protests: Prospects for Industrial Relations

Functioning corporatist structures have numerous institutional prerequisites. As the following account shows, there is little evidence that these
preconditions exist in China's multilevel system. To date, the heterogeneity
of the labor and economic systems and the practices and preferences of
employers and state actors have hampered efficient regulation of the labor
system and an institutionalization of the class conflict.

Detailed reference has already been made to the employer's interest in
preserving low wages and the system of industrial relations at company
level. Although qualification requirements are on the rise, and, to a certain
extent, there is also a labor shortage,[45] these trends have not yet resulted
in qualitative improvements in labor standards, particularly for migrant
workers.

The central state, in contrast, has a vested interest in establishing functioning corporatism. This interest correlates with its attempt to increase
domestic demand. There is a contradiction between ambition and reality,
however. In the trilateral consultative conferences, the state plays a key role.
But the decisions made at the conferences have little binding effect and/or,
compared to functioning forms of corporatism in other countries, are heavily biased toward the employer. Further, the countless consultative conferences at local level promote regional heterogeneity and fragmentation
instead of adopting a coordinating or unifying function (also see Friedman
and Kuruvilla 2015).

Elsewhere, the party-state tends to act through reactive measures and
combat social conflict with a combination of concessions, mediation, and
promises, on the one hand, and threats and physical violence, on the other.

The central government is endeavoring to further develop its labor policy practice, redefined as "social governance" (*shehui guanli*). To date, this practice has been characterized by its conservative paternalistic controlling nature, however. It functions as a system of aftercare, in other words crisis management, primarily put into practice once conflicts have already arisen. With labor law reforms, the state's aim, first and foremost, is to lay the foundations to enable it to better manage China's complex world of work and to be able to limit unpredictable opposition. This does not, however, eliminate the root cause of the problems in implementing the required labor policy measures, namely, a reluctance to do so on the part of the employers (see Gallagher 2017).

The fact that the central state's efforts often fail owing to the diverging predilections of the local governments or the public-private economic alliances has already been described in detail in the present work. However, the central government's halfheartedness cannot solely be attributed to this, as, for example, the reform of the hukou system illustrates. In fact, a transformation of the registration system would technically be perfectly achievable. However, with the current balance of power, the central government's fears of increasing labor costs hamper the implementation of fundamental reform. To this day, Chan and Buckingham's earlier argument remains valid: "there are reasons to believe that even for the national government, maintaining a competitive edge in labour costs is crucial to China's positioning . . . in the global economy. Hukou is obviously central to the current system of sustaining super-low-cost Chinese labour in the international market" (K. Chan and Buckingham 2008, 604).

There is a conflict of objectives between policy approaches that aim to safeguard social justice and those that seek to maintain China's international competitiveness. In this context, Friedman also describes the emergence of an "insurgency trap," which prevents the central state from implementing stronger measures to address the implementation problems at the local level and from allowing independent representation of workers' interests: "The one way to break this alliance [of local governments and companies] and ensure legal compliance—opening up space for the development of a potentially coercive countervailing force at the point of production, i.e. independent worker organization—remains anathema to higher levels of the state since they fear it would threaten their monopoly on power. Hence, the conundrum of insurgency trap" (Friedman 2011, 152).

To bring about the government's aim of rebalancing growth, those representing the labor force need to successfully push through substantial real wage increases. Yet, as mentioned above, the unions still lack both the motivation and ability to do this. To unleash the necessary forces for this development would require a comprehensive transformation of labor union practice and structures. But one question that arises here is whether there are factions within the ACFTU advocating for the strategic implementation of this idea (including all the potential consequences it entails).

There is only minimal evidence that such factions exist: in the traditionally proreform province of Guangdong, which has already acted as a trailblazer on numerous occasions, reformers within the ACFTU have made certain attempts at modernization that could contribute to the establishment of "complete" corporatism in the medium term because of their greater emphasis on representing the interests of the workers. According to reports from the Guangzhou Federation of Trade Unions (GZFTU), for example, there has been a highly promising campaign for the creation of construction worker unions in Guangzhou. Here, in recent years, an almost union-free industry has been unionized with the support of the municipal government. The local unions regularly conduct inspections to monitor occupational safety and compliance with contracts. Moreover, with the help of the unions, schools have been founded for the offspring of migrant workers. It has also become clear from discussions and interviews with Chinese labor unionists that the separation of management and the company union could in fact be feasible in this segment in the future.

The lines of argument of individual labor union officials are in a similar vein. According to their reasoning, employers' (dismissal) policies should not be seen as the misconduct of individuals but rather as a "systemic" dilemma. At public events in the early 2010s, the chair of the GZFTU, for instance, argued for an increase in collective bargaining. For the time being, however, even the majority of reform-minded labor unionists in the province of Guangdong see themselves more as mediators in labor disputes than as spearheading the struggle for fair workers' rights (Friedman and Kuruvilla 2015). As long as the pressure of the workforce on the labor unions cannot offset the pressure of companies, of the party-state, and of internal tendencies toward inertia, we can only anticipate partial reform of the labor union federation.

Can the "fourth party," that is, the workers, develop the necessary pressure to effect significant change? Is corporatism being forced on Chinese society from below? Because the significant protest movements described at the beginning of this chapter represent only the tip of the iceberg of heightened social demands and expectations of fair working conditions, one might think that this would pave the way for a functioning intermediation of interests. However, although the proreform faction of the ACFTU, for instance, is striving toward more autonomy and improved labor union representative authority within companies, and a small number of Chinese experts are in favor of reforming the system of wage determination, the response of large segments of the political and economic power elite has been one of fear and rejection. The concern is that the central government's social guarantees threaten to generate completely "unrealistic" demands from the workers. For this reason, attempts are made to hem in the fourth party, which would be in a better position than anyone to initiate "social upgrading," and far-reaching reform of the unions is put on the back burner.

The historical trajectory of workers' protests suggests that we should discuss the constraints placed on them, that is, we should identify which factors have prevented Chinese capitalism from becoming a new "epicenter" of the labor movement, as some authors had anticipated (Silver and Zhang 2009). To begin with, the process of capitalist modernization triggered only a small number of broad transregional movements (see Y. Cai 2011). In the past, it proved possible to contain workers' protests (with the exception of the 1989 movement). This was done either by successfully isolating the protests, by steering them toward legal disputes, or (in the course of restructuring SOEs, for instance) by containing them through a combination of financial compensation, selective disciplinary procedures against corrupt managers, and repressive measures against protest leaders. Moreover, company party cells and labor union branches had a mitigating effect on industrial unrest.

Two further circumstances are even more important in terms of explaining how workers' protests were contained: first, it was not only the segmentation in different production regimes but also the decentralized power structure of the party-state that brought about an atomization of opposition. The result was a form of "cellular activism" comprising isolated protests:

> Because of uneven local economic development and a tendency of workers to address their grievances vis-à-vis local state institutions, "cellular activism" of geographically limited, atomized protest

is prevalent, not the formation of a generalized class interest. . . . Second, . . . migrant workers characteristically act only when their legal rights are being violated. Accordingly, they mostly direct their claims to the respective local governments, calling for the reinstatement of their rights. . . . Furthermore, migrant workers in most cases protest in defense of their rights, not in support of better payment or working conditions. (Butollo and ten Brink 2012, 422–23; see also C. Lee 2007, 176–94; Shen 2007, 60–62)

The fact that the opposition concentrated on local governments enables the central government to distance itself from the local government, if necessary: by disciplining individual local government decision makers accused of incompetence or corruption, for instance. Thus, the central government even gives the impression of being the more tolerant component of the apparatus of power and is occasionally able to increase its legitimacy through anticorruption measures.

Second, social welfare support mechanisms in crisis situations can (still) limit protest. This applies to those migrant workers in the coastal regions who still own a piece of land in their native villages as a social contingency position. Millions of migrant workers are still able to temporarily return to their homes should they be dismissed, and there they have a certain level of security to fall back on. "Access to land and its associated functions for the social reproduction of migrants' labor power helps reduce employers' burden to pay adequately for workers' survival and limits workers' propensity to sustain labor strife in the cities" (C. Lee 2007, 205; see also Friedman and Lee 2010, 516). Although this security is gradually being eroded as a result of the process of land sales and "land dispossessions" (see C. Lee 2016), because of the trend toward widening of the Chinese social security net mentioned earlier, further welfare support mechanisms have been established at the same time.

Despite their limitations, the "cellular" workers' protests have played a significant role in pressuring the state and employers to make material concessions and in bringing about the normative reorientation of the central government (increasing domestic demand, establishing labor standards, creating corporatist structures, and, last but not least, establishing more progressive sociopolitical norms). Whether or not these changes can create sufficient impetus to translate the government's social and labor policy aims into substantial social improvements remains to be seen. Nevertheless, we can identify certain factors that will shape the further course of social conflict.

First and foremost, it is evident that some groups of workers have become more adept at asserting themselves by acquiring experience. "The spontaneous struggles of workers have achieved the unexpected goal of training small circles of individual activists, and from this milieu occasionally a loose or more integrated network of activists could be forged" (Au 2009; also see Leung and Pun 2009; on the issue of class formation more generally, see Wright 1997, 373–406). Moreover, a number of recent strike movements did indeed spread across regions and sectors, demands were more proactive, and there was a radicalization of individual groups of workers. In the 2000s, migrant workers' hopes were pinned on the enforcement of legal standards and on local governments. Later, however, bitter disappointment with both the inertia of the local authorities and the limitations of labor law prepared the ground for a (fragile) trend toward collective forms of struggle. This development came to a head with the aforementioned strike wave in the early summer of 2010, which caused substantial production losses, particularly in the automobile industry. Because there was a labor shortage in the Pearl River delta region at the same time, this increased the market power of the workers and improved their chances of success (Butollo and Lüthje 2012; Hui 2011; see also A. Chan 2011). Many employers in the Pearl River delta responded to the strike movements (and the Foxconn scandal) with wage increases.

However, "cellular" constraints have prevailed as newer strike movements demonstrate: "The ten-day Yue Yuen strike in 2014 involving 40,000 workers from at least eight factories owned by the world's largest shoe manufacturer in Dongguan shows that staying within the boundaries of the law is still the rule of thumb adopted by ordinary workers, strike leaders, and the most daring NGO activists alike" (C. Lee 2016, 328). Nevertheless, political decision makers have rarely responded to the more recent protests solely with open repression but rather have demonstrated a certain level of willingness to compromise.

Interim Conclusion

This analysis of Chinese industrial relations demonstrates that the relationships between state authorities, labor unions, workers, and employers constitute a fragmented, incomplete form of corporatism. A power structure with four poles has emerged that makes the institutionalization of conflicts difficult. At the company level, soft regulations continue to exist, governing hourly and monthly wages or labor disputes, for instance.

Regulating labor law norms not only founders because of the heterogeneity of industrial production regimes but is also impeded by transnational companies and the public-private growth alliances of variegated state-permeated capitalism, which have a vested interest in preserving the status quo. These growth alliances, which endeavor to use all available means to accelerate capital accumulation and increase the profitability of companies, not only integrate subnational governments but ultimately also influence the central government.

The fundamental problem of China's labor policy is that although the central government supports effective consultation mechanisms and an intact balance of interests, at the same time, it still wants to preserve the competitive advantages of low labor costs (indeed, despite significant wage increases in recent years, these still appear to be relatively "competitive"). Close connections and a consonance of interests with employers perpetuate this. The central government's labor policy measures therefore primarily embody elements of reactive management of industrial relations and, as a rule, do not focus on the production sector itself, which is treated as taboo. The government continues to attempt to shift the responsibility for social conflict to the legal system, to channel that conflict by way of arbitration procedures, and, on the whole, to isolate protest. On balance, the power elite represents a type of benevolent neo-authoritarianism, which advocates for limited reforms but, beyond this, gives no concessions to demands for more far-reaching reforms, such as a fundamental strengthening of the ACFTU—not to mention permitting unofficial political parties or independent labor unions. The government and employers both also essentially still have a vested interest in maintaining a modified version of the hukou system because, as an internal migration control regime, it ensures that labor market segregation and, ultimately, the country's competitiveness is preserved.

At the same time, the country's new working class is prevented from becoming a social counterforce but instead is one that is supposed to consume, not oppose. Admittedly, there are proreform forces within the labor unions that are geared toward Western models of social partnership and advocate for an increase in the efficiency of Chinese corporatism by way of active inclusion of the workforce. However, this strategy has apparently not yet been a great success. For this reason, the mostly young migrant workers in particular constitute a sometimes invisible, sometimes unpredictable "fourth party" in Chinese industrial relations. Their protests hold significant potential for conflict precisely because of the absence of fully functioning collective bargaining or systems of negotiation. This explains why solving the social question has become a key issue in China today.

Conclusion

The present work uses an extended political economy perspective to shed light on the Chinese process of modernization. This enables us to develop a clear picture of the distinguishing features and driving forces of the current system in China as well as its dynamic and paradoxical development trends. The implications of this for political economy and China research are also outlined.

Capitalist Development in China

China's recent developments are fundamentally based on the same drivers of capitalism that can also be observed in processes of modernization in other countries: a boundless and excessive imperative to accumulate, combined with utopian promises, motives for personal advancement, and profit orientation, has fostered considerable economic momentum and has had a decisive impact on institutional change in China. The competition-driven process of accumulation, competitive thinking, and a capitalist logic of acceleration, as well as the attempt to bend and undermine institutions are of central importance for both market-based and non-market-based social relations. These factors have permanently destabilized and changed China's social order. As is the case in other capitalist systems, market activity relies on noneconomic institutions, with the state playing a key role here. We can also identify systematic differences between the strategic capacity for action of the three groups of actors studied (companies, party-state decision makers, and workers), which are the result of inequality in terms of access to resources or class positions. These differences, in turn, create a fundamental tension between market expansion and social coherence in China. Lastly, capitalist dynamics have, to a large extent, absorbed and reshaped non-, pre-, and protocapitalist institutions.

However, it does not suffice to say that the expansion of markets, the imperative of profit maximization, or the accompanying valorization of labor as a commodity are at the crux of social change in China, as in other countries. Although the drivers of capitalist development described earlier do come into play in China, this frequently occurs in a distinctive manner. China's specific socioeconomic conditions and historical traditions, its position in the world system, the conflicts between the key groups of actors, and so on have—influenced by the global trend toward liberalization and transnationalization in the post-1970s—all produced a variety of capitalism that, in the absence of a more fitting term, I refer to as a variegated form of competition-driven state-permeated capitalism. Here, diverse strategic projects implemented by the political power elites and the local public-private growth alliances possessed the capacity to change societal configurations. Against a backdrop of economic underdevelopment and only isolated cases of social opposition, or its suppression, all this resulted in the harsh reality of a capitalist-driven modernization, which, though economically very successful, was simultaneously grim for many. Drawing on historical traditions, yet much more focused on incorporating modern ideas and institutions, and closely linked to domestic and foreign private enterprises (sometimes in the form of a tacit agreement), Sino-Marxism achieved a form of modernization based on a distinctive variety of capitalist development.

Yet China researchers who identify different coexisting varieties of capitalism in China argue that the concept of state-permeated capitalism is juxtaposed with the reality of an internally segmented economy. My response is that this empirical description should not be the only basis for theoretical generalization. As has already been mentioned, the integration of national capitalist systems is never complete: these systems represent an institutional bricolage and do not result in universal homogeneity and constant stability. However, it is often useful to clarify whether certain facets of a given system play a dominant role in terms of overall development and whether this constitutes unity in diversity. In fact, according to my findings, forms of state permeation do represent such an overarching component of economic development. Beyond the constant influence of state permeation of the economy, Chinese capitalism is characterized by the prominent role of state-centric guiding principles. In contrast to the liberalization projects of capitalist democracies, and, during and after the global recession, the massive inevitable state interventions, my research identifies projects that, despite the country's tendency toward liberalization and marketization, are very deliberately centered on macro- and micropolitical regulation.[1] Thus, a segmented, heterogeneous ensemble of business forms and production regimes is, to some extent, embedded in a state capitalist *dispositif*. Here, close public-private relationships are key—in contrast to forms of capitalism where, for instance, market coordination, the "strategic" coordination through associations, or dependence on multinational corporations (in parts of Eastern Europe or Latin America, for example) predominates. Consequently, in the present work, it was possible to analyze dimensions of Chinese capitalism that draw on the diversity aspect without ignoring crosscutting characteristics.

The key, if not the only, historical starting point for this study is the severe crisis at the end of the Cultural Revolution. This provided important stimuli for the reform process initiated at the end of the 1970s, without this symbolizing a complete break with the period of classical Maoism. Contrary to the attempt to explain developments in China by claiming there was a linear transition from a planned to a market economy, frequently interpreted as a systemic break, the transition that actually took place was from one form of national modernization, which already imitated capitalist mechanisms (protocapitalism), to a distinctive new variety of capitalist-driven modernity. The Chinese power elite was therefore far better "prepared" for a transition to capitalist (including private) forms of market activity than the argument of a "communist," "noncapitalist," or "postcapitalist" development logic under Mao might suggest.

Beyond the importance of Maoist protocapitalist institutions and the power elite with its aim of national economic development, other favorable conditions for the dynamic process of capitalist development and gradual institutional change existed at the same time. Further factors emerged as prerequisites for a successful growth path from the late 1970s (measured according to economic criteria)—also compared to other developing and newly industrialized nations. These included the command economy, which was less centralized than the system in the Soviet Union and in reality functioned as a "plan anarchy" and thus already incorporated competitive relationships; the low level of industrialization of this late developer; the virtually inexhaustible army of cost-effective and comparatively well-trained workers; and a relatively functional and adaptive political system; as well as the existence of a modern social structure (created by abolishing unproductive feudal classes as a result of the Maoist land reforms, for instance). Beyond China's borders, East Asian developmental states emerged as new role models of modernization, although this was initially virtually unacknowledged. Additionally, the global crisis of state interventionism opened the eyes of the power elites (particularly the technocratic wing) and the new political and private entrepreneurs to a range of other options. In this sense, China's experimentation with liberalization measures fits into the process of global change since the 1970s, despite the very distinctive manner in which restructuring was implemented there.

As a result of the crisis of classical Maoism and a changed global economic (and geopolitical) landscape, the drivers of capitalism in China developed enormous and unforeseen momentum. I have provided a detailed account of this, covering the period from the 1980s to the 2000s (see Chapter 2) and the years from 2008 to 2016 (see Chapter 3). I will now summarize the key dimensions of capitalism in China. Once again, I will focus on the following areas: (1) corporate relations, (2) industrial relations, (3) the state and other noneconomic institutions, and (4) China's global integration.[2] In each case, I will establish the relevance of the specific area with regard to economic efficiency or revenue growth. In the subsequent section, I will then concentrate primarily on the paradoxes of prosperity.

(1) *Corporate relations.* The present work outlines the primary features and key drivers of the historical evolution of the Chinese economy. In contrast to older concepts of state capitalism where it was perceived as synonymous with a command economy, on the whole, the economic organization of today's China represents a mixed economy, where the principles of competition prevail across all sectors and different forms of ownership. Although certain key sectors of the economy are still controlled by state-owned enterprises (SOEs) or enterprise groups, these coexist with private companies, which now account for around two-thirds of economic growth (domestic and foreign companies combined).[3]

We should remember that juxtaposing private and state actors does not provide an adequate explanation for the growth of the corporate sector. Here, we must draw on the interdependencies between private and state actors. These heterogeneous networks, referred to as public-private economic alliances, created a dynamic setting for profitable investment and thus, at the same time, also contributed to the relative stability of the status quo. This should not be underestimated, particularly in view of the internal disintegration in other emerging countries.

Some studies assert that close public-private links and, in general, an "excess" of state intervention epitomize practices that destabilize the Chinese development model and distinguish it from a "supportive" private entrepreneurial form of capitalism. In contrast to these studies, in the present analysis, close connections with the state are depicted as laying virtually indispensable foundations for the competitiveness of companies. Thus, state institutions play a decisive part, not only in the reproduction of value, but also in increasing economic efficiency in the interests of boundless and excessive accumulation of (now both private and public) capital. Overall, the public-private growth alliances are also more important than the horizontal cooperation between enterprises and their associations (which is a key distinguishing factor in the field of comparative political economy or CPE). If we borrow the wording employed in CPE research, here, a setting that at first glance appears incoherent thus produces institutional complementarities, that is, productive effects on economic development.

In terms of its economic usefulness, the following points can be made with regards to the corporate sector. First, the extensive imperative to compete emerged as a decisive driver of change. This was in fact more important than the privatization processes. It has not only been since China's accession to the WTO in 2001 (which placed domestic enterprises under increased pressure of competition) that companies have had to surrender to competition-driven accumulation. This is why economic development cannot be fully planned by the central government. In the Chinese domestic market, an anarchic competitive dynamic prevails, which, in a sense, has given many economists reason to rejoice. Similarly, an imperative to compete also resonates in the "strategic" SOEs, albeit occasionally to a lesser extent.

Second, China's size and heterogeneity enables economic actors up until this day to profit from uneven accumulation conditions and labor systems, and to "move from region to region to find the most supportive government officials for their private firms, which in turn motivates officials to lend 'helping hands' rather than 'grabbing hands' in the provision of public goods or services (e.g., granting of licenses to start-up firms), or else there will be an outflow of profitable private businesses from the region" (Allen et al. 2012, 44–45).

Domestic and foreign, private and state-owned companies have all benefited from the uneven conditions. The heterogeneous level of development across the country also paved the way for internal competition to attract businesses and investment, where subnational governments reacted to competition from other regions with targeted industrial and fiscal policies.

Third, the Chinese financial system has still managed to secure a successful credit allocation mechanism, despite several bank crises. On the one hand, the state largely exercised control over the banking sector, which particularly benefited the SOEs and strategic industries. On the other hand, the increased importance of the capital markets also bolstered the investment-driven growth regime. "China has managed to create a sustainable Schumpeterian-Keynesian credit-investment-income-creation process, which has led to economic prosperity" (Herr 2011, 25). Moreover, informal credit relationships that do not conform to Western standards and have thus frequently been subject to criticism have in fact proven to be institutionally compatible for some time—particularly in terms of procuring capital to finance private investment.

Fourth, and finally, the Schumpeterian entrepreneur has acquired great significance impacting a range of spheres and involved in a wide spectrum of activities. These include the rule-breaking practice of creating de facto private companies ("wearing a red hat"), the investments of "patriotic" ethnic Chinese, and the risk-taking business activities of mainland Chinese entrepreneurs of diverse provenance. The Schumpeterian entrepreneur can take the form of a former manager of an SOE who now heads an internationally competitive company, a local government official, or a start-up or venture capitalist. Here, the fact remains that the economic success of these entrepreneurs who are focused on pursuing their own narrow individual interests can, however, be fully understood only in the context of their further institutional embedding and support.

(2) *Industrial relations.* In view of the fundamental changes in the labor systems, which brought extensive processes of commodification and precarization in their wake, safeguarding social integration presented a significant challenge during the period of reform. Up until recently, this challenge was being met with relative success, however.

On the whole, employers benefited considerably from the segregation and precarization of the labor force in diverse production regimes, which required primarily low- and medium-qualified labor. A key characteristic of the disparate and heterogeneous production regimes in the Chinese system of industrial relations is the development of a power structure with four poles between the relevant state institutions, the labor unions, the employers, and the workers. A fragmented and incomplete form of quasi-corporatism has evolved. Because the ACFTU has not managed to achieve real independence from the state-party *and* the employers, workers remain underrepresented. A paradoxical consequence of this development, which particularly affects migrant workers, is that, in the midst of a system that, from the outside at least, frequently appears ordered or "collectivist," there has been an assimilation of the neoliberal utopia: "The Party state has created a rough approximation of the neoliberal ideal whereby a disorganized mass of individuals is forced to confront the hegemonic power of state and capital *as individuals*" (Friedman and Lee 2010, 530).

Against a backdrop of workers' protests, at various junctures, the state has pressed for comprehensive legislation on industrial relations—during the course of the reforms, withdrawal of direct or imperative government intervention at the production level was accompanied by a tendency toward more mediated political influence—and strived to create effective corporatist structures. However, all too frequently, legal norms resulted in barely any sanctions, and corporatist institutions were incomplete, primarily because labor union representation of workers' interests was either very limited or nonexistent. Moreover, wages were mainly regulated at the level of the individual companies. There continued to be a lack of effective collective and cross sectoral legislation on labor and social standards. Soft regulations continued to shape the industrial system.

(3) *The state and other noneconomic institutions.* The present study does not interpret the turning point for reform in China from the 1970s as a comprehensive break with the past, but rather as a gradual, albeit ultimately profound, process of restructuring. This applies in particular to the transformation of the party-state, from the final phase of Mao's fragile development dictatorship, into a competent authoritarian agency working to promote economic modernization.

Over the course of reform, the overarching processes of market expansion fostered the establishment of a competition-driven multilevel system of governance (on both the horizontal and vertical levels) and decentralization trends. Yet the central government and the state-party were able to reproduce their power: by controlling essential resources or reserve capacities (including tax revenues, land, and the security apparatus), by influencing the financial system and state-owned and private enterprises,[4] and with the aid of indicative planning policies. During the first phase of reform, the central state tended to be more "reactive," which led to a loss of control. During the second phase from the 1990s onward, however, a more proactive approach saw the central government expand its freedom to act. Thereafter, the power of the party-state did not deplete as such, but rather new configurations evolved between the party and the state, most recently resulting in an increase in the party's power under Xi Jinping (this leads scholars to assume a third reform phase in the making; see L. Chen and Naughton 2017).

New regulatory tasks were anchored at the central government level with the objective of ensuring the order of the market. Thus, the state creates the parameters within which the private entrepreneur, the manager of an SOE or FIE, and also the market-oriented state official operates. Only in this broader sense of an attempt to combine entrepreneurialism and the state's capacity to act can we really refer to a competition-driven and internally heterogeneous state-permeated form of capitalism. Comparable with the transformation and reterritorialization of the state in OECD countries, in China, the party-state mobilized competition between the regions.

The practices of the subnational authorities in particular can be seen as a countertrend to the withdrawal of the state from commercial activities observed internationally. A state-permeated power structure has evolved in the form of local growth coalitions between political functionaries and companies, flanked by informal networks. Local governments share the overall goals of development, upgrading, and innovation with their business partners to such an extent that they reduce (this is not to say prevent) forms of corruption detrimental to economic growth. The opportunity to successfully participate in local "cronyist" growth alliances motivates local politicians to take entrepreneurial risks. Similarly, it fosters individual careers in the political system and within the CCP: the system of cadre evaluation, essential for individual career paths, is mostly based on economic indicators, although some social indicators have also recently been included.

Although this system is fragmented because of its heterogeneity and there are occasional problems with the public-private growth alliances of Chinese capitalism, these alliances—which do not envisage any form of participation rights for the wider population—operate in the interests of boundless and excessive capital accumulation. It is therefore hardly surprising when even the representatives of venture capital in the PRC (frequently classified as antistate in the West) respond to the question as to the need for system change by bluntly stating: "Keep it red" (Li 2010). Despite the rage among investors about the 2015 stock market decline, "most of the Chinese blogosphere was filled with calls for the state to come up with strategies to right Chinese equities rather than calls for economic liberalization" (Kurlantzick 2016, 98). In fact, despite heterogeneity and institutional bricolage in different parts of the country, owing to the developmentalist behavior of the relevant state actors, guaranteed unity in diversity has proven to be a prerequisite for economic growth.

As already argued, over the course of reform, the alliances of companies and subnational political authorities entered into competition with other alliances. A setting evolved that should be viewed as a functional equivalent of a hard budgetary constraint: the economic behavior of local political decision makers and also the managers of state-owned companies and managers or owners of hybrid companies began to resemble that of private owners. What was important here was not their legal status or institutional form—for example, that of a "political actor"—but rather their de facto (entrepreneurial) function. In this sense, the stylized notion of the private/state dichotomy does not really help to clarify the situation.[5] It is much more useful to take into account the wider institutional framework within which these actors operate—in this case, this includes a high degree of competitive pressure and the vested interests of local "developmentalist" political decision makers in a successful accumulation of capital.

Beyond these findings, there are further trends indicative of a transformation of statehood in China. What began as a cautious process of trial and error, characterized by limited violations of the rules at the start of the reform era, evolved into the targeted advancement of market processes and private entrepreneurship from the 1990s onward. At the same time, the central state and party apparatus comprising relatively homogenous technocratic power elites further developed the capacity to roll out positive local experiences across the country.[6] Through fiscal and monetary policy, as well as indicative planning methods, the state regulated the markets. This involved the government exposing SOEs to regulated competition, for instance. As the regulation of the markets was only partially or temporarily successful, sectoral reregulations were undertaken time and again. This is an expression of the impact that market activity has already had to date. Planning policies themselves have become part "of the adaptation of individual government agencies and firms to the continuously evolving signals of the market economy" (Naughton 2011a, 81).

Moreover, the authoritarian state strives to rule the country *with the aid of* the law—not to be confused with the rule *of* law, which would be applied irrespective of the government's view. This is reflected in industrial relations. Today, the state permits associations to have partial autonomy and a certain amount of room to maneuver that is not controlled by the central government apparatus. In this context, however, autonomous civil society space did not emerge automatically, but, instead, the development of elite networked communities between political and private actors was observed. In China, a distinctive pluralization of power elites evolved, which was rooted in the Mao era and even earlier.

Meanwhile, despite various signs of aging and a few temporary losses of legitimacy, the CCP still has an intact monopoly on power. Despite internal conflicts, the CCP as a whole has never been and is still not an impediment to reform but rather a vehicle of reform policy. In the process of modernization resulting in a transition to a more "rational" bureaucracy (in a Weberian sense), the CCP was not called into question. In fact, it recently became stronger under Xi Jinping. The targeted campaigns led by the state-party have a considerable political reserve capacity. Inherent in the leadership legitimacy of Sino-Marxism is syncretism, that is, the linking of various different traditions of thought, even ostensibly anticapitalist ones, to form a pragmatic Sino-Marxist canon that can be described as a non-Western program of capitalist modernization. Here, philosophies of state interventionism and the development of productive forces combine with harmonious thinking (partially derived from Confucianism and resembling notions of social partnership) and nationalist discourse.

To date, it has generally been possible to steer China's process of modernization, determined by dynamic market forces, largely unchallenged, in the interests of the ruling alliance of economic and political elites. In terms of increasing economic efficiency, economic policy crisis management strategies and the adaptive capacity of development planning proved invaluable. In fact—admittedly from an instrumentally rational perspective—during the different phases of reform, China's political system was effectively reorganized through processes of layering and conversion to facilitate institutional learning.

(4) *Global integration.* The historical account of China's global economic integration proved that the country's very high GDP growth rates, long lasting by any international standard, should be viewed as the exception rather than the rule. Here, this work introduces a neglected explanatory factor: without incorporating the favorable global economic and East Asian situation since the 1970s into the analysis, it is impossible to provide a convincing account for the unusually long growth period. On the contrary, an analysis that either fails to consider or only takes limited account of the external causes of the country's economic dynamism risks consisting of biased generalizations and either recounting a condensed success story

of liberal marketization or taking a state-centric perspective that hypostatizes the Chinese leviathan into an omnipotent, visionary driver of the economy.

The emergence of a labor-intensive export-oriented growth regime in the PRC from the 1980s coincided with a phase of extensive global free trade and a new international division of labor. For mainland China, surrounded by the dynamic East Asian economies and companies owned by overseas Chinese entrepreneurs, the concomitant restructuring provided favorable conditions for the policy of reform and opening up. Moreover, in the following decades, the Chinese economy was able to profit from an advanced transnationalization of production and the weak growth or overaccumulation of capital in the old centers of global capitalism, including Japan. Foreign investment promoted the country's domestic economic dynamism and technological upgrading, and, through tax revenues, it underpinned the regulatory capacity of state institutions. At the same time, Chinese producers took advantage of the demand potential of the North. It is also particularly thanks to consumer demand in the major OECD countries that the Chinese economy has not suffered any serious slump since the 1990s.

On the whole, unlike the past experience of other developing and newly industrialized countries, in the PRC, the selective opening up of the economy and its integration into global supply chains has not restricted the government's freedom to act. This paved the way for greater authority of the Chinese state, which controls criteria for market access but is also acting with increasing self-confidence in terms of foreign economic policy.[7]

China's variegated capitalism is now to a large extent, that is, no longer solely in the coastal regions, integrated (albeit selectively) into transnational economic networks. As Chinese firms frequently still function as a subordinate part of transnational brand companies whose products are assembled in China—and are thus dependent on enterprises owned by "patriotic" ethnic Chinese and other foreign companies—in order to be able to paint an accurate overall picture of China's new capitalism, we must take into consideration the evolution of the China Circle (see Chapter 2) and the country's global market integration.

Paradoxes of Prosperity

On balance, adaptive state-permeation has so far acted as an anchor of stability for China's dynamic development. Even Chinese intellectuals who are critical of the party-state quite plausibly describe the country's economic success as the (often unintended and thus paradoxical) realization of the original socioeconomic objectives of Maoism, which, above all, focused on the development and modernization of national productive forces. China has, to all intents and purposes, contrary to the West's "misinterpretation," "achieved its erstwhile objective" (H. Wang 2010, my translation).

However, and this may be an argument against overoptimistic growth forecasts, some of the development trends of Chinese capitalism identified over the course of this study are threatening to undermine China's relatively consistent growth path. It is precisely the features that are deemed to be sources of economic success that also have their downsides. Here we are referring to characteristics such as the local developmental states that are fixated on achieving economic growth as well as policies that ignore wage issues and the lack of a functioning civil society. These drawbacks include (1) problems of socioeconomic development, (2) limitations of state steering capacity, and (3) limitations of Chinese-style subordination.

(1) *Problems of socioeconomic development.* In order to mitigate the effects of capitalist modernization and owing to the global lack of consumer demand, since 2008, the Chinese central government has been pushing for a comprehensive rebalancing of the economy toward a greater focus on the domestic market, technological upgrading, and a socially just economic system. However, it has not yet proven possible to successfully achieve this aim. The significant obstacles to this include the preservation of the low-wage regime and the tendency toward overinvestment and speculative overheating. One reason for this is that domestic and international companies continue to have a vested interest in low wages and taxes and the associated competitive edge for the foreseeable future, and local governments as actors in the powerful local growth alliances are likely to remain prepared to accommodate these needs. While social polarization threatens the growth of domestic demand, the combination of competition-driven accumulation and the decentralization of political governance has exacerbated a trend toward overinvestment and duplication of investment, as is evidenced by the recent ramifications of the country's major economic stimulus packages. Overcapacity, particularly in heavy industry, threatens to bring significant job losses in its wake. According to official statements, there will be millions jobs lost by 2020, due either to closures or to a reduction in capacity.

Here, the country's expansive monetary policy appears to be one of the causes of speculative bubbles in the real estate markets. Although the government attempts to contain overheating in this area, the limitations of national intervention in volatile markets become clear, however. Additionally, because the government and interest groups in the financial sector deem the comprehensive protection of the major state-owned banks as sacrosanct, the problem of banks being "too big to fail" threatens to become critical. In the next few years, a rise in nonperforming loans is likely to increase the susceptibility of the financial system to crisis. This problem also affects informal credit relationships.

It is self-evident that more research on the rebalancing of the Chinese economy and destabilizing dynamics is required. The following are topics of interest here: development policies in rural China, the growth potential of the domestic economy, the results of promoting innovation capacity, the medium-term effects of expanding the social security system and of monetary and fiscal policy measures that mitigate the overheating in the manufacturing industry or in the real estate market, and administrative reforms that, inter alia, are a response to the imbalance between state revenues and expenditures.

(2) *Limitations of state steering capacity.* The overinvestment tendencies in China are reminiscent of typical capitalist crisis mechanisms and are, essentially, an expression of the anarchy of the Chinese economy and its integration into volatile global markets. In addition to this, policies are implemented by competition-driven state institutions that, in some circumstances, exacerbate the crisis. There is evidence of tension between the government's attempts at political steering and the reality of the decentralized economy.

My intention has been to show that the party-state's methods of governance, frequently classed as comparatively efficient—in other words, the attempt of a power elite that refers to itself as communist to make the state to a certain extent precisely the instrument Friedrich Engels had critically referred to as the "ideal collective capitalist"—is thwarted by the very same competition mechanisms that motivated the party-state in the first place. Because local governments repeatedly go against the plan and contradict or undermine national policies or implement a modified version of them, the recent ambitious attempts at recentralizing political regulation result in contradictory effects and adaptive problems. Despite its extensive regulatory capacity, the party-state has thus far failed to gain full control over risky domestic competition to attract business and investment and the associated high-risk growth and finance policies pursued by the subnational governments and financial market actors. The large number of uncoordinated centers of decision making, combined with the uneven levels of development across the country, have resulted in and perpetuated greatly divergent interests.

The dismantling of market barriers in China has been accompanied by central government attempts to link central and subnational bodies in creating a regulatory framework for market activity. The uneven pace of development across the country and the different preferences of the various subnational growth alliances call this framework into question, however. This is also a key factor in understanding the changing relationship between the party and the state over time, in the course of the transition to the Xi administration, for instance, and during its attempts to strengthen the party's power. Because party and state functions are carried out not autonomously by political actors at the central government level but, rather, in conjunction with various different groups of actors at different levels, this repeatedly gives rise to political deadlocks when it comes to practical decisions about action to be taken. This constitutes a distinctive form of the joint-decision trap (Scharpf 1985). In line with my research framework, the latter is not primarily attributed to organizational weaknesses but is linked to the consequences of catch-up capitalist development. Additionally, another research assumption has been substantiated, according to which, in contrast to more stringent laws, soft regulations that are open to interpretation are still of great significance in China.

Overall, therefore, limits to the central state's capacity to take action are revealed, and there is evidence that the regulatory capacity of the central state varies across different policy fields. In recent years, the country's growing sovereign debt has further emphasized these barriers. Moreover, internal party differences in terms of economic policy orientation have recently come to the fore again: the position President Xi Jinping presents demands the end of excessively loose lending practices as well as the repayment of company and local government debt (referred to as "supply-side structural reforms"). Here, in the interests of long-term financial stability, a slight downturn in GDP growth is also tolerated. New growth stimuli are expected to then emerge from the promotion of knowledge- and technology-intensive industries. However, within the party and (primarily local) public administration, there are still a number of advocates for an expansive monetary policy that, in the medium term, promises to maintain high growth rates (see Naughton 2016 on the inconsistent introduction of the supply-side structural reforms and policies addressing local debt). An increasing number of proponents of this position can be found among the administrative cadres who still belong to the previous generation of leaders under Hu Jintao and Wen Jiabao. Since coming to power, President Xi has removed many of the members of this group from office. Xi's anticorruption campaigns played a significant role here.

Nevertheless, especially with regard to the dense "cronyist" networks of economic coordination in China, there is evidence of increasingly frequent tensions and conflict between political and capital fractions. This is reflected in the serious recentralization efforts made by the Xi administration since 2013 to address them. It remains to be seen whether anticorruption measures will only limit economically harmful types of corruption or also adversely affect "productive" cronyism in local growth alliances, as these measures might hamper intra-elite economic decision making in this authoritarian form of capitalism (for a pessimistic outlook, see Pei 2016; for a more optimistic view, see J. Zhu and Zhang 2017).

(3) *Limitations of Chinese-style subordination.* Without a doubt, the reforms that triggered gradual shifts in the social structure of the power elites and the emergence of a consumption-oriented middle class were frequently accompanied by a reinforcement of the powerlessness of the lower social strata. It is therefore hardly surprising that only a small number of China experts explore the limitations of subordination and the potential for change "from below," all the more so in view of the continuing impact of the legacy of elite-centric research on totalitarianism. Statements by prominent scholars such as Minxin Pei illustrate this: "any change is apt to come from the top rather than the bottom" (Pei 2009). However, although the reform processes was essentially shaped "from the top" and through power struggles within the elite, even at an early stage, social discontent and protest created a backdrop for the political endeavors to develop labor law and welfare state standards. This suggests the need to examine the limits of subordination and the emergence of social opposition, and to document the shortcomings of the quasicorporatist balance of interests.

Admittedly, unlike employers in China, the government is endeavoring to complete the country's fragmented quasicorporatism and to effectively balance the various interests. However, the authoritarian social partnership strategies of the Chinese state are not very effective because workers remain severely institutionally underrepresented in the labor system. The working population should only be in a position to increase its consumption and should not be boosted to an oppositional force. The implementation of labor laws and norms not only founders owing to the heterogeneity of industrial production regimes, but it is also impeded by local growth alliances with a vested interest in low wages and poor working conditions. The central government currently finds itself in a conflict of interests, apparently irresolvable for the time being, between a massive upgrading of the aforementioned standards and the competitive edge resulting from low labor costs. Consequently, the government's labor policy measures (more so than its recent comprehensive social policy measures) represent only a system of halfhearted aftercare, in other words, crisis management, primarily implemented once conflicts have already arisen. The government primarily shifts the responsibility for social conflict onto the legal system and channels that conflict through arbitration procedures. Overall, the current power elite represents a type of benevolent neo-authoritarianism that advocates for limited reforms but rejects more far-reaching reforms, such as of the ACFTU or the internal *hukou* migration regime.

By the same token, the production sphere continues to be treated as taboo. The tolerance of a few isolated protests alone is not enough to effectively counteract the huge power imbalances in the production sphere. For the time being, a significant upgrading of collective rights and arguably the most effective labor rights of freedom of association and the right to strike is unlikely, however (C. Lee 2016). Particularly the protests conducted by migrant workers, now the biggest group in the labor force, have the potential to escalate precisely because there is no functioning balance of interests or intact systems of negotiation. The continued absence of an autonomous civil society may very well increasingly be an obstacle to growth here. In the medium term, this might even endanger the political status quo. Although the central government strives to achieve social cohesion using all available means—including guiding principles such as "harmony" or the "Chinese dream," which are used like a semantic glue to hold the fabric of society together and create a sense of common identity—it remains doubtful whether these principles will in fact provide longer-term protection against the shortfalls of Chinese corporatism, social tension, and also the uncontrolled development of social demands and further needs for recognition.

Theoretical Implications for Political Economic
and China Studies

To help explain the key characteristics of the PRC's socioeconomic system
as well as the dynamics and paradoxes of China's development path, a range
of theoretical considerations and assumptions have proven useful.

However, before I summarize these again, I would like to make two
observations. First, several innovative concepts from China studies that I
will not describe in more detail again at this juncture have proven very
helpful. For example, the concepts of fragmented corporatism or tripartism
with four parties were valuable for my analysis of the corporate sector,
industrial relations, and business associations. Moreover, observations on
the distinctive policy cycles of authoritarian pluralism and the adaptive
capacity of institutions contributed to our understanding of the transformation of statehood in China and helped us to move away from the busi-
ness/state or market/plan dichotomies. In fact, China should be viewed as a
prime example of entrepreneurship through state actors and public-private
networks.

Second, the present study, in which I chiefly outline the dynamics of
the capitalist-driven process of modernization in China, ultimately represents only modest groundwork for more in-depth empirical analyses in
the future. Further studies might, for instance, determine more specific
causalities and cross effects between institutions and/or enable individual
variables to be plausibly extracted to help illustrate and explain different
development trends. The historical account of the reform process and the
three groups of actors described in this study as essential to that process
thus contribute to our understanding of China's complex reality and can,
at best, serve as a starting point for more specific comparative and also
sectoral studies.[8]

All in all, the findings of my historical account support the hypotheses
in my extended research framework in which I attempt to plausibly synthe-
size a far-reaching assumption on the role of the universal driving forces of
a variegated capitalist world system. I do this by analyzing the historical
periodization of capitalism and by examining various institutional parameters and constellations of actors. The research framework developed here
can be seen as a contribution to political economy, which provides an
insight into the similarities and differences between political economies
based on a combined analysis of economic and noneconomic factors. This

results in the following implications for research on capitalism and on China:

(1) Transnational analysis has proven useful in avoiding biased generalizations. China's international and transnational integration provides a key prerequisite for explaining the country's growth dynamics, particularly as the transnational character of "Chinese" capitalism and the significant networks of ethnic Chinese, for instance, make it impossible to delineate along national borders. The fact that China became the most attractive production location in the world precisely when real accumulation in the old centers tailed off suggests a correlation that is not mentioned in either liberal marketization success stories or state-centric perspectives. The approach presented here thus supports theoretical assumptions emphasizing the necessity of no longer limiting analyses to national but also taking international complementarities into account when it comes to studies of different forms of capitalism (Bohle and Greskovits 2009, 380). Because temporal-spatial factors promoted the country's socioeconomic growth, the importance of the time factor in profiting from an ideal combination of cost-efficient labor, functional infrastructures of production, and investment from abroad is also underlined.

(2) Drawing on the concept of a heterogeneous capitalist world system that attaches importance to the competition- and crisis-driven rhythms of the global economy, preference is given to a research approach that, in a first step, focuses on similarities between national varieties of capitalism. This analytical strategy helps to refute culturalist concepts of a unique "Chinese" socioeconomic system, for example. At the same time, in a next step, I conduct an analysis of differences and specifics of capitalist development in China. The latter constitute the varying outcomes of a global, capitalist-driven mode of socialization. National/regional economies do not simply converge into a homogenous global economic unit. A network of distinct but connected capitalisms characterized by continual processes of differentiation and adaption constitute the world system.

In a further step, the fundamental drivers of capitalism in the present work are analyzed as being subject to phase-specific variation—these include the state's enhanced role in the economy from the 1930s and the marketization and liberalization tendencies from the 1970s. During its protocapitalist phase after 1949, the Chinese economy was already characterized by imperatives to act in a way that resembled ways in other undeveloped economies and developmental states during the period of state interventionism from the 1930s. Under Deng Xiaoping, however, profound institutional change took place, which was linked to the global liberalization phase set in motion by the 1970s crisis. The fact that this global "reform movement" in China in no way triggered a transition to a textbook liberal market economy is, in turn, the result of entrenched traditions of an exceptionally strong state, a party elite relatively unchallenged by opposition groups, and other path dependencies. As in other capitalisms (in Germany or Japan, for instance), in China, the overarching dynamics of liberalization broke fresh ground in a distinctive manner.

(3) The findings of the present study thus point to the need to link theoretical insights and tools from the disciplines of comparative political economy (CPE) and international political economy (IPE). The emphasis on global and phase-specific drivers of capitalism, mostly derived from IPE studies, should not substitute in-depth comparative research on capitalism and the analysis of distinct institutional regimes but should be combined with these latter approaches in order to provide a proper insight into the regional/national and phase-specific idiosyncrasies of capitalism. I attempted to illustrate these links in the context of Chinese economic policy, the corporate sector, and the financial system.

(4) The present analysis of the outcomes of China's capitalist development has confirmed the assumption that liberal and coordinated market economies must be complemented by other (efficient) varieties of capitalism. The analysis also proved a range of other assumptions:

The focus on the role of and interactions between the three inhomogeneous groups of actors—companies, party-state decision makers, and workers—contributed to a deeper understanding of the PRC's unstable dynamics. While some experts still lean toward elite-centric generalizations, a focus on the role of the subordinated segments of the population and on (inter- and intra-) class conflict can provide additional insights into the course of reform, also in the PRC's authoritarian system. As various examples demonstrate—the social conflict in the late 1970s, in 1989, and from the 1990s onward—these interactions impacted on the direction the reforms took. The same applies to less turbulent phases such as the transfer of power to the Hu/Wen administration at the beginning of this century: although the local public-private growth alliances did not seriously advocate for a change in political direction, nevertheless, this change did come about, against a backdrop of growing social discontent and thus a stronger emphasis on the role of the state as a social equalizer.

By providing a historical-sociological account, the present study underlines the importance of how socioeconomic crises trigger reforms. The reform process took the form of crisis-induced institutional change. Important measures implemented by the central government—such as the reform of the financial system, of corporate organization, or of the labor system—should be interpreted as reactions to smaller sectoral and larger overarching crises. Approaches from crisis and conflict theory are therefore useful in this context. Finally, this has an impact on the analysis of the most recent social tensions that suggest that in a situation where high growth and profit rates bring about only marginal trickle-down effects especially in the interests of migrant workers, there is a lower probability of this situation becoming permanent.

Furthermore, more recent tools from the social sciences that describe and distinguish between different modes and mechanisms of gradual institutional change contribute to a systematic understanding of China's process of reform. While in the 1970s and 1980s, the processes of erosion of the classical Maoist political style, self-definition, and institutions symbolized relevant mechanisms of change, over time, the mode of institutional layering became the predominant form. In a context where establishing radical new institutions was not a simple undertaking, processes of layering formal institutions "from below" (through innovative informal practices of the new de facto private entrepreneurs, for instance) then led to institutional conversion and reforms "from above." Evidence of this can be seen in many local pilot projects that resulted in the creation of institutions alongside and in interaction with existing ones and ultimately, by rolling the projects out across the country, effected substantial changes in the country's institutional architecture. These changes were fostered by competition-driven performance incentives and/or a commitment to company profit maximization. In contrast, the drift phenomenon resulting in the dissolution of institutions now appears to be less relevant than was initially assumed in my research framework. Rather, significant changes appear to have taken place by selectively and creatively learning from a wide variety of sources such as the Silicon Valley model, advanced technologies, or Western corporate governance and social security systems, and via the mechanism of borrowing, in other words, through the successful reintegration of talented entrepreneurs or researchers who had studied and/or worked abroad. The theoretical consequence is that political economy analyses must take the link between path-dependent and path-shaping processes into account.

Ultimately, the notion of uneven, combined, and interconnected development processes has proven to be useful first, to account for China's socioeconomic leap from the 1970s onward, which was also a side effect of development advances in the major global economies: China's political economy was able to profit considerably from the latter (by employing tried and tested technologies and business models, for instance, as well as through foreign investment). Second, a focus on the uneven levels of development across the country and the heterogeneous production regimes provided information on the specific competitive advantages of the PRC. The domestic competition for business and investment is therefore manifested primarily as a struggle for favorable tax and wage systems. Further, the concept of combined development also helped to substantiate the connections between modern forms of economic activity and indigenous traditions, which ensured that business activities progressed relatively efficiently. This enabled me to interpret specific sociocultural resources of China's growth dynamics, such as the *guanxi* networks or traditions of local experimentation, in a nonculturalist manner. My findings demonstrated that older traditions had been reinterpreted and then transformed into modern forms.

(5) With regard to the role of the state and nonmarket institutions, there are a number of theoretical implications that should be integrated into the analysis:

Generally, I have attempted to illustrate that noneconomic institutions must be taken into account in order to explain economic development trends. If it holds true that universal drivers of capitalist development, or phase-specific versions of them, can be seen in China, but the country's political economy continues to exhibit distinctive characteristics, research must also explicitly address the differences between the noneconomic institutions in various countries and regions, so as to be able to explain differing outcomes of capitalist development. Consequently, studies on entrepreneurial activity, for instance, must go beyond a one-sided neoclassical or neo-Schumpeterian understanding of the innovative capacity of the individual entrepreneur and also refer to the institutional and organizational conditions provided, inter alia, by the government: "Entrepreneurialism should be conceived as a more collective process in contrast to the Schumpeterian mainstream. Even when employers see the role of local governments to be of very limited and tangential importance to success, businesses are in truth shaped by numerous supportive institutions" (ten Brink 2011a, 15; see also Deutschmann 2009a).

As emphasized, the Chinese reform process led to a distinctive symbiosis of social development that paradoxically combines aspects that had previously been ascribed to competing projects of modernity—marketization and the party-state. For this reason, we have to reject the assumption of an abrupt transition from a planned economy to a market economy. In reality, China's institutional regime underwent a transformation process that, from the 1970s onward, culminated in a new polycentric mixture of plan, market, and other informal and interpersonal forms of coordination. There are no clear boundaries between public and private institutions, where the separation between free market, sovereign state, and civil society that is typical of Western liberal democracies (although ultimately also often only ideal-typical) occurs analogously. Given this, a logical research strategy appears to be not to assume a strict separation of state and market activity, but rather a semipermeable dividing line. The term *public-private alliance* therefore expressed not only the fact that the established core areas of responsibility of the Chinese government now included the attempts to coordinate economic activity and that government bodies cultivate close links with private actors but that a certain number of state officials also become capitalist actors themselves. Moreover, economic planning can be perfectly compatible with capitalist-driven development. Under certain circumstances, the absence of a powerful autonomous civil society that could modify the substance of government activity, state and private actors emerge as two sides of one and the same capitalist-driven modernization process. Because, under certain conditions, drivers of capitalism have a similar effect on state and private actors—this is abstracted from the various reproduction criteria of the government and enterprises—from this perspective, the owner and manager function can arguably also be assumed by a self-proclaimed member of the communist *nomenklatura*, although these may personally profit less from the wealth generated than private shareholders of a joint-stock company or managers of large corporations.[9]

At a lower level of abstraction, the present study also identifies some methods and mechanisms of government activity that contribute to an understanding of the Chinese multilevel system of governance and could be useful in future for comparative studies, particularly of other nonliberal states and large emerging countries. These include long-term political programs and plans; the importance of local pilot projects and the potential to roll these out nationwide; "regulation for competition," in other words, extensive regulation with the aim of market expansion and promoting competition (inter alia, with the support of sector-specific regulatory authorities); and informal negotiation processes at various administrative levels.

It should also be noted that Chinese capitalism, where interpersonal negotiation has become a crucial tool for consensus making and decision making, is based to a larger extent than in developed OECD countries on networked coordination and demonstrates a lesser degree of formal organization. Going beyond approaches that argue that numerous, mostly small, specialized, private corporate networks spearhead the upgrading of forms of late-developing capitalism, the present work focuses on the significance of state-permeated network structures. Thus, this finding supports the assumption of the value of nonmarket forms of coordination in identifying specific features of capitalism.

Another consequence of the study is that the case of China serves as evidence for the diversity of forms of state intervention. These facts should feed into the discussion on the transformations of the modern state (at least in newly industrialized and large emerging countries). Over time, an increase in the political opportunities and mechanisms for intervention is evident, which contradicts concepts of a "postnational" world or a declining importance of the nation-state. While the mechanisms for intervention at the disposal of the first "late developers" in the nineteenth century, such as Prussia or the German Reich, were still largely limited to influencing the business environment (including through customs, subsidies, and the establishment of monetary policy through the foundation of the Reichsbank), by the twentieth century, the state had more potential room to maneuver. In the phase of state interventionism from the 1930s, particularly prevalent in East Asia, the trend went beyond the manipulation of the business context and moved toward direct replacement of entrepreneurial activity, investment control through government development plans, and industrial policy. This was made possible by a massive increase in administrative capacity and economic acumen. There were also more opportunities to implement labor and social policies through corporatist arrangements. Further, looking more specifically at China, we can see that the mechanisms for crisis management were enhanced from the 1980s, for instance, through party-led campaigns. The same applies to the attempt to organize a controlled opening up and selective integration of the economy into the global market. The power elite also combined governance methods that go beyond the narrower scope of traditional hierarchical state intervention—as mentioned, imperative and indicative economic policies amalgamated with (informal) network- and market-based mediation and negotiation processes.

Finally, the findings presented here have another theoretical implication that is related to the unstable dynamics of capitalist social orders in general. Using mechanisms of experimental adaptation, the process of decentralization in China created a policy regime in which party-state actors play a dominant role to this day. Because this regime is superimposed with diverse external influences, however, it is not subject to unopposed hegemonic state control. Destabilization processes instigated at the national and international level challenge an optimism about the state's regulatory capacity that might be inferred from my analysis only at first glance. Therefore, an appropriate research strategy appears not to reduce political actors to rational action in response to inefficiencies but rather to incorporate crisis-induced insecurity and ambivalence to the behavior of these actors.

A final conclusion can be formulated as follows. In my view, China's current development contributes to a problematic global constellation. A situation prevails where, in capitalist democracies, the "marriage" between capitalism and democracy threatens to disintegrate, where social scientists justifiably diagnose a depletion of democracy or postdemocratic processes ("governance by experts" and uncontrollable supranational agencies) and point to a future where conformist behavior is again in greater demand. Here, China's capitalism, deemed, albeit (still) implicitly, to be the most efficient economic system of the present day, could be stylized as a role model not only for emerging countries but even for highly developed industrial societies.[10]

Consequently, a daunting realization might be that Lenin's earlier conclusion, essentially in anticipation of works by Gramsci on the theory of hegemony, that the "democratic republic [is] the best possible political shell for capitalism" (Lenin 1970, 15), has recently been refuted before the eyes of the world precisely by its purported epigones. In other words, there is a risk that a view of capitalism without democracy as the most beneficial "shell" of economic development might gain influence in the South and West. A further use for the present study might therefore be to oppose such views. This might be done, referring to the exceptionally favorable circumstances of the Chinese "economic miracle," even before enlisting arguments from theories of democracy and normative considerations, by establishing that, in all probability, such a "miracle" will not be repeated in future and is equally unlikely to continue to exist in the long term.

NOTES

Introduction

1. In terms of theoretical literature, I have mostly remained faithful to the original German version of the book. For this reason, very little new work is introduced. The empirical parts of the book, in contrast, have been updated (particularly Chapter 3).

2. On the transformation of the economic system, corporate organization, and the financial system, see, for example, Naughton (2007), Nee (2005), Nolan (2004), Jinglian Wu (2005), and Zweig (2002); on the party-state and political system, see Brodsgaard and Zheng (2004), Fewsmith (2008), Goldman and MacFarquhar (1999a), Lam (2006), Lieberthal (1995), Saich (2004), Shambaugh (2009b), D. Yang (2004), and Zheng (2007); on industrial relations, see A. Chan (1993) and C. Lee (2007).

3. See, for example, K. Chang, Lüthje, and Luo (2008), Heberer and Schubert (2009), Heilmann (2004), Holbig and Reichenbach (2005), and Schubert (2001a).

4. On comparative capitalism research, see, for example, Amable (2003), Coates (2000, 2005), and Streeck (2009); from a regulation theory perspective, see Hollingsworth and Boyer (1997) and Jessop and Sum (2006); on economic sociology, see Beckert, Diaz-Bone, and Ganßmann (2007), Fligstein (2001), and Swedberg (2005).

5. See Arrighi et al. (2003), Beeson (2009), Breslin (2007b), Bunker and Ciccantell (2007), Hung (2009a), ten Brink (2011b, 2014b), van der Pijl (2006), and Zweig and Chen (2007).

6. I am fully aware that the insights presented here are drawn, in part, from quite different theoretical traditions and consequently cannot be combined arbitrarily. In my research framework, I therefore distinguish between theoretical assumptions and heuristic tools and concepts that I borrow from specific theories without automatically adopting their wider theoretical perspectives.

7. In the present study, the terms "workers" and "working class" are used in a broad sense, encompassing people in paid employment in the agricultural, manufacturing, and service sectors.

8. At certain relevant junctures in this text, I employ Chinese terms using the Pinyin romanization system.

9. In China, the delineation between market, sovereign state, and civil society that is typical (albeit ultimately only ideal typical) of liberal democracies does not appear analogously. Because of this lack of clear boundaries between private and public institutions, the present work does not so much refer to a delineation as to a differentiation between market and government action. Building on this, I use the term *public-private regime* to capture the

reality that one of the well-known key mandates of the Chinese government is to ensure far-reaching coordination of economic activity. The term also expresses the close ties between government agencies and private entities and the fact that political actors are occasionally involved in business activity as well.

10. I view this term as an analytical concept (see Nölke 2011), unlike authors and political actors who employ the term "state capitalism" with a political objective in mind, in order to contrast the advantages of the "free" market economies in the West with the disadvantages of the "aggressive" state-capitalist regimes in the East and South (see Bremmer 2010).

11. In the present study, I do not use classical hypotheses testing. However, we can formulate a number of general test criteria that could falsify the hypotheses outlined: if the drivers of capitalism did not play such a central role in the reform process, there would have to be evidence of pre- and/or noncapitalist dimensions of action. First, with respect to the imperative to accumulate, the more traditional subsistence orientation or a conscious steering of growth would then predominate. Second, with regard to competition and individual profit orientation, on the other hand, cooperative and/or solidary courses of action and democratic planning might prevail. Moreover, a premodern system of estates or a grass-roots democratic structure, for instance, would eclipse modern class structures, state institutions and other noneconomic relations would be overshadowed by premodern or also self-determined courses of action. At the same time, the theory of state-permeated capitalism would be invalidated by a simple introduction of liberal market mechanisms. The proposition that external factors must be taken into account to explain the economic dynamics would be refuted by the predominance of endogenous factors, and the notion of continuity in change would be falsified by the significance of radical social schisms. Similarly, the hypothesis on the paradoxes of China's economic development would also be invalidated should relatively coherent development prevail.

12. To shed some light on the labyrinthine institutional change in the PRC with a view to making it easier for readers not involved in China research to understand the historical developments, at numerous different junctures in Chapters 2 and 3, I cite historical accounts and illustrations. Further, for the sake of accessibility, the individual dimensions of the new Chinese capitalism are depicted schematically separately at various points; a certain level of redundancy is therefore unavoidable.

Chapter 1

1. Studies on the development of Chinese industrial relations and the traditions of culturalism in China research are discussed in more detail later in this chapter. More observations can be found in ten Brink (2012a).

2. A more in-depth argument with a greater focus on political struggles and interest groups within the party-state is provided by A. Liu (1986), for instance. As well as studies drawing on theories of totalitarianism, there are also analyses of the unintended consequences of the totalitarian control of the country. According to modernization theory assumptions, confronted with the problem of industrial growth, the party-state was forced to abandon the lion's share of its revolutionary enthusiasm and draw on modern methods of development. This included conventional bureaucratic mechanisms for promoting industrial growth, for instance (see Field 1976).

3. Research on Eastern Bloc countries impacted China research, with Eastern European social scientists such as Kornai and Szelényi publishing advanced studies starting in the 1970s.

Here, research interests centered on topics dealing with the introduction of market economic principles. This included, for instance, the problem of soft budget constraints in public enterprises (Kornai 1992; Szelényi 1982) as well as allocative inefficiencies in planned economies, which had led the forces of reform within the apparatus of power to combine elements of central economy planning with market mechanisms (Stark and Nee 1989; for more information on the importance of market economic principles, in Yugoslavia or the GDR, for example, see Selden 1993; Gey 1985; Solga 1995).

4. An overview of variants of this hypothesis, which range from "socialist" developmental state to "corporatist, regulatory state" and "local corporatist state," can be found in Howell (2006).

5. The same applies to some extent to new institutional economics and evolutionary political economics.

6. Institutional complementarities, as understood in this book, embody the functional institutional cross effects that determine the viability of different types of capitalism from the perspective of dependencies between several institutional forms. The complementarity of various institutions is the historical result of experimenting with hybrid forms proven to be complementary. These observations have similarities with the concept of a systematic congruency as "historical lost property" in regulation theory (see Lipietz 1985).

7. Besides "strong" complementary connections, there are also other "weaker" forms of reciprocal compatibility: "The connections across realms of the economy may be weaker than complementarity, and should also comprise compatibilities, where the existence of one institution does not interfere with or impede another" (Schneider 2008, 19–20).

8. Here, the hypothesis of institutional complementarities in capitalist systems to some extent reflects the assumption that a diversity of modernization models exists. Incidentally, the term "diversity of modernity" is more fitting than "multiple modernities" when it comes to expressing the fact that the different varieties of modernity are to be seen as variations on or modifications of a basic common model (Arnason 2008).

9. The valorization of money or capital in this case appears to be the primary objective of production; the satisfaction of needs is a secondary by-product.

10. The relationship here is based on a "non-traditionalist super-norm": "Actors in a modern-capitalist context, as they confront institutionalized expectations, find themselves encouraged and enabled to proceed on the premise that everything that is not explicitly forbidden is allowed. In traditionalist settings, by comparison, the governing premise is the opposite: Everything that is not allowed is forbidden" (Streeck 2010b, 17).

11. The impact of these forces on other social and personal relationships, on alienation, powerlessness, or individualization phenomena, etc., is not included in the present work.

12. In a similar vein, albeit from the perspective of actor-centered differentiation theory, the term "functionally different *capitalist* societies" has recently been used (Schimank 2009, 256, my translation).

13. "We cannot honestly claim that the British and Dutch East Indian Companies and their subsidiaries were pure market institutions. Physical coercion through military and paramilitary forces were just as powerful in forming market capitalism as the stock exchange. And we should not forget that the neoconservative market economy model was the result of political action driven by ideology and things were no different in the nineteenth century with the Corn Laws and free trade" (Tamás 2007, 11, my translation).

14. This also draws on older insights, which assume the possibility of the parallel expansion of market and state bureaucratic structures and/or private corporate structures converging on bureaucratic structures in the modern era (see Castoriadis 1988; Tilly 1992; Shonfield 1965).

15. This also shows that my research framework focuses on a critical normative social tradition, the essence of which is summarized in the notion "that the process of social rationalization is disrupted or biased by social structural properties that are unique to capitalism, making pathologies" that result in the loss of intact social relations inevitable (Honneth 2007, 45, my translation).

16. The approach used in this work is reminiscent of Boyer's differentiation of five institutional forms (2005, 13–14; see also Becker 2002; ten Brink 2014b).

17. The following dimensions, presented as ideal types, appear in different historical phases of capitalism in diverse combinations. This also applies to the hierarchy between the various dimensions, i.e., historical circumstances can emerge in which certain dimensions have such power that they dominate other basic components (as expressed for instance in the theory of state capitalism or the notion of a finance-dominated accumulation regime: see Boyer 2000).

18. At this point, it should be reiterated that legal ownership and de facto rights to control the means of production in capitalist systems can disintegrate to the degree that the legal owners, fully or partially, voluntarily or involuntarily, accede their control rights to others (managers, states, possibly also bodies of codetermination). For this reason, state nationalization of business enterprises often embodies a change only in the form of appropriation of the surplus product (Solga 1995, 58).

Chapter 2

1. In the mid-nineteenth century, against a backdrop of internal stagnation and external intervention, Chinese civilization fell into a deep crisis that continued until 1949. The capitalist global economy that was evolving during the same period and the transformation of the geopolitics of modern states linked to this process triggered the reciprocal, uneven, and combined interaction between societies at different levels of development on an unprecedented scale. From then on, different civilizations or cultures were heavily influenced by the norms and compulsion to act of capitalist modernity. From this perspective, even the history of China in the first half of the twentieth century can be described as a form of modernization driven by (proto)capitalist imperatives, if characterized by schisms. This process assimilated a rich civilizational tradition that, although abandoned to some extent under Mao, became more prominent again after 1978, albeit in a more modern guise.

2. The "Marxism-Leninism" of the 1940s and after was no longer the expression of an organized anticapitalist endeavor to bring about an international revolution led by the working class. Instead, for the CCP, it served as a model of successful national development. In this sense, Sino-Marxism constituted a specific form of the attempt at party-led national modernization (Arnason 2008, 403–7; see also Arnason 2003b).

3. From a similar perspective, Aoki refers to historical parallels between China's and Japan's development. These similarities were evident despite the different points in time at which that development occurred (Aoki 2011).

4. This perspective has also been useful for the analysis of societies organized predominantly on the basis of private capitalism ever since major corporations have been shaping

economic structures, and thus the legal ownership and the effective power of disposition over production has been separated.

5. "After the Kuomintang's shattering blow to China's Communist Party (CCP) in 1927, 'proletariat' in communist writings came to mean little more than the party itself. The CCP scarcely involved urban classes at all after 1927, and the actual proletarian membership was less than one per cent in Mao's period of leadership before 1948. The cities in general became the rearguard of the revolution, not its vanguard" (Harris 1971, 174). The strategy of an agrarian revolution, the alliances and splits with the nationalist Guomindang, the Chinese Civil War from 1945 to 1949, and ultimately, the assumption of power of the CCP in 1949 transformed the party (Leys 1972; Spence 1995).

6. Another explanation for the appeal of Maoism is that the "big dream of all Chinese revolutionaries from the Opium Wars right up to Mao's generation was for the Fatherland to, some day, occupy its rightful leading position among the people of the world once again. This dream was fulfilled with Mao's proclamation at the official ceremony marking the establishment of the People's Republic of China: *the Chinese people have stood up!*" (J. Lin 2009, 57–58, my translation).

7. As Harris writes: "The prime tasks of the revolution become 'class-less': anti-imperialism abroad and industrialization at home, the two aims being, in a nationalist framework, distinguished in no crucial respect from those of other nationalist movements in an underdeveloped country. As in Stalinism, 'proletarian' refers to friends at home, so abroad it tends to identify whatever force opposes imperialism" (Harris 1971, 178). The segments of the population that supported the CCP regime, or at least tolerated it, constituted the "people." Correspondingly, opponents to the regime were subject to a "democratic dictatorship of the people."

8. Of course, a concise description is possible only at the expense of its historical complexity here (for instance, the many tactical and strategic volte-faces of the Maoist government, the internal power struggles etc.).

9. In Chapter 3, I describe the CCP's current philosophy as a form of syncretism—more accurately speaking, however, it had already taken on this character under Mao, albeit in a different form (see also Arnason 2008, 406).

10. Unlike other factions of the apparatus of power, the technocracy was almost exclusively geared toward the rational implementation of goal-oriented projects, which was the basis of a political-ideological pragmatism.

11. Using the example of the elite Tsinghua University in Beijing, Andreas illustrates how the "Red engineers" were able to rise to the status of ruling power elite. In the 1950s, following the Soviet model, the CCP transformed Tsinghua into a "cradle of Red engineers." Initially, the Communist Party elite took control of the university. However, the introduction of a new centralized national entrance examination (*gaokao*) ensured that only a small minority, primarily the offspring of the old intellectual elite, were awarded places at the university (Andreas 2009, 42–44). Thus, using their social capital, the old intellectual elite and their progeny were able to continue to exercise power. During the Cultural Revolution, the system of gaokao was abolished for some years but was restored in 1977 following an arrangement between the party elites and technocratic intellectual layers. Ultimately, this new alliance also excluded the Maoist rebels and the "left-leaning" party factions.

12. Moreover, the Maoists assumed that, during the initial stage of a "socialist" revolution, a hierarchical division of labor, performance-related wage differences, and other remnants of "feudal" or "peasant" conditions would inevitably prevail. They believed that a new

bourgeoisie would be able to emerge from these remnants, provided that the "class war" against these elements was not continued.

13. The years of the Cultural Revolution, launched in 1966, were mainly shaped by policies involving a renunciation of the economic efficiency maxim. These included a reduction in education spending (in part undertaken by the production brigades in rural areas and the factories in the cities), the dominance of army leaders in civilian institutions, and, during the course of the escalating conflict with the USSR from 1969 onward, a dramatic increase in defense spending. At the same time, the ultraleft excesses of the Cultural Revolution also strengthened the factions that advocated markets in the agricultural sector and saw this as a basis for future development of heavy industry.

14. After 1937, Japanese-controlled Manchuria, in particular, became increasingly important. In 1942, it manufactured over half the country's industrial products (in what is now Chinese territory) and produced the lion's share of electrical energy, iron, and cement (Naughton 2007, 48).

15. A complex mix of imperialist pressure and the need for fundamental internal reform put the CCP and the Guomindang both under enormous pressure to adapt. This forced the two parties, despite being adversaries in a number of bitter struggles, to occupy a similar position in a bid to increase the nation's prosperity: "This mixture . . . could be perceived and adapted in different ways by different parts of the Chinese political spectrum. In this sense, the Chinese Communists and the Guomindang represented two sections of a continuum, with considerable overlap" (Arnason 2008, 405–6; on Sun Yat-sen's concepts of central planning, Bian 2005, chapter 7). At the same time, both parties, albeit in different ways, also drew on ideas from previous forces of reform that inspired the 1911 revolution and aimed at a fusion of Sino-Confucian and Western, i.e., nationalist and Marxist-Leninist, ideology. Further, the famous "Mao suit" (which was more a reminder of the country's poverty than egalitarian principles) had, in fact, already been introduced by Sun Yat-sen.

16. One example of this is the Guangzhou Guangzhong Enterprise Group Corp. (see http://www.gzhm.com), a traditional engineering company in southern China that took on the new rulers from the Guomindang after 1949. Within just a few years, the company, now controlled by the central government in Beijing, replaced its old management with internally recruited party cadre. At a very early stage, a stratification of the workforce developed as a result of a wage differential (admittedly at a very low level). From the 1970s, the company was signed over to the city of Guangzhou. After decades of incremental reform resulting in substantial staff cuts, an increase in flexible wage components (achievable through bonuses), and a series of changes in the company's management, this state-owned enterprise has become one of the largest engineering companies in southern China, even concluding a joint venture with a major German company (factory tour, fall 2010).

17. The regionalization of the Chinese economy also has a long history, which dates back to, inter alia, the establishment of the provinces by the Yuan Dynasty during the thirteenth century (Saich 2004, 158). When, at the close of the nineteenth century, it became possible for the first time to speak of a relatively unified domestic market, this market then collapsed against a backdrop of political unrest, a process that escalated with the fall of the Qing Dynasty in 1911.

18. To a certain extent, this helps us understand the fluctuations in published political opinion: if, at certain junctures, local entities were required to be "independent," this move

might be subject to critical attack shortly afterward; if it were decreed for the workers to "assume control," not much later, justified by the argument that the factory management had the "authority," they might order the workers to surrender that control; if adaptation of Western techniques was being emphasized, it became mandatory to play Beethoven during official functions in Beijing, if at the same time, other members of the power elite emphasized the opposite, Beethoven sporadically became a "capitalist composer," etc.

19. Private entrepreneurs might have invested in light industry because the profit rates were higher. Hence, the "private enterprises were eliminated. This was the only way it was possible to ensure that all surplus flowed directly into the government coffers, which could then be distributed in accordance with the state plan" (J. Lin 2009, 64, my translation).

20. As a result of the opening of company archives of the Guangzhou Guangzhong Enterprise Group Corp. mentioned earlier, for example, we have now been able to establish that the policy of the Great Leap Forward was preceded by worker unrest.

21. The geopolitical dimension mentioned earlier plays a key role here: as part of what was known as the "Third Front" strategy, particularly from the 1960s, the government focused on developing new industrial centers in the Chinese hinterland at the cost of the industrial zones on the coast that were highly developed but very difficult to defend militarily (Taube 2007, 185–86). The Cold War and conflict with the USSR had a major impact on Maoist economic policy.

22. The rigidity of the hukou system is reminiscent of British social legislation in the early nineteenth century (Speenhamland laws, for instance) and the restriction of workers' freedom of movement at the time (Polanyi 2001, 81–90; Walker and Buck 2007, 44).

23. As stated by the journalist Edgar Snow, himself not exactly known for being a particularly harsh critic of China, at the beginning of the 1960s, there were also considerable income differences within the Chinese People's Liberation Army (PLA): while privates earned the equivalent of around $US2.50 per month, the generals received between $US190 and $US230, and commanders-in-chief between $US360 and $US400 (Snow 1963, 289).

24. The dependence of the Chinese people on the danwei unit and the population's limited mobility were compensated by certain rights such as a relatively high level of job security and (partial) codetermination rights at lower levels within the company. In actual fact, voluntarist motivations to work under conditions of deprivation frequently proved to be a barrier to the commitment of the employees (Kosta 1985, 237–38).

25. Overall, the union also had a limited welfare function within companies (A. Chan and Unger 2009, 7). Under Mao, they were instructed to act as "transmission belts" for the common good of society and were responsible for the education and training of the workers. During the Cultural Revolution, the ACFTU was dissolved and not legalized again until 1978.

26. What was decisive for these segments of the working class was that they were required to strictly follow a "quantity over quality approach, adhere to the plan, and show obedience to its cadre representatives. The eight-level wage system that determined wages according to status rather than performance and the associated lack of mobility ('iron rice bowl' and lifelong membership of a danwei) meant that, in terms of their way of life, workers were subjected to the *diktat* of their supervisors" (Grobe-Hagel 1990, 32, my translation). Further, a gender-specific division of labor also prevailed.

27. Welfare benefits were tied to employment type. Those with temporary posts received lower benefits than those with permanent posts. "China shared with capitalist economies the

determination of job status based on the degree of welfare benefits" (Smuthkalin 2011, 179; see also Walder 1986, 43–48). This was similar to the situation in other developing countries labeled as capitalist, "particular segments of an . . . urban sector (full-time state enterprise workers, civil servants, Party and military officers) received welfare provisions, to the exclusion of the rest of the population" (Frazier 2011, 93). At the same time, similar to other "socialist" countries, China also had a certain amount of hidden unemployment (Gey 1985, 47).

28. The comparatively low wage differences between unskilled workers, foremen, and managers are also reminiscent of large Japanese enterprises in the 1960s (A. Chan and Unger 2009, 9).

29. The balance of central-state and subnational control of companies fluctuated over time. For example, in 1958, around 85 percent of all centrally controlled industrial enterprises were delegated to the subordinate institutions. In 1962, this step was reversed (Park 1986, 149).

30. Small and medium-sized enterprises (SMEs) were also more important than in the Soviet Union. With regard to labor force mobility, however, the Chinese system was even more impermeable than the Soviet one.

31. Unfortunately, in the case of China, there is a lack of comprehensive literature because these phenomena are often informal, i.e., there are no archivable records of their occurrence, and they are therefore based on anecdotal evidence.

32. Outside the formal planning process, actors frequently coordinated their economic transactions by way of bartering (Lyons 1990, 49). In rural areas—the agricultural sector was controlled by the central state to a far lesser extent—a shadow economy also played a key role.

33. Justin Yifu Lin elucidates by way of example: "The Ministry of Iron and Steel concerned itself with . . . the fulfilment of plan targets for iron and steel. The actual distribution of the steel was not within the remit of the Ministry for Iron and Steel, however. This was the sole responsibility of the government Committee for Economic Affairs. In practice, this centralist approach obviously repeatedly resulted in ludicrous and completely illogical distributions. In order to put an end to this distribution insanity, the government ultimately decreed that the authority for distribution be transferred from the central government ministry to the provinces making them responsible for the distribution of their steel from that point on" (J. Lin 2009, 135). This resulted in fervent investment activity in the provinces, which were, however, faced with insufficient resources and a lack of transport infrastructure.

34. Mao's and Liu's "battle between two concepts" was reminiscent of Soviet discussions in the 1920s, during which Bukharin and Preobrazhensky, for instance, advocated different views on the issue of economic growth, the relationship between agriculture and industry, etc.

35. Of course, unlike in classical Marxism, under Mao, the CCP's class theory exhibited specific "folkloric" features, where, for example, the industrial working class became one of a group of allies of the "people," and the peasantry was granted revolutionary character. Also, sections of the bourgeoisie focused on "national development" were seen to have broken away from the "bureaucratic capitalists" during the initial phase of the PRC because the latter were in alliance with the imperialist powers.

36. Another conflict-ridden legacy of the "ten lost years" of the Cultural Revolution was that the urban masses, who, as part of the final throes of the Down to the Countryside

Movement (*xiafeng*) (the forced displacement of around fifteen million—mainly young—city dwellers to the countryside to work in agriculture), returned to urban areas.

37. To a certain extent, in the provinces, some reforms were already implemented earlier: "For instance, in the late 1970s, Wan Li, then provincial leader of Anhui, initiated rural reforms without clear central policy guidance" (Xie 1993, 316). This change of course was also accelerated by a severe drought in 1978.

38. Subsequently, in countries such as Egypt, Poland, and Yugoslavia, in various Latin American countries from the mid-1970s onward, in India since the 1980s, and in the former Soviet Bloc and parts of Africa in the 1990s, controversial restructuring processes took place.

39. Castoriadis, for instance, describes real socialist states as "bureaucratic" forms of capitalism because, similar to Western forms of capitalism, they entail the unlimited expansion of control over nature and society as well as the boundless and excessive development of forces of production using all available means (Castoriadis 1988; see also Haynes 2002). Completely counter to the aims of socialist transformation, the subjects of production were treated as objects. By forcibly abolishing the difference between the political apparatus of power and civil society, real socialist states were given a totalitarian structure.

40. In the 1950s, Chinese foreign trade was still on the increase. While foreign trade revenues from Western countries declined, a higher share was contributed by the real socialist states, particularly the USSR. As a consequence of the crisis of the Great Leap Forward, the early 1960s saw foreign trade contract (see Hagemann 1990). However, as a result of a new focus on Western industrialized countries and developmental states, foreign trade subsequently grew again. As early as 1965, over half of all Chinese imports (such as machines and equipment) came from OECD countries. Officially, under Mao, foreign suppliers were attempting to separate China from the world market using the double "airlock" system. The foreign trade monopoly of the central state was assigned another airlock at the level of the currency system: the exchange rate of the RMB was set by the state, and the currency was not convertible. To a certain extent, however, even prior to 1978, production surpluses that exceeded the plan targets were exported (oil and foodstuffs), and modern technologies were imported. Between 1970 and 1980, China's export volume increased eightfold (NBS 1983, 420). In actual fact, rising trade volumes and the import of (first primarily American and then Japanese) technologies provided an incentive for economic reforms from the early 1970s onward (Selden 1993, 34–35). At the same time, even before the creation of the first Special Economic Zones (SEZs) in the early 1980s, a number of companies founded by overseas Chinese nationals invested in the mainland (H. Yeung 2004, 123).

41. In contrast to India or certain Latin American countries, China's land reforms had a greater impact. In addition, compared to China, India's planners somewhat underestimated "the productive role of better health, nutrition, and education and hence underspent on them" (Perry 2007, 4; see also Manor 2009; Kay 2002). Further, the Indian government had more limited capacity to discipline companies in the name of national capitalist development or to prioritize the nation's development above business interests (Chibber 2003).

42. However, for the most part, the following section does not take into account the normative tensions between Maoist dogmas and the increasing need for a distinctive new perception of social governance.

43. After 1978, a new "main contradiction" was described by the government: the contradiction between the country's material or cultural needs and the backwardness of production

(von Senger 2009, 10). The objective was to solve this by the one hundredth anniversary of the founding of the People's Republic of China in 2049.

44. It is interesting to note that it was not always the successful innovations from the coastal provinces that, over the course of time, were promoted as the norm in other provinces. With regard to the professionalization of the administrative units, in the mid-1980s, the rural province of Sichuan proved to be a trendsetter, for instance (Spence 1995, 817).

45. Shirk (1993) attributes the greater significance of the provinces to their gain in power in the Central Committee of the CCP and the state apparatus as a whole. This explains why attempts to recentralize the fiscal system in 1987–88 and from 1989 to 1990 failed, for instance. However, this politics-centered hypothesis has been called into question because of the success of later decentralization measures (D. Yang and Su 2000).

46. The rights of land use, which were assigned by the village leaders, for instance, were (and still are) the subject of intense conflict. The lion's share of rural land is still formally collectively owned to this day.

47. Unger points out that the most significant productivity gains were recorded before comprehensive decollectivization took place—in a brief interim phase from 1978, during which the production teams had substantially more leeway than previously to make their own (planting) decisions (Unger 2002, 224).

48. According to Yasheng Huang, from around the mid-1980s onward, the majority of TVEs could already be classified as private companies (Yasheng Huang 2008, xiv). Tsai writes: "Operating within the collective sector has offered de facto private entrepreneurs many advantages, including favorable tax treatment and preferential access to bank credit. . . . Estimates on privately owned collective enterprises range from one third nationally to as high as 90 percent in some localities" (Tsai 2005, 1136).

49. At this juncture, it is important to reiterate that, before the first reforms in China, SOEs produced a lower share of economic output than in other countries with command economies (Wank 1999, 157).

50. The "management responsibility system" established as part of the 1988 enterprise reforms also aimed to reduce the influence of the company party committees (Saich 2004, 256). From an ideological perspective, the emergence of a new entrepreneurialism was accompanied by a rehabilitation of the role of the "national bourgeoisie" both before and after 1949, as well as a revival of the chambers of commerce (Holbig and Reichenbach 2005, 97).

51. For an analysis of the mass movement and the emergence of independent labor unions, see Selden (1993, 206–30). Under the extreme circumstances of the protest movement in 1989, even the official labor union organization, the ACFTU, was initially forced to support the movement and threaten strike action. Over the course of the campaign, the ACFTU adopted more of a mediatory role again (A. Chan 1993, 56–57). Attempts to create independent labor unions (most notably the Beijing Autonomous Workers' Federation) were ultimately crushed to avert the risk of a development similar to Solidarność in Poland.

52. In the meantime, the government continued with the reforms, in Guangdong, for instance. Within the party, the transformation (particularly of the industrial sector) was evidently controversial, even before 1989. In the 1980s, under the leadership of party veteran Chen Yun, notions were propagated of a modernized command economy that more strictly limited the market.

53. Until 2003, the plan or rather the number of goods distributed by the state bureaucracy significantly limited the role played by market allocation (O'Hara 2006, 402).

54. From the mid-1990s, the "collective" sector also experienced a wave of privatization (H. Li and Rozelle 2003).

55. Although the central government prohibited internal protectionism in 1993 (Shaomin Li, Li, and Zhang 2000, 284), the intense rivalry between the provinces, particularly between the poor regions of China's interior and the wealthier coastal regions, led to over one thousand disputes over the territorial (provincial) borders in 1996 (Saich 2004, 163).

56. Here, we should draw attention to the distinction between "federalism" and "decentralization" that is made in a different context by Ehlert, Hennl, and Kaiser (2007): while the former term comprises clearly defined decision-making powers, the latter refers to the broad scope for implementation of the subnational authorities. Strictly speaking, in the case of China, it therefore makes more sense to replace the term "federalism" with "decentralization."

57. In this process, development of the telecommunications sector was unparalleled. In 1989, only one in one hundred Chinese inhabitants owned a telephone. From 1993, the Ministry of Posts and Communications established the companies China Telecom, China Mobile, and China Netcom. These three businesses were supplemented by another publicly listed company, China Unicom. Together, these companies, all operating under state (competition) control—with SASAC moderating the competition between them—almost entirely dominated the market in China in the 2000s (Ernst and Naughton 2007, 43–44).

58. As Duckett illustrates using the example of the traditional industrial metropolis of Tianjin, government actors set up companies in a wide variety of sectors, even in cities that could not really be classified as particularly reformist during the early 1990s: "These differed enormously in their size and in their spheres of economic activity, ranging from small trading companies or restaurants with only a handful of employees, to large department stores and real estate development companies. . . . Sometimes the businesses were related to the administrative work of the parent department, but many conducted unrelated business. For example, public property departments tended to establish real estate development companies—often more than one—but some had also set up trade companies and one had opened a large department store. . . . The profits generated by the businesses are shared with the parent department and are used to pay officials' bonuses, supplement administrative expenses, and carry out departments' official work" (Duckett 2001, 26).

59. In addition to the factors already mentioned, another circumstance contributed to improving entrepreneurial dynamism: during restructuring, companies were exempt from stringent "social obligations."

60. Anita Chan explains that, because of public land ownership, in the Pearl River delta, there was a particular incentive for local governments to lease land, at a profit, to (often foreign) companies. In Vietnam however, "where land had not been widely collectivized, . . . [local] governments, though they have an interest in attracting foreign investment, do not have a direct stake in renting out land and factory buildings to foreign companies" (A. Chan 2011, 41).

61. As mentioned above, the hard budget constraints local territories are subject to are reflected in the economic downturn between 1988 and 1990, when a large number of TVEs declared bankruptcy.

62. In the early 1980s, this was assisted by a public reappraisal of the Cultural Revolution carried out by the party, which was in stark contrast to the inadequate manner in which the Stalin era was addressed in the USSR: "De-Stalinization in Russia was the sensational but

surreptitious act of a single leader, Khrushchev, who stunned the 20th Congress of his party with a speech denouncing the crimes of Stalin about which he had consulted no-one. . . . This rambling address was never officially published; nor was it followed by any more substantial documentation or analysis from the leadership of that time or later, until the days of *perestroika*. Deng and his colleagues proceeded very differently. Some 4,000 Party officials and historians were involved in a retrospect of the Cultural Revolution, out of whose discussions a drafting group of 20–40 distilled a 35,000 word balance-sheet under Deng's supervision, formally adopted as a resolution by the Central Committee of the CCP in June 1981. While certainly no complete accounting of the Cultural Revolution . . . it offered a reasoned explanation of it, beyond the misdeeds of one man: the peculiar traditions of a party whose road to power had inured it to harsh class struggle, as if this were a permanent task; the distorting effect of conflict with the USSR, fanning fears of revisionism within; and last but not least, 'the evil ideological and political influence of centuries of feudal autocracy' " (Anderson 2010b, 82; see also Breslin 2007b, 42).

63. China research distinguishes between various generations, each of whom attempted to guarantee the stability of the regime. The generations of leaders up until that point were characterized by an extensive homogeneity in terms of their social and professional background: this applied to the cohorts of the first and second generation who were from a farming and/or military background and then joined the professional revolutionaries as well as to the elites from the third and fourth generations, primarily from engineering professions, who climbed to positions in the bureaucracy. The fifth generation, which is establishing itself in the centers of power in the 2010s, seems to be somewhat less homogenous. The cohorts ascending to leading government positions include scientists, lawyers, entrepreneurs, and academics who were also frequently educated abroad. This obviously does not necessarily signify the end of technocratic domination as implied by various authors (C. Li 2009, 17)—, although new leaders expressed greater interest in constitutional reforms (Lam 2006, 285–89).

64. In the debates that followed up until 2001, the refusal to actively integrate into the process of globalization was considered to be an additional reason for the collapse of the Eastern Bloc. Globalization had now come to be perceived as beneficial to "socialist development." At the same time, the liberal policy of "big bang reforms" prevalent in Russia after 1991 was effectively contrasted with China's policy of incremental reform (Wilson 2007b, 280).

65. Many of the taxes and duties introduced during fiscal recentralization (land use tax, building tax, and duties on key projects, for instance) were imposed on state-owned enterprises at subnational level, while private or foreign companies were taxed far less heavily, and, in this respect, therefore had a competitive edge. Another financial burden that was borne by the SOEs was the continuation of a modified version of the company system of social security.

66. The most important authority in this process was China's central executive governmental body, the State Council of the People's Republic of China, which was appointed by the National People's Congress (NPC).

67. From the 1980s, defense companies were given the opportunity to focus on civilian markets, and officers from the People's Liberation Army (PLA) were permitted to take up management positions in companies. This helped promote close-knit networks of former military leaders, members of the state apparatus, family clans, and sometimes even foreign companies (Saich 2004, 152–53).

68. At the same time, between 1997 and 2000, the restructuring trend in the corporate sector accelerated at local level: "Guangdong had 35,899 enterprises (*jingji shiti*) operated by or under the direct supervision (*zhiguan*) of party and government agencies. . . . Of these enterprises or economic entities, 2,510 were transferred (*yijiao*), 4,356 were closed (*chexiao*), 17,723 had their administrative ties (*xingzheng lishu*) removed, and 8,828 ceased their affiliation with party or government agencies. The 20,293 firms that either were transferred or had their administrative ties cut were reorganized into about 200 asset management or fiduciary operating companies subject to government oversight and regulation" (D. Yang 2004, 143–44).

69. During the first phase of reform, the Ministry of Foreign Economic Relations and Trade (MOFERT) was created by merging existing authorities. The plan was that, from 1982, the ministry would provide more efficient administration of foreign trade relations. MOFERT embodied an amalgam of different traditions within the CCP (Chin 2007, 158–64). However, China's clearly emerging move toward exports evident from the mid-1980s secured a compromise within the bureaucracy that initiated a process of institutional conversion. Previous guiding principles of Maoism were eroded and replaced by new economic policies. Within MOFERT, this process took the form of a shift away from strict controls to one of preferential treatment for international economic activities by regulatory means. Because MOFERT now occupied a key position within the government hierarchy (as well as having the backing of the even more powerful State Planning Commission and Ministry of Finance), it (or rather its successor, MOFTEC, renamed in the 1990s) was able to play the role of an intragovernmental avant-garde of modernization.

70. Officially, China's one-party system is described as multiparty cooperation under the leadership of the CCP and is contrasted with the Western "two-party or multi-party system" as an expression of diverging "civilizational traditions." Multiparty cooperation refers to a total of eight Democratic Parties (DPs) representing the interests of specific sections of the population and social classes. Members of these parties sit on the People's Congress committees at various levels. Institutionalized cooperation takes place in the context of the country's political advisory body, the Chinese People's Political Consultative Conference, and its regional committees that extend all the way down to the county level (Kroymann 2009, 20). There are close links with the CCP. The party also controls the DP through the allocation of financial resources. Since the 1990s, the DPs have been upgraded, with thousands of government positions being filled by their members, particularly at the local level. However, in 1998, the opposition China Democracy Party was banned. This party had been established in 1989 by participants in the protest movement, among others (Saich 2004, 184).

71. As early as the 1980s, during Zhao Ziyang's term of office, there was evidence of a very successful practice of consultation. Major proposed reforms were discussed in small working groups with representatives of ministries and commissions and modified where necessary in an attempt to reach consensus (Shirk 1989, 350–54).

72. In actual fact, less than half of the roughly forty million individuals officially designated as cadre (*ganbu*) who work for the public service, companies, the military, or the party itself and whose status entitles them to certain privileges (increasing with rank; here, there is a distinction between leading and nonleading cadres) are members of the CCP (Brodsgaard 2004, 72–73). The share of female cadres is 35 percent, but this figure decreases significantly, the higher the rank.

73. The constitution is at the top of the hierarchy of norms, followed by the laws, orders issued by the State Council, local regulations, and, at the lowest level, local statutes. The decentralization of the nation also resulted in a decentralization of the enactment of norms: on average, 80 percent of norms are enacted at the local level; the laws, in the narrow sense of the word, represent only a small proportion of codified provisions (Kroymann 2009, 22).

74. Consequently, judges are not elected for life, but their appointment is linked to the term of office of the relevant People's Congress. Moreover, judges can be dismissed at any time.

75. It is important to remember here that the notion of an independent legal system in Western industrialized liberal democratic societies did not always correspond to reality and should rather be understood as the (potential) result of a long battle. Before Germany's Civil Code came into force in 1900, in other words, many years after capitalist imperatives took effect in the German Reich, legal fragmentation and, in part, late feudal norms (in the Prussian Land Law, for instance) prevailed. Additionally, in the reality of capitalist-driven societies, the autonomy of the law was frequently only *relatively* independent from broader societal developments. In exceptional cases, the primacy of politics even predominated in capitalist societies—during wartime or phases of authoritarian rule, for instance.

76. Similar to the Chinese enclosure movement, the capitalist development in England or North America progressed in the form of a leasehold (i.e., not originally in a strictly privately owned form). China's speculation booms that were connected with land leasing (and the property trade) also had historical precedents (see Polanyi 2001). Although small farmers in China were allowed to retain a plot of land for themselves during the further course of the reforms, studies confirm that segments of the rural population felt enclosed because their living conditions in the countryside deteriorated compared to those of city dwellers and the area of land that could be farmed decreased (Pun and Lu 2010).

77. This calculation largely disregards informal and nonstandard sources of financing, however.

78. This process also reflected an intrastate power struggle between the Ministry of Finance and the PBOC because the CIC was founded under the auspices of the Ministry of Finance (see Anderlini 2008). Previously Huijin had been under the control of the central bank.

79. Between 2001 and 2007, market capitalization (excluding Hong Kong) was an average of 64 percent of GDP, which was slightly higher than the emerging market average but substantially lower than the average across the large OECD economies (Allen et al. 2012, 7; see also Hansakul 2007).

80. In the 2000s, Huijin and the Ministry of Finance held the largest (equity) shares in the most important government-owned banks (ICBC, CCB, and BOC, for instance). Further, a number of other state actors have shareholdings in banks, such as the National Council of the Social Security Fund and numerous SOEs—particularly in the regional and local banks (Pistor 2012, 42).

81. Naughton elucidates: "In most control-based systems, banks are privately owned, traditionally independent, powerful actors who vigorously enforce their interests. . . . In China, however, banks have very few ways to enforce their interests. . . . Banks are not allowed to own stock directly. Most important, because of their long tradition of passively accommodating government lending policies, banks have neither the capability nor a clear

mandate to aggressively monitor enterprise performance. In China, although the pattern of financing reveals the importance of banks, the system of corporate governance has no corresponding role for bank oversight" (Naughton 2007, 320; see also Conlé 2011, 27).

82. At the same time, to a certain extent, the danwei units also prepared the ground for a gradual transition to market-led forms of employment and ways of life (see Heberer 2008, 97). The egocentricity of many danwei units, where the individual units were primarily intended to take the interests of their members into account, were, to a certain extent, in competition with other "collectives," which, in turn, facilitated the emergence of new systems of competition.

83. The proposition that, in East Asian countries such as China, labor and social policy "were not priorities for the political process" (Schwinn 2009, 462, my translation) owing to values that contradicted those in predominantly Christian Europe, must therefore also be relativized in the same way as the assumption of a historical "acquiescence" of the people (Hartmann 2006, 194–95).

84. On the development of rural areas, see Bernstein 1999; Unger 2002.

85. On the whole, the importance of the danwei significantly declined in the 2000s. However, the lives of workers in the state enterprise sector (in the steel, chemical, and shipbuilding industries, for example) were still frequently bound to the danwei. Here, the danwei continued to be "the basic unit that governs their working and private lives" (Heberer 2008, 95, my translation).

86. The Chinese government also cites a comparatively high life expectancy, which increases slightly over the reform process (70.9 years in 2002). The adult literacy rate is under 10 percent. The values vary from region to region, however.

87. In 2003, 96 percent of the rural population still had no health insurance. Hundreds of millions of people continued to rely on older forms of health care provided on a familial or voluntary basis.

88. Chinese statistics include education spending here. Compared to other large emerging nations, the coverage rate of China's welfare state was positioned somewhere between countries such as Brazil or South Africa (which have higher coverage rates) and India or Indonesia with their lower coverage rates (Frazier 2011).

89. Incidentally, the contribution made by this dichotomy is just as limited as that made by the assumption of perfect competition in the neoclassical theories because soft budget constraints can also be found in "liberal" forms of capitalism.

90. Further, China's catch-up growth was also able to benefit from the fact that the use of tried-and-tested technologies and business models meant that launching innovations incurred only marginal costs.

91. In fact, the first "Free Production Zone" of Taiwan in 1965 was a blueprint for the Special Economic Zones.

92. The Shenzhen Special Economic Zone, which marks the present city center of Shenzhen, was separated from the surrounding area up until the 1990s. Both the tariff walls and the border controls have since been abolished.

93. Various special regulations applied in the SEZs.

94. The Chinese policy of opening up was, however, at the cost of other developing and newly industrialized countries. Only a few economies in the South were able to attract (the limited) FDI on a large scale from the 1990s and, at the same time, become an export platform. Mexico, for instance, was forced out of the clothing market owing to competition from

China. African developing and even South Asian newly industrialized countries lost market shares to the PRC (Cho 2005, 150–51; IMF 2004, 82, 87; see also Gereffi 2009).

95. The Chinese minority communities in Southeast Asian countries arose through migration, partly occurring centuries ago and in waves, in particular from the southern Chinese provinces of Guangdong and Fujian (see Hsing 1998; Meyer-Clement and Schubert 2004; H. Yeung and Olds 2000; H. Yeung 2006). The business networks of overseas Chinese were traditionally characterized by an ascendancy of family-based forms of production, which were professionalized from the 1980s onward under increased competitive pressure (H. Yeung 2004, 80). For the purposes of business expansion on the mainland, they strategically drew on their "Chinese" identity (H. Yeung 2006). One characteristic feature of "ethnic Chinese capitalism" frequently referred to is its "network-like structure" because it largely operated without recourse to state support and formalized contracts and was based on old trade networks (see Redding 1990; H. Yeung 2004).

96. As confirmed by analyses of archive materials, for instance, the People's Bank of China had already begun to establish close economic ties in the city-state back in the 1950s in order to organize currency exchange trading (against the background of international economic blockades) (Tobin 2011). Even during the period of the Cultural Revolution, this bridge to the global market was maintained: "During the Cultural Revolution . . . , it formed a focal point for communist demonstrators in Hong Kong with loud speakers and pro-Mao banners draped from its building in 1967. But this outward show of loyalty to even the most radical of Maoist anti-imperialist and anti-capitalist campaigns concealed the reality of the pragmatic policies which the Beijing leadership expected from this bank whatever the ideological climate on the Mainland" (Tobin 2011, 702).

97. Taiwanese companies frequently have authority over their mainland Chinese partners because they control the industrial or product design of electronic goods, for instance.

98. Authors who use the "pull factor" of low labor costs in particular as an explanation for the increase in FDI (Lardy 2002, 61) are therefore ignoring a significant "push factor" for the (frequently high-risk) investment.

Chapter 3

1. For a long time, this also included fake FIEs, i.e., companies on the mainland that were actually financed through investment from China itself, with the aim of acquiring tax breaks as well as privileged access to land and credit.

2. Limited liability companies employed around twenty-four million people in 2009.

3. Moreover, SOEs also have diverse obligations that makes it impossible to draw a comparison in terms of profitability between private and state-owned enterprises. For instance, for a long time, SOEs had to pay higher income tax and make a larger financial contribution to the social security of their employees than collectively owned enterprises (COEs), privately owned enterprises (POEs), or foreign-invested enterprises (FIEs).

4. Even after the radical wave of restructuring, it is relatively lucrative to work for certain SOEs.

5. In the south of the province of Jiangsu (for an account of the Sunan model, see Huang 2008, 262–64) a dynamic private sector evolved as a result of the privatization of state and collective enterprises, however.

6. One of the electronics companies under the control of the SASAC, China Electronics Technology Corp, originated from the military-industrial complex. It is also no secret that second-tier companies, such as Huawei, maintain close connections with the military.

7. This is why over 40 percent of employees at companies such as Huawei or ZTE are relatively well-paid and well-qualified research staff, and not primarily migrant workers, who are mostly employed by the little-known contract manufacturers.

8. There have also already been tensions with government authorities. In fall 2010, a conflict arose between the NDRC and the employers' association CAAM (China Association of Automobile Manufacturers) over the issue of overcapacity in the automobile industry. The NDRC had previously voiced the possibility of the state reducing automobile production. CAAM argued that overcapacity did not represent a serious problem, however. The association even referred to the procompetitive effects of overcapacity.

9. In joint ventures, for example in the chemical industry, the Chinese frequently have more say when it comes to important personnel and economic policy decisions, however.

10. CEOs with positions in the extended Central Committee of the CCP were not only from state-owned enterprises. They also included, for example, Zhang Ruimin, CEO of Haier, one of China's large model companies, officially run as a listed collective enterprise, and also the CEOs of other flagship companies such as TCL.

11. The CEO of one of the model companies, Haier, Zhang Ruimin, gave a blunt response to a question regarding possible conflict between company party policy and business interests: "I appointed myself party secretary of Haier. So I can't have any conflicts with myself, can I?" (quoted in McGregor 2010, 194).

12. Compared to the previous Seventeenth National Party Congress, seven more delegates with a background in private business have been added. This development, however, is offset by an increase in the general plenum of fifty delegates.

13. Within the party, two motives for attempting to co-opt companies were determined: first, cooperative relationships with the groups responsible for economic growth are in the interests of the political class. This is particularly relevant for party officials in the lower-level regional authorities because their career paths are directly linked to high growth rates. Second, to a certain extent, it is necessary to prevent organized opposition forces from emerging. Further, companies with a "red" executive board are more likely to have company party organizations.

14. Here, cultural traditions continued to have an effect in quite a specific way: "The traditional concept of property in China never supported the absolute property rights familiar in the Western world. . . . Individual property was conceived as a relational category in two senses: First, property belongs to the family, such that the individual owner is only a temporary caretaker who is obliged to increase its value for the coming generations, and second, individual property was perceived as being embedded into a web of social relations in the village, which was a major obstacle to the emergence of land markets in China. Instead, a complex system of tradable and embedded lease-rights emerged" (Herrmann-Pillath 2009, 124).

15. Naughton sums up as follows: "Communist Party leaders have been given a stake in the marketization process, and became reasonably confident that marketization would benefit themselves and their families. If one imagines the Chinese reform process as a Coasian bargain between growth-oriented reformers and vested interest groups, one can capture almost all of the key dynamics" (Naughton 2009, 14).

16. For a description of the pitfalls of official Chinese statistics, see Naughton (2007, 140–42). Naughton assumes that these statistics overestimate GDP growth by around 1 to 2

percent. Because local officials may be promoted if they fulfill plan targets, local statistics are frequently adjusted upward. At the same time, there is also a substantial share of "gray" and "black" markets, which would increase real GDP growth by another few percentage points if they were factored in. Moreover, companies regularly falsify their balance sheets to reduce their tax burden.

17. Another effect of the tendency toward overinvestment was the emergence of speculative bubbles in the acquisition of financial assets, in the real estate sector, for instance. In the wake of the major government stimulus programs, local governments increasingly used land as collateral for loans and as a source of income. This land-induced financialization (Sum 2011) increased the reliance of state and private actors on real estate development. This process was accompanied by rising real estate prices and a property bubble. A real estate coalition comprising local governments, government-owned banks, companies, and foreign investors had been established (Sum 2011, 201–7).

18. Global production networks and foreign enterprises are still dominant in high-tech export sectors. The share accounted for by the processing trade, i.e., the combination and processing of imported intermediate products for export, has declined since the global financial crisis but remains high by international standards.

19. Hong Kong is the business location of around one thousand subsidiaries and regional headquarters of international corporations whose investment partially flows to China via Hong Kong.

20. As Gerschenkron has already pointed out, this aspect of combined development ("borrowed technology") also applied to earlier cases of catch-up development. How effective these practices actually prove to be, however, also depends on indigenous innovative capacity: "In every instance of industrialization, imitation of the evolution in advanced countries appears in combination with different, indigenously determined elements" (Gerschenkron 1966, 26).

21. This practice is regularly criticized by foreign organizations (see EUCCC 2010). In some instances, foreign companies respond to these demands by deliberately providing false information about the construction of technical equipment, for instance.

22. Also in other sectors, links with the domestic market enabled Chinese firms to curb the superior strength of Western companies. One example is the cell phone industry in China, where local providers such as Xiaomi, Oppo, or Vivo now dominate the market.

23. Roughly speaking, the distinction is largely based on the following conditions: importance for national development strategy, high technology and knowledge intensity, high degree of vertical integration, low environmental impact, and high resource and energy efficiency.

24. Prevailing popular discourse views future generations as "human capital": children are seen contributing to an accumulation strategy for the family's economic future. The key question is therefore: "How many points did my child get on his or her test?" This particularly applies to the senior high school entrance examination (*zhongkao*) after ninth grade (until then access to schooling is generally unrestricted) and then later to the university entrance examination (*gaokao*). In the event that the child "fails," the prevailing discourse stigmatizes the "bad" child as well as the "bad" parents.

25. If we calculate the research and development spending in the centers of Chinese capitalism, particularly in the Yangtze River delta, R&D expenditures approach those of the

United States, Germany, or Japan. Another indicator of China's innovation capacity is cross border knowledge acquisition by Chinese experts who spend a number of years working and conducting research in places like Taiwan or Silicon Valley and then later apply their expertise in mainland China. This is very difficult to measure owing to its transnational character, however.

26. Additionally, there was no synchronicity between implementing Five Year Plans (1996, 2001, 2006, 2011, and 2016) and changes of government (1998, 2003, 2008, and 2012–13). Consequently, governments remained bound to previous plan targets, which serves to ensure continuity.

27. There is a risk of these practices being prematurely recognized as policy instruments that can be transferred to other countries, because they make the protracted process of creating legislation "superfluous." The nondemocratic character of this form of policy making and the widespread feedback loops affecting the process of national implementation are testament to the problems of this governance technique, however.

28. Nongovernmental organizations (NGOs) include groups with apolitical objectives or those that do not call the party leadership into question, for instance, consumer rights groups, health organizations, or establishments for children and the disabled. Here, environmental organizations have been the fastest growing in recent years. Unlike the opposition NGOs in the Eastern Bloc, in China, these organizations generally tend to have a loose association with the party-state and are therefore referred to as government-organized NGOs or GONGOs (Béja 2006, 64; Saich 2004, 191).

29. Even classical Maoism had features of Confucianism, in the elements of voluntarism and socialist education it contained, for instance (Anderson 2010b, 69).

30. At the same time, new ethics of consumerism were already created many years ago.

31. China's government (as well as Singapore's, for instance) has already frequently used the argument of "a divergent cultural tradition" to justify its authoritarian rule. Against this backdrop, Dirlik argues that the discourse about "Chinese" culture and "Chineseness" is contributing to the production of a new identity. This results in class or gender differences being concealed within one and the same "culture" (Dirlik 1997, 308, 316).

32. In contrast to Western perceptions, "leftist" positions within the Chinese system of ideas are generally characterized by doctrinaire Maoist values and emphatic support of the party's monopoly on power. The new left effectively argues against the "illusions of the market" and the imminent takeover of society by "neoliberal" patterns of behavior.

33. On the importance of rudimentary forms of democratic participation in the urban neighborhoods (*shequ*) and of village elections, see Heberer (2008, 119–33).

34. The fact that major corporations frequently do not adequately comply with general legal obligations has recently been illustrated by Longmay Mining, based in and owned by the province of Heilongjiang. This SOE has become infamous for missing payments of wages and social security premiums. In early 2016, several days of protests of thousands of angry workers attracted the attention of the Chinese and international media. The company had previously been heralded as a successful case of corporate restructuring in industries plagued by severe overcapacity, low profits, and escalating debts. Workers reportedly chanted "We must live, we must eat" and "Lu Hao lies with his eyes wide open" (referring to the provincial governor, who had claimed the company had met all its obligations) (Buckley 2016). Because events at the mine coincided with a session of the National People's Congress (where Lu is a delegate),

investigation was swift. The governor was forced to admit that he had made an error and promised quick compensation for workers.

35. China has a progressive income tax, which is staggered between 5 percent (on a monthly income of up to five hundred RMB) and 45 percent (for incomes of over one hundred thousand RMB) (Kroymann 2009, 77–78). Although China is no tax haven, there are considerable opportunities for tax deduction and many exemptions for high-income residents.

36. Real economy refers to the industrial sector.

37. As the main providers of social benefits, the subprovincial regional authorities have already had to shoulder an enormous financial burden for some time now. Prefecture-level or county-level cities, for instance, are obliged to bear the cost of elements of social security such as health care. This forces local governments to foster a high capacity for suffering among the local population, which, in turn, is reflected in local governments' poor popularity ratings in the polls—compared to a relatively high level of satisfaction with the central government.

38. To be able to determine the total number, we must also take into account migrant workers in those suburban regions that are effectively urban. These are frequently ignored in the statistics. According to these figures, there are around 270 million internal migrants working in China.

39. The following categorization does not correspond with the production regimes described in the first section of this chapter because this classification differentiates by employment relationships and working conditions rather than ownership structures (for an explanation of the term *production regime* in industrial sociology, see Burawoy 1985).

40. For the time being, the exceptions prove the rule in this field: in some cities in the coastal province of Zhejiang, for instance, there have been sectoral wage agreements (Friedman 2011, 91–111). However, here (in and around Wenzhou, for example), unlike other parts of the country, there are also more active employers' associations.

41. This information was gleaned from discussions with Frederic Speidel.

42. This is not, however, tantamount to active membership or democratic codetermination. One of the reasons for the extremely high number of members is that, according to China's Trade Union Law, workers in companies are classed as union members as soon as a company union exists.

43. The Communist Party of Vietnam granted the state-affiliated central labor union more autonomy than the CCP gave the ACFTU (C. Chan 2011; Clarke and Pringle 2009). In the event that collective bargaining were to fail, there is a right to strike, for instance.

44. The unions and their over five hundred thousand full-time employees are financed through a statutory employer's contribution. This is supplemented by minimal employee contributions.

45. Indeed, in industrial sectors in certain coastal regions there is now a labor shortage. This is partly because not all migrant workers move to the coast but increasingly look for work in the cities in their home provinces. In absolute terms, therefore, the influx of cheap labor from rural areas has not yet petered out.

Conclusion

1. The importance normatively ascribed to government action varies substantially between different types of capitalism. Block recently provided evidence of this on the basis of

a "hidden developmental state" in the United States (Block 2008). In reality, the dominant role of "market fundamentalism" in the United States is counteracted by development policies that make it seem plausible to speak of a "hidden developmental network state," which, particularly on subnational levels, contributes to the advancement of new technologies (Block 2008, 171–74, 188–93). In the PRC, in contrast, the state's management and regulatory function is deliberately not "hidden" but in fact flaunted.

2. I have described the financial system separately in Chapters 1 and 2 as one of the five key dimensions of capitalist systems. Similar to Chapter 3, the following sections integrate aspects of the financial system, particularly in the field of corporate relations and the state.

3. We should also refrain from regarding other contemporary state-permeated capitalisms simply as reincarnations of a command economy (Nölke et al. 2015; Kurlantzick 2016).

4. In general, the bigger the company, the more interested the state tends to be in close cooperation with it, even if it is a private enterprise.

5. The contribution made by this dichotomy is just as limited as that made by the assumption of perfect competition in neoclassical theories because soft budget constraints can also be found in "liberal" forms of capitalism. This was recently confirmed by the problem of banks being "too big to fail." Firms were saved from insolvency because state authorities ascribed them "systemic" relevance.

6. The risky establishment of private property, introduced through processes of institutional layering, is in line with a vested interest of the bureaucracy, which should also be taken into consideration in our analysis: It has "to do with the material interests of this . . . bureaucracy. If there is any continuity between Mao's China and Deng's/post-Deng's China, it is less the continuity of a 'socialist tradition' but more the privileges of the bureaucracy as represented by the CCP: what 'ism' it believes is always of secondary importance; what is paramount is its monopoly of political power. And as time went by the party became more and more conscious of the fact that without the introduction of the right to private property there was always the risk that its monopoly on political power to distribute social surplus would not pass down to its children" (Au 2009).

7. The global consequences of these developments can be summarized as follows: against a backdrop of investment slowdown and capital overaccumulation in the West, companies in developed economies have paradoxically created powerful new competitors while attempting to profit from Chinese economic growth. The result is a restructuring of competitive relationships in international markets, because Chinese companies have now become major international investors themselves. These global economic changes also foster unintended geopolitical shifts (ten Brink 2014a).

8. Thus, using the basis developed here, to give just one example, determinants of wage development and interactions between labor and monetary policy could be systematically examined. Such studies might benefit from the fact that my analysis demonstrated that the labor unions in China (unlike in OECD countries) cannot necessarily be understood as representing workers' interests and also that monetary policy has achieved far less independence in China's state-dominated financial system than is the case in other economies. Additionally, comparative studies with institutional regimes in other large emerging countries might also prove invaluable (Nölke et al. 2015).

9. Assumptions such as the theory of property rights in New Institutional Economics, according to which the key institutional prerequisite of capitalist dynamics is the guarantee

of private property rights through a liberal state or an impartial legal system, hence require modification in the case of China.

10. Nevertheless, the example of China reminds us that capitalism has existed at least as long without representative democracy as with it (for instance, in Europe in the late nineteenth century, and in the first half of the twentieth century).

BIBLIOGRAPHY

ADB (Asian Development Bank). 2011. *Asian Development Outlook 2011: South-South Economic Links*. Manila: Asian Development Bank.

Adorno, Theodor W. 1996. "Über Statik und Dynamik als soziologische Kategorien." In *Gesammelte Schriften*, ed. Theodor W. Adorno, 217–37. Frankfurt/Main: Suhrkamp.

Ahlers, Anna L., and Gunter Schubert. 2009. "'Building a New Socialist Countryside'—Only a Political Slogan?" *Journal of Current Chinese Affairs* 38 (4): 35–62.

Ahrens, Joachim, and Patrick Jünemann. 2006. "Transitional Institutions, Institutional Complementarities and Economic Performance in China: A 'Varieties of Capitalism' Approach." Duisburg Working Papers on East Asian Studies, no. 72/2007. Duisburg: Universität Duisburg-Essen.

Akyüz, Yilmaz. 2011. "Export Dependence and Sustainability of Growth in China." *China and World Economy* 19 (1): 1–23.

Allen, Franklin, Jun Qian, and Meijun Qian. 2003. "Comparing China's Financial System." *China Journal of Finance* 1 (June): 1–48.

Allen, Franklin, Jun Qian, Chenying Zhang, and Mengxin Zha. 2012. "China's Financial System: Opportunities and Challenges." NBER Working Paper, no. 17828. Cambridge, Mass.: National Bureau of Economic Research.

Altvater, Elmar, and Birgit Mahnkopf. 1996. *Grenzen der Globalisierung: Ökonomie, Ökologie und Politik in der Weltgesellschaft*. Münster: Westfälisches Dampfboot.

Amable, Bruno. 2003. *The Diversity of Modern Capitalism*. Oxford: Oxford University Press.

Amelung, Iwo. 2009. "Modernität, Aberglaube und nationale Identität: Überlegungen zur Entwicklung der Wissenschaft in China." *WestEnd: Neue Zeitschrift für Sozialforschung* 6 (2): 96–118.

Anderlini, Jamil. 2008. "China Investment Arm Emerges from Shadows." *Financial Times*, 5 January. https://www.ft.com/content/2ee05a68-baf9-11dc-9fbc-0000779fd2ac.

Anderson, Perry. 2010a. "Sinomania." *London Review of Books* 32 (2): 3–6.

———. 2010b. "Two Revolutions: Rough Notes." *New Left Review* 61 (1–2): 59–96.

Andreas, Joel. 2009. *Rise of the Red Engineers: The Cultural Revolution and the Origins of China's New Class*. Stanford, Calif.: Stanford University Press.

Aoki, Masahiko. 2011. "The Five Phases of Economic Development and Institutional Evolution in China and Japan." Presidential Lecture at the 16th World Congress of International Economic Association, Beijing, 4–8 July.

Aoki, Masahiko, Kevin Murdock, and Masahiro Okuno-Fujiwara. 2005. "Beyond the East Asian Miracle: Introducing the Market-Enhancing View." In *The Role of Government in*

East Asian Economic Development: Comparative Institutional Analysis, ed. Masahiko Aoki, Hyung-Ki Kim, and Masahiro Okuno-Fujiwara, 1–37. Oxford: Clarendon Press.

Arnason, Johann Pall. 2003a. *Civilizations in Dispute: Historical Questions and Theoretical Traditions*. Leiden: Brill.

———. 2003b. "Entangled Communisms: Imperial Revolutions in Russia and China." *European Journal of Social Theory* 6 (3): 307–25.

———. 2005. "The Varieties of Accumulation: Civilisational Perspectives on Capitalism." In *The Economy as a Polity: The Political Constitution of Contemporary Capitalism*, ed. Christian Joerges, Bo Strath, and Peter Wagner, 17–36. London: UCL Press.

———. 2008. "East Asian Modernity Revisited." In *Irmela Hijiya-Kirschnereit zu Ehren: Festschrift zum 60. Geburtstag.*, ed. Judit Árokay, Verena Blechinger-Talcott, and Hilaria Gössmann, 395–407. Munich: Iudicium.

Arrighi, Giovanni. 2008. *Adam Smith in Beijing: Lineages of the Twenty-First Century*. London: Verso.

Arrighi, Giovanni, Po-Keung Hui, and Ho-Fung Hung. 2003. "Historical Capitalism, East and West." In *The Resurgence of East Asia: 500, 150 and 50 Year Perspectives*, ed. Giovanni Arrighi, Takeshi Hamashita, and Mark Selden, 259–333. London: Routledge.

Aspers, Patrik, and Jens Beckert. 2008. "Märkte." In *Handbuch der Wirtschaftssoziologie*, ed. Andrea Maurer, 225–46. Wiesbaden: VS Verlag.

Au, Loong-Yu. 2008. "The New Chinese Nationalism." *Against the Current* 136 (September–October). https://solidarity-us.org/atc/136/p1886/.

———. 2009. "China: End of a Model . . . or the Birth of a New One?" *New Politics* 12 (3) (Summer). http://newpol.org/content/china-end-model%E2%80%A6or-birth-new-one.

Bai, Chongen. 2015. "The Systemic Foundation of China's Economic Development [zhongguo jingji fazhan de zhidu jichu]." *China Economics Education Net*, 6 October. http://chuansong.me/n/1759175.

Bai, Chong-En, Jiangyong Lu, and Zhigang Tao. 2009. "How Does Privatization Work in China?" *Journal of Comparative Economics* 37 (3): 453–70.

Becker, Joachim. 2002. *Akkumulation, Regulation, Territorium: Zur kritischen Rekonstruktion der französischen Regulationstheorie*. Marburg: Metropolis.

Beckert, Jens. 2009. "Die Anspruchsinflation des Wirtschaftssystems." MPIfG Working Paper 09/10. Cologne: Max Planck Institute for the Study of Societies.

———. 2011. "Imagined Futures: Fictionality in Economic Action." MPIfG Discussion Paper 11/8. Cologne: Max Planck Institute for the Study of Societies.

Beckert, Jens, Rainer Diaz-Bone, and Heiner Ganßmann, eds. 2007. *Märkte als soziale Strukturen*. Frankfurt/Main: Campus.

Beeson, Mark. 2009. "Developmental States in East Asia: A Comparison of the Japanese and Chinese Experiences." *Asian Perspective* 33 (2): 5–39.

Béja, Jean-Philippe. 2006. "The Changing Aspects of Civil Society in China." *Social Research* 73 (1): 53–74.

Benson, John, Gospel, Howard, and Ying Zhu, eds. 2013. *Workforce Development and Skill Formation in Asia*. London: Routledge.

Benz, Arthur. 2009. *Politik in Mehrebenensystemen*. Wiesbaden: VS Verlag.

Bernstein, Thomas P. 1999. "Farmer Discontent and Regime Responses." In *The Paradox of China's Post-Mao Reforms*, ed. Merle Goldman and Roderick MacFarquhar, 197–219. Cambridge, Mass.: Harvard University Press.

Beyer, Jürgen. 2006. *Pfadabhängigkeit: Über institutionelle Kontinuität, anfällige Stabilität und fundamentalen Wandel.* Frankfurt/Main: Campus.

Bian, Morris L. 2005. *The Making of the State Enterprise System in Modern China.* Cambridge, Mass.: Harvard University Press.

Bidet, Jacques. 1991. "Für eine metastrukturale Theorie der Moderne." *Deutsche Zeitschrift für Philosophie* 39 (12): 1331–40.

Blecher, Marc. 2008. "When Wal-Mart Wimped Out." *Critical Asian Studies* 40 (2): 263–76.

Block, Fred. 1994. "The Roles of the State in the Economy." In *The Handbook of Economic Sociology,* ed. Neil J. Smelser and Richard Swedberg, 691–710. Princeton, N.J.: Princeton University Press.

———. 2005. "Towards a New Understanding of Economic Modernity." In *The Economy as a Polity: The Political Constitution of Contemporary Capitalism,* ed. Christian Joerges, Bo Strath, and Peter Wagner, 3–17. London: UCL Press.

———. 2008. "Swimming Against the Current: The Rise of a Hidden Developmental State in the United States." *Politics and Society* 36 (2): 169–206.

Bohle, Dorothee, and Béla Greskovits. 2009. "Varieties of Capitalism and Capitalism 'tout court.'" *Archives Européennes de Sociologie—European Journal of Sociology* 50 (3): 355–86.

Bourdieu, Pierre. 1992. *Die verborgenen Mechanismen der Macht.* Hamburg: VSA.

Boyer, Robert. 2000. "Is a Finance-Led Growth Regime a Viable Alternative to Fordism? A Preliminary Analysis." *Economy and Society* 29 (1): 111–45.

———. 2005. "How and Why Capitalisms Differ." MPIfG Discussion Paper 05/4. Cologne: Max Planck Institute for the Study of Societies.

Bradach, Jeffrey L., and Robert G. Eccles. 1991. "Price, Authority and Trust: From Ideal Types to Plural Forms." In *Markets, Hierarchies and Networks: The Coordination of Social Life,* ed. Grahame Thompson, Jennifer Frances, Rosalind Levacic, and Jeremy Mitchell, 277–92. London: Sage.

Brand, Ulrich. 2006. "Die politische Form der Globalisierung: Politische Institutionen und soziale Kräfte im internationalisierten Staat." Kassel: Universität Kassel. Unpublished manuscript.

Brandt, Loren, and Eric Thun. 2010. "The Fight for the Middle: Upgrading, Competition, and Industrial Development in China." *World Development* 38 (11): 1555–74.

Bremmer, Ian. 2010. *The End of the Free Market: Who Wins the War Between States and Corporations?* New York: Portfolio.

Brenner, Neil. 2004. "Urban Governance and the Production of New State Spaces in Western Europe. 1960–2000." *Review of International Political Economy* 11 (3): 447–88.

Brenner, Neil, and Susanne Heeg. 1999. "Lokale Politik und Stadtentwicklung nach dem Fordismus: Möglichkeiten und Beschränkungen." *Kurswechsel: Zeitschrift für gesellschafts-, wirtschafts-und umweltpolitische Alternativen* 2 (99): 103–19.

Brenner, Robert. 2006. *The Economics of Global Turbulence: The Advanced Capitalist Economies from Long Boom to Long Downturn, 1945–2005.* London: Verso.

Breslin, Shaun. 2007a. "Beyond the Disciplinary Heartlands: Studying China's International Political Economy." In *China's Reforms and International Political Economy,* David Zweig and Zhimin Chen, 21–41. London: Routledge.

———. 2007b. *China and the Global Political Economy.* Basingstoke: Palgrave Macmillan.

Brodsgaard, Kjeld Erik. 2004. "Management of Party Cadres in China." In *Bringing the Party Back: How China Is Governed,* ed. Kjeld Erik Brodsgaard and Yongnian Zheng, 57–91. Singapore: Eastern Universities Press.

Brodsgaard, Kjeld Erik, and Yongnian Zheng, eds. 2004. *Bringing the Party Back: How China Is Governed.* Singapore: Eastern Universities Press.

Brückner, Lisa. 2011. "'Papiertiger' oder effektives Sicherungsmodell—Das Sozialversicherungsgesetz der VR China tritt in Kraft." EU-China Civil Society Forum Hintergrundinformationen 1/2011. Cologne: Stiftung Asienhaus.

Bu, Yuanshi. 2009. *Einführung in das Recht Chinas.* Munich: C. H. Beck.

Buckley, Chris. 2016. "Official Admits He Gave Misleading Account of Miners' Plight." *New York Times*, 13 March. https://www.nytimes.com/2016/03/14/world/asia/china-heilong jiang-governor-mine-protest.html.

Bunker, Stephen G., and Paul S. Ciccantell. 2007. *East Asia and the Global Economy: Japan's Ascent, with Implications for China's Future.* Baltimore: Johns Hopkins University Press.

Burawoy, Michael. 1985. *Politics of Production.* London: Verso.

———. 1996. "The State and Economic Involution: Russia Through a China Lens." *World Development* 24 (6): 1105–17.

Butollo, Florian, and Boy Lüthje. 2012. "Drei Seiten—vier Parteien? Arbeitskonflikte, Gewerkschaften und kollektive Arbeitsstandards in China." Unpublished manuscript.

Butollo, Florian, and Tobias ten Brink. 2012. "Challenging the Atomization of Discontent: Patterns of Migrant-Worker Protest in China During the Series of Strikes in 2010." *Critical Asian Studies* 44 (3): 419–40.

Cai, Fang. 2010. "Labor Market Development and Expansion of Rural and Urban Employment." In *Transforming the Chinese Economy*, ed. Fang Cai, 85–114. Leiden: Brill.

Cai, Yongshun. 2010. *Collective Resistance in China: Why Popular Protests Succeed or Fail.* Stanford, Calif.: Stanford University Press.

———. 2011. "Distinguishing Between Losers: Institutionalizing Inequality in China's Corporate Restructuring." In *Going Private in China: The Politics of Corporate Restructuring and System Reform*, ed. Jean C. Oi, 71–93. Stanford, Calif.: Walter H. Shorenstein Asia-Pacific Research Center Books.

Callinicos, Alex. 2006. *The Resources of Critique.* Cambridge: Polity.

Castells, Manuel. 2003. *Das Informationszeitalter. Bd. 3, Jahrtausendwende.* Opladen: Leske und Budrich.

Castoriadis, Cornelius. 1988. "The Relations of Production in Russia." In *Political and Social Writings*, ed. Cornelius Castoriadis, 107–58. Minneapolis: University of Minnesota Press.

Chan, Anita. 1993. "Revolution or Corporatism? Workers and Trade Unions in Post-Mao China." *Australian Journal of Chinese Affairs* 29 (1): 31–61.

———. 2001. *China's Workers Under Assault: The Exploitation of Labor in a Globalizing Economy.* Armonk, N.Y.: M. E. Sharpe.

———. 2006. "Arbeitsbeziehungen in China: Zwischen organisiertem und neoliberalem Kapitalismus." *Das Argument* 268: 92–97.

———. 2008. "The Evolution of China's Industrial System, the Japanese-German Model, and China's Workers' Congress." *Labour Relations Journal* 1: 52–65.

———. 2011. "Strikes in China's Export Industries in Comparative Perspective." *China Journal* 65 (1): 27–51.

Chan, Anita, and Jonathan Unger. 2009. "A Chinese State Enterprise Under the Reforms: What Model of Capitalism?" *China Journal* 62 (2): 1–26.

Chan, Chris King-Chi, and Ngai Pun. 2009. "The Making of a New Working Class? A Study of Collective Actions of Migrant Workers in South China." *China Quarterly* 198 (June): 287–303.

Chan, Kam Wing, and Will Buckingham. 2008. "Is China Abolishing the Hukou System?" *China Quarterly* 195 (September): 582–606.

Chang, Eric C., and Sonia M. L. Wong. 2004. "Political Control and Performance in China's Listed Firms." *Journal of Comparative Economics* 32 (4): 617–36.

Chang, Kai, Boy Lüthje, and Siqi Luo. 2008. "Die Transformation der Arbeitsbeziehungen in China und ihre Besonderheiten." HBS Research Project "Sozialökonomische Transformation und industrielle Beziehungen in China," Working Paper. Düsseldorf: Hans-Böckler-Stiftung.

Chen, Jiagui, and Qin Wang. 2010. "The Reform, Opening, and Development of China's Industrial Economy." In *Transforming the Chinese Economy*, ed. Fang Cai, 39–83. Leiden: Brill.

Chen, Ling, and Barry Naughton. 2017. "A Dynamic China Model: The Co-Evolution of Economics and Politics in China." *Journal of Contemporary China* 26 (103): 18–34.

Chen, Minglu. 2015. "From Economic Elites to Political Elites: Private Entrepreneurs in the People's Political Consultative Conference." *Journal of Contemporary China* 24 (94): 613–27.

Chen, Wenhong. 2007. "Does the Colour of the Cat Matter? The Red Hat Strategy in China's Private Enterprises." *Management and Organization Review* 3 (1): 55–79.

Chen, Xiangming. 2005. *As Borders Bend: Transnational Spaces on the Pacific Rim.* Lanham, Md.: Rowman and Littlefield.

Chibber, Vivek. 2003. *Locked in Place: State-Building and Late Industrialization in India.* Princeton, N.J.: Princeton University Press.

Chin, Gregory T. 2007. "Between 'Outside-In' and 'Inside-Out': The Internationalization of the Chinese State." In *China's Reforms and International Political Economy*, ed. David Zweig and Zhimin Chen, 155–70. London: Routledge.

China Daily. 2014. "Potential of the Chinese Dream." *China Daily*, 26 March.

Cho, Hyekyung. 2005. *Chinas langer Marsch in den Kapitalismus.* Münster: Westfälisches Dampfboot.

Chu, Yin-wah, ed. 2010. *Chinese Capitalisms: Historical Emergence and Political Implications.* Houndmills: Palgrave Macmillan.

Clarke, Simon, and Tim Pringle. 2009. "Can Party-Led Trade Unions Represent Their Members?" *Post-Communist Economies* 21 (1): 85–101.

CLB (China Labour Bulletin). 2009. *Going It Alone: The Workers' Movement in China (2007–2008).* Hong Kong: China Labour Bulletin.

———. 2011. *Unity Is Strength: The Workers' Movement in China (2009–2011).* Hong Kong: China Labour Bulletin.

———. 2016. "Strikes and Protests by China's Workers Soar to Record Heights in 2015." Hong Kong: China Labour Bulletin. http://www.clb.org.hk/en/content/strikes-and-pro tests-china%E2%80%99s-workers-soar-record-heights-2015.

Coates, David. 2000. *Models of Capitalism: Growth and Stagnation in the Modern Era.* Cambridge: Polity.

———, ed. 2005. *Varieties of Capitalism, Varieties of Approaches.* Houndmills: Palgrave Macmillan.

Conlé, Marcus. 2011. "The Continuity and Change of China's Capitalism: An Evolutionary Perspective." Paper presented at Annual Conference of the Society for the Advancement of Socio-Economics, 23 June, Madrid, Spain.

CPC Central Committee. 2013. "Decision of the Central Committee of the Communist Party of China on Comprehensively Deepening Reforms Targeting Several Key Problems." *CPC News*, 15 November (in Chinese). http://cpc.people.com.cn/n/2013/1115/c64094-23 559163.html.

Crouch, Colin. 2005. *Capitalist Diversity and Change: Recombinant Governance and Institutional Entrepreneurs.* Oxford: Oxford University Press.

Crouch, Colin, Martin Schröder, and Helmut Voelzkow. 2009. "Regional and Sectoral Varieties of Capitalism." *Economy and Society* 38 (4): 654–78.

Dale, Gareth. 2004. *Between State Capitalism and Globalisation: The Collapse of the East German Economy.* Bern: Peter Lang.

Davies, Ken. 2013. "China Investment Policy—an Update." OECD Working Papers on International Investment, 2013/01, Paris: OECD.

de Haan, Arjan. 2010. "The Financial Crisis and China's 'Harmonious Society.'" *Journal of Current Chinese Affairs* 39 (2): 69–99.

Derichs, Claudia, and Thomas Heberer. 2008. "Grundlagen politikwissenschaftlicher Komparatistik." In *Einführung in die politischen Systeme Ostasiens: VR China, Hongkong, Japan, Nordkorea, Südkorea, Taiwan*, ed. Thomas Heberer and Claudia Derichs, 1–20. Wiesbaden: VS Verlag.

Deutschmann, Christoph. 2009a. "The Entrepreneur in Economic Sociology." Paper presented at Annual Conference of the Society for the Advancement of Socio-Economics, 15–19 July, Paris.

———. 2009b. "Soziologie kapitalistischer Dynamik." MPI Scholar in Residence Lectures 09/2. Cologne: Max Planck Institute for the Study of Societies.

Deyo, Frederic C. 1993. *Beneath the Miracle: Labor Subordination in the New Asian Industrialism.* Berkeley: University of California Press.

Dickson, Bruce J. 2003. *Red Capitalists in China: The Party, Private Entrepreneurs, and Prospects for Political Change.* Cambridge: Cambridge University Press.

———. 2007. "Integrating Wealth and Power in China: The Communist Party's Embrace of the Private Sector." *China Quarterly* 192 (December): 827–54.

———. 2016. *The Dictator's Dilemma: The Chinese Communist Party's Strategy for Survival.* Oxford: Oxford University Press.

Dirlik, Arif. 1997. "Critical Reflections on 'Chinese Capitalism' as Paradigm." *Identities* 3 (3): 303–30.

Dittmer, Lowell. 1987. *China's Continuous Revolution: The Post-Liberation Epoch, 1949–1981.* Berkeley: University of California Press.

Dörre, Klaus, Stephan Lessenich, and Hartmut Rosa, eds. 2009. *Soziologie, Kapitalismus, Kritik: Eine Debatte.* Frankfurt/Main: Suhrkamp.

Dreyer, June Teufel. 1996. *China's Political System: Modernization and Tradition.* Boston: Allyn and Bacon.

Duan, Haiyan, and Vivian Zhan. 2011. "Fiscal Transfer and Local Public Expenditure in China: A Case Study of Shanxi Province." *China Review* 11 (1): 57–88.

Duckett, J. 2001. "Bureaucrats in Business, Chinese-Style: The Lessons of Market Reform and State Entrepreneurialism in the People's Republic of China." *World Development* 29 (1): 23–37.

Durkheim, Emile. 1988. *Über soziale Arbeitsteilung: Studie über die Organisation höherer Gesellschaften.* Frankfurt/Main: Suhrkamp.

Edmonds, Christopher, Sumner J. La Croix, and Yao Li. 2007. "China's Rise as a Trading Power." In *China's Emergent Political Economy: Capitalism in the Dragon's Lair*, ed. Christopher A. McNally, 169–89. London: Routledge.

Ehlert, Niels, Annika Hennl, and André Kaiser. 2007. "Föderalismus, Dezentralisierung und Performanz: Eine makroquantitative Analyse der Leistungsfähigkeit territorialer Politikorganisation in entwickelten Demokratien." *Politische Vierteljahresschrift* 48 (2): 243–68.

Eifler, Ulrike. 2007. *Neoliberale Globalisierung und die Arbeiterbewegung in China*. Stuttgart: Ibidem.

Eisenstadt, Shmuel N. 2006. *Theorie und Moderne: Soziologische Essays*. Wiesbaden: VS Verlag.

Ernst, Dieter. 2006. *Innovation Offshoring: Asia's Emerging Role in Global Innovation Networks*. Honolulu, HI: East-West Center.

Ernst, Dieter, and Barry Naughton. 2007. "China's Emerging Industrial Economy: Insights from the IT Industry." In *China's Emergent Political Economy: Capitalism in the Dragon's Lair*, ed. Christopher A. McNally, 39–59. London: Routledge.

EUCCC. 2010. *European Business in China Position Paper 2009/2010*. Beijing: European Union Chamber of Commerce in China.

Evans, Peter. 1995. *Embedded Autonomy: States and Industrial Transformation*. Princeton, N.J.: Princeton University Press.

Eyal, Gil, Iván Szelényi, and Eleanor Townsley. 2000. *Making Capitalism Without Capitalists: Class Formation and Elite Struggles in Post-Communist Central Europe*. London: Verso.

Fan, Peilei. 2011. "Innovation, Globalization, and Catch-Up of Latecomers: Cases of Chinese Telecom Firms." *Environment and Planning A* 43 (4): 830–49.

Felipe, Jesus, Editha Laviña, and Emma Xiaoqin Fan. 2008. "The Diverging Patterns of Profitability, Investment and Growth of China and India During 1980–2003." *World Development* 36 (5): 741–74.

Feng, Chen. 2003. "Between the State and Labour: The Conflict of Chinese Trade Unions' Double Identity in Market Reform." *China Quarterly* 176 (May): 1006–28.

Fewsmith, Joseph. 2008. *China Since Tiananmen: From Deng Xiaoping to Hu Jintao*. New York: Cambridge University Press.

———. 2011. The Elusive Search for Effective Sub-County Governance. In *Mao's Invisible Hand*, ed. Sebastian Heilmann and Elizabeth J. Perry, 269–96. Cambridge, Mass.: Harvard University Press.

Field, Mark George. 1976. *Social Consequences of Modernization in Communist Societies*. Baltimore: Johns Hopkins University Press.

Fligstein, Neil. 2001. *The Architecture of Markets: An Economic Sociology of Twenty-First-Century Capitalist Societies*. Princeton, N.J.: Princeton University Press.

Fligstein, Neil, and Jianjun Zhang. 2011. "A New Agenda for Research on the Trajectory of Chinese Capitalism." *Management and Organization Review* 7 (1): 39–62.

Frazier, Mark W. 2010. *Socialist Insecurity: Pensions and the Politics of Uneven Development in China*. Ithaca, N.Y.: Cornell University Press

Frazier, Mark W. 2011. "Welfare Policy Pathways Among Large Uneven Developers." In *Beyond the Middle Kingdom*, ed. Scott Kennedy, 89–109. Stanford, Calif.: Stanford University Press.

Friedman, Eli. 2011. "Rupture and Representation: Migrant Workers, Unions and the State in China." PhD thesis, University of California–Berkeley.

Friedman, Eli, and Sarosh Kuruvilla. 2015. "Experimentation and Decentralization in China's Labor Relations." *Human Relations* 68 (2): 181–95.

Friedman, Eli, and Ching Kwan Lee. 2010. "Remaking the World of Chinese Labour: A 30-Year Retrospective." *British Journal of Industrial Relations* 48 (3): 507–33.

Fröbel, Folker, Jürgen Heinrichs, and Otto Kreye. 1988. "Die Entwicklungsländer in der internationalen Arbeitsteilung." In *Die Armut der Nationen: Handbuch zur Schuldenkrise von Argentinien bis Zaire*, ed. Elmar Altvater, Friedhelm Wachs, Kurt Hübner, and Jochen Lorentzen, 92–101. Berlin: Rotbuch.

Fu, Xiaolan. 2015. *China's Path to Innovation*. Cambridge: Cambridge University Press.

Gallagher, Mary E. 2017. *Authoritarian Legality in China: Law, Workers, and the State*. Cambridge: Cambridge University Press.

Gallagher, Mary E., and Yue Ma. 2011. "FDI and Corporate Restructuring in China: Is the Medicine Worse Than the Disease?" In *Going Private in China: The Politics of Corporate Restructuring and System Reform*, ed. Jean C. Oi, 135–73. Stanford, Calif.: Walter H. Shorenstein Asia-Pacific Research Center Books.

Gao, Qin, Yang, Sui, and Shi Li. 2013. "The Chinese Welfare State in Transition: 1988–2007." *Journal of Social Policy* 42 (4): 743–62.

Gates, Hill. 1996. *China's Motor: A Thousand Years of Petty Capitalism*. Ithaca, N.Y.: Cornell University Press.

Gaulier, Guillaume, Francoise Lemoine, and Deniz Ünal-Kesenci. 2007. "China's Integration in East Asia: Production Sharing, FDI and High-Tech Trade." *Economic Change and Restructuring* 40 (1–2): 27–63.

Gereffi, Gary. 2009. "Development Models and Industrial Upgrading in China and Mexico." *European Sociological Review* 25 (1): 37–51.

Gereffi, Gary, John Humphrey, and Timothy Sturgeon. 2005. "The Governance of Global Value Chains." *Review of International Political Economy* 12 (1): 78–104.

Gerschenkron, Alexander. 1966. *Economic Backwardness in Historical Perspective: A Book of Essays*. Cambridge, Mass.: Belknap Press of Harvard University Press.

Gey, Peter. 1985. "Planwirtschaft und Industrialisierung—Probleme sozialistischer Wirtschaftssysteme in Entwicklungsländern am Beispiel Polens, Jugoslawiens, Chinas und Kubas." In *Sozialismus und Industrialisierung: Die Wirtschaftssysteme Polens, Jugoslawiens, Chinas und Kubas im Vergleich*, ed. Peter Gey, Jiri Kosta, and Wolfgang Quaisser, 15–55. Frankfurt/Main: Campus.

Glyn, Andrew. 2006. *Capitalism Unleashed: Finance, Globalization, and Welfare*. Oxford: Oxford University Press.

GM (Globalization Monitor). 2010. *Complicity, Campaigns, Collaboration, and Corruption: Strategies and Responses to European Corporations and Lobbyists in China*. Hong Kong: Globalization Monitor.

Goldman, Merle, and Roderick MacFarquhar. 1999a. "Dynamic Economy, Declining Party-State." In *The Paradox of China's Post-Mao Reforms*, ed. Merle Goldman and Roderick MacFarquhar, 3–29. Cambridge, Mass.: Harvard University Press.

———. 1999b. *The Paradox of China's Post-Mao Reforms*. Cambridge, Mass.: Harvard University Press.

Goodman, David S. G. 2016. "Locating China's Middle Classes: Social Intermediaries and the Party-State." *Journal of Contemporary China* 25 (97): 1–13.

Grobe-Hagel, Karl. 1990. "Die Elite der Partisanen: Mit den Mitteln von 1935 ins dritte Jahrtausend." In *Nachdenken über China*, ed. Ulrich Menzel, 23–47. Frankfurt/Main: Suhrkamp.

Gruin, Julian Y. 2016. "The Social Order of Chinese Capitalism: Socio-Economic Uncertainty, Communist Party rule and Economic Development, 1990–2000." *Economy and Society* 45 (1): 24–50.

Guangdong Province. 2016. "Guangdong Province Statistics Bulletin on the Economic and Social Development of Guangdong Province in 2015 [2015 nian guangdong guomin jingji he shehui fazhan tongji gongbao]." *Guangdong Provincial Government*, 16 May. http://www.gdstats.gov.cn/tjzl/tjgb/201605/t20160516_327975.html.

Guo, Di, Yan Guo, and Kun Jiang. 2016. "Government-Subsidized R&D and Firm Innovation: Evidence from China." *Research Policy* 45 (6): 1129–44.

Guo, Dingping. 2009. "The Changing Nature of Chinese Socialism Comparative Perspectives." *European Journal of East Asian Studies* 8 (1): 1–29.

Guthrie, Doug. 2002. *Dragon in a Three-Piece Suit: The Emergence of Capitalism in China.* Princeton, N.J.: Princeton University Press.

Hagemann, Ernst. 1990. "Öffnung mit Zugluft: Getrübte Aussichten in der Außenwirtschaft." In *Nachdenken über China*, ed. Ulrich Menzel, 105–25. Frankfurt/Main: Suhrkamp.

Hall, Peter A. 2008. "Systematic Process Analysis: When and How to Use It." *European Political Science* 7 (3): 304–17.

Hall, Peter A., and David Soskice. 2001. "An Introduction to Varieties of Capitalism." In *Varieties of Capitalism: The Institutional Foundations of Comparative Advantage*, ed. Peter A. Hall and David Soskice, 1–68. Oxford: Oxford University Press.

Hamilton, Gary G. 2006a. *Commerce and Capitalism in Chinese Societies.* London: Routledge.

———. 2006b. "Hong Kong and the Rise of Capitalism in Asia." In *Commerce and Capitalism in Chinese Societies*, ed. Gary G. Hamilton, 129–45. London: Routledge.

Hamilton, Gary G., and Nicole Woolsey Biggart. 1997. "Market, Culture, and Authority: A Comparative Analysis of Management and Organization in the Far East." In *The Economic Organization of East Asian Capitalism*, ed. Marco Orru, Nicole Woolsey Biggart, and Gary G. Hamilton, 111–50. Thousand Oaks, Calif.: Sage.

Hamilton, Gary G., Misha Petrovic, and Robert C. Feenstra. 2006. "Remaking the Global Economy: U.S. Retailers and Asian Manufacturers." In *Commerce and Capitalism in Chinese Societies*, ed. Gary G. Hamilton, 146–83. London: Routledge.

Hancké, Bob, Martin Rhodes, and Mark Thatcher, eds. 2007. *Beyond Varieties of Capitalism: Conflict, Contradictions, and Complementarities in the European Economy.* Oxford: Oxford University Press.

Hansakul, Syetarn. 2007. *Chinas Bankensektor: Bereit für die nächste Runde?* Frankfurt/Main: Deutsche Bank Research.

Harman, Chris. 2009. *Zombie Capitalism: Global Crisis and the Relevance of Marx.* London: Bookmarks.

Harris, Nigel. 1971. *Beliefs in Society: The Problem of Ideology.* London: Penguin Books

———. 1978. *The Mandate of Heaven: Marx and Mao in Modern China.* London: Quartet Books.

———. 1986. *The End of the Third World: Newly Industrializing Countries and the Decline of an Ideology.* Harmondsworth: Penguin Books.

Hartig, Falk. 2008. *Die Kommunistische Partei Chinas heute: Von der Revolutions- zur Reform-partei.* Frankfurt/Main: Campus.

Hart-Landsberg, Martin, and Paul Burkett. 2006. "China and the Dynamics of Transnational Accumulation: Causes and Consequences of Global Restructuring." *Historical Materialism* 14 (3): 3–43.

Hartmann, Jürgen. 2006. *Politik in China: Eine Einführung.* Wiesbaden: VS Verlag.

Harvey, David. 1989. "From Managerialism to Entrepreneurialism: The Transformation in Urban Governance in Late Capitalism." *Geografiska Annaler: Series B, Human Geography* 71 (1): 3–17.

———. 2010. *The Enigma of Capital and the Crises of Capitalism.* London: Profile Books.

Hay, Colin. 2002. *Political Analysis: A Critical Introduction.* Houndmills: Palgrave Macmillan.

Haynes, Mike. 2002. "Marxism and the Russian Question in the Wake of the Soviet Collapse." *Historical Materialism* 10 (4): 317–62.

He, Jianwu, Louis Kuijs. 2007. "Rebalancing China's Economy: Modeling a Policy Package." World Bank China Research Paper 7. Washington, D.C.: World Bank.

He, Qinglian. 2006. *China in der Modernisierungsfalle.* Hamburg: Hamburger Edition.

Heberer, Thomas. 2002. "Strategische Gruppen und Staatskapazität: Das Beispiel der Privatunternehmer in China." Duisburg Working Papers on East Asian Studies, no. 46. Duisburg: Universität Duisburg-Essen.

———. 2007. "Institutionelle Defizite gefährden Chinas soziale und politische Stabilität: Von der Rolle einer Supermacht des 21. Jahrhunderts ist das Land noch weit entfernt." *Zeitschrift für Politik* 54 (2): 162–78.

———. 2008. "Das politische System der VR China im Prozess des Wandels." In *Einführung in die politischen Systeme Ostasiens: VR China, Hongkong, Japan, Nordkorea, Südkorea, Taiwan,* ed. Thomas Heberer and Claudia Derichs, 21–177. Wiesbaden: VS Verlag.

Heberer, Thomas, and Gunter Schubert, eds. 2009. *Regime Legitimacy in Contemporary China: Institutional Change and Stability.* London: Routledge.

Heberer, Thomas, and Anja Senz. 2009. "Reform, Demokratisierung, Stabilität oder Kollaps? Literaturbericht zur Entwicklung des chinesischen Herrschaftssystems." *Politische Vierteljahresschrift* 50 (2): 306–26.

Heilmann, Sebastian. 2004. *Das politische System der Volksrepublik China.* Wiesbaden: VS Verlag.

———. 2008. "Policy Experimentation in China's Economic Rise." *Studies in Comparative International Development* 43 (1): 1–26.

———. 2009. "Weltwirtschaftliche Integration und politisch-administrative Modernisierung: Die Volksrepublik China als lernendes autoritäres System?" In *Ostasien in der Globalisierung,* ed. Hanns W. Maull, Martin Wagener, 155–68. Baden-Baden: Nomos.

———. 2010. "The Reinvention of Development Planning in China. 1993–2010." Paper presented at Joint International Conference of the Research Network "Governance in China" and the Association for Social Science Research on China, 26–28 November, Würzburg, Germany.

Heilmann, Sebastian and Matthias Stepan, eds. 2016. *China's Core Executive Leadership Styles, Structures and Processes Under Xi Jinping.* Berlin: MERICS (Mercator Institute for China Studies).

Heilmann, Sebastian, and Oliver Melton. 2013. "The Reinvention of Development Planning in China. 1993–2012." *Modern China* 39 (6): 580–628.

Heilmann, Sebastian, and Elizabeth J. Perry, eds. 2011a. "Embracing Uncertainty: Guerilla Policy Style and Adaptive Governance in China." In *Mao's Invisible Hand*, ed. Sebastian Heilmann and Elizabeth J. Perry, 1–29. Cambridge, Mass.: Harvard University Press.

———. 2011b. *Mao's Invisible Hand: The Political Foundations of Adaptive Governance in China*. Cambridge, Mass.: Harvard University Press.

Heinrich, Michael. 2003. *Die Wissenschaft vom Wert: Die Marxsche Kritik der politischen Ökonomie zwischen wissenschaftlicher Revolution und klassischer Tradition*. Münster: Westfälisches Dampfboot.

Herd, Richard, Vincent Koen, and Anders Reutersward. 2010. "China's Labour Market in Transition: Job Creation, Migration and Regulation." OECD Economics Department Working Paper, no. 749. Paris: OECD.

Herr, Hansjörg. 2002. "Tastendes Suchen statt beherztes Springen: Chinas erfolgreicher Reformprozess." *Internationale Politik und Gesellschaft* 3: 26–48.

———. 2008. "Das chinesische Wechselkurssystem." *Aus Politik und Zeitgeschichte* 7: 27–32.

———. 2011. "Perspectives on High Growth and Rising Inequality." In *China's Labor Question*, ed. Christoph Scherrer, 7–27. Munich: Rainer Hampp Verlag.

Herr, Hansjörg, and Silke Tober. 1999. "Unterschiedliche Marktkonstellationen: Was unterscheidet die Entwicklung in der VR China von den Ländern der ehemaligen Sowjetunion und den Visegrádstaaten?" In *Der "lange Marsch" in die Marktwirtschaft: Entwicklungen und Erfahrungen in der VR China und Osteuropa*, ed. Hansjörg Herr and Kurt Hübner, 77–118. Berlin: Edition Sigma.

Herrigel, Gary, Ulrich Voskamp, and Volker Wittke. 2017. *Globale Qualitätsproduktion. Transnationale Produktionssysteme in der Automobilzulieferindustrie und im Maschinenbau*. Frankfurt/Main: Campus.

Herrigel, Gary, Volker Wittke, and Ulrich Voskamp. 2013. "The Process of Chinese Manufacturing Upgrading: Transitioning from Unilateral to Recursive Mutual Learning Relations." *Global Strategy Journal*, 3: 109–25.

Herrmann-Pillath, Carsten. 1995. *Marktwirtschaft in China: Geschichte—Strukturen—Transformation*. Opladen: Leske und Budrich.

———. 2001. "Staatliche Kapazität, Regulation und Krise: Systemerbe und Globalisierung in der chinesischen Transformation." In *China: Konturen einer Übergangsgesellschaft auf dem Weg in das 21. Jahrhundert*, ed. Gunter Schubert, 183–234. Hamburg: Institut für Asienkunde.

———. 2009. "China's Path-Dependent Transition: Culture Mediating Between Market and Socialism." In *Market and Socialism in the Light of the Experiences of China and Vietnam*, ed. János Kornai and Yingyi Qian, 110–34. London: Palgrave.

Hirsch, Joachim. 2005. *Materialistische Staatstheorie: Transformationsprozesse des kapitalistischen Staatensystems*. Hamburg: VSA.

Holbig, Heike. 2003. "Gelingt die politische Steuerung der wirtschaftlichen Dynamik in China?" *China aktuell* 32 (1): 43–51.

———. 2004. "The Party and Private Entrepreneurs in the PRC." In *Bringing the Party Back: How China Is Governed*, ed. Kjeld Erik Brodsgaard and Yongnian Zheng, 239–68. Singapore: Eastern Universities Press.

———. 2005. "'Wissenschaftliches Entwicklungskonzept,' 'Harmonische Gesellschaft' und 'Eigenständige Innovation': Neue parteipolitische Prioritäten unter Hu Jintao." *China aktuell* 34 (6): 13–19.

———. 2009. "Ideological Reform and Political Legitimacy in China: Challenges in the Post-Jiang Era." In *Regime Legitimacy in Contemporary China*, ed. Thomas Heberer and Gunter Schubert, 13–34. London: Routledge.

Holbig, Heike, and Bruce Gilley. 2010. "In Search of Legitimacy in Post-Revolutionary China: Bringing Ideology and Governance Back In." GIGA Working Paper, no 127. Hamburg: German Institute of Global and Area Studies.

Holbig, Heike, and Thomas Reichenbach. 2005. *Verbandliche Interessenvermittlung in der VR China: Der Bund für Industrie und Handel zwischen staatlichem Kontrollanspruch und privatwirtschaftlicher Selbstbehauptung*. Hamburg: Institut für Asienkunde.

Hollingsworth, J. Rogers, and Robert Boyer, eds. 1997. *Contemporary Capitalism: The Embeddedness of Institutions*. Cambridge: Cambridge University Press.

Holz, Carsten A. 2008. "China's Economic Growth 1978–2025: What We Know Today About China's Economic Growth Tomorrow." *World Development* 36 (10): 1665–91.

Honneth, Axel. 2007. "Eine soziale Pathologie der Vernunft: Zur intellektuellen Erbschaft der Kritischen Theorie." In *Pathologien der Vernunft: Geschichte und Gegenwart der Kritischen Theorie*, ed. Axel Honneth, 28–56. Frankfurt/Main: Suhrkamp.

Honohan, Patrick. 2008. "Finance for Urban Centers." In *China Urbanizes: Consequences, Strategies, and Policies*, ed. Yusuf Shahid and Tony Saich, 105–23. Washington, D.C.: World Bank.

Höpner, Martin. 2005. "What Connects Industrial Relations and Corporate Governance? Explaining Institutional Complementarity." *Socio-Economic Review* 3 (2): 331–58.

Howell, Jude. 2006. "Reflections on the Chinese State." *Development and Change* 37 (2): 273–97.

Hsing, You-tien. 1998. *Making Capitalism in China: The Taiwan Connection*. Oxford: Oxford University Press.

Hsueh, Roselyn. 2011. *China's Regulatory State: A New Strategy for Globalization*. Ithaca, N.Y.: Cornell University Press.

Hu, Angang. 2010. "Government Transformation and Public Finance." In *Transforming the Chinese Economy*, ed. Fang Cai, 149–99. Leiden: Brill.

Hu, Shuli. 2016. "Liaoning Scandal Uncovers Twisted Government-Business Relations." *Caixin*, 20 September. https://www.caixinglobal.com/2016-09-20/100992730.html.

Huang, Xiaoming. 2011. "Institutional Analysis and China's Transformation: Issues and Concepts." In *The Institutional Dynamics of China's Great Transformation*, ed. Xiaoming Huang, 1–24. New York: Routledge.

Huang, Yanjie, and Shaofeng Chen. 2010. "Pearl River Delta in a Crisis of Industrialisation." In *China and the Global Economic Crisis*, ed. Yongnian Zheng and Sarah Y. Tong, 67–87. Singapore: World Scientific.

Huang, Yasheng. 2008. *Capitalism with Chinese Characteristics: Entrepreneurship and the State*. Cambridge: Cambridge University Press.

Hui, Sio-ieng. 2011. "Understanding Labour Activism: The Honda Workers' Strike." In *China's Labor Question*, ed. Christoph Scherrer, 133–51. Munich: Rainer Hampp Verlag.

Hung, Ho-fung. 2008. "Rise of China and the Global Overaccumulation Crisis." *Review of International Political Economy* 15 (2): 149–79.

———, ed. 2009a. *China and the Transformation of Global Capitalism*. Baltimore: Johns Hopkins University Press.

———. 2009b. "The Three Transformations of Global Capitalism." In *China and the Transformation of Global Capitalism*, ed. Ho-fung Hung, 1–21. Baltimore: Johns Hopkins University Press.

———. 2010. "Uncertainty in the Enclave." *New Left Review* 66 (11–12): 55–77.

Hürtgen, Stefanie, Boy Lüthje, Wilhelm Schumm, and Martina Sproll. 2009. *Von Silicon Valley nach Shenzhen: Globale Produktion und Arbeit in der IT-Industrie.* Hamburg: VSA.

Hurtienne, Thomas. 1988. "Gibt es für den verschuldeten Kapitalismus einen Weg aus der Krise?" In *Die Armut der Nationen: Handbuch zur Schuldenkrise von Argentinien bis Zaire*, ed. Elmar Altvater, Friedhelm Wachs, Kurt Hübner, and Jochen Lorentzen, 128–51. Berlin: Rotbuch.

IMF. 2004. *World Economic Outlook, April 2004: Advancing Structural Reforms.* Washington, D.C.: International Monetary Fund.

———. 2011. *People's Republic of China: Financial System Stability Assessment.* Washington, D.C.: International Monetary Fund/World Bank.

———. 2016. "Article IV Consultation Staff Report on the People's Republic of China." IMF Country Report, no. 16/270. Washington, D.C.: International Monetary Fund.

Itoh, Makoto. 2003. "Sozialistische Marktwirtschaft und der chinesische Weg." *Zeitschrift Sozialismus* 7–8 (supplement). https://www.sozialismus.de/vorherige_hefte_archiv/supplements/liste/detail/artikel/der-chinesische-weg-sozialistische-marktwirtschaft/.

Jacques, Martin. 2009. *When China Rules the World: The End of the Western World and the Birth of a New Global Order.* New York: Penguin.

Jessop, Bob. 2002. *The Future of the Capitalist State.* Cambridge: Polity.

———. 2007. *State Power: A Strategic-Relational Approach.* Cambridge: Polity.

———. 2009. "Cultural Political Economy: Rethinking the Linkages Between Culture and the Political Economy of Variegated Capitalism in a World Market Organized in the Shadow of Neo-Liberalism." Paper presented at Ringberg Conference on Varieties of Capitalism, 17–19 November, Ringberg Castle, Germany.

———. 2010. "Cultural Political Economy and Critical Policy Studies." *Critical Policy Studies* 3 (3–4): 336–56.

Jessop, Bob, and Ngai-Ling Sum. 2006. *Beyond the Regulation Approach: Putting Capitalist Economies in Their Place.* Cheltenham: Edward Elgar.

Jiang, Julie, and Jonathan Sinton. 2011. *Overseas Investment by Chinese National Oil Companies: Assessing the Drivers and Impacts.* Paris: International Energy Agency.

Jiaxing City. 2016. "Concise Analysis of the Situation of Economic Development of the Yangtse River Delta in 2015 [2015 nian changsanjiaoqu jingjing fazhan qingkuang jianxi]." *Jiaxing City Administration*, 1 April. http://www.jiaxing.gov.cn/stjj/tjxx_6433/tjfx_6436/201604/t20160401_584644.html.

Jung, Joo-Youn. 2011. "Reinvented Intervention: The Chinese Central System and State-Owned Enterprise Reform in the WTO Era." In *Going Private in China: The Politics of Corporate Restructuring and System Reform*, ed. Jean C. Oi, 119–34. Stanford, Calif.: Walter H. Shorenstein Asia-Pacific Research Center Books.

Kaldor, Nicholas. 1972. "The Irrelevance of Equilibrium Economics." *Economic Journal* 82 (328): 1237–55.

Karl, Rebecca E. 2010. *Mao Zedong and China in the Twentieth-Century World: A Concise History.* Durham, N.C.: Duke University Press.

Kay, Cristóbal. 2002. "Why East Asia Overtook Latin America: Agrarian Reform, Industrialisation and Development." *Third World Quarterly* 23 (6): 1073–102.

Kennedy, Scott. 2007. "Transnational Political Alliances: An Exploration with Evidence from
China." *Business and Society* 46 (2): 174–200.

———, ed. 2011a. *Beyond the Middle Kingdom: Comparative Perspectives on China's Capitalist
Transformation.* Stanford, Calif.: Stanford University Press.

———. 2011b. "Fragmented Influence: Business Lobbying in China in Comparative Perspective." In *Beyond the Middle Kingdom,* ed. Scott Kennedy, 113–35. Stanford, Calif.: Stanford University Press.

King, Lawrence P., and Iván Szelényi. 2005. "Post-Communist Economic Systems." In *The
Handbook of Economic Sociology,* ed. Neil J. Smelser and Richard Swedberg, 205–29.
Princeton, N.J.: Princeton University Press.

Knöbl, Wolfgang. 2007. *Die Kontingenz der Moderne: Wege in Europa, Asien und Amerika.*
Frankfurt/Main: Campus.

Kornai, János. 1992. *The Socialist System: The Political Economy of Communism.* Oxford:
Oxford University Press.

Kosta, Jiri. 1985. "Die chinesische Volkswirtschaft vom 'Großen Sprung nach vorne' bis zur
gegenwärtigen Wirtschaftsreform: Ein Kampf zwischen zwei Konzepten." In *Sozialismus
und Industrialisierung: Die Wirtschaftssysteme Polens, Jugoslawiens, Chinas und Kubas im
Vergleich,* ed. Peter Gey, Jiri Kosta, and Wolfgang Quaisser, 229–47. Frankfurt/Main:
Campus.

Kroymann, Benjamin. 2009. *Das Kapitalgesellschaftsrecht der VR China: Analyse der
Rahmenbedingungen für ausländische Investoren.* Tübingen: Mohr Siebeck.

Krug, Barbara. 1993. *Chinas Weg zur Marktwirtschaft: Eine politisch-ökonomische Analyse der
Wirtschaftstransformation 1978–1988.* Marburg: Metropolis.

Kurlantzick, Joshua. 2016. *State Capitalism: How the Return of the State Is Transforming the
World.* New York: Oxford University Press.

Lam, Willy Wo-Lap. 2006. *Chinese Politics in the Hu Jintao Era: New Leaders, New Challenges.*
Armonk, N.Y.: East Gate.

———. 2015. *Chinese Politics in the Era of Xi Jinping: Renaissance, Reform, or Retrogression?*
New York: Routledge.

Lane, David. 1976. *The Socialist Industrial State: Towards a Political Sociology of State Socialism.*
London: Allen and Unwin.

Lane, David, and Martin Myant, eds. 2007. *Varieties of Capitalism in Post-Communist Countries.* Houndmills: Palgrave Macmillan.

Lane, Philip R., and Sergio L. Schmukler. 2007. "International Financial Integration of China
and India." In *Dancing with Giants: China, India, and the Global Economy,* ed. L. Alan
Winters and Yusuf Shahid, 101–32. Washington, D.C.: World Bank.

Lardy, Nicholas R. 1998. *China's Unfinished Economic Revolution.* Washington, D.C.:
Brookings.

———. 2002. *Integrating China into the Global Economy.* Washington, D.C.: Brookings.

———. 2014. *Markets over Mao: The Rise of Private Business in China.* Washington, D.C.:
Peterson Institute for International Economics.

Lawrence, Thomas B., and Roy Suddaby. 2006. "Institutions and Institutional Work." In *The
Sage Handbook of Organization Studies,* ed. Steward Clegg, 215–54. London: Sage.

Lee, Ching Kwan. 2007. *Against the Law: Labor Protests in China's Rustbelt and Sunbelt.* Berkeley: University of California Press.

———. 2016. "Precarization or Empowerment? Reflections on Recent Labor Unrest in China." *Journal of Asian Studies* 75 (2): 317–33.

Lee, Ching Kwan, and Mark Selden. 2007. "China's Durable Inequality: Legacies of Revolution and Pitfalls of Reform." *Japan Focus: The Asia-Pacific Journal* 5 (1). https://apjjf.org/-Mark-Selden/2329/article.html.

Lee, Eun-Jeung. 1997. *Konfuzianismus und Kapitalismus: Markt und Herrschaft in Ostasien.* Münster: Westfälisches Dampfboot.

Leibfried, Stephan, and Michael Zürn, eds. 2006. *Transformationen des Staates.* Frankfurt/Main: Suhrkamp.

Lenin, Vladimir I. 1970. "Staat und Revolution." In *Lenin Studienausgabe.* Bd. 2, ed. Iring Fetscher, 7–100. Frankfurt/Main: Fischer.

Leung, Pak Nang, and Ngai Pun. 2009. "The Radicalisation of the New Chinese Working Class: A Case Study of Collective Action in the Gemstone Industry." *Third World Quarterly* 30 (3): 551–65.

Lewis, John W. 1963. *Leadership in Communist China.* Ithaca, N.Y.: Cornell University Press.

Leys, Simon. 1972. *Maos neue Kleider: Hinter den Kulissen der Weltmacht.* Munich: Verlag Kurt Desch.

Li, Cheng. 2009. "The Chinese Communist Party: Recruiting and Controlling the New Elites." *Journal of Current Chinese Affairs* 38 (3): 13–33.

Li, Eric. 2010. "A Color Revolution in China? Keep It Red." *International Herald Tribune,* 7 December. https://www.nytimes.com/2010/12/07/opinion/07iht-edli.html.

Li, Hongbin, and Scott Rozelle. 2003. "Privatizing Rural China: Insider Privatization, Innovative Contracts and the Performance of Township Enterprises." *China Quarterly* 176 (December): 981–1005.

Li, Peilin. 2011. "China's New Stage of Development." *China: An International Journal* 9 (1): 133–43.

Li, Shaomin, Shuhe Li, and Weiying Zhang. 2000. "The Road to Capitalism: Competition and Institutional Change in China." *Journal of Comparative Economics* 28 (2): 269–92.

Li, Shaomin, and Jun Xia. 2008. "The Roles and Performance of State Firms and Non-State Firms in China's Economic Transition." *World Development* 36 (1): 39–54.

Li, Shiyu, and Shuanglin Lin. 2011. "The Size and Structure of China's Government Debt." *Social Science Journal* 48 (3): 527–42.

Li, Weisen. 2011. "China's Road to Rechtsstaat: Rule of Law, Constitutional Democracy and Institutional Change." In *The Institutional Dynamics of China's Great Transformation,* ed. Xiaoming Huang, 98–109. New York: Routledge.

Li, Xiaoxi. 2008. "30 Years of Reform Transforms China Beyond Recognition." *China Economist* 16 (9–10): 84–94.

Liang, Yan. 2010. "China and the Global Financial Crisis: Assessing the Impacts and Policy Responses." *China and World Economy* 18 (3): 56–72.

Lieberthal, Kenneth. 1995. *Governing China: From Revolution Through Reform.* New York: W. W. Norton.

Lieberthal, Kenneth, and Michel Oksenberg. 1988. *Policy Making in China: Leaders, Structures, and Processes.* Princeton, N.J.: Princeton University Press.

Lim, Kean Fan. 2010. "On China's Growing Geo-Economic Influence and the Evolution of Variegated Capitalism." *Geoforum* 41 (5): 677–88.

Lin, Chun. 2006. *The Transformation of Chinese Socialism*. Durham, N.C.: Duke University Press.

Lin, Justin Yifu. 2009. *On China's Economy: Der chinesische Weg zur Wirtschaftsmacht*. Heidelberg: ABC Verlag.

Lin, Nan. 1995. "Local Market Socialism: Local Corporatism in Action in Rural China." *Theory and Society* 24 (3): 301–54.

———. 2011. "Capitalism in China: A Centrally Managed Capitalism (CMC) and Its Future." *Management and Organization Review* 7 (1): 63–96.

Lipietz, Alain. 1985. "Akkumulation, Krisen und Auswege aus der Krise: Einige methodische Überlegungen zum Begriff 'Regulation.'" *Prokla* 58: 109–37.

Lippit, Victor D. 1997. "Market Socialism in China?" *Review of Radical Political Economics* 29 (3): 112–23.

Liu, Alan P. L. 1986. *How China Is Ruled*. Englewood Cliffs, N.J.: Prentice-Hall.

Liu, Xielin, Boy Lüthje, Peter Pawlicki. 2007. "China: Nationales Innovationssystem und marktwirtschaftliche Transformation." In *Innovationspolitik: Wie kann Deutschland von anderen lernen?*, ed. Frank Gerlach and Astrid Ziegler, 222–49. Marburg: Schüren Verlag.

Lo, Dic, and Yu Zhang. 2011. "Making Sense of China's Economic Transformation." *Review of Radical Political Economics* 43 (1): 33–55.

Lockett, Hudson. 2016. "China Local Government Revenues Boosted by Real Estate." *Financial Times*, 13 June. https://www.ft.com/content/deab335b-b8a8-3c6a-bd75-b26c0c1f3d41.

Luo, Siqi. 2011. "Collective Contracts, but No Collective Bargaining." In *China's Labor Question*, ed. Christoph Scherrer, 49–69. Munich: Rainer Hampp Verlag.

Lüthje, Boy. 2009. "Tripartism with Four Parties? Regimes of Production and Industrial Relations in Chinese Core Industries." Paper presented at conference "Work and Inequality in the Global Economy: Mexico, China, and the United States," 8–10 October, University of California, Los Angeles.

———. 2010. "Arbeitsbeziehungen in China in der Wirtschaftskrise: 'Tripartismus mit vier Parteien'?" *WSI-Mitteilungen* 9: 473–79.

Lüthje, Boy, Siqi Luo, and Hao Zhang. 2013. *Beyond the Iron Rice Bowl—Regimes of Production and Industrial Relations in China*. Frankfurt/Main: Campus.

Lütz, Susanne. 2003. "Governance in der politischen Ökonomie." MPIfG Discussion Paper 03/5. Cologne: Max Planck Institute for the Study of Societies.

Lyons, Thomas P. 1990. "Planning and Interprovincial Co-ordination in Maoist China." *China Quarterly* 121 (March): 36–60.

Ma, Guonan, and Wang Yi. 2010. "China's High Saving Rate: Myth and Reality." BIS Working Papers 312. Basel: Bank for International Settlements.

Mackert, Jürgen. 2006. *Ohnmächtiger Staat? Über die sozialen Mechanismen staatlichen Handelns*. Wiesbaden: VS Verlag.

Mahoney, James, and Kathleen Thelen. 2010. "A Theory of Gradual Institutional Change." In *Explaining Institutional Change: Ambiguity, Agency, and Power*, ed. James Mahoney and Kathleen Thelen, 1–37. Cambridge: Cambridge University Press.

Mann, Michael. 1990. *Geschichte der Macht: Von den Anfängen bis zur griechischen Antike*. Vol. 1. Frankfurt/Main: Campus.

———. 1998. *Geschichte der Macht: Die Entstehung von Klassen und Nationalstaaten.* Vol. 3–1. Frankfurt/Main: Campus.

Manor, James. 2009. "Politics and Experimentation in India: The Contrast with China." China Analysis, no. 74. Duisburg: Universität Duisburg-Essen.

Marx, Karl. 1986. "Das Kapital: Kritik der politischen Ökonomie; Dritter Band." In *MEW*, *Band 25*, ed. Karl Marx and Friedrich Engels. Berlin: Dietz.

May, Christian, Andreas Nölke, and Tobias ten Brink. 2013. "Institutionelle Determinanten des Aufstiegs großer Schwellenländer: Eine global-politökonomische Erweiterung der 'Varieties of Capitalism.'" *Politische Vierteljahresschrift, Sonderheft 54: Entwicklungstheorien*, 67–94.

Mayntz, Renate. 1996. "Politische Steuerung: Aufstieg, Niedergang und Transformation einer Theorie." *Politische Vierteljahresschrift, Sonderheft 26: Politische Theorien in der Ära der Transformation*, 148–68.

———. 2002. "Zur Theoriefähigkeit makro-sozialer Analysen." In *Akteure—Mechanismen—Modelle: Zur Theoriefähigkeit makro-sozialer Analysen*, ed. Renate Mayntz, 7–43. Frankfurt/Main: Campus.

McGregor, Richard. 2010. *The Party: The Secret World of China's Communist Rulers.* New York: HarperCollins.

McMillan, John, and Barry Naughton. 1996. "Elements of Economic Transition." In *Reforming Asian Socialism: The Growth of Market Institutions*, ed. John McMillan and Barry Naughton, 3–15. Ann Arbor: University of Michigan Press.

McNally, Christopher A., ed. 2007a. *China's Emergent Political Economy: Capitalism in the Dragon's Lair.* London: Routledge.

———. 2007b. "The Institutional Contours of China's Emergent Capitalism." In *China's Emergent Political Economy: Capitalism in the Dragon's Lair*, ed. Christopher A. McNally, 105–25. London: Routledge.

———. 2007c. "Introduction: The China Impact." In *China's Emergent Political Economy: Capitalism in the Dragon's Lair*, ed. Christopher A. McNally, 3–16. London: Routledge.

———. 2011. "State Capitalism Is Dead! Long Live State Capitalism! Rebalancing China's Political Economy." Paper presented at annual meeting of the Association of Asian Studies, 31 March–3 April, Honolulu, Hawaii.

McNally, Christopher A., and Yin-Wah Chu. 2006. "Exploring Capitalist Development in Greater China: A Synthesis." *Asian Perspective* 30 (2): 31–64.

McNally, Christopher A., Hong Guo, and Guangwei Hu. 2007. "Entrepreneurship and Political Guanxi Networks in China's Private Sector." East-West Center Working Papers: Politics, Governance, and Security Series, no. 19. Honolulu: East-West Center.

Meerwaldt, Kerstin. 2010. "Von wirtschaftlicher Stärke und politischer Macht nach der Krise: Ein Bericht von der Expertentagung 'The Economic Crisis as a Litmus-Test—Will the West Gain or Lose?'" *Zeitschrift für Außen- und Sicherheitspolitik* 3 (1): 119–23.

Meyer, Marshall W. 2011. "Is It Capitalism?" *Management and Organization Review* 7 (1): 5–18.

Meyer-Clement, Elena, and Gunter Schubert. 2004. "Greater China—Idee, Konzept, Forschungsprogramm." Greater China Occasional Paper, no. 1. Tübingen: Eberhard Karls Universität.

Montinola, Gabriella, Yingyi Qian, and Barry R. Weingast. 1995. "Federalism, Chinese Style: The Political Basis for Economic Success in China." *World Politics* 48 (1): 50–81.

National People's Congress. 2016. "Outline of 13th National Five-Year Programme for Economic and Social Development of the People's Republic of China [zhonghua renmin gongheguo guomin jingji he shehui fazhan di shisan ge wunian guihua gangyao]." *National People's Congress*, 17 March.

Naughton, Barry. 1995. *Growing Out of the Plan: Chinese Economic Reform 1978–1993*. Cambridge: Cambridge University Press.

——, ed. 1997. *The China Circle: Economics and Electronics in the PRC, Taiwan, and Hong Kong*. Washington, D.C.: Brookings.

——. 2007. *The Chinese Economy: Transitions and Growth*. Cambridge, Mass.: MIT Press.

——. 2009. "Singularity and Replicability in China's Developmental Experience." China Analysis, no. 68. Duisburg: Universität Duisburg-Essen.

——. 2010. "The Policy Challenges of Post-Stimulus Growth." *Global Asia* 5 (2). https://www.globalasia.org/v5no2/cover/the-policy-challenges-of-post-stimulus-growth_barry-naughton.

——. 2011a. "China's Distinctive System: Can It Be a Model for Others?" In *In Search of China's Development Model: Beyond the Beijing Consensus*, ed. S. Philip Hsu, Yu-Shan Wu, and Suisheng Zhao, 67–85. London: Routledge.

——. 2011b. "China's Economic Policy Today: The New State Activism." *Eurasian Geography and Economics* 52 (3): 313–29.

——. 2016. "Supply-Side Structural Reform at Mid-Year: Compliance, Initiative, and Unintended Consequence." *China Leadership Monitor* 51 (Fall). https://www.hoover.org/sites/default/files/research/docs/clm51bn.pdf.

——. 2017. "The Regulatory Storm: A Surprising Turn in Financial Policy." *China Leadership Monitor* 53 (Spring). https://www.hoover.org/sites/default/files/research/docs/clm53bn.pdf.

NBS (National Bureau of Statistics of China). 1983. *China Statistical Yearbook 1983*. Beijing: China Statistics Press.

——. 2010. *China Statistical Yearbook 2010*. Beijing: China Statistics Press.

——. 2011. *China Statistical Yearbook 2011*. Beijing: China Statistics Press.

——. 2015a. *China Industry Statistical Yearbook 2015* [zhongguo gongye tongji nianjian 2015]. Beijing: China Statistics Press.

——. 2015b. *China Statistical Yearbook 2015*. Beijing: China Statistics Press.

——. 2016. "China Monthly Statistics." *National Bureau of Statistics of China*, 24 February. http://www.stats.gov.cn/english/publications/201202/t20120224_72337.html.

NDRC. 2008. *The Outline of the Plan for the Reform and Development of the Pearl River Delta (2008–2020)*. Beijing: National Development and Reform Commission. http://en.ndrc.gov.cn/policyrelease/P020090120342179907030.doc.

——. 2011. *Report on the Implementation of the 2009 Plan for National Economic and Social Development and on the 2010 Draft Plan for National Economic and Social Development*. Beijing: National Development and Reform Commission.

NDRC and MOFCOM. 2015. Catalogue for the Guidance of Foreign Investment Industries, order 2015, no. 22 (in Chinese).

Nee, Victor. 1989. "A Theory of Market Transition: From Redistribution to Markets in State Socialism." *American Sociological Review* 54 (5): 663–81.

——. 2005. "Organizational Dynamics of Institutional Change: Politicized Capitalism in China." In *The Economic Sociology of Capitalism*, ed. Victor Nee and Richard Swedberg, 53–74. Princeton, N.J.: Princeton University Press.

Nee, Victor, and Sonja Opper. 2007. "On Politicized Capitalism." In *On Capitalism*, ed. Victor Nee and Richard Swedberg, 93–127. Stanford, Calif.: Stanford University Press.

Nee, Victor, and Sijin Su. 1996. "Institutions, Social Ties, and Commitment in China's Corporatist Transformation." In *Reforming Asian Socialism: The Growth of Market Institutions*, ed. John McMillan and Barry Naughton, 111–34. Ann Arbor: University of Michigan Press.

Ngok, Kinglun, and Chak Kwan Chan, eds. 2016. *China's Social Policy: Transformation and Challenges*. New York: Routledge.

Nolan, Peter. 2004. *Transforming China: Globalization, Transition and Development*. London: Anthem Press.

Nölke, Andreas. 2011. "Die BRIC-Variante des Kapitalismus und soziale Ungleichheit: Das Beispiel Brasilien." In *Soziale Ungleichheiten in Lateinamerika: Neue Perspektiven auf Wirtschaft, Politik und Umwelt*, ed. Ingrid Wehr and Hans-Jürgen Burchardt, 137–52. Baden-Baden: Nomos.

Nölke, Andreas, Tobias ten Brink, Simone Claar, and Christian May. 2015. "Domestic Structures, Foreign Economic Policies and Global Economic Order: Implications from the Rise of Large Emerging Economies." *European Journal of International Relations* 21 (3): 538–67.

———. 2018. "State-Permeated Market Economies in Large Emerging Countries." Unpublished manuscript.

Nölke, Andreas, and Arjan Vliegenthart. 2009. "Enlarging the Varieties of Capitalism: The Emergence of Dependent Market Economies in East Central Europe." *World Politics* 61 (4): 670–702.

North, Douglass C. 2005. "The Chinese Menu (for Development)." *The Wall Street Journal*, 7 April. https://www.wsj.com/articles/SB111283514152300351.

Obinger, Herbert, Stefan Traub, Andreas Etling, Karsten Mause, Carina Schmitt, Katharina Schreeb, and Philipp Schuster. 2010. "Der Rückzug des Staates aus unternehmerischen Tätigkeiten: Eine Zwischenbilanz." *Der Moderne Staat* 3 (1): 209–33.

OECD. 2016. *OECD Statistics*. http://stats.oecd.org/Index.aspx.

Offe, Claus. 2006. *Strukturprobleme des kapitalistischen Staates: Aufsätze zur Politischen Soziologie*. Frankfurt/Main: Campus.

Office of the United States Trade Representative. 2016. *The People's Republic of China: U.S.-China Trade Facts*. https://ustr.gov/countries-regions/china-mongolia-taiwan/peoples-republic-china.

O'Hara, Phillip Anthony. 2006. "A Chinese Social Structure of Accumulation for Capitalist Long-Wave Upswing?" *Review of Radical Political Economics* 38 (3): 397–404.

Oi, Jean C. 1995. "The Role of the Local State in China's Transitional Economy." *China Quarterly* 144 (December): 1132–49.

———, ed. 2011. *Going Private in China: The Politics of Corporate Restructuring and System Reform*. Stanford, Calif.: Walter H. Shorenstein Asia-Pacific Research Center Books.

Oi, Jean C., and Chaohua Han. 2011. "China's Corporate Restructuring: A Multi-Step Process." In *Going Private in China: The Politics of Corporate Restructuring and System Reform*, ed. Jean C. Oi, 19–37. Stanford, Calif.: Walter H. Shorenstein Asia-Pacific Research Center Books.

Osterhammel, Jürgen. 1989. *China und die Weltgesellschaft: Vom 18. Jahrhundert bis in unsere Zeit*. Munich: C. H. Beck.

Pang, Cuiping. 2005. *Investmentbanken in China: Performanz und Eigentumsformen.* Taunusstein: Dr. H. H. Driesen.

Panitch, Leo. 2009. "Giovanni Arrighi in Beijing: Eine Alternative zum Kapitalismus?" *Sozialismus* 36 (1): 17–24.

Park, Sung-Jo. 1986. "Die VR China und ihre Entwicklung zu einer "sozialistisch-marktwirtschaftlichen" Leistungsgesellschaft." In *Gesellschaftssysteme der Gegenwart: Politökonomische Systemanalysen im internationalen Kontext*, ed. Wilfried Röhrich, 138–55. Opladen: Westdeutscher Verlag.

Pearson, Margaret M. 2010. "The Impact of the PRC's Economic Crisis Response on Regulatory Institutions: Preliminary Thoughts." China Analysis, no. 78. Duisburg: Universität Duisburg-Essen.

———. 2011. "Variety Within and Without: The Political Economy of Chinese Regulation." In *Beyond the Middle Kingdom*, ed. Scott Kennedy, 25–43. Stanford, Calif.: Stanford University Press.

Pei, Minxin. 1994. *From Reform to Revolution: The Demise of Communism in China and the Soviet Union.* Cambridge, Mass.: Harvard University Press.

———. 2006. *China's Trapped Transition: The Limits of Developmental Autocracy.* Cambridge, Mass.: Harvard University Press.

———. 2009. "Will the Chinese Communist Party Survive the Crisis? How Beijing's Shrinking Economy May Threaten One-Party Rule." *Foreign Affairs*, March. https://www.foreign affairs.com/articles/asia/2009-03-12/will-chinese-communist-party-survive-crisis.

———. 2016. *China's Crony Capitalism: The Dynamics of Regime Decay.* Cambridge: Harvard University Press.

Perry, Elizabeth J. 2007. "Studying Chinese Politics: Farewell to Revolution?" *China Journal* 57 (1): 1–22.

Perry, Elizabeth J., and Mark Selden, eds. 2003. *Chinese Society: Change, Conflict and Resistance.* New York: Routledge.

Pickles, John, and Adrian Smith, eds. 1998. *Theorising Transition: The Political Economy of Post-Communist Transformations.* London: Routledge.

Pissler, Knut B. 2009. "Sozialistisches Recht." In *Handwörterbuch des Europäischen Privatrechts*, ed. Jürgen Basedow, Klaus J. Hopt, and Reinhard Zimmermann, 1421–24. Tübingen: Mohr Siebeck.

Pistor, Katharina. 2012. "The Governance of China's Finance." In *Capitalizing China*, ed. Joseph P. H. Fan and Randall Morck, 35–60. Chicago: University of Chicago Press.

Pohlmann, Markus. 2002. *Der Kapitalismus in Ostasien: Südkoreas und Taiwans Wege ins Zentrum der Weltwirtschaft.* Münster: Westfälisches Dampfboot.

Polanyi, Karl. 2001. *The Great Transformation: The Political and Economic Origins of Our Time.* Boston: Beacon Press.

Pollock, Friedrich. 1975. Staatskapitalismus. In *Friedrich Pollock: Stadien des Kapitalismus*, ed. Helmut Dubiel, 72–100. Munich: C. H. Beck.

Pomeranz, Kenneth. 2000. *The Great Divergence: China, Europe, and the Making of the Modern World Economy.* Princeton, N.J.: Princeton University Press.

Prud'homme, Dan. 2016. "Dynamics of China's Provincial-Level Specialization in Strategic Emerging Industries." *Research Policy* 45 (8): 1586–603.

Pun, Ngai, and Huilin Lu. 2010. "Unvollendete Proletarisierung: Das Selbst, die Wut und die Klassenaktionen der zweiten Generation von BauernarbeiterInnen im heutigen China." *Sozial.Geschichte Online* 4: 36–69.

Pye, Lucian W. 1998. *The Spirit of Chinese Politics*. Cambridge, Mass.: Harvard University Press.

Redding, Gordon. 1990. *The Spirit of Chinese Capitalism*. Berlin: de Gruyter.

Redding, Gordon, and Michael A. Witt. 2007. *The Future of Chinese Capitalism: Choices and Chances*. Oxford: Oxford University Press.

Robins, F. 2010. "China: A New Kind of "Mixed" Economy?" *Asian Business and Management* 9 (1): 23–46.

Rosenberg, Justin. 2006. "Why Is There No International Historical Sociology?" *European Journal of International Relations* 12 (3): 307–40.

Rowen, Henry S. 2007. "When Will the Chinese People Be Free?" *Journal of Democracy* 18 (3): 38–52.

Sablowski, Thomas. 2009. "Die Ursachen der neuen Weltwirtschaftskrise." *Kritische Justiz* 42 (2): 116–31.

Sachs, Jeffrey, and Wing Thye Woo. 1999. "Zum Verständnis der Reformerfahrungen in China, Osteuropa und Russland." In *Der "lange Marsch" in die Marktwirtschaft: Entwicklungen und Erfahrungen in der VR China und Osteuropa*, ed. Hansjörg Herr and Kurt Hübner, 19–44. Berlin: Edition Sigma.

Saich, Tony. 2004. *Governance and Politics of China*. New York: Palgrave Macmillan.

———. 2008. "The Changing Role of Urban Government." In *China Urbanizes: Consequences, Strategies, and Policies*, ed. Yusuf Shahid and Tony Saich, 181–206. Washington, D.C.: World Bank.

SASAC. 2016. "List of Central Enterprises." *State-Owned Assets Supervision and Administration Commission of the State Council*, 3 August. http://www.sasac.gov.cn/n86114/n86137/index.html.

Sauer, Dieter, and Christa Lang, eds. 1999. *Paradoxien der Innovation: Perspektiven sozialwissenschaftlicher Innovationsforschung*. Frankfurt/Main: Campus.

Saxenian, AnnaLee. 2005. "Brain Circulation and Capitalist Dynamics: Chinese Chipmaking and the Silicon Valley-Hsinchu-Shanghai Triangle." In *The Economic Sociology of Capitalism*, ed. Victor Nee and Richard Swedberg, 325–51. Princeton, N.J.: Princeton University Press.

Scharpf, Fritz W. 1985. "Die Politikverflechtungs-Falle: Europäische Integration und deutscher Föderalismus im Vergleich. " *Politische Vierteljahresschrift* 26: 323–56.

Scharping, Thomas. 1988. "Sprünge im Spiegel: Das China-Bild im Wandel der westlichen Forschung." *Kölner China-Studien* 1: 1–28.

Schimank, Uwe. 2009. " 'Vater Staat': Ein vorhersehbares Comeback; Staatsverständnis und Staatstätigkeit in der Moderne." *Der Moderne Staat* 2 (2): 249–70.

Schmidt, Dirk, and Sebastian Heilmann. 2010. "Dealing with Economic Crisis in 2008–09: The Chinese Government's Crisis Management in Comparative Perspective." China Analysis, no. 77. Duisburg: Universität Duisburg-Essen.

Schmidt, Vivien A. 2000. "Still Three Models of Capitalism? The Dynamics of Economic Adjustment in Britain, Germany and France." In *Die politische Konstitution von Märkten*, ed. Roland Czada and Susanne Lütz, 38–73. Wiesbaden: Westdeutscher Verlag.

———. 2009. "Putting the Political Back into Political Economy by Bringing the State Back In Yet Again." *World Politics* 61 (3): 516–46.

Schmidt-Glintzer, Helwig. 2008. *Kleine Geschichte Chinas*. Munich: C. H. Beck.

Schneider, Ben Ross. 2008. "Comparing Capitalisms: Liberal, Coordinated, Network, and Hierarchical Varieties." Unpublished manuscript.

Schubert, Gunter, ed. 2001a. *China: Konturen einer Übergangsgesellschaft auf dem Weg in das 21. Jahrhundert.* Hamburg: Institut für Asienkunde.

———. 2001b. "Still in Search of Wealth and Power? Nationalismus und nationale Identität im China des beginnenden 21. Jahrhunderts." In *China: Konturen einer Übergangsgesellschaft auf dem Weg in das 21. Jahrhundert,* ed. Gunter Schubert, 55–80. Hamburg: Institut für Asienkunde.

Schucher, Günter, and Kawsu Ceesay. 2011. "Wird China zum neuen Modell für soziale Stabilität?" *GIGA Focus Asien* 8: 1–8.

Schwinn, Thomas. 2009. "Multiple Modernities: Konkurrierende Thesen und offene Fragen." *Zeitschrift für Soziologie* 38 (6): 454–76.

Selden, Mark. 1993. *The Political Economy of Chinese Development.* Armonk, N.Y.: M. E. Sharpe.

Selden, Mark, and Chih-ming Ka. 1993. "Original Accumulation, Equality, and Late Industrialization: The Cases of Socialist China and Capitalist Taiwan." In *The Political Economy of Chinese Development,* ed. Mark Selden, 109–36. Armonk, N.Y.: M. E. Sharpe.

Selden, Mark, and Aiguo Lu. 1993. "The Reform of Landownership and the Political Economy of Contemporary China." In *The Political Economy of Chinese Development,* ed. Mark Selden, 187–205. Armonk, N.Y.: M. E. Sharpe.

Selwyn, Ben. 2011. "Trotsky, Gerschenkron and the Political Economy of Late Capitalist Development." *Economy and Society* 40 (3): 421–50.

Shahid, Yusuf, Kaoru Nabeshima, and Dwight H. Perkins. 2006. *Under New Ownership: Privatizing China's State-Owned Enterprises.* Stanford, Calif.: Stanford University Press.

Shambaugh, David. 2008. "Training China's Political Elite: The Party School System." *China Quarterly* 196 (December): 827–44.

———. 2009a. "The China Quarterly and Contemporary China Studies." *China Quarterly* 200 (December): 911–16.

———. 2009b. *China's Communist Party: Atrophy and Adaptation.* Berkeley: University of California Press.

———. 2016. *China's Future.* Cambridge: Polity Press.

Shao, Sijun, Chris Nyland, and Cherrie Jiuhua Zhu. 2011. "Tripartite Consultation: An Emergent Form of Governance Shaping Employment Relations in China." *Industrial Relations Journal* 42 (4): 358–74.

Shen, Jie. 2007. *Disputes and Their Resolution in China.* Oxford: Chandos.

Shih, Victor. 2008. *Factions and Finance in China: Elite Conflict and Inflation.* New York: Cambridge University Press.

Shih, Lea. 2015. *Chinas Industriepolitik von 1978–2013: Programme, Prozesse und Beschränkungen.* Wiesbaden: Springer.

Shirk, Susan L. 1989. "The Political Economy of Chinese Industrial Reform." In *Remaking the Economic Institutions of Socialism: China and Eastern Europe,* ed. Victor Nee and David Stark, 328–62. Stanford, Calif.: Stanford University Press.

———. 1993. *The Political Logic of Economic Reform in China.* Berkeley: University of California Press.

Shonfield, Andrew. 1965. *Modern Capitalism: The Changing Balance of Public and Private Power.* Oxford: Oxford University Press.

Shue, Vivienne. 1988. *The Reach of the State: Sketches of the Chinese Body Politic.* Stanford, Calif.: Stanford University Press.

Silver, Beverly J., and Lu Zhang. 2009. "China as an Emerging Epicenter of World Labor Unrest." In *China and the Transformation of Global Capitalism*, ed. Ho-fung Hung, 174–87. Baltimore: Johns Hopkins University Press.

Smith, Richard. 1993. "The Chinese Road to Capitalism." *New Left Review* 199: 55–99.

Smuthkalin, Worawut. 2011. "The Politics of Social Security Reform in Corporate Restructuring in China." In *Going Private in China: The Politics of Corporate Restructuring and System Reform*, ed. Jean C. Oi, 175–202. Stanford, Calif.: Walter H. Shorenstein Asia-Pacific Research Center Books.

Snow, Edgar. 1963. *The Other Side of the River: Red China Today.* London: Victor Gollancz.

Solga, Heike. 1995. *Auf dem Weg in eine klassenlose Gesellschaft? Klassenlagen und Mobilität zwischen Generationen in der DDR.* Berlin: Akademie Verlag.

Sombart, Werner. 1921. *Der moderne Kapitalismus. Historisch-systematische Darstellung des gesamteuropäischen Wirtschaftslebens von seinen Anfängen bis zur Gegenwart*, 1. Band, 1. Halbband., Munich: Duncker und Humblot.

Spence, Jonathan D. 1995. *Chinas Weg in die Moderne.* Munich: Hanser.

Stark, David. 1996. "Recombinant Property in East European Capitalism." *American Journal of Sociology* 101 (4): 993–1027.

Stark, David, and Victor Nee. 1989. "Toward an Institutional Analysis of State Socialism." In *Remaking the Economic Institutions of Socialism: China and Eastern Europe*, ed. Victor Nee and David Stark, 1–31. Stanford, Calif.: Stanford University Press.

State Council. 2016. "Circular Concerning the Promulgation of the Work Plan for Lowering the Cost of Enterprises in the Real Economy [guowuyuan guanyu yinfa jingdi shiti jingji qiye chengben gongzuo fang'an de tongzhi]." Ministry of Finance of the People's Republic of China, GuoFa 2016, no. 48, 8 August. http://www.mof.gov.cn/zhengwuxinxi/caizhengxinwen/201608/t20160823_2398378.htm.

Steinherr, Alfred. 2008. "Großer Sprung im zweiten Anlauf: 30 Jahre Wirtschaftsreformen in China." *Wochenbericht des DIW Berlin* 75 (51–52): 825–36.

Streeck, Wolfgang. 2009. *Re-Forming Capitalism: Institutional Change in the German Political Economy.* Oxford: Oxford University Press.

———. 2010a. "E Pluribus Unum? Varieties and Commonalities of Capitalism." MPIfG Discussion Paper 10/12. Cologne: Max Planck Institute for the Study of Societies.

———. 2010b. "Taking Capitalism Seriously: Toward an Institutionalist Approach to Contemporary Political Economy." MPIfG Discussion Paper 10/15. Cologne: Max Planck Institute for the Study of Societies.

Streeck, Wolfgang, and Kathleen Thelen. 2005. "Introduction: Institutional Change in Advanced Political Economies." In *Beyond Continuity: Institutional Change in Advanced Political Economies*, ed. Wolfgang Streeck and Kathleen Thelen, 1–39. Oxford: Oxford University Press.

Sum, Ngai-Ling. 1999. "Rethinking Globalisation: Re-Articulating the Spatial Scale and Temporal Horizons of Trans-Border Spaces." In *Globalisation and the Asia-Pacific: Contested Territories*, ed. Kris Olds, Peter Dicken, Philip F. Kelly, Lily Kong, and Henry Wai-chung Yeung, 124–39. London: Routledge.

———. 2011. "Financial Crisis, Land-Induced Financialization and the Subalterns in China." In *China's Labor Question*, ed. Christoph Scherrer, 199–208. Munich: Rainer Hampp Verlag.

Swedberg, Richard. 2005. "The Economic Sociology of Capitalism: An Introduction and Agenda." In *The Economic Sociology of Capitalism*, ed. Victor Nee and Richard Swedberg, 3–40. Princeton, N.J.: Princeton University Press.

Szelényi, Iván. 1982. "The Intelligentsia in the Class Structure of State-Socialist Societies." In *Marxist Inquiries: Studies of Labor, Class, and States*, ed. Michael Burawoy and Theda Skocpol, 287–326. Chicago: University of Chicago Press.

Szelényi, Iván, and Erie Kostello. 1996. "The Market Transition Debate: Toward a Synthesis?" *American Journal of Sociology* 101 (4): 1082–96.

Tamás, Gáspár Miklós. 2007. "Ein ganz normaler Kapitalismus." *Grundrisse—Zeitschrift für linke Theorie und Debatte* 22: 9–23.

Tang, Xiangjun, Ruiming Liu, and Guanghui Ma. 2015. "The Fight Against Corruption and Economic Transformation—Theory and Proof from China's Experience [fanfu yu zhuanxing—lilun yu zhongguo jingyan zhengju]." *Nankai Economic Studies* 5: 140–53.

Taube, Markus. 2001. "Fit für das nächste Jahrhundert? Die Wachstumsfaktoren der chinesischen Volkswirtschaft auf dem Prüfstand." In *China: Konturen einer Übergangsgesellschaft auf dem Weg in das 21. Jahrhundert*, ed. Gunter Schubert, 135–81. Hamburg: Institut für Asienkunde.

———. 2007. "Prinzipien der Entstehung eindeutiger Verfügungsrechtsstrukturen in der VR China: Das Beispiel der Township Village Enterprises." *Zeitschrift für Politik* 54 (2): 179–214.

———. 2009. "Ökonomische Entwicklung in der Volksrepublik China: Nachholendes Wachstum im Zeichen der Globalisierung." In *Ostasien in der Globalisierung*, ed. Hanns W. Maull and Martin Wagener, 111–30. Baden-Baden: Nomos.

Taube, Markus, and Peter Thomas in der Heiden. 2015. "Assessment of the Normative and Policy Framework Governing the Chinese Economy and Its Impact on International Competition." *AEGIS EUROPE*, June. http://www.aegiseurope.eu/news/china-is-not-a-market-economy-confirms-new-in-depth-study.

ten Brink, Tobias. 2010. "Strukturmerkmale des chinesischen Kapitalismus." MPIfG Discussion Paper 10/1. Cologne: Max Planck Institute for the Study of Societies.

———. 2011a. "Institutional Change in Market-Liberal State Capitalism: An Integrative Perspective on the Development of the Private Business Sector in China." MPIfG Discussion Paper 11/2. Cologne: Max Planck Institute for the Study of Societies.

———. 2011b. "Kooperation oder Konfrontation? Der Aufstieg Chinas in der globalen politischen Ökonomie." MPIfG Working Paper 11/7. Cologne: Max Planck Institute for the Study of Societies.

———. 2012a. "Kontinuität und Wandel: China in der westlichen Chinaforschung." *Geographische Revue* 14 (2): 36–52.

———. 2012b. "Überlegungen zum Verhältnis von Kapitalismus und Staatenkonkurrenz." *Zeitschrift für Außen- und Sicherheitspolitik* 5 (1): 97–116.

———. 2013. "Paradoxes of Prosperity in China's New Capitalism." *Journal of Current Chinese Affairs* 42 (4): 17–44.

———. 2014a. "The Challenges of China's Non-Liberal Capitalism for the Liberal Global Economic Order." *Harvard Asia Quarterly* 16 (2): 36–44.

———. 2014b. *Global Political Economy and the Modern State System*. Leiden: Brill.

———. 2015. "Chinese Firms 'Going Global': Recent OFDI Trends, Policy Support, and International Implications." *International Politics* 52 (6): 666–83.

Thompson, Grahame, Jennifer Frances, Rosalind Levacic, and Jeremy Mitchell, eds. 1991. *Markets, Hierarchies and Networks: The Coordination of Social Life.* London: Sage.

Tian, Major. 2014. "The Role of Land Sales in Local Government Financing in China." *Cheung Kong Graduate School of Business*, 3 September 2014. http://knowledge.ckgsb.edu.cn/2014/09/03/policy-and-law/the-role-of-land-sales-in-local-government-financing-in-china/.

Tilly, Charles. 1992. *Coercion, Capital, and European States, AD 990–1992.* Oxford: Blackwell.

Tobin, Damian. 2011. "Austerity and Moral Compromise: Lessons from the Development of China's Banking System." *World Development* 39 (5): 700–711.

Tong, Sarah Y. 2010. "China's Decisive Response to the Economic Crisis Bears Fruits." In *China and the Global Economic Crisis*, ed. Yongnian Zheng and Sarah Y. Tong, 47–65. Singapore: World Scientific.

Tsai, Kellee S. 2005. "Capitalists Without a Class: Political Diversity Among Private Entrepreneurs in China." *Comparative Political Studies* 38 (9): 1130–58.

———. 2006. "Adaptive Informal Institutions and Endogenous Institutional Change in China." *World Politics* 59 (1): 116–41.

———. 2007. *Capitalism Without Democracy: The Private Sector in Contemporary China.* Ithaca, N.Y.: Cornell University Press.

Unger, Jonathan. 2002. *The Transformation of Rural China.* Armonk, N.Y.: M. E. Sharpe.

———. 2007. "The Cultural Revolution at the Grass Roots." *China Journal* 57 (1): 109–37.

Unger, Jonathan, and Anita Chan. 1995. "China, Corporatism, and the East Asian Model." *Australian Journal of Chinese Affairs* 33 (1): 29–53.

———. 1999. "Inheritors of the Boom: Private Enterprise and the Role of Local Government in a Rural South China Township." *China Journal* 42 (2): 45–74.

van der Pijl, Kees. 2006. *Global Rivalries from the Cold War to Iraq.* London: Pluto Press.

von Senger, Harro. 2009. "Demokratie aus Sicht des Sinomarxismus." *Schweizer Monatshefte, Sonderthema 5. Wege des Ostens: Japan, China und die Krise*, 8–11.

Wade, Robert. 1990. *Governing the Market: Economic Theory and the Role of Government in East Asian Industrialization.* Princeton, N.J.: Princeton University Press.

Walder, Andrew G. 1986. *Communist Neo-Traditionalism: Work and Authority in Chinese Industry.* Berkeley: University of California Press.

———. 1995. "Local Governments as Industrial Firms: An Organizational Analysis of China's Transitional Economy." *American Journal of Sociology* 101 (2): 263–301.

———. 2015. *China Under Mao: A Revolution Derailed.* Cambridge, Mass.: Harvard University Press.

Walker, Richard, and Daniel Buck. 2007. "The Chinese Road: Cities in the Transition to Capitalism." *New Left Review* 46 (7–8): 39–66.

Walter, Carl E., and Fraser J. T. Howie. 2011. *Red Capitalism: The Fragile Financial Foundation of China's Extraordinary Rise.* Singapore: John Wiley and Sons.

Wang, Fei-Ling. 2011. "China's Evolving Institutional Exclusion: The Hukou System and Its Transformation." In *The Institutional Dynamics of China's Great Transformation*, ed. Xiaoming Huang, 110–29. New York: Routledge.

Wang, Hui. 2008. "Das Vergessen der sechziger Jahre: Entpolitisierte Politik und Hegemonie im neuen China." *Prokla* 152: 459–77.

———. 2010. "China hat keine klare Ideologie mehr: Reformen müssen von innen kommen. Gespräch mit Wang Hui, einem der gewichtigsten Intellektuellen seines Landes." *Neue*

Zürcher Zeitung, 5 November. https://www.nzz.ch/china_hat_keine_klare_ideologie_
mehr-1.8276681.

Wang, Shaoguang. 2009. "Adapting by Learning: The Evolution of China's Rural Health Care
Financing." *Modern China* 35 (4): 370–404.

Wank, David L. 1996. "The Institutional Process of Market Clientelism: Guanxi and Private
Business in a South China City." *China Quarterly* 147 (September): 820–38.

———. 1999. *Commodifying Communism: Business, Trust, and Politics in a Chinese City.*
Cambridge: Cambridge University Press.

Weber, Max. 1991. *Die protestantische Ethik.* Gütersloh: Gütersloher Verlagshaus.

Wedeman, Andrew. 2011. "Crossing the River by Feeling for Stones or Carried Across by the
Current? The Transformation of the Chinese Automotive Sector." In *Beyond the Middle
Kingdom*, ed. Scott Kennedy, 66–88. Stanford, Calif.: Stanford University Press.

Weggel, Oskar. 1997. *China im Aufbruch: Konfuzianismus und politische Zukunft.* Munich:
C. H. Beck.

Wen, Jiabao. 2011. "Report on the Work of the Government." Speech delivered at the Fourth
Session of the 11th National People's Congress, 5 March. http://online.wsj.com/public/
resources/documents/2011NPCWorkReportEng.pdf.

Wenten, Frido. 2011. "Restructured Class-Relations Since 1978." In *China's Labor Question*,
ed. Christoph Scherrer, 28–48. Munich: Rainer Hampp Verlag.

Werner, Jenni. 2010. "Die politische Förderung technologischer Innovation in der VR China."
China Analysis, no. 81. Duisburg: Universität Duisburg-Essen.

Whyte, Martin. 1989. "Who Hates Bureaucracy? A Chinese Puzzle." In *Remaking the Economic
Institutions of Socialism: China and Eastern Europe*, ed. Victor Nee and David Stark, 233–
54. Stanford, Calif.: Stanford University Press.

Wilson, Jeanne L. 2007a. "China's Transformation Towards Capitalism." In *Varieties of Capitalism in Post-Communist Countries*, ed. David Lane and Martin Myant, 239–57. Houndmills: Palgrave Macmillan.

———. 2007b. "The Impact of the Demise of State Socialism on China." In *The Transformation of State Socialism: System Change, Capitalism or Something Else?*, ed. David Lane,
269–85. Houndmills: Palgrave Macmillan.

Witt, Michael A. 2010. "China: What Variety of Capitalism?" INSEAD Working Paper
no. 2010/88/EPS. Fontainebleau: INSEAD.

Woetzel, Jonathan, Yougang Chen, Jeongmin Seong, Nicolas Leung, Kevin Sneader, and Jon
Kowalski. 2016. *China's Choice. Capturing China's $5 Trillion Productivity Opportunity.*
McKinsey Global Institute.

Woetzel, Jonathan, and Jeffrey Towson. 2015. *The One Hour China Consumer Book: Five Short
Stories That Explain the Brutal Fight for One Billion Chinese Consumers.* Cayman Islands:
Towson Group.

Wong, Christine. 2007. "Budget Reform in China." *OECD Journal on Budgeting* 7 (1): 1–24.

———. 2009. "Rebuilding Government for the 21st Century: Can China Incrementally
Reform the Public Sector?" *China Quarterly* 200 (December): 929–52.

World Bank, ed. 2009. *Global Economic Prospects: Commodities at the Crossroads.* Washington,
D.C.: World Bank.

———. 2016. "Gross Fixed Capital Formation (% of GDP): World Bank National Accounts
Data, and OECD National Accounts Data Files." *World Bank Data Catalogue.* http://
data.worldbank.org/indicator/ne.gdi.ftot.zs.

Woronov, T. E. 2011. "Learning to Serve: Urban Youth, Vocational Schools and New Class Formations in China." *China Journal* 66 (July): 77–100.

Wright, Erik Olin. 1997. *Class Counts: Comparative Studies in Class Analysis*. Cambridge: Cambridge University Press.

———. 2000. "Working-Class Power, the Capitalist-Class Interests, and Class Compromise." *American Journal of Sociology* 105 (4): 957–1002.

Wu, Jieh-Min. 2001. "State Policy and Guanxi Network Adaptation in China: Local Bureaucratic Rent-Seeking." *Issues and Studies* 37 (1): 20–48.

Wu, Jinglian. 2005. *Understanding and Interpreting Chinese Economic Reform*. Singapore: Thomson.

Xiamen Municipal Statistics Office. 2015. "Rise by Embracing Difficulty—Steadily Progress—Output Situation of Enterprises Above Designated Size [ying nan er shang—webu fazhan—2014 nian Xiamen guimo yishang gongye shengchan qingkuang]." *Xiamen Municipal Statistics Office*, 3 February. http://www.stats-xm.gov.cn/tjzl/tjfx/201502/t20150203_25068.htm.

Xie, Weizhi. 1993. "The Semihierarchical Totalitarian Nature of Chinese Politics." *Comparative Politics* 25 (3): 313–30.

Xinhuanet. 2016. "In 4 Years Implementation of the Eight Rules 187,000 Individuals Have Been Processed." *Xinhua*, 17 October. http://news.xinhuanet.com/legal/2016–10/17/c_1119727856.htm.

Yang, Dali L. 1996. "Governing China's Transition to the Market: Institutional Incentives, Politicians' Choices, and Unintended Outcomes." *World Politics* 48 (3): 424–52.

———. 2004. *Remaking the Chinese Leviathan: Market Transition and the Politics of Governance in China*. Stanford, Calif.: Stanford University Press.

Yang, Dali L., and Fubing Su. 2000. "Political Institutions, Provincial Interests, and Resource Allocation in Reformist China." *Journal of Contemporary China* 9 (24): 215–30.

Yang, Mayfair Mei-hui. 2000. "Putting Global Capitalism in Its Place: Economic Hybridity, Bataille, and Ritual Expenditure." *Current Anthropology* 41 (4): 477–95.

———. 2002. "The Resilience of Guanxi and Its New Deployments: A Critique of Some New Guanxi Scholarship." *China Quarterly* 170 (June): 459–76.

Yergin, Daniel, and Joseph Stanislaw. 1999. *Staat oder Markt: Die Schlüsselfrage unseres Jahrhunderts*. Frankfurt/Main: Campus.

Yeung, Godfrey. 2009. "How Banks in China Make Lending Decisions." *Journal of Contemporary China* 18 (59): 285–302.

Yeung, Henry Wai-chung. 2004. *Chinese Capitalism in a Global Era: Towards Hybrid Capitalism*. London: Routledge.

———. 2006. "Change and Continuity in Southeast Asian Ethnic Chinese Business." *Asia Pacific Journal of Management* 23 (3): 229–54.

Yeung, Henry Wai-chung, and Kris Olds. 2000. "Globalizing Chinese Business Firms: Where Are They Coming from, Where Are They Heading?" In *Globalization of Chinese Business Firms*, ed. Henry Wai-chung Yeung and Kris Olds, 1–28. New York: Palgrave Macmillan.

Young, Jason. 2011. "China's Changing Hukou System: Institutional Objectives, Formal Arrangements, and Informal Practices." In *The Institutional Dynamics of China's Great Transformation*, ed. Xiaoming Huang, 130–51. New York: Routledge.

Yu, Hong. 2010." Impact of the Global Economic Crises on the Pearl River Delta and Yangtze River Delta Regions." In *China and the Global Economic Crisis*, ed. Yongnian Zheng and Sarah Y. Tong, 89–112. Singapore: World Scientific.

Yuan, Lei. 2008. "Policy Recommendations for Developing Foreign-Invested Enterprise in China." *China Economist* 16: 95–106.

Zeng, Jin, and Kellee S. Tsai. 2011. "The Local Politics of Restructuring State-Owned Enterprises in China." In *Going Private in China: The Politics of Corporate Restructuring and System Reform*, ed. Jean C. Oi, 39–69. Stanford, Calif.: Walter H. Shorenstein Asia-Pacific Research Center Books.

Zhang, Jingxiang, and Fulong Wu. 2006. "China's Changing Economic Governance: Administrative Annexation and the Reorganization of Local Governments in the Yangtze River Delta." *Regional Studies* 40 (1): 3–21.

Zhao, Suisheng. 2004. *A Nation-State by Construction: Dynamics of Modern Chinese Nationalism*. Stanford, Calif.: Stanford University Press.

———. 2017. Whither the China Model: Revisiting the Debate." *Journal of Contemporary China* 26 (103): 1–17.

Zheng, Yongnian. 2007. *De Facto Federalism in China: Reforms and Dynamics of Central-Local Relations*. Singapore: World Scientific.

———. 2010. *The Chinese Communist Party as Organizational Emperor: Culture, Reproduction, and Transformation*. London: Routledge.

Zhu, Andong, and David M. Kotz. 2011. "The Dependence of China's Economic Growth on Exports and Investment." *Review of Radical Political Economics* 43 (1): 9–32.

Zhu, Jiangnan, and Dong Zhang. 2017. "Does Corruption Hinder Private Businesses? Leadership Stability and Predictable Corruption in China." *Governance* 30 (3): 343–63.

Zhu, Zhichang. 2007. "Reform Without a Theory: Why Does It Work in China?" *Organization Studies* 28 (10): 1503–22.

Zurndorfer, Harriet T. 2004. "Confusing Confucianism with Capitalism: Culture as Impediment and/or Stimulus to Chinese Economic Development." Unpublished manuscript.

Zweig, David. 2002. *Internationalizing China: Domestic Interests and Global Linkages*. Ithaca, N.Y.: Cornell University Press.

Zweig, David, and Zhimin Chen, eds. 2007. *China's Reforms and International Political Economy*. London: Routledge.

INDEX

ACKNOWLEDGMENTS

A whole host of individuals and institutions supported me with the analysis and observations in this project. I would first like to thank Andreas Nölke, Heike Holbig, and Wolfgang Streeck, the reviewers of the German edition of this work. Grants from the Fritz Thyssen Foundation and the Max Planck Institute for the Study of Societies (MPIfG) in Cologne followed by a position as a research associate at MPIfG enabled me to realize the full potential of this project. My work at the institute from 2009 until 2012, which was intellectually so instructive, and MPIfG's superb infrastructure provided an extremely favorable foundation for the completion of my project. I would therefore also like to thank MPIfG's two directors at the time, Jens Beckert and Wolfgang Streeck, as well as Martin Höpner, with whom I worked very closely, and all other members of staff at the institute.

I am also greatly indebted to Axel Honneth and his colleagues at the Institute for Social Research in Frankfurt, where I conducted parts of my analysis. Here, the pioneering work of Boy Lüthje in the field of China's industrial relations provided a key impetus for my work. The institute also provided me with invaluable support and an environment for stimulating discussions ranging far beyond my own area of study. Further, Ulrich Rödel was, once again, an extremely competent adviser and thorough critic.

I would also like to thank Iwo Amelung, Johann P. Arnason, Hauke Brunkhorst, Sonja Buckel, Florian Butollo, Anita Chan, Lee Chun-Yi, Christoph Deutschmann, Kai Enzweiler, He Gaochao, Laura Gruss, Julian Gruin, Peter Hall, Annika Hennl, Christoph Hoffmeier, Martin Höpner, Cho Hyekyung, Bob Jessop, Roy Karadag, Boy Lüthje, Christian May, Chris McNally, Daniel Mertens, Guido Möllering, Sascha Münnich, Sum Ngai-Ling, Thomas Paster, Johannes Petry, Geny Piotti, Susanne Rühle, Thomas Sablowski, Armin Schäfer, Stefan Schmalz, Alexander Schröder, Luo Siqi, Frederic Speidel, Kathleen Thelen, René Trappel, and Jia Wenjuan for their invaluable and inspiring discussions, for their willingness to help, and for their critical commentary. Special thanks go to Peter in der Heiden, who helped me to update the present volume.

The translation of this work was funded by Geisteswissenschaften International—Translation Funding for Humanities and Social Sciences from Germany, a joint initiative of the Fritz Thyssen Foundation, the German Federal Foreign Office, the collecting society VG WORT and the Börsenverein des Deutschen Buchhandels (German Publishers & Booksellers Association).

Carla Welch was my extremely supportive and sensitive translator, and Linda Jayne Turner my very meticulous copy editor. Further, I would like to thank Peter Agree and Noreen O'Connor-Abel from the University of Pennsylvania Press for their friendly editorial support.

This book is dedicated to my dearest Dražena.

Lightning Source UK Ltd.
Milton Keynes UK
UKHW040914280419
341725UK00007B/444/P